THE PRINTED PAGE IS EVERYMAN'S UNIVERSITY

THE CIVILIZATION OF THE AMERICAN INDIAN

OTHER BOOKS BY GEORGE E. HYDE

CORN AMONG THE INDIANS OF THE UPPER MISSOURI
(in collaboration with George F. Will)
Cedar Rapids, 1917

THE EARLY BLACKFEET AND THEIR NEIGHBORS
Denver, 1931

THE PAWNEE INDIANS
Denver, 1951

RANGERS AND REGULARS
Columbus, Ohio, 1953

A SIOUX CHRONICLE
Norman, 1956

SET UP AND PRINTED AT NORMAN, OKLAHOMA, U.S.A.
BY THE UNIVERSITY OF OKLAHOMA PRESS
PUBLISHING DIVISION OF THE
UNIVERSITY

FROM AN ORIGINAL ETCHING BY LYMAN BYXBE
BY PERMISSION OF JOHN VANMALE

Red Cloud

Red Cloud's Folk

Folk

A History of the Oglala Sioux Indians

GEORGE E. HYDE

UNIVERSITY OF OKLAHOMA PRESS

To

My Sister

Mabel L. Reed

Whose

Assistance Made this Work

Possible

PREFACE

THE object of the present volume is to present a complete history of one of the Teton Sioux tribes from the time of its origin until it came to the reservation and was broken to pieces by the policy then favored by the United States government. Up to this time no such work has appeared in print; numerous books have been published dealing with certain episodes in Sioux history, but none of these works has attempted to present a complete history of any of the Sioux tribes. Most of these books are histories of the wars from 1854 to 1890 and do not attempt to cover any other material.

In setting down the story of the migrations and early history of the Oglalas and their Teton kindred, the author has had to treat a subject which has been ignored by nearly all historians of the Sioux. Yet without a clear knowledge of these early events we cannot understand the later history of this people or that of the tribes with which they came into contact. It was during their migration from Minnesota across the coteau to the Missouri and out toward the Black Hills that the Oglalas and other Tetons developed from little camps of poor people afoot in the vast buffalo plains into seven powerful tribes of mounted Indians. This westward advance of the Tetons was led by the Oglalas; they were the first Sioux to pass west of the Missouri, the first to reach the Black Hills and the first to turn southward to the Platte. Their history is perhaps more strikingly representative of the story of their race than that of any of the other Teton tribes would be. This volume attempts to present that history clearly and fairly.

The chapters of the book which tell of the establishment of Red Cloud Agency and the early years on the reservation have been compiled from official reports, from Indian accounts and material obtained from former agency employes, traders, interpreters, and other whites who were at the agency in early days. This part of the book presents a phase of Sioux life which has been much neglected by our writers of Indian history, although it forms a very interesting and important part of the story of this people. For the period 1870-1879 practically every book on the Teton Sioux is concerned almost exclusively with events connected with the little bands of wild rovers generally known as the Sitting Bull and Crazy Horse camps. The agency Sioux, who greatly exceeded the wild bands in numbers, are generally ignored until the time comes to make the stereotyped assertion that in the spring of 1876 every able-bodied agency Sioux rushed out to join Sitting Bull and Crazy Horse. In the chapters covering this period the author has attempted to give the agency Sioux the attention their position as the major group of their people warrants, to set forth their attitude and conduct during this war which had been thrust upon them, and to clear these friendly Indians of the oft-repeated charge that in 1876 all of their warriors flocked out to the hostile camps. The refutation of the latter charge is important, because the officials justified their harsh treatment of the agency Sioux and the seizure of the Black Hills and all other Sioux lands worth having by painting the friendly agency bands as hostiles whose warriors—fed, armed, and equipped by government agents—had taken a leading part in the attacks on Crook and Custer. When examined, the facts are clear. In 1876, the agency Sioux were friendly; it was not their war; they tried to keep out of it, and with few exceptions they did so.

In writing Indian history much use must be made of Indian information. Such materials, coming directly from the Indians themselves, are invaluable aids to the author, if properly employed and checked with other sources. In some quarters there seems to be a belief that the Plains Indian could retain in his memory details of historical events that had occurred two or three hundred years back. Ninety years, in a very few instances one hundred years, would be nearer the truth. In 1916, the Oglalas had no historical memory of the events leading up to and following the killing of their great chief Bull Bear in 1841; in 1933, they could give a few petty incidents connected with the cholera of 1849, but they were incapable of giving a historical account of that dreadful event. The Cheyennes in 1910 had no historical memory back of the Crow battle of 1820, and the same was true of the Arapahoes. Captain

L. H. North who knew the Pawnees intimately informed me that about the year 1865 the earliest event of which these people had a clear historical memory was the fight with the Skidis on Loup Fork, an event which occurred after the year 1770. In the case of the Teton Sioux we have a people who kept pictographic records or "winter counts" to assist their memories; but when the counts were explained by their keepers soon after the year 1875 it became apparent that these tribal record-keepers had no better memories than the rest of the people. They knew the names of the pictographs that represented the main events of each year, but when they got farther back than sixty years they were much in doubt as to what the pictographs really stood for. The memory of the Indians for tradition, of course, goes back much farther than their historical memory; but the scene of tradition is a misty land in which rivers, lakes, and hills are dimly seen, their location and names generally unknown. The dates of traditional events are broadly stated, the names of the principal actors are unknown or made up, and often the very names of the tribes engaged have been forgotten. Such traditions are of great value in studying the period of early migrations, but they are hardly to be classed as historical material. From the Oglalas who are now living nothing very useful can be obtained on the history of their people back of the year 1850. The earlier period must be covered from other sources. Even for the later period the memory of these people is far from satisfactory and their statements often require careful checking with other sources. Their memories are largely personal; few men can tell clearly of any events of their fathers' time, and the period when their grandfathers were young is almost a blank in their minds. This is not poor memory; it is the frailty of human nature.

The author has used the English plural in writing tribal and band names: Oglalas, Tetons, Kiyuksas. The custom followed by many writers of using what may be termed the Indian plural and writing "one Oglala," "seven Oglala," is supposed for some reason to be scholarly; but surely this Indian grammatical form has no place in the writing of English prose. There is no more sense in writing "seven Oglala" than in writing "seven Spaniard" or "seven western state."

Many persons have given me assistance in the preparation of this book. My thanks are due to my sister, Mabel L. Reed, and to Mr. John VanMale of Denver for aid and encouragement. To

Dr. Scudder Mekeel of Harvard, formerly of Yale, I am indebted for some new information on early Oglala chiefs and bands. The late Captain L. H. North of Columbus, Nebraska, and Mr. George F. Will of Bismarck, North Dakota, have also supplied me with much Indian information. To Miss Edith Tobitt and Miss Bertha Baumer, Librarians, and to the staff of the Omaha Public Library my thanks are due for their assistance in obtaining many old books and official reports.

GEORGE E. HYDE

Omaha, Nebraska, April, 1936.

TABLE OF CONTENTS

PART I: MIGRATION AND EARLY HISTORY

PART II: THE ERA OF WHITE ENCROACHMENT

PART III: RED CLOUD AGENCY

PART I

MIGRATIONS AND EARLY HISTORY

"The Buffalo North and the Buffalo South: that is the game that has brought our Nation where it now stands."

—RED CLOUD, 1875.

CHAPTER I

OVER THE COTEAU TO THE MISSOURI
1650-1770

THE Dakotas or Sioux came originally from the South, and in the sixteenth century established themselves on the headwaters of the Mississippi in a region of lakes and marshes through which travel was mainly by means of bark canoes. These people, who sometimes spoke of themselves as the *Otchenti Chakowin* or Seven Council Fires, were the most savage and warlike of the Siouan tribes, and when we get our first glimpses of them early in the seventeenth century, we see them vigorously attacking the Algonquian tribes who dwelt beyond them, toward the north and northeast. At first the Sioux had the better of these encounters, but the Algonquians, coming in contact with the French in Canada and somewhat later with the English on Hudson Bay, obtained metal weapons and firearms and by means of their superior equipment turned the scales against the Sioux and gradually pressed them back into southern Minnesota.

A study of the available materials discloses the fact that the Sioux retirement from the head of the Mississippi was made in two distinct waves. The first of these, consisting of the Yanktonais, then including the Yanktons, and Tetons, began to move after the middle of the seventeenth century; the second wave, made up of the *Sioux de l'Est,* did not move until after 1735. There is no absolute proof as to the causes of the first wave of Sioux retirement; but from the date, direction, and circumstances of the movement it would seem a fair inference that at about the date 1670 the Yanktonais group and the Tetons were attacked in their old home near the head of the Mississippi by the Crees and their allies, who now were armed with guns, and were compelled to retire southward.

As we piece together the story from the fragments of information obtainable from the early French records and a few vague Indian traditions, it appears that sometime around 1650 the Sioux began to raid the Crees who dwelt north of them in the district around Rainy Lake. As Nicolas Perrot, who was in the Indian country at this time, tells the tale, these tribes were still in the stone age and untouched by white influence at the time of the beginning of these wars; but the Sioux were the fiercer warriors and soon gained the upper hand. The Sioux who were nearest to the Crees were that division of the Yanktonais who later became a separate tribe under the name of the Assiniboins. These people were inclined to be friendly with their Cree neighbors; indeed, they even intermarried with the Crees. A war-party of Sioux, coming to the Assiniboin camp, found some Crees there and attacked them. They also mistreated the Assiniboins for being on good terms with the alien Crees. The Assiniboins soon found themselves in the uncomfortable position of neutrals in a merciless war between their own tribe and the Crees; and this position becoming intolerable, they presently were compelled to decide whether to stay with their own people or join the Crees. They joined the Crees; and the French statement that by this date the Crees were obtaining guns and European goods and were supplying the Assiniboins with these articles affords us the only possible explanation for the Assiniboin decision to throw in their lot with these alien Algonquians. Kinship ties were very strong among the Indians in early times, but we have many instances of bands deserting their own tribe when material interests strongly impelled them to do so. The arrival of the English on Hudson Bay was the turning point in the wars between the Sioux and the Crees. The French were just beginning to penetrate the region west of Lake Superior, but they had few guns to trade to the Indians, poor stocks of everything else, and their trade was very irregular. The English, on the other hand, had plentiful supplies, especially of good guns, and from the time the *Nonsuch* entered Hudson Bay in 1668 large flotillas of canoes began to come to the bay each summer to trade. The most numerous of the Upland Indians who came down to trade with the English were from the first the Crees and Assiniboins, and it was undoubtedly here on Hudson Bay that these tribes obtained the weapons which enabled them to defeat the Sioux. We can easily follow these events in outline. Perrot's statement indicates that the Sioux first attacked the Crees before 1650 and soon "ruined them." Radisson speaks of a bloody fight between the Sioux and Crees in 1658; Marquette met the Crees in 1670 and found them armed only with bows, but four years later these same Crees, all armed with guns, attacked and massacred the Sioux envoys at Sault de Ste Marie. The Sioux in this party had only flint knives and similar primitive weapons. In 1673, Father Nouvel reported that the Upper Algonquins, including the Crees, were going constantly to trade with the English at Hudson Bay, and he predicted that the French would lose these tribes and their trade. In 1684, a great flotilla of Cree canoes, including four hundred Assiniboin men, went down Hayes River to trade with the English at the bay. The trade there was to a large extent for guns and ammunition, which the Indians highly prized, for with good guns in their hands they had the hated Sioux at their mercy. It was at about this time, as de la Potherie reports, that the Crees came frequently in canoes and drove the Sioux from their villages, forcing them to take refuge in waste places where they had only acorns, roots, and bark to eat. Anyone who doubts the extreme effectiveness of firearms when used against people who were still living in the stone age should read Sir Alexander Mackenzie's account of the reign of terror which these same Crees created in the Athabasca country toward the close of the eighteenth century. Small parties of Crees armed with good guns hunted the unfortunate natives like rabbits and had them so terrorized that they fled at the mere sight of a strange smoke miles away. Truteau in 1795 stated explicitly that the fear in which the Teton Sioux were held by the other tribes on the Missouri and out near the Black Hills was mainly due to the fact that the Sioux had many guns while the other tribes had practically none.

We have no details of these early wars, but it would seem probable that the Sioux of the Yanktonais group, who dwelt nearest the Crees, suffered most when that people obtained guns and assumed the offensive. The Tetons appear to have dwelt south of the Yanktonais in the tall-grass prairies west of the Mississippi, near Sauk Rapids, where they still dwelt about 1680. A retirement of the Yanktonais southward naturally would have exposed the Tetons to the attacks of the Crees and Assiniboins, forcing them to remove; and something of this sort seems to have occurred, for in 1700 we find the Yanktonais, Yanktons, and Tetons all far to the south of their old homes. The Sissetons and other Eastern Sioux were not greatly affected by the Cree war, perhaps because of their location in marshes where it was difficult to get at them, although there is reason to believe that the Crees and their allies felt a greater animosity toward the Yanktonais and Tetons than toward the Eastern Sioux. In the early eighteenth century we find the Eastern Sioux blaming their western kinsmen for these wars and, as the French assert, even offering to aid the Crees and Assiniboins against the turbulent Western Sioux.[1]

Our Sioux traditions dealing with this period come entirely from the Eastern Sioux; they are lacking in detail, and having been recorded mainly by missionaries who knew little of early Indian history they are of but slight service in attempting to follow the movements of the Western Sioux, first southward to the Minnesota Valley, and then west toward the Missouri. The French records help us a little, but we are left to surmise the details of this movement.

Driven from their homes between the head of the Mississippi and Red Lake sometime after 1670, the Yanktonais group retired southward through the tall-grass prairies west of the Mississippi and came into the great elbow-bend of the Minnesota River, in the Swan Lake district. Here we may assume that they separated, the Yanktons crossing the Minnesota and occupying the country from the Blue Earth River toward the Pipestone Quarry, while the Yanktonais (the parent group) migrated slowly up the Minnesota River. The Tetons, either preceding or following the Yanktonais group, on reaching the elbow-bend also appear to have divided into two groups, those later known as the Brulés and Oglalas crossing the river and occupying the prairies from the Blue Earth River westward, the Teton-Saones going up Minnesota River to its head.

Since the Tetons and Saones were later in advance of the Yanktons and Yanktonais in their westward migration, it may be that they led this movement from the first. The French maps, which

1. The sources for this early period are so numerous that only a few of them can be indicated here. The French documents, which are so useful, will be found in Margry's volumes, in the Canadian Archives and in Thwaites' *Jesuit Relations*. A good reprint of Perrot and de la Patherie is in Blair's *Indian Tribes of the Upper Mississippi*, Volume I. The Indian traditions collected in the middle of the nineteenth century hardly reach so far back in the form of detailed narrative and give us only vague and fleeting glimpses of this far-off time. An excellent idea of the character of the old homeland of the Sioux at the head of the Mississippi may be obtained from the Coues edition of Zebulon Pike's journals, Volume I.

are regarded by some scholars as excellent authority for the location of these Sioux tribes at various dates, may be quoted to prove it one way or the other, as you choose; but most of these maps are very poor material to draw upon, and some of them have been added to by later hands, so that the dates they bear are snares to entangle the unwary. The famous de l'Isle map "of 1708" has led historians and ethnologists into endless misstatements.

That the Tetons divided to form two groups on reaching the elbow-bend seems obvious. The Yanktons certainly separated from the Yanktonais group here; and when (after 1735) the Sissetons, migrating southward by the same route through the prairies which the Tetons and Yanktonais had followed at a much earlier date, came to this bend they are known to have divided, one group crossing the river to hunt in the Blue Earth district, the parent group going on up the Minnesota to its head. Indeed, this great elbow in the river seems to have been a kind of trap, designed by nature, into which one migrating horde after another came, to find itself faced with the problem of whether to cross the river here and occupy the open prairies to the southward or to go up the river toward its head, keeping to the more wooded country; in each instance the Sioux appear to have settled the matter as they usually settled any controversy, by quarreling and breaking up into factions, each of which went its own way. The evidence suggests that in each case the conservative element, representing the parent group of the tribe, stuck to the river and went on up its banks, while the others formed new bands and went off southward into the prairies where the buffalo were to be found in greater abundance.

In crossing south of the Minnesota at the elbow-bend the Yanktons, and that portion of the Tetons who also crossed here, came into buffalo plains and soon drifted out onto the Coteau des Prairies. The rest of the people of these groups, those who migrated up Minnesota River, kept more in the wooded country, and this fact probably gave rise to the nickname Saone (from *Tchanona* and *Tchankute*: "Shooters among the Trees"), a term of derision applied to them by their bolder and more adventurous kinsmen of the buffalo plains. As we shall see farther on, this name was applied both to the Teton-Saones and to a part of the Yanktonais.

Viewing the Teton migration from the Minnesota angle, we have little to go on other than the vague statements of the Eastern Sioux, made in the middle of the nineteenth century, to the effect that the Tetons were formerly in Minnesota but gradually drifted westward. The Tetons themselves had lost most of their memories of the old home on the Mississippi by 1840, for in that year Riggs came across the coteau to Fort Pierre on the Missouri and there questioned these Indians and their traders, learning that only a vague memory was retained that the Tetons had come from the east and that their chiefs had formerly sat in council with those of the Eastern Sioux. It is nevertheless true that when we take our stand near the Great Bend of the Missouri, looking eastward, we can trace the routes by which these people migrated, we can date the movement, and by noting the Sioux tribes with which the Tetons were most closely associated and certain other clues we gain a fairly clear idea of the Teton migration.

The trading-fairs at which the Western Sioux obtained their guns and European goods were of vital importance to these people, and the location of these fairs is one of our best means for tracing their movements. About 1750 these annual fairs were held on the extreme headwaters of the Minnesota River, but as late as 1700 the fairs were at the mouth of this stream, on the Mississippi. We must therefore conclude that the Tetons and Yanktons, who were still without horses, were not very far toward the west. For this reason one is led to infer that Lesueur in 1700 met the Tetons, and it even seems probable that one of the bands which wintered near his stockade on the Blue Earth were the Oglalas, for he terms these people the *Ojalespoitans* or Village Divided into Many Small Bands. There is no "j" in the Sioux tongue, this sound being represented in the Teton dialect by "gl." This name was therefore *Oglales-poit-ton*: from *Oglala* (scattered or divided) and *ton* (village). The *poit* is puzzling, but seems to be an Algonquian word (*poituc,* "men" or "people") which the early French often employed in writing Sioux tribal names. Examples are Assinipoit, for Assiniboin, and Mascoutepoit ("Prairie Men") an old name for the Teton Sioux. As close as the name given by Lesueur is to Oglala, this resemblance would mean little if taken alone. It is his translation of the name, Village Divided into Many Small Bands, that is really significant, for we have always known that the name *Oglala* meant scattered, divided. It would be difficult to conceive of a more sensible explanation for this tribal name than that indicated by Lesueur, this people having crossed south of Minnesota River and then scattered out in little camps in the prairies. The most popular of several stories explaining the origin of this name which were current among the Sioux after the middle of the nineteenth century was to the effect that two chiefs quarreled and one insulted the other by scattering dust in his face. There is no sense in this tale, and it is in all probability apocryphal.[2]

That Lesueur in 1700 did not mention the Brulés is not strange; for our evidence points strongly to the fact that this name (*Sichangu,* Brulés or Burnt Thighs) did not originate until after 1750. The Brulés were probably near the Blue Earth in Lesueur's day, but under some other name.

These clues, and some others, point to the fact that at the opening of the eighteenth century the Tetons of the Oglala and Brulé group were hunting in the prairies west of the Blue Earth, were wintering in the wooded valley of that stream, and each spring were going to a point near the mouth of the Minnesota to do their trading. These Tetons were all afoot, and their closest associations were with the Yanktons, who had already gone far enough afield to acquire the name Village of the Red Stone, from their frequenting of the district in southwestern Minnesota in which the Red Pipestone Quarry is situated.

The occupation of the lands bordering on Minnesota River by these Sioux of the West was evidently not a peaceful process. From Sioux tradition we gather that they found part or all of the Cheyenne tribe in the upper valley, near Yellow Medicine, and pressed them farther toward the northwest. Even in 1700 the Iowas and Otoes claimed the lands along the Blue Earth, but finding the Sioux uncomfortable neighbors these tribes had recently withdrawn westward, to join the Omahas. The latter tribe had formerly dwelt in the district near the Pipestone Quarry where (apparently after 1680) they had been attacked and, as their traditions state, slaughtered by the Yanktons. Fleeing westward, they built new villages on the west bank of the Big Sioux, near Sioux Falls; but here they were again attacked and massacred, the survivors fleeing to the Missouri and establishing themselves near the mouth of the Big

2. It may seem a hard saying to assert that the Oglalas in later days did not know how their own tribal name had originated, but the evidence indicates that this was the case. They had three or four contradictory and rather trivial tales dealing with this subject, and most of the other Teton tribes also had several explanations of the origin of their tribal names. Many of these tales seem to be of late origin and some of them exhibit an astonishing ignorance on the part of these Indians as to the conditions under which their ancestors lived in the seventeenth and eighteenth centuries.

Sioux. The Omahas at this period were without horses or metal weapons, the easy prey of any tribe which was supplied with fire-arms; the traditions clearly state that the people were slaughtered or massacred and fled into the west to seek a safer dwelling-place. All of this is borne out by the French records, which indicate that at this date the Sioux of the West and their allies who dwelt on the Upper Mississippi were accustomed to make up very large war-parties, armed with guns, to go against the Omahas and certain other western tribes. From Lesueur's report it would seem that the Omahas had been driven to the Missouri before 1700.

What little has been written on the history of the Sioux at this early date has spread the false impression that after driving the Omahas to the westward the Yanktons and Tetons at once advanced in the same direction and established themselves on the Missouri in South Dakota. This view, which is suggested if not actually stated in Hodge's *Indian Handbook,* is based entirely on the supposition that the de l'Isle map was made and completed sometime around the year 1708; but this is not true. The map has been added to at a much later date than the one it bears and, as Justin Winsor has stated, it has even been corrected by someone who wrote on it in English. The map does show the Tetons and Yanktons on the Missouri below the Great Bend; but it also shows the Ponkas, a people who in 1708 were a part of the Omaha tribe and who did not become known to the French under their own name until after 1780. To anyone familiar with the sources, this map bears the clear indications of having been added to by someone who had information which J. B. Monier and J. B. Truteau brought back from the Upper Missouri between 1787 and 1797. The opinion that the Tetons and Yanktons established themselves on the Missouri below the Great Bend at a date prior to 1708 does not take into account that the Omahas, after being driven to the Missouri near the mouth of the Big Sioux, advanced up the river and settled in the very district in which their Teton and Yankton enemies are supposed to have been already established. These people moved up there after 1723 and remained until about 1750, when they retired down the west bank of the Missouri into northern Nebraska.

If we accept the view that the Sioux of the West met by Lesueur on the Blue Earth in 1700 were the Tetons of the Brulé and Oglala group, we must seek an explanation for the fact that the Yanktons, who at this date were roving the prairies far west of the Blue Earth, permitted these Tetons to pass them in their westward migration and reach the Missouri first. The reason for this is not far to seek. In 1700 buffalo and other game were in great abundance near the Blue Earth, but bands of Eastern Sioux were coming here each season to hunt, and by the end of the first quarter of the eighteenth century this district had become a poor hunting country. The traditions of the Eastern Sioux state explicitly that the Tetons migrated westward in quest of buffalo, and as we know that the herds were first cleared out of the country farthest toward the east, near the Blue Earth, we have a simple explanation as to why the Tetons who occupied that district were the first to withdraw westward. In making this movement they passed the Yanktons, whose hunting-grounds near the Pipestone Quarry and the head of the Des Moines River were still well supplied with game.[3]

The Oglalas and Brulés were now hunting far out on the Coteau des Prairies and even beyond, to the valley of James River (the *Tchan-sansan* as they termed it). To picture this movement as a conquering advance would be ridiculous, for the people (in many little camps) were simply drifting here and there on the coteau in quest of the shifting buffalo herds. They were still without horses, and the coteau was a very hard country for people afoot who had to transport all of their camp equipment on the backs of their dogs and women, even the tiny girls of six or seven having to carry burdens on the march. They could not move more than about five miles a day in any comfort with their impedimenta; and as there was little fuel or shelter on the coteau, when winter drew on they had to retire eastward to seek refuge in some wooded valley. In the spring they took their furs to the annual *rendezvous* or trading-fair, where they met the Sioux from the Mississippi, who brought them guns, ammunition, and European goods. At this period, toward the middle of the eighteenth century, the trading-fair was held near the head of Minnesota River. Jonathan Carver in 1766 evidently heard of this trading-fair from the white traders on the Upper Mississippi. This author's account of his trip

3. Truteau in 1794 found a few Yanktons in the Teton camp on the Missouri, but he clearly indicates that they were visitors from the Des Moines. In 1858 the Yanktons ceded to the United States the lands on the Missouri below the Great Bend, and the Tetons on learning of this cried out furiously that these were their lands. They said that long ago the Yanktons had come to beg for meat and horses, that they had permitted that tribe to occupy Teton lands on the Missouri, and that the Yanktons had now stolen these lands and sold them to the whites.

up the Minnesota River and the spending of a winter among the Indians of that region bears all the marks of falsehood. Like LeRaye at a later period, Carver seems to have picked up some information from traders on which to base his imaginary sojourn among the Western Sioux.

The Saones during all this time appear to have been in the upper valley of Minnesota River, taking no part in the movements of their Oglala and Brulé kindred. These people of the wooded valley certainly called themselves Tetons, and they probably looked on the Oglalas and Brulés as seceders; indeed, the Saones had in their possession an ancient pipe and some sacred objects which seem to have belonged to the original Teton tribe before it quitted its old home on the Upper Mississippi. At the period 1690-1720 the French map-makers placed the Tetons (evidently the Saones) near Big Stone Lake at the head of Minnesota River. They seem to have centered here until they began their migration toward the Missouri, while the Yanktonais frequented Lac qui Parle, some distance farther down Minnesota River.

As the origin of the name Saone has been regarded as somewhat inexplicable during the past fifty years, and as this matter has a direct bearing on the early history of the Tetons, a few words on the subject may not be out of place here. The name does not occur in the early French records dealing with the Sioux, and this fact bears out what S. R. Riggs was told at Fort Pierre in 1840; namely, that Saone (or *Sanyona*) was a nickname which the Oglalas and Brulés had applied to five Teton tribes: the Miniconjous, Sans Arcs, Two Kettles, Hunkpapas, and Blackfoot-Sioux. The name was therefore little used in Minnesota but was familiar on the Upper Missouri where we find Truteau using it in the form *Chahony* in 1795. Truteau also bears out Riggs' statement that the name was applied to five Teton tribes, for he speaks of the Saones as five tribes, the "Northern Indians." The Arikaras and Mandans were in such close contact with the Saones that they applied that name to all the Sioux. In 1840 the name was still in common use and large camps of Sioux were still called Saones; but fifty years later the name was almost forgotten, and when the missionaries made inquiries in 1889 they were given vague and conflicting information concerning the name and its application. Thus some of the Sioux stated that Saone came from *Sanyoni wichasha* ("Saone Men") and was a nickname formerly applied by the Oglalas and Brulés to the

Miniconjous, Sans Arcs, and Two Kettles, while others insisted that the name came from *Sanyona* and was not applied to the Tetons at all but to part of the Yanktonais. As to the meaning of the name, these Indians could only guess, but they all seem to have suspected that Saone referred in some way to shooting.

Studying these clues, we find that in the early eighteenth century the Sioux loved to give their bands names referring to shooting, and that Saone was clearly a name of this type, invented by the Oglalas and Brulés of the treeless plains and applied by them to their kindred who kept near the woods in the Minnesota River valley. The name was therefore given to both Tetons and Yanktonais. Examining the older lists of Sioux band-names we find that the Yanktons formerly had a *Tchankute* band (from *tchan*, "tree," and *kute*, "to shoot"); we also find a *Tchankute* band among the Sissetons (the name being translated "Shooters in the Woods"); while among the Upper Yanktonais this same name, transformed in their dialect into *Tchanyona* (translated "Shooters among the Trees"), was given to a band of their people. *Tchanyona* is merely a different spelling of *Sanyona*, the name which Riggs gave to the Saones in 1840.

This evidence indicates that the name Saone was given to large groups of Sioux who dwelt on the upper Minnesota River early in the eighteenth century. When these groups broke up, the Saones of Teton blood took the name with them to the Missouri; part of the Yanktonais who migrated in the same direction also retained the name; some Saones joined the Yanktons, while enough people called by this name remained on Minnesota River to form a Saone-band made up of people from several Sioux tribes. This latter band was mentioned by Lewis and Clark in 1804.

Near these Saones ("Shooters among the Trees") on the headwaters of Minnesota River were the Wazikutes ("Shooters among the Pines") and a people called Masikotas whose name clearly comes from the Sioux words *mazi* ("iron") and *kute* ("to shoot") and refers to their early use of guns. When the Teton-Saones migrated towards the Missouri not only the Yanktonais but also a part of the Wazikutes and Masikotas went with them. In 1840 some of the Wazikutes were with the Yanktonais roving between Devil's Lake and the Missouri, while part of the Masikotas had joined the Two Kettle Saones. From Cheyenne tradition we know that the Masikotas were Sioux who in early times roved on the headwaters of the Minnesota and Red rivers; that part of them migrated to the Missouri with the Cheyennes, with whom they remained, many Cheyennes of today counting their descent from Masikota ancestors.

During the period 1700-1750 while they were slowly drifting westward, following the buffalo, the Oglalas and Brulés must have often taken part in the periodical expeditions which the Sioux of the West and their allies from the Upper Mississippi made against the tribes on the Missouri. These great war-parties seem to have used the Big Sioux and Little Sioux rivers as their roads to the Missouri, probably going in canoes, and these streams had acquired the name *Rivières des Sioux* long before that tribe came to the Missouri to dwell. The French reports mention several of these expeditions, aimed at the Omahas and their neighbors, between the years 1700 and 1740, and in some of these reports, reprinted in Margry's volumes, we find the Sioux of the West referred to as turbulent trouble-makers, who would not listen to French advice and should be destroyed. The first results of these Sioux operations were the flight of the Omahas to the Missouri and the withdrawal of the Iowas and Otoes from their old home in northern Iowa and southern Minnesota. Lesueur states that the latter tribes went to the Missouri in the year 1700, to live near the Omahas, and this statement is borne out by the Omaha and Iowa traditions. The Otoes, however, did not join the Omahas, but moved farther toward the south and crossed the Missouri into southern Nebraska.

Thus, about the date 1700-1725, the Omahas and part of the Iowas were settled on the north side of the Missouri near the mouth of the Big Sioux, and above them on the same side of the river were the Arikaras, a people closely akin to the Skidi Pawnees. These Arikaras had been driven out of northeastern Nebraska, evidently by the Padoucas. This group of Indians on the Missouri above the Big Sioux constituted quite a large population. The Arikaras had many villages of earth-lodges; the Omahas were also a large tribe, and there was at least one strong village of Iowas in the group. But these people, except for the Iowas, were without firearms and were practically living in the stone age; therefore, when attacked by large parties of the Sioux and their allies, all armed with guns, they had no recourse except flight.

Soon after 1723 these Indians moved up the Missouri into Dakota, the movement evidently forced, for they were agricultural tribes who would not move except under compulsion, and by going up into South Dakota they were leaving a good farming country to enter one in which the raising of crops was a very uncertain proposition. Indeed, when we study this event we can find no more reasonable explanation for the removal of these tribes into Dakota than the fact that they were being raided by the Sioux and their allies; and on examining the French records we find that the Sioux of the West are reported to have been preparing such an expedition against the tribes on the Missouri in 1727, and again in 1729.

The result of this movement was that by about 1730-1740 the Arikaras had established themselves in new settlements on both banks of the Missouri, from a point near the present Chamberlain up to the site of the present Pierre, while the Omahas and Iowas had crossed the Missouri and built villages on the north bank of White River. At this time the Ponkas, who had formed a part of the Omaha tribe, left the others and went up Bad River, where they seem to have joined the Arikaras, going on hunting trips out toward the Black Hills. Here they were assailed by mounted warriors (evidently the Kiowas) and were so badly frightened that they presently left Bad River and rejoined the Omahas and Iowas at the mouth of White River. These tribes now moved down the west bank of the Missouri into northern Nebraska (about 1750), but they had hardly built new villages when they were again assaulted by large forces of Sioux. The Iowas now withdrew southward, while the Omahas moved a short distance farther south and settled on Omaha Creek, below the mouth of the Big Sioux on the Nebraska side. The Ponkas remained near the mouth of the Niobrara, building a village in a strong position and fortifying it after the Arikara fashion.

This was the situation on the Upper Missouri at the period when the Tetons of the Oglala and Brulé group made their first appearance in that region. Having drifted westward by slow stages, these little Teton bands finally reached the James River, where they must have come into contact with the Arikaras. Finally, toward the middle of the eighteenth century, these Sioux left the James River, crossed the low Coteau du Missouri and came down into the great valley beyond. They were no conquerors, but poor people afoot in the vast plains, and from both the Sioux and Arikara statements, it seems probable that the Teton bands first came to the Missouri in a hard season, to beg at the Arikara towns. But the Teton Sioux was always a hardy beggar with nothing humble about him; and if these people came to the Arikaras one day to beg, they returned on another day to waylay the Arikaras and kill them, and from the very first they must have proved bad neighbors.

At the date 1760 when the Tetons made their first appearance on the Upper Missouri, the Arikara towns contained a population perhaps equal to that of the entire Sioux nation. Beginning on the east bank of the river within the limits of the present city of Pierre, these villages extended down this bank to a point near the upper end of the Great Bend. The ruins, which are still to be seen, indicate that the larger villages were strongly fortified with ditch, earth wall, and cedar log stockade. Below the Great Bend, on the east bank near the mouth of Crow Creek, was a very large and heavily fortified village, a kind of southern outpost city. On the west bank was a group of three fortified villages on the site of Old Fort George, opposite the town of DeGrey, and just above the mouth of Bad River was a second group of three fortified towns. The remains left by the Arikaras in this district have been described by archæologists as amazing in their extent, some of the forts being termed tremendous in their impressiveness. The great fortress-town, on the east bank about seven miles below the city of Pierre, occupied a commanding position on a plateau, and although protected in most places by steep ravines and other natural features, it was made still stronger by a great earth wall with many bastions or loops, the whole work exhibiting much ability on the part of its builders and a good understanding of the art of fortification. This village covered from 130 to 150 acres, indicating a population much larger than any Missouri River Indian village of the historic period. Anyone who has studied these Arikara remains will not doubt the truth of what these Indians said to Truteau in 1795: that about the year 1760 they had 4,000 warriors, or a total population of some 20,000 souls.[4]

By 1760 the Arikaras were plentifully supplied with horses. Although an agricultural tribe dwelling in fixed villages, they had the custom of making two extended buffalo hunts in the plains each year, going out toward the Black Hills and probably also eastward toward the James River. In the spring they planted their crops and remained at their villages long enough to give the corn one

4. A detailed description of these Arikara remains near Pierre will be found in the *South Dakota Historical Society Collection*, Vol. III.

hoeing; they then deserted their villages and went in pursuit of the buffalo. Returning home in time to harvest their crops, on the approach of winter they set out on another hunt, remaining away until spring. These people were on friendly terms with the Kiowas and some other wandering tribes of the Black Hills region, from whom they obtained horses and also a few articles of Spanish manufacture. Up to about the year 1790 the Kiowas frequently visited the Arikara villages, to trade their horses and Spanish goods for corn and other articles.

Thus when the first little camps of Teton Sioux began to filter across from James River toward the Great Bend of the Missouri, about the date 1760, they found their way blocked by this powerful Arikara nation. The Arikaras were no longer the timid folk, without horses or metal weapons, who had been driven up the Missouri into Dakota by the Sioux raiders after the year 1725. They now were mounted; they had Spanish sabre-blades with which to point their long, heavy buffalo-lances, and in the open plains they could ride down and destroy any small body of Sioux, that people still being afoot. The Sioux possessed the advantage of having large numbers of guns, and by coming from Minnesota in war-parties of several hundred men they might drive the Arikaras into their fortified villages; but they could not storm these places, and after taking a few scalps and horses and plundering the corn patches they had to withdraw. Another phase of the situation about this period was this: the French and Indian War had compelled the French to abandon their trade on the Upper Mississippi, and until about 1770 the Sioux were starved for goods. Without a regular supply of arms and ammunition they lost for a time the great advantage which the possession of firearms had given them in their wars against the tribes on the Upper Missouri. We may therefore accept without hesitation the statement made by the Arikaras to Lewis and Clark in 1804; namely, that they had not formerly feared the Sioux, that it was the smallpox that had destroyed their power, and that it was only after this disease had carried off most of their people that the Sioux had begun to annoy them seriously. These Indians had suffered from three great epidemics of smallpox between the years 1772 and 1780, and during that brief period they had seen four-fifths of their population destroyed by this dreadful plague.

We may therefore assume that when the Tetons of the Oglala and Brulé group first reached the Missouri near the Great Bend they came to the Arikara towns as poor suppliants rather than as bold enemies. Teton tradition states that the people obtained their first horses from the Arikaras, and some of the earlier entries in the Teton winter-counts indicate that the Teton attitude toward the Arikaras was often friendly. Truteau found the Tetons coming on friendly visits to the Arikaras and even warning that tribe that some other Sioux bands were planning to attack their villages. We may therefore picture the little Teton camps about the year 1760 coming in on foot, with their little tipi poles tied in bundles to the sides of their big dogs, and their women and little girls loaded with packs, to visit at the villages, to beg for corn, dried pumpkins, and native tobacco, and also obtaining a few horses from the friendly people. But these Tetons, being the wild, fickle folk that they were, also raided the villages, and probably paid the penalty; for in the Brulé winter-count it is set down that at this early period the Tetons were much troubled by mounted warriors who came and attacked them in their own camps. As these attacks were evidently made in the lands east of the Missouri, the Arikaras must have made them, for they were the only people in this region who had horses.

At this period the Tetons of the Saone group were also drifting westward. Coming from the headwaters of the Minnesota River, their route across the coteau was farther north than that taken by the Oglalas and Brulés. They came by way of the Kettle Lakes, where their Two Kettle division is said by tradition to have acquired its peculiar name; in their rear their Yanktonais allies were advancing, just as the Yanktons were migrating westward in the rear of the Oglalas and Brulés. The Saones and Yanktonais were engaged between 1725 and 1750 in a savage warfare with the Crees and Assiniboins who dwelt to the north of them. The Cheyennes, who had an earth-lodge village on the Sheyenne Fork of Red River, were directly between these contending tribes, and having been mauled by both parties they were forced, about 1740, to flee beyond the Missouri. Perhaps because of these events, the Saone advance-guard appears to have reached the Missouri at a somewhat later date than the Oglalas and Brulés, and while the latter people struck the river below the Arikara villages the Saones reached it above those settlements.

By 1770 the drift westward of all these Teton groups had been temporarily halted by the Arikaras, who blocked any further advance in that direction. Very few in number and still mainly on foot, the Tetons could not venture to cross the Missouri and go on westward leaving the Arikaras in complete control of all the river-crossings in their rear. But Fate now played into the hands of the Tetons, and within a few years the Arikaras were broken and swept out of the way. First the smallpox struck this strong nation a staggering blow; then the Sioux of Minnesota, having obtained fresh supplies of firearms, resumed their old practice of making long-distance expeditions in force against the tribes on the Upper Missouri. The strong Arikara village on the east bank below the Great Bend was destroyed by these Sioux, and the weak remnants of population in the other Arikara towns could no longer hold out against them; they therefore combined to form new villages, retiring slowly up the river; and by 1786 what was left of the people were living in five or more villages on the west bank of the Missouri, just below the mouth of Cheyenne River. With the river-crossing below the Great Bend now safe from Arikara interference, the Oglalas passed the river at a point near the mouth of Crow Creek and began a new movement westward, going up Bad River. The Brulés soon followed them across; but the movement of the Arikaras up to the mouth of Cheyenne River put them directly in the way of any further Saone advance, and the westward movement of this group of Tetons was held up until the Arikaras were forced to draw farther northward in 1795.[5]

5. Up to the present time no extended account of the Teton and Saone migration to the Missouri has been published. The author has attempted to utilize in the present chapter all available material and to write a rational account of these events, checking the movements of one tribe with those of the others. For fifty years past the Tetons have had no memory of this early period, but up to 1910 the people of the Saone group retained some recollection of events as far back as 1740. The Beede tradition (still in manuscript) are mostly from Saone sources and contain enough material on the early period to indicate that the Saones migrated to the Missouri by a northern route. The lack of references in these traditions to the Tetons of the Oglala and Brulé group is a clear indication that the latter tribes were not with the Saones during the movement to the Missouri.

I now (1957) think that the origin of the name Oglalas is founded in an event Tabeau records (p. 104). He says that the Oglalas and Shiyos settled among the Arikaras and grew crops. The name Oglala refers to scattering dust, and a sensible explanation would be that it was given to the tribe in derision by the camps of roving Sioux hunters, who thought it shameful for Sioux to settle down and dig in the soil. So they called the Oglalas "Dust Scatterers." Tabeau adds that a war between the Sioux and Arikaras forced the Oglalas to resume roving and hunting.

CHAPTER II

IN THE BLACK HILLS COUNTRY
1775-1834

WITH the Arikara villages destroyed and that tribe out of the way, the Tetons were now ready for a new advance westward. The Oglalas led the movement, taking their camp across the river at the Sioux Pass, just below the Great Bend in the Crow Creek neighborhood. The date of this event is not exactly known. S. R. Riggs was told by the traders at Fort Pierre in 1840 that the Oglala crossing was quite recent in time, probably having occurred as late as 1800, but this date is too late.[1] The Arikaras seem to have deserted the country near the Great Bend at about the date 1775, and the Oglala crossing was probably made at that time. At just this date the Tetons were sending war-parties beyond the Missouri, and in 1775 or 1776 an Oglala war-party led by Standing Bull went far enough toward the west to discover the Black Hills.

The Brulés soon followed their Oglala kinsmen across the river, and the west bank of the Missouri from the mouth of White River up to the Arikara towns just below Cheyenne River was now in the hands of the Tetons. Choosing their own line, the Oglalas began a movement up Bad River toward the Black Hills, while the Brulés turning farther to the south selected White River as their field of operation. Most of these Indians were still without horses, marching on foot and living in little tipis whose small poles and leather covers could be transported by their dogs. The Cheyennes, who occupied the Black Hills district at this period, have a tradition that the first Sioux who came into their country arrived in little groups, all afoot. They came to beg for horses, and each season

1. S. R. Riggs' Journal, in *South Dakota Historical Collections,* Vol. XIII, p. 339.

returned in increasing numbers, until presently they were in sufficient strength to begin attacking the other tribes.

These Tetons still regarded the Minnesota country as their home, and as it was also their only source of supply from which they obtained guns, ammunition and other European articles, they had to return eastward each year to do their trading. During the first few years they appear to have gone west of the Missouri only for the summer buffalo hunt and to obtain horses from the tribes out near the Black Hills. As winter drew on they recrossed the Missouri and retired eastward. When Truteau met them in the autumn of 1794 they were mainly on the east side of the river below the Great Bend; but at least a part of them seem to have wintered on the Missouri, for in the winter of 1795-1796 James Mackay met them in council somewhere near the mouth of the James River.[2] Truteau states that the Tetons of the Missouri each spring visited the Sioux trading-fair on the head of Minnesota River. Ten years later the Tetons had become accustomed to living on the Missouri and did not care to make annual journeys as far east as the Minnesota River; a new trading-fair was therefore established for their convenience on James River, only a short journey east of the Great Bend of the Missouri.

When the Oglalas first crossed the Missouri they were evidently a little group of a score or two of lodges. If they had formerly included a larger number of people in their organization, and this is indicated in their name, Village Divided into Many Small Bands, they had left most of them behind during their hard migration across the coteau. Once across the Missouri their small numbers did not deter them from pushing boldly out into the open plains where they quickly obtained horses and were soon roving widely, hunting the buffalo, and fighting enemies on all sides. Their camp was now spoken of wherever the Sioux met at a rendezvous, and their reputation for daring and success in obtaining abundant meat and large numbers of fine horses presently began to attract to their camp the bolder spirits from the Sioux bands which still lingered in the country east of the Missouri.

The country which the Oglalas had now taken possession of was not a good one, even when judged by Dakota standards, and

2. For Mackay consult the notes to the Truteau journals. He was coming up the river to join Truteau but failed to accomplish this. To the Teton chiefs he gave Spanish medals and flags some of which were found among the Brulés by Lewis and Clark in 1804.

the Sioux name for its principal stream, *Shicha Wakpa* (Bad River), clearly indicates this. The river, which headed due east of the Black Hills, was a typical plains stream, full to overflowing in early spring, but almost dry in summer, with pools of rather brackish water standing here and there in its bed. To the north of the river the plains stretched away unbroken to the valley of the Cheyenne River, the Good River of the Indians. In early spring these plains were delightfully green; but by late May or early June the grass was dry and brown; and when a little later in the season the prairie fires came the nights were made weird by the long lines of advancing flame which slowly climbed every prairie hillock, forming a circle of fire around its flanks. The fires turned great tracts of land into blackened wastes for a time; but game abounded in these plains, and as long as the Oglalas had plenty of meat they did not care much about the appearance of the country. Indeed, the Oglalas soon learned to love their new home with its high, dry, and windy plains—a hard country where men had to be fully alive to avoid perishing. They spoke with contempt of the better lands nearer the Missouri and nicknamed the Sioux who lingered in that district *Kutawichasha* (Lowland Folk), a name which in time became the special designation of the Lower Brulés.

But a few miles away to the south of Bad River was a country which was too bad even for the Oglalas: the Big Badlands, a vast tract set with a jumble of clay buttes carved into fantastic forms with mysterious and lonesome valleys lying between them; and here and there great alkali flats, snowy white in the sunlight and strewn with the gigantic bones of prehistoric monsters. In the heat of summer the hills and buttes of this region danced and swam about and seemed to invert themselves in the sky. This was also a land of spirits, where men were led astray to die of thirst or cold, never to be seen again by their friends.

To the south of this badland barrier lay the White River country, where the Brulés were now taking possession. This was a better land than that along Bad River, and why the Oglalas who had first choice should have taken Bad River is difficult to explain. Perhaps the buffalo on Bad River were at the moment nearest to hand, and having found good hunting there the Oglalas remained.

For twenty years after they crossed the Missouri we have practically no information concerning the Oglalas and Brulés except that given in the Sioux winter-counts. The winter-count was an *aide-mémoire* in the form of colored pictographs painted on a buffalo robe, each picture representing the event by which that particular year, or "winter" as the Sioux called it, was to be recalled. From internal evidence it would seem that these records were started soon after the Oglalas crossed the Missouri; some of them appear to have been copied in part from the others, and only one of them (the Brulé count kept by Baptiste Good) attempts to cover the period back of the year 1775. Of the three Oglala counts that have been published, American Horse's count was kept by a family belonging to the True Oglala division, which was therefore with the tribe from the start. The other two counts, those of Cloud Shield and White Cow Killer, belonged to families of the division known as the Smoke People, who do not appear to have joined the Oglalas until after 1825.[3]

The first entry in American Horse's count refers to the discovery of the Black Hills by a war-party of Oglalas led by Standing Bull in 1775-1776. Cloud Shield records the same event, but puts it in the following winter. The counts do not mention meeting the Kiowas at this time, but Kiowa tradition has much to say of the attacks made on their people by the Tetons at this period. One entire division of the Kiowas was cut off in a battle with the Sioux, and the Kiowas had to abandon their old custom of going to the Arikara villages on the Missouri to trade. In 1795 Truteau heard that the Kiowas were hovering about, far up Cheyenne River, fearing to venture nearer to the Missouri because of the hostility of the Tetons.

The Omahas and Ponkas, who had been so often slaughtered and driven from place to place by the Tetons and their allies and were now strongly established in northeastern Nebraska, had obtained horses and were regularly supplied with guns and ammunition by the Sacs and Foxes of the Mississippi, who made annual trips to the Omaha village to trade for furs. American Horse's count states that the Ponkas, about 1778, made peace with the Oglalas and then came with a war-party and treacherously attacked the camp. They were beaten off and pursued, losing sixty of their warriors. According to Cloud Shield, an Omaha woman who was

3. The winter-counts will be found in the fourth and tenth annual reports of the Bureau of American Ethnology. The interpretations of the counts printed in these volumes are very faulty and exhibit clearly the fact that even with the aid of these pictured records the Sioux memory for events more than fifty years back was poor.

living in the Oglala camp was killed in the winter of 1784-1785. Led on by their great chief Blackbird, the Omahas attacked the Oglalas and Brulés, and fighting went on until peace was again made in 1791-1792.

At this period the Oglalas and Brulés were fighting the Arikaras, who occupied the west bank of the Missouri to the north of them, and also the Omahas and Ponkas who occupied a similar position to the southward; while at the same time they were engaged in wars with the Kiowas, Crows, and some other tribes in the Black Hills country to the westward. Raids and counter-raids were constantly taking place and now and then peace was made, only to be broken within a few months. The trouble with the Crows started in earnest in 1785-1786 when Bear's Ears, a Brulé who was visiting in the Oglala camp, and Broken-Leg-Duck, a famous Oglala, were killed while engaged in stealing horses from a Crow camp. The Crows at this date occupied the country from the Black Hills northward, evidently centering along the Little Missouri; but they were soon forced by the Tetons to remove westward into the country beyond Powder River.

The Cheyennes were the next to receive attention from the Oglalas and Brulés. In its initial stage the Cheyenne war seems to have been a Brulé affair. Owner-of-Flute, a prominent Brulé leading a war-party against the Cheyennes, had bad luck and was killed, probably with most of his men. The Brulés and Oglalas now, about 1794, made up a great war-party and going into the country south of the Black Hills they surprised a band of Cheyennes, killing many of the people and capturing their camp with all its contents. That the winter-counts give the correct date for this Cheyenne war is proven by the references in Truteau's journal (1795) to hostilities then going on between the Cheyennes and Tetons.

In these early wars in the plains, the Oglalas and Brulés made a distinction between some of their neighbors and the rest, hating some of the tribes bitterly and exhibiting an inclination to tolerate the presence of the others. Thus they drove away the Crows and Kiowas but soon made peace with the Cheyennes and permitted them to remain in the Black Hills district. With the Arikaras they seem to have been on moderately good terms, at least a part of the time. During the first seasons the Oglalas spent on Bad River they probably withdrew eastward toward Minnesota as winter came on. Thus they had to cross the Missouri twice each year, passing quite near to the lands held by the Arikaras, and their love for corn, dried pumpkins, and tobacco probably drew them often to the Arikara towns. After 1785 the Oglalas seem to have given up the practice of retiring east of the river in the autumn; they wintered on or near the Missouri, and the winter-counts indicate that they occasionally wintered at the Arikara villages.

The Arikaras although terribly reduced in numbers still had plenty of fight left in them, and sometimes—either alone or aided by the Mandans—they even attacked the Tetons in their own camps. Thus American Horse records that in 1783-1784 the Arikaras and Mandans attacked the Teton camp but were driven away with a loss of twenty-five killed. Flame's count states that in 1786-1787 a Saone chief who wore an iron cap was killed by the Arikaras, while American Horse asserts that in the winter of 1788-1789 Last Badger, a famous Oglala, was killed in a fight with the Arikaras. The winters of 1789-1790 and 1790-1791 were very cold, with deep snows; the Oglalas could not hunt and nearly starved to death. In 1792-1793 the Tetons and Arikaras were at peace and, as Flame states, camped together. This probably refers to a large gathering of Tetons at the Arikara towns. At this time Jacques d'Eglise, the first white trader to come up the Missouri this far, was in the Arikara villages, and the Tetons may have gone there on the news of his arrival. For this period when the French from St. Louis first began to come up to the Arikara towns we have several entries in the winter-counts, extending from 1792 to 1795, referring to the Tetons camping at the Arikaras all winter. One winter-count shows an earth-lodge, representing the Arikara villages, and a gun, which is explained as meaning that the Tetons camped at the villages and fought the Arikaras all winter; but this is certainly untrue—the gun more probably refers to trading for guns with the whites who were visiting the Arikaras.

The references in the winter-counts to the Good Whiteman are very puzzling. This man could not have been Truteau; perhaps he was Jacques d'Eglise. American Horse's count states that the Good Whiteman came with two other men to a Teton camp in 1794-1795; he was treated well and on departing was given a load of furs. In 1797-1798 he sent a trader named Little Beaver, Registre Loisel, to trade with the Tetons, and in 1799-1800 he returned in person with many guns to trade. D'Eglise is the only French trader who is known to have been on the Upper Missouri at all the dates indicated.

When Truteau came up the Missouri in the autumn of 1794 he was stopped and robbed at the lower end of the Great Bend by a band of Tetons who had a few Yanktons visiting in their camp. These people were evidently stay-behind Brulés who were afraid to cross west of the Missouri. They had been hunting on the coteau, had found little game, and were living mainly on wild rice which they had gathered in some prairie lake. They told Truteau that one band of their people, twenty-two lodges, was hunting west of the Missouri on White River. This little band was probably made up of the most adventurous of the Brulés, who hunted on White River and wintered on the Missouri. They were on White River again in the following autumn, when John Evans, one of Mackay's men, ran into them and was chased and almost captured.

The Tetons who stopped Truteau attempted to dissuade him from visiting the Arikaras, whom they described as a poor, mean-spirited race. They spoke of the Saones, who roved on the east side of the Missouri farther to the north, as a group distinct from their own, calling them Northern Indians. They asserted that during the past summer these Northern Indians, in five bands, had driven the Arikaras out of their villages, that people not even staying to harvest their crops. After escaping from these Tetons, Truteau took his party on foot up the west bank to the Arikara villages, just below the mouth of Cheyenne River. He found the towns deserted. He saw many signs of Tetons along the west bank from the Great Bend northward.

Having wintered farther down the Missouri, in the spring of 1795 Truteau came up again and this time found the Arikaras at home. He speaks of this tribe being on good terms with part of the Saones, one of the bands of that people having actually settled down to live at the villages. This band must have been Miniconjous, whose name refers to their attempting to settle on the river and grow corn. Truteau also records that in June, 1795, a band of Tetons called Ta Corpa came to the villages to warn the Arikaras that several bands of Sioux were gathering a force of 500 warriors to come and attack them. This band seems to be Lewis and Clark's Ta-co-eh-pa, the third band of the Miniconjous. From these facts it appears that the Miniconjous were the first of the Saones to cross west of the Missouri, coming over at the Arikara villages near the mouth of Cheyenne River. By 1804 this Teton tribe had roved far up the Cheyenne River. As for the Oglalas, they were certainly the band of Tetons which Truteau mentions as being out in the plains near the Cheyennes. He gives no further information concerning them.

From Truteau's reports and the winter-count records it is clear that in 1795 the Oglalas were far out near the Black Hills, engaged in terrorizing the tribes of that region; the Brulés were beginning to hunt on White River, but not in any considerable numbers; while the Saones, still mainly in the country east of the Missouri, were alternately attacking the Arikaras in force and coming to pay friendly visits at their villages. Part of the Saones, by keeping on good terms with the Arikaras, had managed to establish themselves on the west side of the river and were ready to commence their migration westward as soon as these village-dwellers were out of their way. In the summer of 1794 the Saones had attacked the Arikaras and driven them from their villages. Truteau states that at that time one band of Arikaras went up the river to seek protection from the Mandans, while a second band fled southward to join the Skidi Pawnees in Nebraska. These bands were still away a year later when the Ta Corpa Tetons came to the village with the warning that the Sioux were preparing a great attack on the Arikaras. This attack was probably made; for in the following year, 1796, Evans found all of the Arikaras living with the Mandans. There are many evidences that at this time the Arikaras were much divided in counsel, part of the people wishing to remain near the Mandans and part preferring the rather doubtful friendship of the Teton Sioux. These Tetons now began to visit the Arikaras in their new villages, and presently we hear of a battle in which the Tetons joined the Arikaras against the Mandans and their Hidatsa allies. Soon after this, the Tetons having gone off into the plains again, the Mandans and Hidatsas attacked the Arikaras and drove them from their villages. Thus about 1799 the Arikaras, having fled down the Missouri again, built three new villages at a point a little above the mouth of Grand River. Here they held out against all their enemies until about the year 1825.[4]

4. The first part of the Truteau journals (1794) will be found in *The American Historical Review*, Vol. XIX, No. 2. The second part is in *Missouri Historical Collections*, Vol. IV, No. 1, and is reprinted in *South Dakota Historical Collections*, Vol. VII. I have not quoted Charles LeRaye's journal, in the latter collections, Vol. IV, as I regard it as a forgery. Of the score or more of traders mentioned by LeRaye not one is known in the records of the Upper Missouri fur-trade, and this man's account of the Tetons is a grotesque distortion of truth.

The events just referred to are of prime importance in recording the early history of the Oglalas, for the removal of the Arikaras from near the mouth of Cheyenne River opened up the valley of that stream as a line of migration for the Saones, whose advance-guards were soon far enough out in the plains to co-operate with their Oglala kinsmen in all their warlike undertaking. Indeed, the Saones soon began to join the Oglalas in large numbers, and by the year 1840 perhaps a full half of all the people who called themselves Oglalas were of Saone blood. The movement up Cheyenne River was led by the Miniconjous, with the people later known as the Sans Arcs and Two Kettles in their rear. The rest of the Saones—those later known as the Hunkpapas and Blackfoot-Sioux—remained on the east side of the Missouri, frequently visiting the new Arikara villages to trade, but evidently afraid to attempt to occupy the lands lying west of the villages; for the Arikaras claimed that country as their own and were still strong enough to keep these Saones from encroaching on their territory.

Between 1795 and 1804 the French from St. Louis began to trade among the Tetons, establishing temporary trading-houses at various points near the Great Bend, the Oglalas and Brulés usually wintering with these traders near the mouth of Bad River, and the Saones near the mouth of Cheyenne River. Some of the Yanktons by this date had moved to the Missouri and established themselves on Teton land below the Great Bend. A part of the Brulés, evidently the Lower Brulés of later days, were closely associated with these Yanktons; indeed, Lewis and Clark's French interpreters termed these Yankton, Yankton-Bois Brulés, giving to the true Brulés the name Teton-Bois Brulés.[5]

When Lewis and Clark came up the river in the autumn of 1804 they found that the situation described by Truteau had developed still further. The Brulés were now across the Missouri and their old lands on the east side of the river were occupied by bands of Yanktons who had migrated from the Des Moines country; the Brulés and Oglalas were now rendezvousing at the mouth of Bad River, where they traded with the French from St. Louis; the Arikaras had removed from the mouth of Cheyenne River to a point above Grand River, and with their villages out of the way

5. The use of the name Bois Brulé indicates that of the several Brulé tales explaining the origin of their name the one which tells of the people being caught in a fire in the lands east of the Missouri was most probably true. S. R. Riggs in 1840 terms this people Sichangus or Yakora, Tetons of the Burnt Wood.

the Saones, led by the Miniconjous, had crossed the Missouri in force and were roving far up Cheyenne River.

Lewis and Clark met the Brulés at the mouth of Bad River and heard of another camp some distance up this stream which was evidently an Oglala camp. These explorers gave to the Oglalas only sixty lodges, 120 warriors, 360 people, and they gave the other Teton tribes of the Upper Missouri similar amazingly small numbers. For many years scholars have been divided on the question of the Lewis and Clark estimates of Teton population; some authorities accept the figures while others reject them as absurd and insist that there were many members of these tribes who were overlooked when the estimates of population were compiled. These Tetons had come across from the Mississippi and had driven the strong Arikara tribe out of their way; they had crossed the Missouri and invaded the Black Hills country, driving out the powerful Crows, the Kiowas, and some other tribes. The invasion of the Black Hills had been the work of the Oglalas and Brulés alone, and to assume that they could do this with a force of only 200 or 300 warriors does not seem reasonable. This is one view of the matter. On the other hand, it is known that Lewis and Clark in making these estimates had the assistance of all the French traders, some of whom had spent years among the Upper Missouri tribes, and it is also known that there were no hidden pockets in which bands of Tetons unknown to the traders could be concealed. All other evidence points to the small number of Tetons in early times, and it is not unreasonable to surmise that such little bands could invade successfully the Trans-Missouri country, for at this very time tiny groups of Crees armed with guns were haunting the Athabasca country, taking their women and children with them on journeys of hundreds of miles through a hostile territory whose inhabitants ran away at the mere sight of a Cree and his gun. It is true that Atkinson's estimate of the Oglalas in 1825 indicates a fourfold increase in population during the twenty years following 1804, but this astonishing growth is not difficult to account for. It was mainly due to the fact that large bands from other Teton tribes came to join the Oglalas, and to a lesser extent to a rising birth rate and a falling off of infant mortality. Before they crossed the Missouri the Tetons had led a very hard life, marching afoot with the women and small girls who were heavily burdened, generally in a state of want and often faced with long periods of real starvation. After they had crossed the Missouri and had been supplied with horses, life was much easier, especially for the women, and the use of horses in hunting made it possible to keep the camps abundantly supplied with meat during most seasons. The birth rate increased rapidly, and from 1800 onward the Teton camps contained many healthy children. In 1875 a member of the Black Hills commission made a careful estimate of the Oglala birth rate and stated that from births alone the tribe would double in number every twenty years.[6]

Lewis and Clark divided the Oglalas into two bands, the She-o and the O-kan-dan-dahs. The She-o (*Shiyo*: "Sharp-tail Grouse") were the first band and their chief, Wah-tar-par, was the head-chief of the tribe. This man, also called Wah-char-par, "On His Guard," was probably Wachape, "Stabber," for there has always been an Oglala chief of this name, while On His Guard is a name unknown among these Indians. According to Cloud Shield's winter-count a prominent Oglala named Stabber froze to death in the winter of 1783-1784. Lewis and Clark's chief may have been this man's son. Another chief named Stabber was met by Francis Parkman among the Oglalas in 1845, and in 1875 there was a band of Oglalas called the Stabber Band, named after its chief. The second band, the O-kan-dan-dahs (*Oglalas*: the True Oglala band of later times) was led by Chief O-ase-se-char (*Owashicha*: "Bad Wound"), and here again we have a man whose name has always been borne by an Oglala chief. In 1856 General Harney made Bad Wound (perhaps the son or grandson of Lewis and Clark's chief) head-chief of the Oglalas.[7] Lewis and Clark do not mention White Blanket or Shenouskar (*Shinouska*: "White Blanket" or "White Robe") who is termed head-chief of the Oglalas by Zebulon Pike in 1805. Pike's information, obtained on the Mississippi, may have been a year or two out of date and White Blanket may have been dead when Lewis and Clark wrote their account of the tribe.

The Kiyuksas were not noted among the Oglalas by Lewis and Clark, although by 1825 they were the most important division of the tribe. They seem to have been among the first of the Tetons to cross west of the Missouri, for Le Borgne, the brother of Bull Bear, told Francis Parkman in 1846 that as a boy he had had his

6. *Report of the Commissioner of Indian Affairs,* 1875, p. 200.
7. Owawicha Creek (mentioned by Nicollet) must have been named for this Bad Wound of 1804. It is on the west side of the Missouri just below Bad River and is the stream Lewis and Clark called Smoke Creek.

dream in a cave among the Black Hills. Judging from the known age of this man, he must have been in the Black Hills as early as 1782, and his family had always been Kiyuksas. This band can be traced back to the Mississippi and to the year 1750. A portion of this tribe drifted westward and early in the nineteenth century were divided in two groups, one located near the head of Des Moines River and the second between Devil's Lake and the Missouri. The Kiyuksas who appeared among the Oglalas and Brulés after 1804 probably came from the group at the head of the Des Moines. Another band which turned up among the Oglalas after 1825, the Red Water (Minisala or Minisha) was listed as a Brulé band by Lewis and Clark. This shifting of bands from tribe to tribe was nothing extraordinary, for these Tetons were one people, speaking the same dialect and having the same customs. When they pressed into the plains beyond the Missouri, families and whole bands shifted from one tribe to another as their personal interests drew them.

At the time of Lewis and Clark's coming among them, the Oglalas and their Teton kindred were engaged in a new war against the Crows. Sometime around the year 1785 the Oglalas had driven the Crows out of the lands lying north of the Black Hills and had forced them to retire west of Powder River. The Crows, being now a rather distant tribe, were not much troubled by the Tetons for some years, that people contenting themselves with making up little parties now and then to go into the Crow country to steal horses. At times the Crows came eastward in large camps and attempted to reach the Mandan and Hidatsa villages on the Missouri, near the mouth of Knife River, where they wished to trade horses for British goods, and sometimes the Tetons caught them on the march and attacked them. In this fashion the feud between the tribes was kept alive for fifteen or twenty years without any very striking episodes; but about the year 1801, according to the winter-counts, a war-party of Tetons which had ventured into the Crow country was attacked by that tribe near the mouth of Powder River, losing thirty warriors. The Tetons now sent around a war-pipe, assembling a great force of Oglalas, Brulés, Miniconjous, and Cheyennes; they then moved into the Crow country, where they surprised and captured a Crow camp. Some years after this, about 1820, the Crows killed every man in a war-party of Cheyenne Bow String warriors in a fight on Tongue River, and on learning of this the Cheyennes sent around a pipe and induced the Oglalas and some other Teton tribes to come to their aid. The Indians moved westward to Powder River, and having discovered a camp of one hundred lodges of Crows on the Tongue they made a march in the night and surprised and captured the camp soon after daybreak.[8]

During these early wars any disaster, such as the destruction of a war-party or the killing of a prominent man, was sure to lead to a great gathering of the camps and a movement in force against the enemy. The customs that were observed on these occasions were fixed and were about the same among both the Tetons and the Cheyennes. The expedition did not set out as soon as news was received that a party of their warriors had met disaster; the people waited "one winter" and during that time the relatives of the dead men took the war-pipe to neighboring camps where they publicly mourned their dead and pleaded with the people to help them. In each camp the leading men held councils and decided whether their chiefs should accept the pipe or reject it. The pipe was nearly always accepted, and when it had been smoked by the chiefs the camp was pledged to take part in the forthcoming expedition. In the following summer the camps assembled and moved as secretly and swiftly as they could into the enemy's country, with scouts out ahead to look for hostile camps. Having arrived near one of these camps, a halt was made on some stream; here the camps with the women, children, and old men were left, while the warriors made a rapid advance in the night and attempted to surprise the enemy camp at dawn. These operations were generally very successful, resulting in the capture of entire camps; many of the enemy were killed, large numbers of women and children were taken alive, and herds of horses and other property fell into the hauds of the victors. After the Crow village was captured in 1820 the Oglala and Cheyenne camps were full of Crow women and children, most of whom were adopted.

The Teton Sioux had another method of conducting war with large forces. They waited until the summer buffalo hunt was over and then held their annual Sun Dance. Immediately after this ceremony they got up a war-party of several hundred men and ad-

8. George Bird Grinnell, *The Fighting Cheyennes*, Chapter III, gives a detailed account of the capture of this Crow village. From a passage in Lewis and Clark it would appear that the Sioux warriors who were killed about 1801 were Crazy Dogs who staked themselves out with dog-ropes and remained where they were until killed.

vanced into the enemy's country where they struck a heavy blow. The Tetons seem to have employed this method while they were living in Minnesota and still were on foot, going to the Missouri each year to attack the Omahas, Arikaras, or Mandans.

During the period 1800-1825 the Oglalas were hunting each summer in the plains immediately east of the Black Hills, in close association with the Saones of Cheyenne River and the Cheyenne tribe. The latter people were sometimes on the head-branches of Cheyenne River and sometimes down on the North Platte, where one of their favorite camping places was on Horse Creek just west of the present Nebraska-Wyoming line. The Kiowas no longer dared to venture near the Black Hills, for fear of the Sioux, but they often came to the North Platte to trade horses and Spanish goods with the Cheyennes and other friendly tribes. The name Horse Creek probably originated from the custom of holding such horse-fairs at its mouth. In 1815 the Kiowas came to hold a fair at this spot with the northern tribes. The Sioux then made their first appearance on the Upper Platte, evidently being brought to the fair by the Cheyennes, who seem to have had the idea of making a peace between the Kiowas and Sioux; but the fair had hardly started when a Brulé quarreled with a Kiowa and killed him with a war-club. The Sioux then attacked the Kiowas and their friends and drove them into the mountains at the head of the North Platte. It was apparently at this time that a band of Arapahoes and Cheyennes joined the Kiowas and went down to the Red River with them. Thus was formed the queer mixed-camp of trading Indians: Kiowas, Comanches, Prairie-Apaches, Cheyennes, and Arapahoes, who continued for some years to pass north and south through the plains. These trading Indians went north again about 1821 and were camped with the Cheyennes on the Platte when the Crows came to recover their women and children who had been captured in 1820.

During this period, 1800-1825, the Oglalas had a regular beat, passing back and forth between the Black Hills and the mouth of Bad River. At first they wintered on the Missouri, trading during that season with Loisel at Cedar Island below Bad River or with some other French traders from St. Louis; but soon after 1805 they began to spend their winters in the eastern edge of the Black Hills, usually near Bear Butte. In the spring they would go down Bad River, hunting as they went along; and on reaching the Missouri they joined the Saones and Brulés and took part in the pastime of stopping and robbing traders who were going up-river to the Arikaras and Mandans. At times the annual Sun Dance was held on the Missouri, at other times out near the Black Hills; the summer's activities were then concluded by getting up a great war-party to go against the Crows or some other tribe. As cold weather set in the Oglalas were back in their winter camps near Bear Butte, usually with camps of friendly Saones and Cheyennes for neighbors.

It was during these years that the Kiyuksas were first mentioned as being with the Oglalas, and several bands of Brulés and Saones had also come to join the tribe. Red Water and his band seem to have come from the Brulés, and soon this chief was aiding Bull Bear of the Kiyuksas in getting control of the Oglala tribe and assuming the position of head-chief. From the Brulés also came the band led by Lone Man, Red Cloud's father, one of whose chiefs is said to have been Man-Afraid-of-His-Horse, the father of the chief of that name who was born in the Oglala camp the winter of 1814-1815. Red Cloud was born in this country between the Black Hills and the Missouri during the winter of 1821-1822.[9]

With the exception of a few French traders whom they regarded as their friends, the Tetons did not welcome any of the whites who came up the Missouri after 1804; indeed, from a variety of circumstances, they showed a growing disposition to treat all white men as enemies. The French traders from St. Louis had learned to accept with as good a grace as they could muster the pleasant Teton custom of stopping traders and either robbing them outright or forcing them to remain and trade their goods at rates which the chiefs themselves often set; but the Americans who now began to come up the river were of a starker breed, and any attempt of the Tetons to rob or mistreat them was likely to be met with grim looks and a prompt handling of rifles. In 1807 Ensign Pryor was sent to escort home the Mandan chief who had been induced by Lewis and Clark to go to Washington. At the Arikara

9. He was born the winter the blazing star passed over the Sioux country and was named Red Cloud because of the lurid light in the sky caused by the passage of this ball-of-fire meteorite. I have found that this meteorite was observed at Fort Snelling near the mouth of Minnesota River, the night of September 20, 1822. (See Keating: *Expedition to the Sources of the St. Peters River*, Philadelphia, 1824, Vol. 1, p. 316.) In 1870 Red Cloud stated that he was born at the forks of the Platte. This assertion is negatived by every bit of evidence we have and was clearly a political prevarication of the type this chief often indulged in. He said what he did hoping that it would convince the officials that he and his people had a right to live on the Platte.

villages Pryor's party was attacked by that tribe and some Tetons who were present, and after a sharp fight he was forced to retreat down the river. In this affair an Oglala chief named Red Shirt was killed by the American fire. The killing angered the Tetons greatly, and in 1810 they attempted to stop and rob the American traders Crooks and McClellan at a point below the Great Bend. Six hundred Oglala and Saone warriors took part in this affair, but the traders eluded them, slipping into their boats after nightfall and dropping back down the river. In this same year Carson, a trapper, fired across the river from the Arikara villages where he was stopping and killed a famous Teton chief, evidently Blue Blanket.[10] In revenge the Oglalas and Saones killed three whites, and in 1811 they made a bold attempt to halt and rob the very strong Astorian party. The Brulés, Miniconjous, and some Yanktons made this attempt, below the Great Bend, and finding themselves too few in number to deal effectively with the whites they coolly requested that the Astorians wait until the Oglalas and Saones, who were hunting out in the plains, could arrive. The Americans, however, declined to wait to have their feathers plucked and pressed on and reached the Arikara towns safely. At this time the Oglalas, whenever they came to the Missouri, were with the Saones from the upper Cheyenne River, while the Brulés were usually accompanied by some camps of Miniconjous, also from Cheyenne River.

From 1800 to 1817 the Teton trade was almost entirely in the hands of the French from St. Louis, men with whom the Sioux maintained friendly relations. Registre Loisel's old stand on Cedar Island near the mouth of Bad River was occupied in 1809 by Manuel Lisa from St. Louis, who built a post there for the Teton trade. The winter-counts record the burning down of a post in this locality at this date, and as they state that Little Beaver (seemingly their name for Loisel) was burned to death in this disaster, it may be that Loisel was here, either as Lisa's partner or factor. We have very little information on the Tetons at this period, and the winter-count outline is not as useful as it might be, for by the time these counts were interpreted, soon after the year 1877, the count-keepers themselves were very hazy as to the meaning of many of the pictographs. Thus it is stated that in 1815-1816 the Oglalas built a house like a white man's house and lived in it all winter; in 1818-

10. The Brulé winter-count says, "Blue Blanket's father killed winter." I have heard that the father was also called Blue Blanket.

1819 they built another house, and in the following winter a third one. These entries in the counts of course refer to the building of trading-posts by the whites, near which posts the Oglalas wintered. The counts state that several posts were built by Choze, the Teton name for Joseph LaFramboise, a favorite trader of theirs at this period.

American companies entered the trade after 1817; competition became keen, and the traders resorted to the use of the weapon which was most effective in such a trade war and flooded the Teton camps with bad liquor. It was evidently at this time that Red Cloud's father died, for Red Cloud said on many occasions that his father died of drink. This event must have occurred around the year 1825, for Red Cloud is said to have been a little child at the time and was brought up by his older sisters.

As has been indicated, about the year 1799 the Arikaras had established themselves in three new villages on the west bank of the Missouri not far north of the mouth of Grand River. By 1810 the number of villages was reduced to two; but these were strongly fortified, and although often beset by large bodies of Teton warriors they were never in any danger of being taken by assault. As long as the Arikaras maintained a friendly relationship with the whites and were supplied by the traders with arms and ammunition they could hold out against the Sioux; but with astonishing ineptitude these village Indians now proceeded to arouse the anger of all the traders by a series of acts of hostility, culminating in 1823 in a seemingly unprovoked and treacherous attack on Ashley's large party of trappers which had come to the villages to trade for horses. Ashley managed to extricate his men from the trap they were in with the loss of only thirteen and beat a hasty retreat down the river. Halting at a safe distance below the hostile villages he sent expresses in every direction to summon all the white trappers and traders to his support, while at the same time a message was sent down the river to request aid from the military. The white men on the Upper Missouri quickly responded to Ashley's call, but the troops were much slower, and several weeks passed before they finally arrived—a small force of infantry and riflemen under the command of Colonel Henry Leavenworth.

The traders had been at work in all the Teton camps, urging these Indians to join in the crusade against the Arikaras, and by the time the regular troops came up in their boats the Teton warriors had assembled in great numbers: Oglalas, Miniconjous, Saones, and some Brulés and Yanktons. Fire Heart's Saones from east of the Missouri had come in full force, but they had the reputation of being flighty folk, not very friendly toward the whites and likely to desert them and join the Arikaras if they saw the chance of any profit in such a move. Colonel Leavenworth, who had taken over command of all these forces, now had about eleven hundred men, almost twice the number of the Arikara warriors.

From his camp about eight miles below the hostile villages, Colonel Leavenworth started his advance on August 9. The Arikara warriors had all come out on horseback, boldly barring the way; but the Tetons rushed upon them and after a hard fight pushed them back inside their defenses. Having performed their own part handsomely, the Tetons now drew back to watch the white soldiers of whose deeds the traders had been telling them so much, storm the Arikara fortifications; but Colonel Leavenworth was cautious and made no move to assault, and presently the Tetons in considerable disgust left the whites and invaded the Arikara corn patches, where they spent the remainder of the day in feasting. "Helped the white soldiers and get plenty Arikara corn" is the entry in the winter-counts for this year.

On the morning of August 10, Colonel Leavenworth drew up his forces in line of battle, the Tetons still occupying a strategic position in the corn patches, where they kept the pots boiling and hopefully watched for the white soldiers to drive the Arikaras out in the open where they could get at them. But Colonel Leavenworth was very slow to act. He drew his men up in line ready to assault, then shifted them to another position. A few shots were fired into the villages by the artillery, but the Arikaras though frightened stood to their defenses, ready to resist any attack. Thus most of the day was wasted. In the afternoon most of the traders and trappers and some of the troops, who were all very hungry, joined the Sioux in the corn patches. This was too much for the Tetons. Hastily loading their ponies with all the corn they could carry they withdrew, stealing eight of Colonel Leavenworth's horses to take home as trophies.

Late in the day the Arikara chiefs came out with peace pipes. Colonel Leavenworth received them well, but some of the traders refused to smoke and made open threats that they would ignore any peace that was made. The chiefs grew frightened and went back to the villages, but the following day they came out again and concluded a peace with the colonel. They, however, showed no disposition to restore the property they had taken in their attack on Ashley's party, and as this was a violation of the terms of peace Colonel Leavenworth was unwillingly forced to order an assault; but he postponed this until the following day, and when morning came it was found that the entire Arikara population had slipped out of the villages during the night and made their escape.[11]

This inglorious campaign against the Arikaras filled the Tetons with a feeling of contempt for the white soldiers; yet the expedition had frightened the Arikaras badly enough to induce them to desert their villages, which were then partly destroyed by fire. When the tribe came home again they were more troubled than ever by the Tetons, who were evidently urged on by the vindictive traders; drought destroyed their crops, and presently they made the extraordinary decision to move to Nebraska and rejoin their kinsmen, the Skidi Pawnees. How they managed to get safely through the hostile Teton country that barred their way is a mystery—there is some reason for supposing that they took the Powder River route, west of the Black Hills—but they finally reached Nebraska, only to find themselves faced again by the hostility of the traders and Tetons. The Skidi Pawnees were a very friendly tribe, and by telling them what bad Indians the Arikaras were the traders finally induced them to order that tribe to leave; at the same time the Oglalas moved down to the Upper Platte in force and seem to have attacked and defeated the Arikaras, who were also alarmed by the march of Colonel Henry Dodge's dragoons up the Platte. Thus the unfortunate Arikaras, about 1835, decided to return to the Upper Missouri; but they did not attempt to reoccupy their old villages above the mouth of Grand River, going much further north and in the end settling down in the deserted Mandan village near Knife River.

The flight of the Arikaras from the Grand River villages had at last opened the way for the Tetons who still lingered on the east side of the Missouri to advance westward. These Saones, mainly people of the Hunkpapa and Blackfoot-Sioux divisions, now crossed the river and occupied the old Arikara lands lying between Cheyenne River and the Cannonball.

11. The official reports on the Arikara campaign of 1823 are reprinted in full in *South Dakota Historical Collection,* Vol. I. In the same series, Vol. III, there is an extended account of these events.

In 1825 the Oglalas saw their first steamboat and signed their first treaty with the United States. The boat came up the river in early summer, bringing the Atkinson expedition, which stopped at various points to meet the Teton tribes in council and obtain the chiefs' assent to the treaty, which was a simple agreement of peace and friendship. On June 22 the Brulés, Yanktons, and some Yanktonais signed the treaty at Fort Lookout, on the west bank below the Great Bend, where the Oglalas had first crossed the river. At the mouth of the Bad River the Oglala chiefs gave a dog feast on July 4 for the officers of the expedition, and the following day the Oglala and Saone chiefs signed the treaty. Passing on up the Missouri this expedition met the Fire Heart Saones on the east bank of the mouth of Hidden Creek; the Saones of the Hunkpapa division were met at the old Arikara villages near the mouth of Grand River.

Unfortunately, no one with sufficient literary ability to prepare a detailed narrative accompanied this expedition and from the brief reports we obtain no information on the Tetons beyond a bare statement of the location and numbers of the several tribes and the names of some of the chiefs.[12] In these meager reports we are told that the Brulés, estimated at 3,000 persons, wander up the White River to the Black Hills region and rendezvous at Fort Lookout below the Great Bend. The Oglalas, estimated at 1,500 persons, including 300 warriors, rove up Bad River to the Black Hills and rendezvous near Fort Teton at the mouth of Bad River. With the Oglalas at the time they signed the treaty of 1825 were some bands of Saones (from the names of their chiefs they were clearly Miniconjous and Sans Arcs) and the reports state that the Saones, numbering 3,000 persons, were in two divisions and ranged on both sides of the Missouri from Bad River to a point fifty miles north of the mouth of Cheyenne River; one division, mainly Miniconjous and Sans Arcs, roving on Cheyenne River, the other bands, Fire Heart Saones and Hunkpapas, roving mainly on the east side of the Missouri as far eastward as the head of Minnesota River. These Saones of the east bank usually traded on James River, while the Saones of Cheyenne River sometimes traded at the mouth of that stream. From these statements it is clear that the Saones who later were known as the Hunkpapas, Blackfoot-

12. The Atkinson report is in *American State Papers, Indian Affairs*, Vol. II, p. 606; the treaties are in C. J. Cappler, *Indian Laws and Treaties*, Vol. II.

Sioux, and Two Kettles were still mainly on the east side of the river in 1825; but the Arikaras who had so long held the west bank of the river were now about to withdraw, leaving the way open for a new Saone advance.

From a study of the names attached to the Oglala treaty of 1825 we obtain some valuable clues as to the organization of the tribe at that date. The treaty was signed by four chiefs and four head-warriors, which indicates that there were four bands. The first band, led by Standing Bull, Tatanyka Najin, whose head-warrior was Black Elk, was clearly the old True Oglala division, now once more recognized as the head--band. The chief was probably the son of that Oglala warrior Standing Bull who had discovered the Black Hills about the year 1775. The second band whose chief was Shoulder and head-warrior Lone Bull— names known among the Oglalas in later times—was seemingly the old Shiyo or Sharptail Grouse band which by 1845 appears to have merged into the True Oglalas. The third division of 1825 was certainly the Kiyuksa band, for its head-warrior was that famous man Bull Bear, Mato Tatanyka, who within the next few years was to win the position of head-chief of the Oglalas. The chief of this band in 1825 was Crazy Bear, Mato Witko. He is called in the treaty, Full White Bear, which is an error for Fool White Bear, *mato* meaning the white or grizzly bear and *witko* meaning either foolish or crazy. There were several men named Crazy Bear among the Oglalas in later times. The fourth band of 1825 cannot be identified. The chief was given as Wa-na-re-wag-she-go, Ghost Boy. This seems to be Wanonrechege, Ghost Heart, a name known among the Oglalas as late as 1876. The head-warrior of this band is given as Na-ge-nish-ge-ah, Mad Soul, which seems to be the common Oglala name, Mad Shade. *Nagi* means ghost or shade. The family bearing this name belonged to the True Oglala division after 1870.

These four bands of the 1825 treaty clearly were people who after 1835 were known as the Bear People—the followers of Bull Bear. The other half of the Oglala tribe of later days, the Smoke People, including the bands of Chief Smoke, of Red Cloud's father, and some others, are not mentioned in the treaty of 1825. They, and also Red Water's band, were associated at this time with the Oglalas but were still being rated, apparently, as Saones and Brulés. They must have first taken the name Oglala when they left their own tribes permanently and followed Bull Bear to the Platte in 1834.

From 1825 to 1835 the winter-count records are devoted to events which seem trivial, although they were clearly regarded by the Oglalas of that day as important. They indicate that the main interest was still the war with the Crows; a war with the Pawnees was just starting. In 1832 that foolish fellow George Catlin visited the Indians at the mouth of Bad River, but there is nothing to be gained from his romantic and rather addle-headed pages further than the names of two or three individuals, these names being so badly mutilated that they are almost unrecognizable. His one statement of any interest is that Whirlwind, the well known chief of later times, was an Oglala of the Kiyuksa band.

At this period, around 1830, Fort Teton, the old Oglala trading-post, at the mouth of Bad River, had been abandoned and Fort Tecumseh had been erected in the same locality. The company that controlled this post was now engaged in establishing branch-posts out near the Black Hills, to save the Indians the trouble of coming all the way to the Missouri to do their trading. One of these branch-houses, Brulé Post, was at Butte Caché on White River, very near the present Oglala agency at Pine Ridge. On Cheyenne River there was a post for the Cheyennes, evidently at the mouth of Cherry Creek; above this location was Saone Post, near the forks of Cheyenne River, while Ogala Post was on the South Fork of Cheyenne River near the mouth of Rapid Creek, east of Bear Butte. The small fur companies did not build branch-posts but sent their traders to live in the Indian camps.

Oglala Post was evidently built about 1829. Thomas L. Sarpy, who was called Red Lake by the Oglalas, was in charge of this place. On the night of January 19, 1832, while he and his men were at work in the trade-room a candle was upset and fell into an open keg of powder. There was a violent explosion which killed Sarpy and injured his three companions, James Parker, Pineau le Yankton, and Louison le Brulé. Pineau was the man for whom Pineau Springs, a water-hole near the head of Bad River, was named. This little post was soon rebuilt, and the Oglalas continued to trade there until 1834.[13]

During the generation from 1805 to 1835 the Oglalas were probably happier than they ever were in later times. Dwelling in

13. The Fort Tecumseh journals are in *South Dakota Historical Collections,* Vol. IX, p. 93 *et seq.* In the same collections, Vol. XI, pp. 282-83, the location of Oglala Post on Rapid Creek is clearly indicated.

remote sections on the plains, they were untroubled by the whites, only a few French traders whom they looked upon as their good friends came into their country. They were now plentifully supplied with horses, game abounded in their territory, the camps were usually overflowing with fresh and dried meat, and the call to come and feast was heard all day long. The quantity of food that these Indians could consume was astonishing. Even the wars of this golden time were pleasant affairs, dragging along from year to year with their little horse-stealing raids and illuminated now and then by some lurid happening such as the killing of an entire war-party, the capture of an enemy camp, or the mysterious killing during the night of all the horses belonging to Chief Standing Bull. During these years the Oglala camps were almost always within sight of the Black Hills, which from a distance in the plains appeared as a faint blue shape on the horizon, but seen near at hand rose grim and black against the sky. In winter the camps were located in sheltered stream valleys close to the eastern edge of the hills, and sometimes the people went into the mountain valleys to hunt deer and elk or to cut lodge-poles; but *Pa Sapa,* the Black Hills, was sacred ground, the heart of the Teton land, where people did not often venture to camp. A whole epoch in the life of the Tetons has been lost through the failure to record in writing at an earlier date the tale of the Sioux migration to the Black Hills and their early life in that region. Here and there we catch a glimpse of the rich materials we have lost, as in the mention of the Race Track. This was a lodge-trail that ran completely around the base of the Black Hills. When the Indians surrendered the Hills in 1876, they said: "We give the lands as far as the Race Track." The Bear's Lodge, Medicine Pipe Mountain, the Old Woman's Hill, the Dancers' Hill, and the Buffalo Gate: behind each of these names lies a story of those early times, but most of the stories have been lost.

CHAPTER III

FROM THE BLACK HILLS TO LARAMIE
1834-1841

WE have now come to the time when the white traders were to induce the Oglalas to move down to the Platte to live, and in order to understand this event some account of the operations of the fur-traders must be given here. During the period 1825-1835 the American Fur Company had a practical monopoly of trade with the Teton Sioux, conducting their business from their central post, Fort Tecumseh, later Fort Pierre, at the mouth of Bad River. This company's policy was to trade with the Indians; that is, it depended on Indians to collect its furs, and although it purchased furs from white trappers it did not encourage trapping by parties of whites on the Indian lands. On the other hand, from 1824 onward General Ashley and his partners took large brigades of white trappers into the field, and by going farther toward the west, to Powder River and into the Rockies, they discovered rich fur regions which had never been trapped and brought back to St. Louis such quantities of fine beaver and other furs that the other fur-traders were amazed at their success. This Rocky Mountain Company, as it came to be called, paid little attention to the Indians, merely attempting to keep on good terms with them and trading with them occasionally to obtain horses. They kept their brigades of trappers in the field the year round, camping out like Indians and wandering from stream to stream in search of good trapping grounds. Thus was brought into existence within a few years that unique type of American, the Rocky Mountain trapper, a white Indian often with an Indian wife. For many years these men in large brigades or little parties of two or three combed every nook and cranny of the mountains and plains in quest of beaver, making friends with the Indians when they could, fighting them with ferocious courage when they had to.

The American Fur Company was soon alive to the great profits which the Rocky Mountain trappers were reaping and decided to enter this new field. Organizing a brigade of trappers and putting some of its most enterprising leaders in command, it sent the outfit to the mountains. Getting on the trail of the Rocky Mountain trappers, these newcomers dogged their footsteps, following them wherever they went, to learn their secrets and discover the richest trapping grounds. They were even accused of setting the Indians on their rivals in order to hamper their operations. Enraged by these tactics, the Rocky Mountain Company attempted to strike back by sending a fine outfit of trade-goods to the Upper Missouri to compete with the American Fur Company in its own field for the Indian trade; but the older company kept a firm hold on the Sioux and other tribes and presently forced its rivals to withdraw.

The Rocky Mountain Company had now reorganized; some of the partners withdrew from the mountains and devoted their time to the marketing of the furs and the supplying of brigades of trappers with the articles they required. These men were really not partners, merely having an agreement with the Rocky Mountain Company to take the furs it collected and to bring out to the mountains each year the goods that were needed. In 1834 these men, William Sublette and Robert Campbell, decided to bring their goods to the mountains by way of the Santa Fe Trail, for at this time the Arikaras were on the Platte and the traders were afraid of being attacked and robbed by these hostile Indians if they took the Platte route to the mountains. Being much delayed on their journey, Sublette and Campbell began to fear that they would arrive too late for the Rocky Mountain Company's annual rendezvous; Sublette therefore pushed on ahead, but on reaching the mountains he found that the Rocky Mountain Company had purchased the supplies it required from other parties, thus leaving him and his partner with a large stock of goods on their hands for which they had no market. Meantime Robert Campbell had reached the mouth of Laramie Fork, and while waiting there for the return of Sublette he set his men to work building a little stockade on the site of the later Fort Laramie. This stockade he named Fort William in honor of his partner.

Failing to dispose of the goods to the Rocky Mountain Company, Campbell, who was a resourceful man, then decided to draw the Oglalas down from the Black Hills, to live on the Platte and trade at the new stockade. Lucien Fontenelle, returning from the mountains, passed down the Platte at this time and on reaching Bellevue, just south of the present city of Omaha, he wrote to warn his own firm, the American Fur Company, of Campbell's plans. Stating that Campbell intended his post to be a central point for the Sioux and Cheyenne trade, Fontenelle continued: "He has now men running after these Indians to bring them to the River Platte. Buffalo is in abundance on that river during all seasons of the year and the situation may turn out to be an advantageous one for the trade."[1]

Fontenelle and the other American Fur Company leaders clearly regarded Campbell's operations as an attempt to steal their Indians, for they had held control of the Sioux and Cheyenne trade for so long that they regarded any attempt of rival traders to deal with these Indians as poaching. They had already suffered in this fashion, for between 1827 and 1829 the Bent brothers, having built a post on the Arkansas River, had come up to the Black Hills and persuaded several bands of Cheyennes and Arapahoes to move south and trade with them.

In 1895, Major Powell wrote an article on the early history of Fort Laramie and published it in Frank Leslie's Weekly. Much of his information had been obtained from General Carlin, who had served at the fort in early days, and this material included the statement that when the first stockade on Laramie Fork was completed two men, Kiplin and Sabille, were sent to Bear Butte in the Black Hills, where they induced Bull Bear with one hundred lodges of Oglalas to move to the Platte, "and this was the first appearance of the Sioux in that region."[2] A search of the records discloses that Kiplin was C. E. Galpin, usually called Gilpin, who was still trading in the Fort Laramie neighborhood in 1842. He later went back to the Upper Missouri where he continued to trade among the Sioux for many years. John Sabille was another trader for whom a branch of Laramie Fork and also a valley, Sybille's Hole, were named. In 1843 Sabille was trading on the Missouri again, near the mouth of Cheyenne River.

1. H. M. Chittenden, *History of the American Fur-trade of the Far West* (New York, 1902), p. 305.
2. Powell's article is reprinted in *Wyoming Historical Collection*, Vol. I.

Thus the Oglalas in 1834 were suddenly uprooted and taken from their old home in the Black Hills country to a new land on the North Platte. Their long-established relations with the American Fur Company were broken off; but Sublette and Campbell soon turned over their post to the Rocky Mountain Company and that concern, finding that it was losing money, sold out to the American Fur Company; so within a few months the Oglalas were trading with their old friends again. The stockade on Laramie Fork was now remodelled and given the name Fort John. The Sioux soon forgot these events. In 1870 the government sent a commission to Fort Laramie to deal with the Oglalas, and during the councils one of the chiefs assumed an air of great importance and began to tell the white men how ignorant they were. "Who built the first post on this ground!" he shouted; and to his amazement one of the white-haired commissioners said quietly, "I built the first post here." It was Robert Campbell of St. Louis, who in 1834 had built the first little stockade on the site of Fort Laramie.

From the story told by Major Powell it appears that Bull Bear came to the Platte in the fall of 1834 with one hundred lodges, and since the Oglalas at that period were rated at two hundred lodges or more, it is apparent that only a part of the tribe came to the Platte at first. Bull Bear, having wintered near the new stockade, was evidently joined in the spring of 1835 by most of the other Oglala bands, for when Samuel Parker came up the Platte that summer he met two thousand Oglalas there, about two hundred lodges.[3] These people had been hunting buffalo near the forks of the Platte and were on their way up to Laramie Fork to do their trading. A few Oglalas are known to have remained in the Black Hills. They gradually drifted back to the Missouri, where they still maintained a tiny camp of their own as late as 1865.

The lands along the Upper Platte which the Oglalas had occupied were claimed by the Cheyennes and Arapahoes. Many of the bands of these two tribes had gone down to the Arkansas to live; but there were still several of their camps in the Platte country, and even as late as 1855 the district between the forks of the Platte was known as Cheyenne and Arapaho territory though the Oglalas had long been in full possession.

Before they moved south the Cheyennes had become engaged in

3. Samuel Parker, *Journal of an Exploring Tour Beyond the Rocky Mountains* (Ithaca, N. Y., edition of 1842), p. 66.

a lively war with the Pawnees, whose earth-lodge villages were on the Loup Fork of the Platte in eastern Nebraska. The Skidi Pawnees had long been accustomed to winter near the forks of the Platte, the lands in that district being their favorite hunting field; here they had come into frequent collision with the Cheyennes, sometimes one tribe and again the other having the better of it. Just prior to 1830 the Pawnees had killed an entire war-party of Cheyennes and that tribe, as was its custom, waited "one winter" and then "moved the Arrows" against the Pawnees. In the meantime they sent around a war-pipe to all friendly camps, and when they started into the Pawnee country in the following summer they were accompanied by a large body of Arapahoes and Sioux. Advancing to the headwaters of Loup Fork these Indians ran into the Skidi Pawnees and attacked them, the Cheyennes taking their sacred Medicine Arrows into the battle tied to the head of a lance which was carried by a medicine-man. A Pawnee who was suffering from ill health and wished to die had gone out between the lines and sat down on the ground to await his death; but when the Cheyenne medicine-man rode at him and tried to strike him with his lance, the sick man grasped the lance and jerked it out of his hand. The Pawnees then made a charge, getting possession of the lance and of the Medicine Arrows which were attached to it. This misfortune so disheartened the Cheyennes that they and their allies gave up the fight and withdrew, the Cheyennes mourning and wailing over the loss of their great tribal medicine.[4]

The Medicine Arrow fight seems to have drawn the attention of the Tetons to the Pawnees, for from this time on the winter-counts frequently record important fights with that tribe. In these affairs the Brulés appear to have played the leading part in attacks on the Pawnee earth-lodge villages, while the Oglalas, after they moved to the Platte, devoted much of their attention to harrying the Pawnees when they came westward into the plains on their semi-annual buffalo hunts. By 1832 the Pawnees had been so mauled by the Brulés that they abandoned Loup Fork and built

4. Grinnell, *The Fighting Cheyennes,* gives a good account of the Medicine Arrow fight. I have other accounts from the Cheyennes and Pawnees in manuscript. The statement in the Brulé winter-count that their tribe recaptured the medicine arrows from the Pawnees is incorrect. Captain L. H. North of the Pawnee Scouts tells me that the old Skidis always said that their chiefs gave two of the medicine arrows to the Yanktons at a peace council and the Yanktons traded or gave these arrows to the Brulés. The Skidis still had the other medicine arrows some years ago.

new villages on the south bank of the Platte; but the United States government did not want them there, as it was feared that they would annoy the fur-traders and emigrants who used the route up the Platte; for this reason the government agents, some years later, induced the Pawnees to return to Loup Fork. It was said by the Indians that they were promised protection from the Sioux, but no effort whatever was made to afford them any relief.

Part of the Pawnees were still on the Platte, and those bands which had gone back to the Loup were engaged in building new villages when, in June, 1845, a great force of mounted Sioux was observed early in the morning on a ridge overlooking a new Pawnee village of sixty earth-lodges. This mass of warriors charged down the slope into the village, killing some Pawnees and capturing a number of horses. They then retired to their ridge, left their plunder there, formed up and charged again. Many Pawnees hearing of the fight rode from the old villages on the Platte eighteen miles away to aid their kindred, but the Skidi Pawnees whose village was near the one being attacked fortified themselves and did not go to the assistance of the other Pawnees. The Sioux would charge into the village, kill some Pawnees, set fire to a few lodges and ride back to their ridge, taking many captured horses with them; then form up and charge again. Most of the Pawnees had taken refuge in the head-chief's house, a very large earth-lodge, and cutting loop-holes in the walls they fought desperately against the overwhelming force of Sioux. The horse-pens surrounding this lodge were full of Pawnee horses which the Sioux were trying to obtain, riding boldly up almost to the muzzles of the Pawnee guns. Here several Sioux were killed, but their friends threw their bodies across the backs of horses and carried them off to prevent the Pawnees scalping them. This fight went on for hours, and when the Sioux finally drew off with their plunder the Pawnees were so badly frightened that they threw their dead into corn-caches and ravines, gathered up a few of their belongings and fled from the village. The Pawnees had about seventy killed in this affair, including Middle Chief, another head-chief, and LaChapelle the interpreter. Thirty lodges were burned and a great number of horses were taken by the Sioux.[5]

When the Oglalas moved to the Platte they began hunting buffalo near the forks of that stream, and as the Skidi Pawnees hunted

5. The best account of this fight will be found in *Nebraska Historical Society Transactions*, first series, Vol. II, pp. 152-56.

in the same district the two tribes came to blows almost at once. As we have seen, Bull Bear came to the Platte with one hundred lodges of Oglalas. He wintered near the new trading post on Laramie Fork and in the spring went down the Platte to hunt buffalo, being joined on the way by another one hundred lodges of his tribe. There is no record of a fight with the Pawnees at this time, the Oglalas completing their hunt and in July returning to Laramie Fork to trade; but during the ensuing winter, as the winter-counts record, the Oglalas had a battle with the Pawnees on the ice of the frozen Platte and defeated them.

It is well known that the Sioux often called the Arikaras Pawnees (Padani), and in the winter-counts we have several instances of the Arikaras and Pawnees being confused one with the other. At this time, the summer of 1835, the whole Arikara tribe left the Skidi Pawnee village on Loup Fork and moved up to the forks of the Platte. Here they were met by Colonel Henry Dodge and his dragoons, and they seem to have settled down in this district to spend the winter. As we have a record of the fact that the Skidi Pawnees wintered much farther down the Platte, near Grand Island, and as it is stated that they had only a small fight with the Sioux that winter, it seems obvious that the Oglala battle with the Pawnees on the ice was really a fight with the Arikaras. Rufus Sage referring to this battle states that it took place near Ash Hollow on the North Platte, that the Pawnees were badly defeated and retired to their village on Cedar Bluff, near the present city of North Platte, where they hurriedly gathered up part of their belongings and fled to escape further attacks from the Sioux.[6] This story fits in well with the known movements of the Arikaras at this time and it supplies an explanation for their leaving Nebraska and presently turning up near the Mandan and Hidatsa villages on the Upper Missouri.

The Oglalas now began to attack the Skidi Pawnees, and within a few years compelled this tribe to abandon its ancient custom of wintering and hunting near the forks of the Platte. The other three Pawnee tribes hunted on the branches of Kansas River, and the Skidis now obtained permission to hunt with them.

American Horse records that in the winter of 1837-1838 an

6. Rufus B. Sage, *Rocky Mountain Life* (Boston, 1857), p. 196. Samuel Parker's party, led by Lucien Fontelle, passed Cedar Bluffs in July, 1835, and saw no Pawnee village there. They heard that the Arikaras were in the vicinity. I suspect that the traders, disappointed when Colonel Dodge failed to attack the Arikaras, set the Oglalas on that tribe.

Oglala named Paints-His-Cheeks-Red and all his family were killed by Pawnees on the North Platte; the Brulé winter-count records the same event, stating that five Oglalas were killed. Spotted Horse, a nephew of Paints-His-Cheeks-Red, then took a war-pipe around to the Sioux camps, to recruit a party to go into the Pawnee country and take vengeance for the killing of his uncle's family. This raid on the Pawnees seems to have been made in 1838, and the winter-counts state that the party got to the Pawnee villages, had a fight, and captured some horses, but on the way home their supply of provisions was exhausted and they were compelled to eat the Pawnee horses which they were bringing back as trophies.

In the following summer the Sioux and their allies went to the Pawnee hunting grounds on the branches of Kansas River where they surprised and defeated that tribe, killing eighty persons, the Sioux losing only one man. This must have been the usual Sioux performance of watching the Pawnees until they left their camp to hunt, permitting them to chase buffalo and tire out their horses, and then when the Pawnees were scattered in little groups butchering the game, the Sioux on fresh horses would suddenly charge them, surrounding some parties and chasing the others back to their camp. The Pawnees, who had women and children with them, were very much scattered and could make no stand until they all got back to camp; meanwhile the Sioux would cut off one little party after another and kill them. Such were the scenes that lay back of the simple entry so often repeated in the winter-counts: "Killed one hundred Pawnees."

Bull Bear himself led this expedition of 1839 and was on his way home when his party met the German traveler Wislizenus on the South Platte. In the Wislizenus journals we have our only description of the personal appearance of this great Oglala chief. "Rather aged, and of a squat, thick figure." He is described as a good friend of the whites who was much liked and respected by the traders.[7]

For some unexplained reason the Oglalas of Bull Bear's following, including the Kiyuksas, True Oglalas, Red Water's band, and some small camps, now began to hunt westward from Laramie Fork, going into the Laramie Plains near the extreme head of the North Platte. Their hunting grounds near the forks of the Platte

7. Wislizenus, *A Journey to the Rocky Mountains in 1839* (St. Louis, 1912), pp. 58, 138.

from 1840 onward were occupied by the Oglalas of the Smoke People division and by several camps of Brulés who now began to desert their old range on the head of White River and move down to the Platte to live.

The result of this shifting of range was that the Oglalas of Bull Bear's group came into conflict at once with the Snakes who inhabited the country west of the mountains and owned large herds of fine horses. These herds irresistibly attracted the Oglalas. The Northern Arapahoes and Northern Cheyennes, who roved often in the country near the headwaters of the Platte, joined the Oglalas in attacking the Snakes, while the Crows from the Bighorn country at times came down to make raids on the Oglalas and Cheyennes. Thus when the Oglalas of Bull Bear's division went to the Laramie Plains to hunt they found themselves in a kind of debatable land which was crossed by the war-parties of several tribes. It was a good hunting country, but notoriously a place where trouble was easily brewed, and these Sioux soon found an abundance of trouble.

Raiding the Snakes and taking up again their old war with the Crows where they had dropped it ten years before, the Oglalas soon found themselves also embroiled with the white trappers. In 1840 the Rocky Mountain trappers held their last rendezvous; some of the men left the country, others continued to trap in little independent groups. Beaver trapping was no longer profitable for the large companies; the days of the big trapping brigades were over, but many of the men were unfitted for any other kind of life, and they remained in the mountains, doing some trapping and usually living in the Indian camps when the season's work was ended. As most of these men were living among the Snakes and Crows, the Oglalas who were raiding these tribes often saw white men helping their enemies, and they suffered considerable losses which they attributed to the fire of the trappers.

This feeling of hostility toward the whites, at first directed toward the trappers who were taking sides with the Snakes and Crows, quickly spread among the Oglalas and other Indians of the Upper Platte, who were soon talking of killing or driving out of their country all the whites except a few favored traders. The conduct of many of the whites was a sufficient justification for such action on the part of the Indians. The Indian trade, like beaver trapping, seemed to be dying, and year after year the number of trading-posts decreased; yet in the midst of this period of declining trade there were many foolish men who thought only of the large profits which had been made in the trade in past years, and these men now entered the field to compete with the older companies at a time when those firms were only holding on in the hope that after a few years conditions might improve.

In 1835 the little stockade on Laramie Fork was the only trading-post in the Upper Platte country, but within the next few years several new posts were established and the American Fur Company, which had at first enjoyed a monopoly of the Indian trade of the region, soon found itself engaged in a bitter trade-war with the rival companies. As was always the case in such struggles for control of the Indian trade, liquor was the principal weapon employed. At first traded at high prices, as competition increased liquor was given to the Indians without charge. The Oglalas had already been through a trade-war of this kind on the Upper Missouri about the year 1822, and had seen scores of their tribesmen killed in drunken brawls. These poor Indians knew that liquor was a very bad thing, and most of them did not wish to have it brought to their camps, but when it was pressed upon them they did not have the moral strength to refuse it. Beginning about 1840, this struggle among the traders kept the Oglalas, Brulés, and Cheyennes of the Upper Platte in a state of utter demoralization for several years. In ordinary times the killing of a Sioux by a fellow-tribesman was an event of rare occurrence, but with liquor entering the camps freely such murders happened every day. The list of killings recorded in the winter-counts and by Rufus Sage is appalling, and it is evident that these accounts tell only a portion of the sordid story.

It was at this time that John Richards, a fiery little Frenchman who was to play such a large part in the later history of the Oglalas, made his first appearance on the scene. This man, described as a desperado, was the first to start the flow of liquor in the Indian camps, for he is reported to have smuggled a supply of whiskey across the boundary from the Mexican settlements south of the Arkansas River. He carried the stuff along mountain trails to his employers, Pratte, Cabanne & Company, who now had a post near the American Fur Company's Fort John on Laramie Fork. With this stock of liquor, Pratte and Cabanne began to debauch the Indians, rapidly getting their trade away from the American Fur Company. That concern, assuming a highly moral attitude, made a formal complaint to the United States government and urged that a special Indian agent should be sent to the Upper Platte to put a stop to this liquor peddling; then, being a wise old corporation, it quickly provided itself with a large supply of liquor and began fighting fire with fire. This company managed to have one if its own employes appointed as Indian agent, but when he arrived on Laramie Fork the traders, who had been warned, hid their stock of liquor and greeted him with innocent faces. He seems to have managed, however, to smoke John Richards out, for this reprobate was now supplied by his company with a stock of goods, including a liberal supply of liquor, and went up to trade in the Black Hills country, where his trail from camp to camp was marked by dead Sioux killed in drunken brawls. On Laramie Fork the traders brought out their alcohol again as soon as the Indian agent's back was turned and resumed operations, the American Fur Company, as it was said at the time, drugging its stock of liquor, probably by adding laudanum to it. This was supposed to be a humane practice, as such drink usually stupified the Indians and prevented quarrels and killings.[8]

It was during this period of liquor peddling in the Oglala camps that the feud between Bull Bear and Smoke finally reached a crisis. Bull Bear was a great chief but something of a tyrant, holding his turbulent followers in check by roaring at them and promptly putting a knife into any man who did not heed his orders. He had never paid for a wife, taking the girls that pleased his eye and letting their parents whistle for the customary payment. He would not endure a rival, and when the traders put forward that plump and jovial chieftain Smoke and encouraged him to oppose the old chief, Bull Bear paraded through the length of the camp and stationing himself in front of Smoke's lodge, loudly challenged him to come out and fight. No one appearing, Bull Bear in a fury stabbed and killed Smoke's favorite horse which was tethered in front of the lodge and then marched back to his own camp. Thus affronted and injured, Smoke did not dare voice an objection; but he and his friends, young Red Cloud among them, devised a plan and awaited their time.

In the autumn of 1841 their chance came. Old Bull Bear with only a few followers rode into Smoke's camp on the Chugwater, an eastern branch of Laramie Fork a few miles southeast of Fort

8. The letters of the Indian agent, Andrew Drips, bearing on the liquor trade among the Sioux, will be found in *South Dakota Historical Collection*, Vol. IX, p. 170 *et seq*. Chittenden and Sage also print much material on this subject.

John. Some of the American Fur Company's men from the fort were in this camp trading liquor, and Smoke's men started Bull Bear's warriors to drinking and embroiled them in a quarrel. The old lion, hearing the uproar, rushed out of his lodge to stop the fight and was instantly shot down, some say by young Red Cloud. A wild fight ensued; Red Cloud's brother, a chief named Yellow Lodge, and six warriors were killed and many others wounded before the encounter was stopped.

Francis Parkman heard this story five years later from Rouleau, who was in the camp when the fight broke out. Rufus Sage gives the date as November, 1841. The Oglalas today have almost no memory of the killing of Bull Bear, an event which split their tribe into two hostile factions and profoundly influenced its later history. Dr. Charles A. Eastman, himself a Sioux full-blood, has set down the story as it was told to him in later years by the Oglalas. As an example of the poor memories of these Indians Dr. Eastman's narrative is a classic. Thus we find him stating that the cause of the trouble was the arrival of General Harney at Fort Laramie for the purpose of making a treaty with the Sioux. In actual fact, there was no Fort Laramie at the time; General Harney first came to that vicinity fourteen years after Bull Bear's death, and he did not come to make a treaty. The story goes on to relate that the Oglalas refused to sign the treaty; General Harney then bribed the wicked chief "Bear Bull" and he attempted to bully the people into accepting the treaty. Red Cloud's father (who had been dead for many years), now stepped forward and defied the chief, who at once killed him. Young Red Cloud then killed the tyrant Bear Bull, for which deed he was hailed as a hero.[9]

American Horse's winter-count records this event under the

9. Charles A. Eastman, *Indian Heroes and Great Chieftains* (Little, Brown & Company, Boston, 1920), p. 11. This book is worth studying. Written by a full-blood Sioux, mainly from information obtained directly from the older people of his tribe, it presents a spectacle of poor and distorted memory that is appalling, as nearly every date and statement of fact is incorrect. The stories of the early lives of Red Cloud and the other chiefs do not ring true, and wherever we can check them from reliable sources they turn out to be apocryphal. The attempt to belittle Spotted Tail is surprising, coming as it does from a Sioux, but it carries no weight, the assertions made being so glaringly incorrect that no scholar will credit them.

There is a water color portrait of Bull Bear reproduced in *The West of Alfred Jacob Miller* (Norman, University of Oklahoma Press, 1951). The chief is shown as a handsome, strong-featured man of commanding appearance. Little Wound is said to have been a son of Bull Bear and to have hated Red Cloud all his life for killing his father. Little Wound became head chief of the Bear People, and even in 1890 he was bitterly opposing Red Cloud.

correct date: winter of 1841–42. It states that the Oglalas got drunk while encamped on the Chugwater and had a fight, after which the Kiyuksas, Bull Bear's band, seceded from the rest of the tribe. The True Oglalas, Red Water's band, and some others went along with the Kiyuksas; fully half the tribe seceded, and even forty years later on the reservation the Oglalas were divided into two sections which were still known as the Bear People, Bull Bear's followers, and the Smoke People, Smoke's faction. From the day in November, 1841, when the old chieftain was slain in Smoke's camp the two divisions of the tribe drifted apart, the Bear People moving gradually toward the southeast and in the end occupying the lands in Nebraska and Kansas between the Platte and the Smoky Hill Fork, while the Smoke People shifted northward from Fort Laramie and presently occupied the headwaters of Powder River, in northern Wyoming, as their home-country.

When, five years after the fight on the Chugwater, Francis Parkman came to spend a summer in the Oglala camps, he found the people wandering about, leaderless and divided. Eagle Feather, the son of old Red Water, said that since the time of the great chief's death the Oglalas had been like children who did not know their own minds. Whirlwind, the man who was met by George Catlin on the Upper Missouri in 1832, had been chosen to succeed Bull Bear; but he was leading only his own band, the Kiyuksas. The other chiefs were in a similar position, each acting for himself and for his own little group, and when the people came together in large camps to decide upon some important action, it was only to quarrel and separate again, each band going off hating all the others.

CHAPTER IV

THE DRIFTING YEARS
1842-1851

IT was just after the time of Bull Bear's death that the Oglalas had to face new conditions with the coming of the emigrants. At first a few white-topped wagons creeping slowly up the Platte; then many more; then a flood, an army of strange white people all going toward the west. The Oglalas had usually found the traders and trappers comfortable companions, but these new white people were different. They had women and children with them and their attitude toward the Indians was one of distrust and fear. The Sioux noticed that these newcomers did not get on well with the old white men, the traders and trappers. They seemed to distrust the whites they found living among the Indians, and the traders in their turn cursed the men with the wagon-trains who were coming in to spoil the country. The Oglalas were puzzled by the coming of the emigrants. They did not understand this movement toward the west. Gradually they became aware that the whites were spoiling the Platte valley, destroying the grass and timber, driving off the game, and turning the valley into a white man's country where the Indian was only tolerated as an unwelcome intruder and was expected to conform to the white man's laws and regulations, which he did not understand.

It is absurd to blame the emigrants for all the Indian hostility toward the whites in the early forties. The records show that this hostility was at first aimed at the white trappers. The Indians had been attacking the trappers for several years before the emigrants came in sufficient numbers to attract notice. As far as the Oglalas were concerned, this growing feeling of hostility toward the whites was largely an outgrowth of the demoralization of the tribe brought about by the liquor traffic. Then too, many trappers were living among the Snakes and Crows in the early forties just at the time when the Oglalas were vigorously raiding these tribes, and this made it a simple matter for the trappers to become embroiled, for sometimes they aided the Snakes and Crows, and often the Oglalas ran off the trappers' horses.

In 1841 the Oglalas and Cheyennes stopped Dr. E. White's party of emigrants, who were being guided by Thomas Fitzpatrick, west of Independence Rock on the Sweetwater. The Indians counciled all night as to whether the emigrants should be attacked or not. Most of the warriors were for attacking. In the end the chiefs informed Fitzpatrick that his party might proceed, but they warned him that no more wagon-trains would be permitted to pass through the country. This same summer 500 Sioux, Cheyenne, and Arapaho warriors attacked a large party of trappers under Fraeb's leadership on the present Battle Creek near the Colorado-Wyoming line west of Laramie Plains, and in a pitched battle killed Fraeb and four of his men. Their loss in this fight enraged the Indians, and during the winter war-pipes were sent around.[1]

When Fremont reached Fort John on Laramie Fork in July, 1842, he was warned of this growing hostility of the Indians and was told that 800 lodges of Oglalas, Cheyennes, and Arapahoes had gone up the North Platte with the avowed intention of "cleaning out" a camp of trappers and Snakes on the Sweetwater in revenge for the killing of some Indians by Fraeb's trappers in '41. The chiefs, who were at Fort John, tried to keep Fremont there. It is apparent that they could not control their own people and were afraid an attack would be made on the whites. Fremont, however, went on westward. He soon met many sulky Oglalas returning toward Laramie Fork, who stated that the big camp of Oglalas, Cheyennes, and Arapahoes had quarreled among themselves. Some of the warriors had wished to attack an emigrant-train near Independence Rock, the rest had other views, and after carrying the quarrel almost to the point of fighting each other they had crossed south of the Platte near the mouth of the Sweetwater and were now hunting in Laramie Plains.

At this time Bull Bear had been dead but a few months, yet the Oglalas had already split into quarreling factions and were showing the effects of lack of strong leadership. We cannot fol-

1. Hafen & Ghent, *Broken Hand* (Denver: The Old West Company, 1931), p. 133.

low these events in detail, the evidence being too scanty, but we have enough information from Fremont, Sage, Parkman, and some others to make it clear that part of the Oglalas were hunting and camping west and southwest of Fort John and were associating with the Northern Cheyennes and part of the Arapahoes, while other Oglala bands were hunting and camping east and southeast of the fort and were associating with the Brulés and some Miniconjous from the Black Hills. In June, 1843, Fremont met an Oglala near Bijou Creek on the South Platte who said that his band was moving south to visit the Arapahoes, who were hunting on the head of Bijou. In August of this year Sage found about 1,000 lodges of Indians camped on the South Platte attending the Cheyenne medicine-lodge ceremonies, and he speaks of a large body of Sioux being present.

When Fremont came up the Platte again in 1845 he found the Sioux very angry with the emigrants, who had driven the buffalo away from the North Platte, compelling the Indians to go beyond the Laramie Mountains to hunt. The emigrants were also complaining that they were being threatened and robbed by the Sioux, and during this same summer Colonel S. W. Kearny was sent up the Platte with a force of U. S. dragoons to quiet the tribes by a display of strength. On Laramie Fork he met the Sioux in council and warned them sternly that if they molested the emigrants they would be severely punished. At this council old Bull Tail, a Brulé chief, spoke for the Sioux. It is to be noted that on this occasion, as at the council in 1851, the Brulés took the leading part, although the councils were held on Oglala lands. One suspects that the Brulés, who down to 1825 seem to have been considered the true Tetons, being usually called Tetons and not Brulés, were regarded by the Oglalas as the elder, perhaps the parent group. There are many little clues pointing in this direction, but actual proof is wanting.

Smoke's division of the Oglalas must have been present during the council with Colonel Kearny, for Red Cloud always claimed that he was there and saw the dragoons parade, and he lived with Smoke's people. The Bull Bear group, now led by Whirlwind, were hunting on the Laramie Plains and were not at the council. On their way back they stopped among the foothills of the Laramie Mountains to cut new lodge-poles. From this camp Whirlwind's son, Male Crow, set out with a war-party to go against the Snakes. Not a man of this party returned, for in the Snake country they were attacked by a superior force and were all killed. American

Horse records this event in the winter 1844-1845, but Cloud Shield, who belonged to Smoke's faction, merely says, "Crazy Horse says his prayers and goes to war." This man must have been the father of the Crazy Horse who led in the Custer battle, for Frank Grouard the scout stated that the name Crazy Horse had been handed down in this chief's family from father to son for several generations. Parkman informs us that the Snakes, fearing the vengeance of the Sioux, induced Vaskiss to bring to Whirlwind the scalp of his son Male Crow with a present; but Whirlwind put aside the Snake peace-offering and that winter sent a war-pipe as far as the Missouri River, summoning the Tetons to a crusade against the Snakes. In the following summer, 1846, two villages of Miniconjous arrived to take part in this grand expedition into the Snake country; but in the meantime Whirlwind had let Bordeaux, the trader at Fort John, talk him out of his purpose. He had summoned these warriors and now would not lead them. He clearly could not control his own people, for in July when the question of going on a buffalo hunt in Laramie Plains was brought up Whirlwind was entirely against it; yet the people went on the hunt beyond the mountains, leaving the sulky chieftain and his half-dozen lodges to do as they pleased. That summer Whirlwind's little camp and the family of Bull Bear almost starved, as there were no buffalo on the Chugwater and Horse Creek where they were encamped.

Smoke's people and some Cheyennes finally set out for the Snake country; but they appear to have quarreled amongst themselves, as they did in 1842, and the expedition broke up with nothing accomplished. Edwin Bryant found 600 lodges, 3,000 Sioux, camped near Fort John. This was the Snake expedition ready to start. Later in the summer Dr. White, coming east from Oregon, ran into a village of 250 lodges, Sioux and Cheyennes. This was the remnant of the great Snake expedition. Smoke's people were in this village and Dr. White was informed by Galpin, who was with the Indians, that the Sioux and Cheyenne warriors were out looking for white men and Snakes, intending to kill all they were able to find, in revenge for the killing of seven Sioux who were supposed to have been attacked by Snakes and whites.[2]

This summer, 1846, is the one which Francis Parkman spent among the Oglalas, and it is to this sojourn that we owe that splendid

2. A. J. Allen, *Ten Years in Oregon; the Travels of Dr. E. White & Lady* (Ithaca, N. Y., 1850); Edwin Bryant, *What I Saw in California* (New York, 1849).

book *The California & Oregon Trail.* Parkman had an instinctive understanding of the Indians; they were neither Noble Red Men nor scurvy savages to him, but human beings each with his own characteristic faults and virtues. Considering it as a whole, it would be difficult indeed to find another work, written by a contemporary, with as full and true a picture of the old West: the Indian, the trader, the trapper, and the emigrant. Parkman spent part of the summer with the Bull Bear group of Oglalas, hunting on Laramie Plains. There is no other picture of these people in their wild, free state that is to be compared with his.

In the summer of 1931 Dr. Scudder Mekeel of the Institute of Human Relations, Yale University, took a copy of Parkman's book to Pine Ridge and read the passages which refer to the Oglalas to some of the old people. They were much interested and had a long discussion as to the Indians and whites mentioned in the book. At first they had the idea that Parkman was the man who married Bear Robe, the daughter of Bull Bear. They called him Yellow Whiteman, but in the end they decided that this man was Henry Chatillion, Parkman's guide. Here again we have a test of the Indian's memory. These people in 1931 had only the haziest recollection of the important men of their own tribe who were living in Parkman's day, only eighty-five years previously. One day a man named Frank Man-Afraid-of-His-Horse came to ask Dr. Mekeel if he could help him to discover who his white grandfather was. After some talk, it was found that Frank was the grandson of Henry Chatillion. There could be no doubt of this. His mother, the daughter of Yellow Whiteman and Bear Robe, became the wife of Young-Man-Afraid-of-His-Horse and Frank was the child of this union. Young-Man-Afraid-of-His-Horse had another wife, a full-blood Oglala woman, and she was the mother of Amos Man-Afraid-of-His-Horse, the present head of this famous family. Frank Man-Afraid-of-His-Horse is married to one of Red Cloud's younger daughters.

The winter-count of American Horse says that in 1845-1846 White Bull and thirty Oglalas were killed by the Crows and Snakes. In White Cow Killer's count this leader is called White Buffalo Bull, and he and his party are said to have been killed by the Crows; Cloud Shield says by the Snakes, while the Brulé count says thirty-eight Oglalas were killed by Crows.

In the summer of 1847 the Tetons made their annual attack on the much-bedeviled Pawnees. Four hundred mounted Sioux attacked a hunting-camp of 216 Pawnees and killed eighty-three persons. For this year American Horse's winter-count merely records a great feast given by Big Crow and Conquering Bear, at which many horses and other presents were given away. Cloud Shield records that Long Pine, a Sioux, was murdered by another Sioux; White Cow Killer says "Diver's neck broken." Except for the Pawnee slaughter it seems to have been a dull year on the Upper Platte.

But still the flood of emigrants poured westward. In this very year of 1847 a new movement was starting. Kimball with 143 Mormon men and seventy-three women came up the Platte this spring, reached Salt Lake in July, and began farming operations. The following summer Brigham Young passed along the Platte with 397 wagons, 1,200 people, and was followed by two other trains which included 395 wagons, 1,188 people. The damage done by the hordes of emigrants was by this time becoming noticeable even to the most unobserving of the Indians. The growing scarcity of buffalo alarmed the chiefs. The Indian Affairs Reports for these years are full of foreboding. The agents and superintendents felt that the dwindling of the buffalo herds meant a crisis in the plains, but the government showed little interest in anything except the keeping of the emigrant road open.

The emigrants on the Platte were annoying enough to the Sioux and their neighbors, but the natural feeling of the Indians against them seems to have been greatly increased by the talk of many of the traders, who blamed the emigrants for all the ills from which they and the Indians suffered. As the emigrant road touched the buffalo range along the Platte for only one hundred miles, the traders' talk of the slaughtering of game by the emigrants was absurd. These men either had not the brains or the honesty to observe that the dwindling away of the great herds had begun long before the first emigrant-trains appeared on the Platte. The traders themselves were largely to blame for the reckless killing-off of the buffalo. Catlin in 1832 saw a herd of 1,500 of these animals slaughtered by Indians near Fort Pierre on the Upper Missouri because a trader wanted a boat-load of salted tongues to ship to the St. Louis market. Catlin states that only the tongues were taken, the rest of the meat and the skins being left for the wolves. These foolish Indians received only liquor in exchange for the tongues.

In 1832 buffalo were often very scarce on the Missouri and the Indians had long periods of semi-starvation; then the herds would come back to the river for a time. Prince Maximilian noted that the Tetons camped near Fort Pierre in the winter of 1833 nearly starved to death because there were no buffalo near. There were plenty of buffalo on the Niobrara and White River in 1841 and for some years after that date; along the Platte from near Grand Islands to the forks the herds, disturbed by the emigrants, began to dwindle after 1843, but great herds were not far to seek, both north and south of the emigrant trail. This fact explains the origin of the Oglala geographical terms, the Buffalo North and the Buffalo South. To these Indians the country north of the Platte was the Buffalo North.

When we look at the figures showing the number of buffalo robes traded to the fur companies during the forties, the number of animals killed for food by emigrants along the Platte seems an insignificant part of the great slaughter that was going on. Fremont estimated that for eight or ten years prior to 1843 about 90,000 buffalo robes were brought to market annually by the fur companies. These were all cow skin winter-robes, November to March, the summer-skins not making good robes. Bull-hides were not traded for. In 1847, 110,000 cow skin robes were shipped to St. Louis. Considering that it was estimated that the whites (the traders, trappers, and emigrants) killed only about 5,000 buffalo a year during the fifties, it is evident that the Indians, urged on by the traders, were themselves the principal offenders in the slaughtering of the herds. It should be remembered that the skins traded represented only a fraction of the buffalo destroyed each year. The Indians had to provide themselves with robes, clothing, lodge-covers, and a great many other articles made from buffalo skins.

A great deal of nonsense has been written concerning the care the wild Indian took never to waste a particle of the buffalo he killed. This was the version set forth by the reservation Indians after the last buffalo herds had been destroyed by white hunters. Men who saw the wild Indian at work among the herds were under no such delusions. In 1850 Captain H. Stansbury and his party saw a band of Oglalas killing buffalo on Laramie Fork and were shocked to observe that these people took only a few choice parts of the meat and left the great carcasses unskinned on the ground for the wolves. At this very time these Oglalas were complaining bitterly about the destruction of game by the emigrants.

During this period, from 1840 to 1855, the Oglala tribe was drifting like a ship with a disabled rudder. Most of these Indians detested the emigrants, yet a strange attraction drew them back to the Platte Valley each season, to camp beside the Oregon Trail, to watch the passing trains, to frighten the more timid of the whites into giving them presents, and to beg from those whom they could not intimidate. Bull Bear, who had taken the traders' advice and brought his people down from the Black Hills with the idea that he was taking them to a better country, had really led them into a trap, but a trap which neither he nor the traders could have foreseen. That the Oglalas were not benefiting from their association with the whites along the emigrant trail was apparent even to many of the Indians themselves; yet with no strong leadership these people seemed incapable of breaking the spell that held them on the Platte, where they drifted here and there and every year became more entangled in the web of events which Fate seemed to be weaving for their ruin.

In the early summer of 1849 the greatest rush of whites that had so far taken place began to flow up the Platte. To the Oregon emigrants and the Mormons were now added the thousands who were heading for California and the new gold fields. Asiatic cholera had made its appearance in the United States; the disease raged on the steamboats which brought the emigrant parties up the Missouri, and these groups carried the plague up the Platte, where it was at once communicated to the Indians. "Many died of cramps" is the grim entry in the winter-counts for this year. Captain Stansbury's party came up the Platte this summer and found the cholera in all the Sioux camps. Part of these Indians had been stricken while encamped on the South Platte and had fled to the North Fork, the disease killing them as they hastened northward. They then camped along the Oregon Trail, begging for medicine and receiving no attention from the churlish emigrants. The Sioux believed that the whites had poisoned them in some mysterious manner, but they were too sick and frightened to attempt to make reprisals. Near Ash Hollow, Stansbury saw five deserted lodges filled with dead Sioux; a little farther on he met a small camp whose people were recovering from the cholera but were in deadly fear of its return; while some distance farther along the road he came on a large camp of Sioux with the cholera raging among the lodges. He sent his physician to minister to the Indians who swallowed the medicines eagerly, for most of them believed firmly that they would thereby be saved.

During this epidemic the Oglalas of the Smoke division fled north to White River, and while they were encamped there near the site of their present agency at Pine Ridge, Red Cloud is said to have attempted to devise a remedy for the cholera. He finally prepared a decoction of cedar leaves which was considered helpful to the sufferers. This incident has been quoted by some authors as proof that Red Cloud was a doctor. The truth is that all the Sioux were desperately afraid and many of the men and women were trying to find something which would relieve their sufferings.

The Indian agents' reports show that the cholera lingered among the Western Sioux for over a year and was followed by severe epidemics of smallpox and measles. As most of the Indians believed that these diseases were forms of magic which the whites were employing against them, the resentment produced by the flood of emigrants coming up the Platte was naturally increased. The United States government had a full realization of this growing hostility among the Indians of the Upper Platte, and it now purchased the old trading-post on Laramie Fork—now quite generally known as Fort Laramie—and garrisoned it with troops. The year 1849 thus witnessed the ending of the fur-trading period in this region. The American Fur Company built a small trading-house just west of Horse Creek on the south bank of the Platte and put Andrew Drips in charge. This place was the new center for the Oglala and Brulé trade. Joseph Bissonette was also trading with these tribes, having had the stock of Pratte, Cabanne & Company, his old employers, turned over to him when that firm abandoned the field. Several other men were trading in this district, dealing both with the Indians and the emigrants, for the trade with the whites by this time was in some respects more profitable than that with the Indians.

For several years prior to 1850 the Superintendent of Indian Affairs at St. Louis, T. H. Harvey, had been urging the government to hold a grand council on the Upper Platte with the northern tribes of the plains and mountains, the object being to quiet the Indians on the Platte who were becoming restless because of the throngs of emigrants passing through their country, and to take the first steps toward bringing the tribes under government control. Mr. Harvey reiterated each year in his reports that the buffalo were dwindling away, and he warned the government that the disappearance of the herds would bring on a great crisis among the plains and mountain tribes. D. D. Mitchell, who succeeded Mr. Harvey as superintendent at St. Louis, continued the plea for the assembling of a council on the Upper Platte, and Congress finally made an appropriation for this purpose in February, 1851.

Early in the season of 1851 the Indian Office sent men up the Arkansas, Platte, Missouri, and even up the Yellowstone, to inform the tribes of the great council to be held on the Upper Platte and induce them to send delegations; but the Indians did not seem to be much interested, even after the list of fine presents which would be distributed at the council had been described to them. To the Pawnees, Snakes, Crows, and other enemies of the Sioux the prospects of venturing their lives among that vindictive people with the object of making a white man's peace must have appeared as a foolish proceeding; but the agents and traders coaxed and cajoled and in the end succeeded in bringing to Fort Laramie several delegations, including a party of Snakes from the mountains and some Crows and other Indians from the Yellowstone. The Pawnees would not come. The entire Oglala tribe was present, the council being held on their land; most of the Brulés were also there, and some camps of Cheyennes and Arapahoes. For two weeks this great body of Indians remained encamped on Horse Creek, some miles east of Laramie, where they feasted on white man's food, provided free by the government, visited each other's camps and at the urging of the whites, pledged eternal peace among the tribes. They finally "touched the pen" for the treaty-signing, received their presents, and started on their return journey.

A great deal of happy sentiment was expended on this Horse Creek council by writers such as De Smet, who heralded it as the dawn of a new day of peace and brotherhood among the western tribes. The peace really lasted no longer than the two weeks during which the Indians were camped together with the troops on guard to prevent trouble; but for several years after this gathering the Sioux agents repeatedly stated in their annual reports that their Indians were faithfully adhering to the peace pledge which they had given during the council at Horse Creek. This was not true. The Sioux were as busily engaged as ever in fighting the Crows, Pawnees, and other enemies; but the agents were profiting by the annual distribution of presents provided for in the treaty and they were eager to make it appear that the money being expended by the government was bringing good results. The real situation was that year after year the Upper Missouri Sioux openly repudiated the treaty and begged these dishonest agents to tell the Great Father that they did not want his annual presents which they considered as a bribe offered them to restrict their freedom of action. They also stated emphatically that they intended to continue the Crow war. Suppressing these facts, the agents each spring took the annuity goods up the river on a steamboat and appropriated most of them for their own uses, persuading some of the tame chiefs who hung about the trading-posts to sign receipts for all the goods.

The agents might have saved themselves the trouble of devising many false reports if they had read the treaty a little more carefully; for it is apparent that the officials at Washington were not particularly interested in intertribal peace and brotherhood. When these hard-headed gentlemen provided $100,000 for the purpose of holding the council, and further sums each year, as provided for in the treaty to be enforced, they did so with the very practical object of putting the Indians along the Platte in a good humor, safeguarding the Platte road from Indian attack, and obtaining by treaty the right to establish military posts in the Sioux country. The pretty scheme for a peace among the tribes was adopted for the edification of certain classes of good people in the East who believed in such improbable things as eternal peace among warlike tribes of wild Indians.

During the council at Horse Creek the boundaries between the several tribes were discussed at great length by the chiefs and the most experienced traders, and in the treaty the lands of each tribe were carefully defined. Thus we learn that in 1851 the Sioux claimed no lands south of the Platte, the boundary running from the forks of the river up the North Platte to Red Buttes near the mouth of the Sweetwater. The Powder River country, soon to become the home of the northern bands of Oglalas, was set down in the treaty as a part of the Crow territory.

The Sioux appear to have been lumped together as one nation at the signing of this treaty, and only a few chiefs, who were selected by the traders as the most important men, were permitted to "touch the pen."[3] Brave Bear of the Brulés headed the list of signers, the other chiefs being Brulés and Missouri River Sioux. In later years the Oglalas talked of this treaty as if it had been first and last an Oglala affair, yet none of their chiefs signed the treaty.

3. Each chief put his hand on the pen while one of the whites signed his name. This was sometimes termed "taking hold of the stick."

It was during this council that Brave Bear, the chief of the Wazha-zha band of Brulés, was made head-chief of all the Teton Sioux. Why Whirlwind, Smoke, and Red Water of the Oglalas were passed over we do not know. Brave Bear was a traders' chief who in 1841 was employed by the American Fur Company traders to annoy their Fort Platte rivals in the Brulé winter-camps on White River; a commission which he fulfilled conscientiously by stealing these traders' horse-herds, by shooting up their camp, and finally by boldly attempting to assassinate them. However, ten years later, this man was accepting responsibility. He made an excellent chief of the Bull Bear type, controlling his wild followers by roaring at them and promptly resorting to the use of weapons when any man dared to oppose his will.

Our information concerning the Oglala chiefs between the time of the cholera of 1849 and the Grattan affair of 1854 is so scanty that we cannot tell when or how the leadership of the tribe was changed. Whirlwind and Red Water appear to have survived the cholera, for we find them in the list of chiefs in Schoolcraft's *Indian Tribes*.[4] This list, dated 1850, shows four Oglala chiefs, six bands, and a total of 400 lodges. Whirlwind is the first chief and old Red Water, at that time over eighty-five years of age, is second. Smoke's name is not in the list, his rivals of the Bull Bear faction seemed to have control of the tribe; yet only four years after the date of this list we find Man-Afraid-of-His-Horse, a young leader in Smoke's division of the tribe, recognized by everyone as the head of the Oglalas. This sudden change in leadership is very puzzling. Whirlwind and Red Water apparently died soon after 1850. Smoke was then the only one of the old chiefs left; a man still physically vigorous and popular both among the Indians and the traders. Why was he passed over and a young chief of his camp selected? And why was Smoke's nephew, Red Cloud, only five years younger than Man-Afraid-of-His-Horse, also passed over? The oldest Oglalas now living have no knowledge of these events, but they do insist very earnestly that the whites have never understood their system of tribal government, or the rank and duties of the chiefs and other leaders; they assert that they never had a head-chief until after 1850, when the whites persuaded them to choose a chief with whom the government might deal as the head of the tribe. This seems to be true. Man-Afraid-of-His-Horse, re-

4. Volume III, p. 629.

garded by the whites as a head-chief, was called by the Oglalas themselves simply "our Brave Man." And in that title we may see the reason why he and not one of the older chiefs was considered head of the tribe, for he, like Brave Bear of the Brulés, was the recognized leader of the all-powerful class of warriors.

This famous chief was born about 1815 and, as He Dog asserts, belonged originally to the little camp of which Red Cloud's father was chief. He is first mentioned in the written records in 1845 when as head of a small camp of Oglalas on the North Platte he receipted for some annuity goods. In this receipt his name is written Man-Afraid-of-The-Dog, Ta-chonce-ko-ki-te, and the second chief of the camp is set down as White Cottonwood, Wagi-ensca.[5] He is next mentioned in 1854 as head-chief of all the Oglalas. His family, like those of many other famous chiefs, have attempted to make out that his name was given to him after he became a leading man and that it is a sort of title of honor. They explain that it does not refer to a man who is afraid of his horse but to the fact that this man was so brave that his enemies grew alarmed at the mere sight of his horse; "They-Fear-His-Horse," or "Even-His-Horse-is Feared." This view has been accepted by most of our authors, who seem to believe whatever the Indians tell them. It may be noted, however, that the Sioux did not have the custom of giving their chiefs new names of honor after they had become famous, and also that according to the statements of the Man-Afraid-of-His-Horse family the name was handed down from father to son for several generations; in fact it goes back to the period around 1760 when the Sioux were obtaining their first horses and were having difficulty in learning to ride these strange animals. Knowing as we do how much more ready the Sioux were at inventing nicknames of a humorous turn than they were at giving beautifully expressed titles of honor, we may readily conjecture how this famous name really originated.

Man-Afraid-of-His-Horse is said to have been originally a Kiyuksa, but by 1865 he was head of the band known as the Hunkpatila, Those-Who-Camp-at-the-Horn, the horn or end of the camp-circle being the position of honor. After this chief's position had been taken from him by the government officials and given to Red Cloud, Man-Afraid-of-His-Horse's band was termed the Payabya, meaning Pushed Aside, a name which probably refers to the fact that the chief had been discarded as head of the tribe.

5. Drips papers in *South Dakota Historical Collections,* Vol. IX, p. 199.

CHAPTER V

BLOOD ON THE GROUND

1852-1856

THE purchase of Fort Laramie by the government and the garrisoning of it with troops in 1849 inaugurated a new era in the relations between the Oglalas and the whites. At first the Indians appear to have welcomed the coming of the soldiers who, they had been told, were to protect their country from the devastation being wrought by the emigrants. They very quickly learned that it was the emigrants' complaints which the Great Father had in mind in sending the soldiers and that the purpose of the whites was not to control the emigrants but to dominate the tribesmen.

Agent Thomas Fitzpatrick of the Upper Platte and Arkansas Agency protested from the first against the placing of little garrisons at Laramie and at the new post near the crossing of the Arkansas. This agent had been a trapper and fur-trader in the plains and mountains for over thirty years and was one of the most experienced men in handling Indians to be found in the West. He protested very strongly and repeatedly in his annual reports against stationing a skeleton company of infantry at a tiny post in the heart of the Indian country, where the garrison at any moment could be rendered helpless by a swarm of warriors. He ridiculed the use of a few foot-soldiers to protect emigrants from the mounted plains Indians. His suggestion was a force of three hundred mounted men on the Platte and a similar force on the Arkansas, to march here and there as required; and it was his belief that if such forces were maintained in the field for a few seasons and were judiciously used the troops could then be withdrawn, for the tribes would have learned the power of the government and would think twice before committing any depredations on the whites.

Some of the military men apparently objected as strongly as did Fitzpatrick to this policy of placing infantry detachments in the Sioux country six hundred miles from the nearest supporting force. Thus Colonel Fauntleroy, First Dragoons, in 1852 recommended that Fort Laramie, Fort Kearney on the Lower Platte, the new small post on the Arkansas, and Fort Leavenworth should all be abandoned and that a force of ten companies of dragoons should be concentrated at a new post near the mouth of the Republican, where Fort Riley was later established. This post would be much nearer the Indian country than Fort Leavenworth and from it the troops could take the field early in the spring and strike quickly if required to do so. His opinion was that the dragoons from this post could control both the emigrants and the Indians, and by making annual marches through the plains could overawe any tribe that showed signs of restlessness.[1]

Colonel Fauntleroy had hardly sent in his recommendation and Fitzpatrick was still penning his protests against the little posts of infantry when the first trouble occurred at Fort Laramie. This was in June, 1853. There was then at the post one company of the Sixth Infantry, about fifty officers and men, under the command of First Lieutenant R. B. Garnett. That summer there was the usual huge assembly of Sioux and Cheyennes near the fort, probably from five hundred to six hundred lodges with one thousand to twelve hundred warriors, waiting for the Indian agent and the annuity goods. One day a Miniconjou, from a little camp of this tribe which was visiting the Oglalas and Brulés, fired across the river at a soldier who was in the skiff which was used as a ferry by the troops. There were only twenty men at the fort when this incident occurred; yet an officer with four or five infantrymen was sent at once to the Indian camp to arrest the Miniconjou. There were about forty lodges of Miniconjous, and near them were several much larger camps of Oglalas and Brulés. Most of the Indian men were out hunting, and when the soldiers approached the camps the people started to flee. The usual trouble-maker was present and fired a shot at the men in uniform who replied promptly, killing five Sioux. They returned to the fort without their prisoner.

1. *Report of the Secretary of War*, 1852. The heavy cost of transporting grain for horses was the reason for using infantry at Fort Laramie, and the equally great cost of transporting supplies for the infantry was the excuse for reducing the garrison to a mere handful of men. In 1850 it cost $27.72 to feed a horse for one month at Fort Kearney on the lower Platte, the cost at Fort Laramie being $34.24.

The whites who were passing along the road at the time were greatly alarmed by this affair, fearing that the Sioux would attack the wagon-trains. These emigrants blamed the military for starting the trouble, stating that the Miniconjou had asked the soldier in the boat to take him across the stream and had only fired his gun after being roughly repulsed.[2] The diary of Maria A. Belshaw, who was with an emigrant train that passed Fort Laramie at this time, states that four or five days after this affair the Indians in revenge attacked a small emigrant camp near the fort, killing a man and his wife and their two children. A few of the soldiers then went out and attacked the first Indians they met, killing one and wounding another.[3] This second affair is not mentioned in the military reports.

When Agent Fitzpatrick arrived on September 10, he found the Sioux in such an ugly humor that he requested the officer in command of two companies of the Mounted Rifles, who were encamped near the fort on their march east from Oregon, to remain while he counciled with the chiefs and quieted the Indians. He had brought with him the amendments to the treaty of 1851 for the Sioux to sign, but the chiefs cried out in a rage that they would have nothing to do with any more pieces of paper; they demanded that the troops leave their country, saying that these white soldiers who had been brought here to keep the peace were now the first to make the ground bloody. The agent stated in his report that the relatives of the dead Indian were making threats against the whites, and he again protested strongly against the policy of placing small infantry garrisons in isolated positions among these powerful tribes of mounted Indians.

It is quite apparent that on this occasion Fitzpatrick and the friendly chiefs prevented serious trouble. As for the military, it was depending, as it usually did in dealing with Indians, on force alone, and it had not sufficient force to accomplish anything further

2. Diary of Mrs. Maria A. Belshaw, in *New Spain & the West* (Lancaster, Pa., 1833), Vol. II, p. 225. "June 16th .... A great many Indians traveling; the reason I suppose is they are fixing for a battle with the whites. They are moving their families where they can be safe. One wanted to cross the river with a soldier, but the soldier refused to take him. The Indian shot at him, the soldier returned to the Fort, raised the soldiers. They pursued the Indians 3 miles. Shot 5 dead, wounded 2, took 2 prisoners; now they think they are making ready for a battle. The Indians no more look smiling, but have a stearn solumn look. We feel this evening that we are in danger. We pray the kind Father to keep us safe this night."

3. *Ibid.*, p. 227.

than the stirring up of trouble. With their usual ineptitude, the troops at the fort had employed an interpreter whom the Indians disliked and even hated. This man, who was the only channel through which the officers could negotiate with the chiefs, was a drunken bully who spent much of his time in insulting and threatening the Indians and encouraging the young officers in the peculiar belief that their skeleton company of infantry had been stationed at Laramie for the purpose of fighting and subduing the Sioux. Second-Lieutenant J. L. Grattan was the leading-spirit among these youthful warriors. He was fresh from West Point, of Irish descent, and eager to show his mettle. He talked constantly of Indian-fighting and of what he would do if he got the opportunity to "crack it to the Sioux."

It was in the following summer, 1854, that he got his chance. The Sioux had assembled as usual to await the agent and their annuity goods and were camped in great force on the Platte some miles below the fort. The same little group of Miniconjou mischief-makers was camped with the Brulés, and on August 17 they found the opportunity to make trouble. A Mormon train on its way to Utah was passing the Brulé camp when a cow or ox got away from the man who was driving it. The Mormon, afraid of the Indians, hurried after the train; a Miniconjou then shot the cow and butchered it. This incident was reported at the fort, with embellishments, by the Mormons, and the Brulé head-chief Brave Bear also came to give his version in an attempt to settle the matter. With the affair of the previous year fresh in his mind, this chief suggested leaving the business where it was until the Indian agent arrived, but the young officers would not hear of this. They were for immediate action. Brave Bear then offered to attempt to induce the Miniconjou to surrender. At night the subject was still under discussion. Some time before this Lieutenant Fleming, who was in command at the fort, had promised Lieutenant Grattan the leadership of any detachment which had to be sent to the Indian camps in case of trouble, and Grattan was now eagerly seeking permission to go to the Brulé camp and seize the Miniconjou.

The chiefs and traders knew that any such attempt was almost certain to bring on a fight. This fatal policy of attempting to arrest wild Indians for minor offenses was typical of our military dealings with the tribes from first to last. There was nothing in the treaties to justify the military in making such arrests, and the Sioux treaty of

1851 which was at this time in effect states explicitly that in case of an offense by an Indian against the whites, his tribe, through its chief, should offer satisfaction. Brave Bear was doing this very thing. Men of experience knew that the average wild Indian would not submit to arrest. He had a great fear of this mysterious custom of the whites, suspecting that he was to be taken from his own people and killed in some terrible manner. He therefore usually refused to surrender, preferring to die in the open like a man. An order for a wild Indian's arrest was thus in effect an order for his death and should not have been issued except in case of dire necessity.

On August 19 when Man-Afraid-of-His-Horse, the Oglala head-chief, arrived at the fort he found that the decision had been made and that Grattan was preparing to go to the camp to arrest the Miniconjou. The lieutenant called for volunteers for dangerous service, selected twenty-nine men, and with these and two howitzers crossed Laramie River and marched down the emigrant road. Man-Afraid-of-His-Horse went with the soldiers to help Brave Bear keep the Indians quiet and to try to prevent a fight. The post interpreter also went along. He was drinking before they left the fort, obtained more whiskey on the road, and reached the Brulé camp roaring drunk and yelling insults and threats at the Indians.

Four and one-half miles from Fort Laramie the party passed the little trading post of Gratiot, and just east of there the road climbed a spur of bluff. From the top of this spur the soldiers had a view down the valley, which was crowded with Indian lodges and herds of ponies. Just east of the spur was the Oglala camp of 300 or more lodges; three miles or so below was Bordeaux's trading post with a village of 200 lodges of Brulés immediately east of it, and a little further on stood a second camp of 100 lodges, eighty lodges of Brulés and twenty of Miniconjous. In all there were over 600 lodges in plain view; two warriors to a lodge, a total of at least 1,200 warriors and 4,800 Indians.

As the soldiers marched past the Oglala camp the Indians began driving in their pony herds, an ominous sign, if the lieutenant had known enough to heed it. At Bordeaux's place, in the western edge of the first Brulé village, a halt was made and a conference held with Bordeaux, who was urged to go into the hornet's nest with Grattan, but the wily trader made excuses and at most gave a vague promise to follow the troops in a few minutes. Bordeaux was a fine trader and a man of sense, but he had little liking for a fight. When he was in charge of Fort John on Laramie Fork in 1846 he was challenged by an irate trapper to a duel with rifles, but he hid in his bedroom and to the great disgust of his squaw and her relatives refused to stir until the trapper had gone away. He now gave Lieutenant Grattan the sound advice to get the Brulé chief, Brave Bear, to coax the Miniconjou into submitting to arrest. The trader also asked him to shut up the drunken interpreter or send him back to the fort. This fool was riding his horse up and down at a hard run and giving war-whoops. As the Indians always ran their horses in this way just before a fight, to get them out of breath and give them their second-wind, they of course regarded the man's conduct as a certain sign that the troops had come to fight. To make this clearer the man was shouting at them in their own tongue that he would have them all killed, that he would eat their hearts before sundown, and similar pleasantries. Grattan paid no attention to Bordeaux's advice, but marched on through the Indian camps.

Brave Bear joined the troops in the edge of his own village, near Bordeaux's place, and accompanied them to the lower camp which was that of a different band of Brulés with whom the twenty lodges of Miniconjous were living. Here the lieutenant lined up his handful of infantry and put his two howitzers into position facing the Indian lodges. A long conference then took place. Brave Bear and Man-Afraid-of-His-Horse went back and forth between the troops and the lodges, talking earnestly to both parties, trying to get the Miniconjou warrior to surrender and attempting to induce Grattan to leave the trouble for the Indian agent to settle. The Miniconjou would not submit to arrest; he had the wild Indian's usual feeling of horror at the thought of placing himself in his enemies' hands. He acted like a man, telling the chiefs that he wished to die where he was and asking the Indians to draw off and leave him for the soldiers to deal with, as he did not wish to get anyone into trouble. Meanwhile a messenger had been sent by the chiefs to get Bordeaux, to tell him that the interpreter was behaving very badly and was not giving their words to the officer. A saddled horse was offered to Bordeaux, but the Frenchman said that the stirrups were not adjusted properly. While he stood fussing with the straps shots were heard, and he prudently climbed to the flat roof of his house and stayed there.

Grattan had lost what little patience he possessed. He gave an order and his men, who were lying on the ground resting, stood up and fired some shots toward the Miniconjou lodges. Brave Bear leaped forward and shouted to the Indians not to return the fire; but at that moment the soldiers fired again and also discharged the two howitzers, and the Brulé chief fell mortally wounded. The howitzers had been laid too high and the grape-shot tore through the tops of the lodges without doing any harm. The Indians in the lodges and those who had taken refuge among the bushes now poured a sudden fire into the troops. Grattan and all the men near the howitzers fell; the remnant of the little group turned and fled, some in a wagon, the others afoot. The Brulés and Miniconjous mounted and rode up the road rapidly after the soldiers. The whites appear to have succeeded in passing Bordeaux's houses, where one of the wounded men hid himself. The rest rushed on up the road, but hardly had they passed the second Brulé camp when the warriors in their rear caught up with them, and at the same moment the Oglalas from the camp above came surging over the spur of bluffs and charged down on them. Here the remnant of Grattan's party died in the midst of two converging waves of mounted warriors. The only man who escaped was the soldier who had taken refuge at Bordeaux's, and he was mortally wounded.[4]

All that night there was a seething mass of Sioux gathered about Bordeaux's place. Here Brave Bear, mortally wounded, had been brought and many of the other chiefs had assembled; and behind these men Bordeaux placed himself and talked—talked for his life and the lives of all the whites on the Upper Platte. He talked all night, wheedling and coaxing, handing out gifts from his stock to the more important warriors. He sacrificed most of his stock, but with the aid of the chiefs kept the Indians from starting a general slaughter of the whites. They were determined to attack Fort Laramie (there were ten men at the post, waiting in silent fear for news of Grattan's party) but they were persuaded not to do this. The next day they broke into the American Fur Company's houses and plundered them, taking all the Indian annuity goods which

4. The testimony of officers and traders at Fort Laramie concerning the Grattan affair is printed in *House Documents, Thirty-third Congress, second session,* doc. 63. The *Report of the Commission of Indian Affairs* for 1854 reproduces an affidavit signed by Bordeaux and the other traders which gives a very fair account of the Grattan fight. As far back as 1912 the Oglalas and Brulés had only a confused memory of these events, and I have made little use of their information. Mr. Stanley Vestal in *New Sources of Indian History* (University of Oklahoma Press, Norman, 1934), pp. 210-11, gives a modern Sioux version of the Grattan affair. It is a good example of Indian embroidery work but of little historical value.

were stored there. The day after this looting of the stores, they broke up their camps and moved away to their hunting grounds.

We do not know when or where Brave Bear died. This chief sacrificed his life in a vain attempt to prevent useless killing, and he was recompensed by the spreading of a story which averred that he had laid a plot and had led Lieutenant Grattan's party into a trap. The very traders whom he had protected and faithfully aided for many years started this tale, fearing that if they told the truth they would be regarded by the whites as friends and allies of the savages who had murdered Grattan's men.

The first news of this affair near Fort Laramie was brought to the Missouri frontier in September by traders from the Upper Platte. These men placed all the blame on Brave Bear and spread the report that all the Sioux were hostile. The agent for the Indians of the Upper Platte, John W. Whitfield, next appeared and took the same ground as the frightened traders, blaming the Indians and demanding that a strong military force march against them. He termed the little infantry detachment at Laramie "a perfect nuisance" which caused trouble but was unable to render the slightest aid to the emigrants, who had to bribe the Indians to permit them to pass through their country. He asserted that the Sioux were hostile. A few days later this peculiar person wrote a second report in which he strongly regretted that a decision on the Mormon cow affair had not been delayed until his arrival at Fort Laramie, as he could have settled the trouble peacefully. He declared that the military did not have any right to arrest an Indian for killing a cow or for any other offense, gave the hasty action of the soldiers as the cause of all the trouble, and asserted that up to the time of the Grattan killing the Sioux had always had the reputation of being the most friendly Indians on the Platte, who had never injured an emigrant in any manner. This second report of Agent Whitfield agrees with his first in one respect only: a repetition of the statement as to the uselessness of small infantry posts.

Most of the Sioux spent this autumn and winter quietly in their hunting grounds and there was no evidence of any hostile intentions except in the case of a small band of Brulés made up of Brave Bear's relatives and close friends who were determined to have vengeance for the death of their chief. There can be no doubt at all that the whites in the Indian country were greatly alarmed, and rumors of serious Indian troubles were passing along the Platte and Upper Missouri. In October, Agent Vaughan reported from the Missouri that the Indians who had killed Grattan were now north of the Platte and had sent around a war-pipe to induce all the Tetons to join them in a war on the whites. He stated that the Hunkpapas and Blackfoot-Sioux were very hostile in their attitude toward the whites and urged that a military expedition be sent up the Missouri as well as one up the Platte.

The government certainly had to take strong action now that its hand had been forced by the Grattan affair. Brave Bear's relatives and friends were determined to be avenged for his killing, and if they were permitted to raid with impunity, other bands would undoubtedly soon grow bold enough to make attacks on the whites. In November, 1854, five Brulés of the Brave Bear faction, led by Long Chin, attacked the mail-wagon on the road below Fort Laramie, twelve miles west of Horse Creek, and killed two drivers and a passenger. There was a sum of $20,000 in the mail pouches, which the Indians are said to have carried off, though what they did with it was never learned. Young Spotted Tail and young Red Leaf, both famous Brulé chiefs in later days, took part in this attack. Another party of Brulés made a raid at Ward & Guerrier's trading store on the emigrant road just west of Fort Laramie. The Indians now withdrew to their wintering grounds; but in the spring they returned, and as the military had taken no action the same little group of Brulé malcontents began to plan further raids along the road.

The traders were in a grave situation. If the government did not act the Indians would soon be bold enough to rob them of their goods; if there should be a military expedition against the Sioux their trade would be ruined for the time being. As summer approached the traders on the Upper Platte were very nervous. The little band of Brulé raiders were growing bolder in their hostility toward all white men; there were rumors of a military expedition in preparation, but nothing definite could be learned.

On August 10 the new Indian agent, Thomas Twiss, suddenly appeared at Fort Laramie. A graduate of West Point and a former officer of the regular army, Twiss was not the usual politically appointed Indian agent but had been selected because of his special fitness to aid the military in dealing with the Sioux. The great wagon-freighting firms which had such large sums invested in the business of transporting goods along the Platte road were determined that the Sioux should be taught such a lesson that they would never again interfere with travel along the road. These firms evidently used their great influence at Washington to secure the appointment of General W. S. Harney to command the troops and of Twiss to act as Indian agent. The Indian Office officials did not approve of this procedure and attempted to recall Twiss as soon as the fighting was over, but they failed and he retained his position until Lincoln removed him in 1861.

This agent's action was purely military. On reaching Fort Laramie he declared the North Platte River a deadline and sent expresses to the Indian camps warning all friendlies to move south of the river at once and to report to him for orders. Most of the Sioux came in promptly, and Twiss had a talk with Man-Afraid-of-His-Horse and the Oglalas at Ward & Guerrier's, eight miles west of the fort, and one with the Brulés at Bordeaux's trading house. In the latter conference, August 19, he told the chiefs that he knew the names of the warriors who had attacked the mail-wagon and had also been informed as to which Brulé band was hostile. He stated that these hostiles must not come south of the river, but that the friendly Brulés would be welcome and could count on being well treated. He now formed a friendly camp for the Brulés on "Cherry Creek," a tributary of Laramie Fork, ten miles above the fort.[5]

Here he assembled seventy lodges. The Oglalas began moving in at once in little bands from north of the river, and by August 28 Twiss had a camp for them established on Laramie Fork twenty-five miles above the fort. On the thirtieth Stabber came in with a band of Wazhazhas, the Brulé band to which the dead chief Brave Bear had belonged. These people seem to have been under suspicion, but the traders informed Twiss that Stabber was a good Indian who had always been opposed to the big Bear chief, Brave Bear, and had driven that chief's family out of his camp soon after the Grattan affair. Stabber was therefore taken under the agent's wing and joined the friendly camp; but the Brulés did not forget or forgive his treatment of Brave Bear's family, and we soon find his band living with the Oglalas and rated as belonging to that tribe.

By September 8 Twiss had assembled 400 lodges of Brulés and Oglalas at a camp on Laramie Fork thirty-five miles above the fort. With the aid of the traders and the friendly chiefs he

5. Chug Creek? There is no Cherry Creek in this district.

had done his work well and swiftly, and the way was now prepared for the march of General Harney's column. The government clearly did not credit the report that all of the Indians along the Upper Platte were hostile, and whatever we may think of General Harney's action we must admit that the authorities did all that was possible to avoid involving the friendly Sioux in a clash with the troops.

Little Thunder of the Brulés had not come in. Twiss had warned him to come, if he were friendly, but he disregarded this message and was now encamped with some other Brulé groups and a handful of Oglalas on the Blue Water, a few miles north of the North Platte and not far from Ash Hollow. If this chieftain's intentions were hostile he was certainly not very wise, for he was in about the most dangerous position he could have found and he seems to have taken no precautions.

Harney's march was swift and secret. His scout, Joe Tesson, easily found Little Thunder's camp, which was in a locality known to everyone as a favorite camping place of the Brulés. On the night of September 2 Harney moved his mounted troops to a position in the rear of the Indians, and before dawn on the third he started with his infantry, advancing up the creek with no attempt to conceal his movement. As day broke the Sioux caught sight of the troops, and Little Thunder and some other chiefs went forward to draw Harney into a conference, evidently hoping to delay his movement and give the people time to take down the lodges and get out of the way; but Harney's infantry came straight on, and now the Indians to their dismay discovered a force of mounted dragoons up the creek in their rear. Charged vigorously from two directions, the Sioux simply dropped everything and ran over the bluffs in wild flight, the dragoons pursuing them for over five miles. Harney reported eighty-six Indians killed, including some women and children. Seventy women and children were captured, and the camp and all its contents fell into the hands of the troops.

Whether Little Thunder deserved his whipping or not has always been a debatable question. In the following year General Harney told the Sioux in open council that he regretted that his troops had attacked the camp of a friendly chief. He said that when he marched up the Platte he was "very mad" and had struck at the first camp he found north of the river. The testimony taken in connection with the killing of Grattan and his party proves that when Brave Bear was mortally wounded Little Thunder took charge and did everything in his power to prevent further acts of hostility. Harney, however, reported that he found in this chief's camp articles taken from the men who were murdered when the mail-wagon was captured and also two fresh scalps supposed to be those of white women. Twiss had certainly warned Little Thunder very clearly either to come south of the river and join the friendly camp or to take the consequences. We evidently have here a situation that was not at all uncommon—a friendly chief who could not control all of his people and was forced to follow when he should have led.

Before the Civil War broke its heart, the regular army used to sing joyously:

> *We did not make a blunder,*
> *We rubbed out Little Thunder,*
> *And we sent him to the other side of Jordan.*

Sir Richard Burton met Little Thunder in 1860, not on the other side of Jordan but on the other side of Laramie Fork. The old man was hale and hearty and was making the most outrageous charges against Agent Twiss, who was regarded as a thief by many of the chiefs.[6] Little Thunder's last appearance was in the friendly Sioux camp near Fort Laramie in the spring of 1865, and he was probably one of the chiefs who were killed by their own people for taking the side of the whites when this camp suddenly revolted, attacked their guard of troops, and fled north to join the hostiles.

The news of the attack on Little Thunder reached Fort Laramie on September 8 and Agent Twiss at once informed the Oglala and Brulé chiefs of this event. They took it quietly, but they must have felt very uneasy when they learned that General Harney was marching in their direction with his troops. On reaching the fort, however, Harney did nothing to alarm the Sioux. He made no attempt to punish them for the killing of Lieutenant Grattan's party, but demanded the surrender of the Brulés who had attacked the mail-wagon in the autumn of 1854. The chiefs appealed to these men to sacrifice themselves for the good of all the people, and some days later Spotted Tail and the others rode into the fort dressed in all their war finery and singing their death songs. They undoubtedly

6. Sir Richard Burton, *The City of the Saints* (New York: Harper & Brother, 1862), p. 132.

expected to be killed, but they were taken to Fort Kearney on the lower Platte, where they spent two years as prisoners but were not confined, even going out with the troops on scouting excursions. During his captivity Spotted Tail learned to know the whites and appreciate their power as no other Sioux chief ever did, and in later times only the most outrageous injustice could drive him into hostility, for he realized the futility of struggling against a government whose resources were so vast.

General Harney now gave any of the Teton Sioux who desired a fight full opportunity to obtain one. He marched from Fort Laramie through the heart of the Sioux country to Fort Pierre on the Upper Missouri, and not a shot was fired. His troops wintered at Fort Pierre, and in the following spring, 1856, he held councils with all of the Teton tribes, appointing new chiefs, and drew up a treaty which they signed. This treaty was not ratified by the Senate, and as the Indians did not understand this and still regarded the agreement as being in force, much confusion resulted.[7]

Some of the military men and also some traders did not think that Harney had gone far enough with his expedition against the Sioux. The Platte road had been rendered safe for the time being by the Blue Water fight, but many of the Sioux of the Upper Missouri were openly hostile and it was considered unfortunate that Harney broke up his expedition without striking at least one more blow. The traders pointed to the Hunkpapas as the Tetons who most deserved a drubbing and the history of later years seems to bear out their views, for from 1856 to the end of the Sioux wars these Hunkpapas, Sitting Bull's people, were the most consistently hostile of all the Tetons. Lieutenant G. K. Warren, who explored the Sioux country at this time, greatly regretted that Harney did not keep in the field longer. Warren advised the War Department to seek a fund of $50,000 with which to make a thorough military exploration of the Sioux lands before the encroachment of the whites should so embitter the Indians as to make such an examination of the country impossible.

Warren was quite right. Up to 1855 the Sioux had been watching the whites along the Platte and Missouri like children excited by the passing of troops and quite unaware of the meaning back of the spectacle they were witnessing. Their eyes had been opened by

7. For the Harney campaign see the *Report of the Secretary of War* for 1855 and 1856; J. S. Morton, *History of Nebraska*, Vol. II; *South Dakota Historical Collections*, Vol. XI.

Harney's attack on the Brulés, an event which had rung from one end of the Teton country to the other. When in all their history had they suffered such losses in a single fight—nearly one hundred dead, the women and children carried off as captives, and a Teton camp in the hands of an enemy! Teton pride was sadly taken down, and it was not restored when Harney marched through the heart of their land, daring them to come and fight him and finding no band willing to take up the challenge. While General Harney was bullying them at Fort Pierre in 1856, the chiefs were talking quietly among themselves, and no sooner had the troops left their country than a pipe was sent around, this time no war-pipe but a greater matter—a pipe summoning all the Tetons to council.

This great council, the only one of its kind of which we have any knowledge, met in the northern edge of the Black Hills near Bear Butte in the summer of 1857. The chiefs brought all their people with them, and when the lodges had been pitched the Tetons were amazed and pleased to see how numerous they were. The sight of the great camps made their hearts strong again, and in the council that followed the chiefs decided that they had given in too quickly to General Harney, that they should have united and opposed him. They were fully aroused now to the danger of white invasion, and before the conference ended the leaders pledged themselves to resist any further encroachments on Teton lands.

Just after this council had broken up, part of the Miniconjous and Hunkpapas were hunting buffalo west of the Black Hills when they discovered Lieutenant Warren's party engaged in making a survey for military routes. The Sioux were furious and wished to kill all the whites, but Bear's Rib and the other chiefs persuaded them not to do this. Bear's Rib warned Warren to go at once and to tell the whites that they must keep out of the Sioux country. He also asked the lieutenant to inform the Great Father that if the annuities which were being sent to the Sioux were intended as a payment to secure to the whites permission to enter the Sioux country the people would not accept the presents in future, and if these annuities were intended to stop the Sioux war with the Crows they did not want the goods and would not take them, for they were determined to continue fighting the Crows.[8]

While the Sioux were pondering the lessons of the Grattan affair and the Harney campaign these matters were made clearer in their

8. G. K. Warren, *Explorations in Nebraska and Dakota* (Washington, 1875).

minds by fresh happenings on the Platte. Harney had hardly gone when the Cheyennes became involved in trouble. It was the Brulé affair all over again; this incident being caused by the soldiers of the little detachment at Platte Bridge attempting to arrest some Cheyennes for picking up strayed horses which the emigrants claimed. The usual shooting ensued; the angry Indians went away and made some small raids; and presently a large force of troops came up the Platte, defeated the Cheyennes, and pursued them down to the Arkansas River. In these events the military agent, Thomas Twiss, played the same rôle that he had in the Brulé difficulties of 1855, carefully moving the Indians into a position in which the troops could strike them. The Sioux kept aloof from these events but watched closely and shook their heads over the white man's peculiar ideas of right and wrong.[9]

It was during these years that the rush of settlers was filling up the lands along the Missouri in Kansas, Nebraska, Iowa, and Dakota. The Missouri River lands were settled as far up as Sioux City in 1856, and in 1857 twenty-three steamboats were in regular service as far up as that town. During the fifties attempts were constantly being made to extinguish the titles of the Indians to lands in Kansas, Nebraska, and southeastern Dakota. Some of the Indians refused to sell their lands, and popular sentiment was stirred up against these tribes. The whites began to maltreat the border tribes, especially in Kansas, and mobs of so-called militia were sent out to harry the Indians. There was also a strong sentiment in favor of removing the tribes to Indian Territory, and when the Indian Office opposed this idea the whites attempted to have the unfortunate Indians cooped up on their reservations although they had by treaty agreements the right to go to the buffalo range on annual hunts. The Pawnees, Kaws, and other border tribes were at this period undoubtedly much worse off than the tribes out in the plains.

The Teton chiefs were not ignorant of what was happening to the tribes along the Missouri, and it was the news of the ruin wrought to these peoples by the coming of white settlers added to their own experience with the emigrants along the Upper Platte which produced the feeling among the Tetons that if they were to save themselves they must resist any further encroachment of the whites on their territory. They had hardly reached this conclusion

9. For a detailed account of these Cheyenne troubles see George Bird Grinnell, *The Fighting Cheyennes*, Chapter X.

when the news came that the Yanktons had signed a treaty ceding lands on the Missouri. This Yankton treaty produced a furious outburst of protest from the Tetons of the Upper Missouri and Black Hills region. They bitterly denounced the Yanktons, saying that they had come to the Missouri long ago to beg from the Tetons and had been permitted to occupy Teton lands which they had now stolen and traded to the whites. From 1855 to 1868 the one thing that might be termed the policy of the Teton chiefs was this almost universal determination to oppose any further white encroachments on their lands.

CHAPTER VI

THE OGLALAS MOVE AGAIN
1856-1860

ALTHOUGH the Oglalas were not much involved in the troubles near Fort Laramie in 1852-1855 these events influenced the later history of the tribe. Since the time of Bull Bear's killing in 1841 the Oglalas had been drifting aimlessly about, keeping near the Platte, watching the whites passing along the road, and each year becoming more fascinated by the strange people and their ways. A few more years and the Oglalas would have found it impossible to break the spell that held them, but the violent shock of the Grattan affair and the Harney compaign had awakened them to the fact that the Platte Valley was now a white man's land where they could remain only on sufferance and by submitting to the domination of the whites. Neither the Oglalas nor the Brulés were willing to accept such a situation, and the moment the leaders' eyes were opened to the facts these Indians turned their backs on the Platte and moved into the buffalo country to the north and south of the river.

Thus, soon after 1854, the Oglalas of the old Bull Bear group who in 1846 had been hunting on Laramie Plains and wintering near Fort Laramie, now suddenly shifted their range toward the southeast and were soon established on the branches of the Republican Fork, in northern Kansas and southern Nebraska. With them went the Brulés of the Little Thunder and Spotted Tail group. The leaders of this group of Oglalas were Bad Wound, selected by General Harney in 1856 to succeed Man-Afraid-of-His-Horse as head-chief of the tribe, Little Wound, Whistler, and Pawnee Killer, the last man being a war leader and not a real chief. Associating themselves with the Southern Cheyennes, these Sioux of the Republican Fork often went as far south as the Arkansas River. They soon began to lose touch with their northern kinsmen, and as they found it difficult to go as far as Fort Laramie to get their annuity goods they wished to have a new agency established for their use on the Platte below the forks.

When this movement away from the Platte began, the Smoke People, comprising the bands which recognized Old Smoke as their leader, turned northward and occupied the lands on the headwaters of the South Fork of Cheyenne River, just to the southwest of the Black Hills. Man-Afraid-of-His-Horse was regarded both by the Indians and the whites as the leader of this group. Old Smoke's position is a puzzling question. This division of the tribe was named for him and we would naturally expect him to be the leader, yet his name is not even included in the list of chiefs in 1850 and 1856. He was now a very old man and spent most of his time at Fort Laramie. Perhaps he had retired, as some of the older chiefs did. This northern group of Oglalas was closely connected with the Miniconjous and Northern Cheyennes.

When this movement into new country occurred, a small group of Oglalas, including some Brulés, remained near Fort Laramie. These people were the ones who had become so entangled with the whites that they could not leave them. Coming from different bands, some of them Bear People and others Smoke People, they formed a new group and were soon being called by their more independent tribesmen, Waglukhe, followers or loafers, a name which fitted them neatly, for they usually hunted close to the emigrant road and then hurried back, to follow the wagon-trains and beg from the whites or to go to Fort Laramie and loaf about, living on what they could get from the soldiers. To this group belonged all of the families whose daughters were married to white men. Some of the officers had taken Indian wives, according to the Sioux marriage customs, and many a prominent family in the East and South had unknown relatives in the Waglukhe camp. Thus we hear of General ———'s squaw and Captain ———'s woman who were well known on the Upper Platte after the Civil War.

During the fur trade period there had been no stigma attached to the Sioux families who lived at the fort; indeed, marriage with a trader was considered an honorable position for any Sioux girl to gain and her family were looked upon with considerable envy. This feeling must have continued for some years after the troops took charge at Fort Laramie, for we find Old Smoke living at the post with a band of his people, clearly the Bad Faces in whose camp Red Cloud was living. These folk were no loafers. They left the fort as soon as they realized what remaining there any longer meant, and within a few years they became the leading band of the warlike Northern Oglalas.

Red Cloud had lived in the Fort Laramie district, from about the age of twelve, the post itself being the center of interest at which he spent most of his time. He lived in Smoke's camp, a camp which after 1850 was led by one of Smoke's sons. He Dog, the son of one of Red Cloud's sisters, was born in this camp. He states that the chief, the son of Old Smoke, had a very jealous wife who often quarreled with him, filling the lodge and indeed the whole camp with her angry accusations. Her favorite epithet was to tell her husband that he had a bad face, and this she repeated so often and in such shrill tones that it soon became a standing joke, the people giving the chief the nickname of Bad Face, Iteshicha. The name stuck and was soon being applied to the camp itself.[1]

Red Cloud said on several occasions that he was present when Lieutenant Grattan was killed in 1854, but he evidently did not take a leading part in this affair. He seems to have remained near Fort Laramie for a year or two longer and then joined the exodus of those Oglalas who did not wish to remain on the Platte as the vassals of the whites. Until the last few years we have had no information bearing on this period of Red Cloud's life, but recently Mr. L. B. Dougherty in his recollections of his life as a trader at Fort Laramie has definitely placed this chief in the Sioux camp which was a permanent fixture at the fort, about the year 1856. On one occasion, as Mr. Dougherty relates, Red Cloud was preparing a feast for some prominent chiefs who were visiting at the fort, and wishing to make a real impression on his guests he went to the post surgeon and asked him for a bottle of whiskey. This he received, and in return he gave the officer two finely ornamented buffalo

---

1. He Dog neglected to give the name of this son of Smoke who was nick-named Bad Face, but said that he was the father of Woman's Dress, the Oglala who in 1877 stopped General Crook and warned him that Crazy Horse was planning his death. Lieutenant Caspar Collins evidently heard a form of the story He Dog gives, on the Upper Platte in 1863, for he says in his notes, "The Bad Faces come from the Oglalas. The Oglalas got the name of the bad faces because of their quarrelsome disposition and because they quarreled with their own nation." This is the earliest recorded mention of the Bad Faces (Spring: *Life of Caspar Collins*, p. 177).

robes. When the feast began Red Cloud produced the bottle and handed it with a flourish to the chief guest, who took a drink, looked hard at his host, and quickly passed the bottle. Each guest in turn had a drink, but they did not seem to like it. The bottle finally reached the puzzled Red Cloud; he took a hasty swallow and found that the bottle contained nothing but water, a little whiskey having been applied to the cork to trick him. Leaving his guests, Red Cloud went angrily to the surgeon's office, but that officer was expecting him and had taken cover. A few days later the matter was smoothed over, the surgeon making his excuses and presenting Red Cloud with sufficient gifts to heal his injured pride. But as long as Red Cloud remained at the fort he was known as Two Robes, in memory of the day on which he had given a white man two fine robes for a bottle of water.[2]

By moving south to Republican Fork the Oglala Bear People possessed themselves of the best hunting grounds the Pawnees had, and these Oglalas and their Brulé and Cheyenne friends were constantly being raided by the Pawnees. They returned the compliment by attacking the Pawnees whenever they ventured into the plains to hunt and by going to raid them in their earth-lodge villages on Loup Fork. It was at this period, after 1855, that the Southern Oglalas appear to have first come into contact with the Utes, occasionally going with the Cheyennes into the mountains of Colorado to raid that tribe. Charles A. Eastman asserts that as early as 1835 or 1840 the Oglalas were much engaged in warring on the Utes and that Spotted Tail, Red Cloud, and the other young men of the day won most of their early successes in fights with the Utes. These tales seem to have their source in the faulty memory of the Sioux. The winter-counts and other contemporary records are silent as to any fighting with the Utes at the period indicated.

When the Oglalas of the Smoke People turned their backs on the Platte and started northward, about 1855, the country near the Black Hills was already rather crowded with Sioux who had migrated westward from the Missouri, and buffalo were no longer plentiful. These Indians had for some time fixed covetous eyes on the fine game lands toward the west; the Powder River and Bighorn countries. This region had been recognized by the treaty of 1851 as Crow territory, the divide between Powder River and the Little Missouri being the line that separated the Crow country

2. L. B. Dougherty, in *Missouri Historical Review*, July, 1930.

from that of the Sioux. The Crows as far back as 1800 had found Powder River unsafe because of the constant attacks the Sioux and other enemies were making on them; they therefore usually hunted in the lands west of Powder River. They were still able, however, to prevent any other tribe occupying their old lands, and Powder River was for long a kind of No Man's Land through which war-parties cautiously made their way and into which occasionally some band of Indians ventured to bring their camp, for a season, and then withdrew before enemies learned of their presence.

When the treaty of 1851 was made, the Sioux already had designs on the Crow lands, and this was why the Hunkpapas and some others so strongly objected to the peace with the Crows which was a feature of that agreement. The Hunkpapas stated emphatically that they would not abandon their war on the Crows, and they did not do so. Year after year they crossed Powder River and attacked the Crows, being aided in these raids by the Miniconjous and Sans Arcs from the Belle Fourche (North Fork of Cheyenne River). The agent for the Upper Missouri tribes reported each year that his Sioux were all loyally keeping peace with the Crows. Men in the Indian country must have smiled at this, for they knew how much this agent was profiting from the Sioux annuities and that his greatest fear was that the officials at Washington would learn the truth and stop the Sioux presents.

No sooner had the northern bands of Oglalas moved into the lands north of the Platte than the Crow war became their principal interest. They presently shifted westward, hunting on the head of Powder River, where they came into close alliance with the Miniconjous and Sans Arcs from the Black Hills country and also with the Northern Cheyennes. Agent Twiss of the Upper Platte Agency must have known this very well, but his reports are innocent of any reference to a war which the Sioux were waging on the Crows. Like the Upper Missouri agent, he had nothing but praise for the manner in which his good Sioux were keeping the peace pledge they had made in 1851.

At this period the Crows were in great trouble, for they were being pressed by the Blackfeet from the north at the same moment when the Sioux were assailing them from the east and south. One can hardly avoid sympathizing with the Crows, a brave people who had generally been very friendly in their dealings with the whites for fifty years past. It is true that they had now and then robbed parties of white men passing through their country and had occasionally killed a white man; but compared with the Sioux, their southeastern enemies, and the Blackfeet, their northwestern enemies, the Crows were good people who got along well with the whites. Their location far up the Yellowstone made it difficult to supply them with the goods they required, and after the Laramie treaty there was always trouble in getting the annuity goods to the Crows.

In 1854 part of the Crows were induced to come all the way to Fort Union at the mouth of the Yellowstone for their annuities, but on the way home they were attacked by enemies and had many people killed. The following year they did not come, and when the agent came up to Fort Union in a steamboat in 1856 he found the Crow annuity goods for the previous year still in store at the fort. He formed a small party to accompany him, went up the Yellowstone and Bighorn, and finally found the Crows hunting above the mouth of the Little Bighorn. They told him that they were afraid to come to Fort Union for their goods, and stated that white men had told them that smallpox was on the Missouri and that the smallpox poison was in their annuity goods. They were afraid of enemies and afraid of the smallpox. Agent Vaughan assured them that these tales about the smallpox were the invention of wicked men, and he finally induced the chiefs to come with 350 warriors, a party strong enough to fight off any war-party they were likely to encounter, with pack ponies to the fort. There the Crows obtained their annuities for two years. They also received the smallpox, and many of their people died. The "unscrupulous white men" the agent had denounced in his report for spreading the rumor of smallpox germs had been perfectly right. The next season the Crows refused to come to Fort Union.

In the summer of 1859, Captain W. F. Raynolds found the two largest band of Crows, the Mountain Crows under Red Bear and the Lower or River Band under Two Bears, trading at Fort Sarpy near the mouth of the Bighorn. They were very friendly. One year later, in August, 1860, a part of Raynolds' expedition led by Lieutenant Mullins, Second Dragoons, was proceeding from Fort Benton to Fort Union. On August 3 their camp on the Big Dry Sandy south of the Missouri was approached by a large body of Crows. Jim Bridger, the guide, went out and induced some of the warriors to come into camp; they came with scowling faces, and after saying that their hearts were bad they suddenly fired three guns, at which signal 250 mounted Crows appeared and charged the camp, attempting to stampede the herd. Mullins and Bridger succeeded with the greatest difficulty in saving the horses and preventing a pitched battle. At the end of the uproar, the Crow chief was induced to come in and talk. He was Mato Luta, the same Red Bear, head-chief of the Mountain Crows, who had been so friendly to Raynolds' party in August, 1859. He said that his warriors' hearts were black because the whites had betrayed them to their enemies. On inquiry, Lieutenant Mullins discovered that the fools at the Indian Office had ordered the Crow annuity goods sent to the Upper Platte Agency—to the agency of the Oglalas, the bitter enemies of the Crows! The latter tribe had then been informed that they might obtain their goods by making a 300 mile journey through hostile territory. At about the same time the Crow trading post on the Bighorn, Fort Sarpy, had been abandoned by the fur company, and the tribe was without goods and without ammunition for their guns. These Mountain Crows were now encamped on the Big Dry Sandy, far from their homeland on the Bighorn. They had ventured into that territory with the evident object of trading at Fort Union, but they were afraid to go to that post because of the Sioux and the smallpox.[3]

It is little wonder that the hearts of the Crows were black. At the moment when they were defending their country from enemies pressing in on them from the south, east, and north all supplies of arms and ammunition were suddenly cut off by the white men who were supposed to be their loyal friends, and they were compelled to leave their home on the Bighorn and take refuge north of the Yellowstone for the time being. In the matter of a regular supply of arms and ammunition, the situation of the Sioux was very different from that of the Crows. Besides the supply of these articles obtained from the government in the form of annuities, the Oglalas and some of the other Teton tribes were within easy reach of the great Overland Road along the Platte where at the numerous trading houses, stage stations, and ranches they could obtain all the ammunition and new guns that they were able to pay for with buffalo robes, horses, and other articles of trade.

3. W. F. Raynolds, *Exploration of the Yellowstone and Missouri Rivers in 1859 and 1860* (Fortieth Congress, first session, Senate Ex. Doc. 77, 1868). It was at Agent Twiss' suggestion that the Crow annuities were sent to his agency on the Upper Platte. What he did with the goods is not stated. The Crows never saw them.

The idiotic action of the Indian officials in 1859, together with the abandonment of the Crow post, probably cost that tribe a large portion of the Powder River country. They had to go far away, seeking ammunition and other necessaries, and when they returned to their own land they found that the Sioux had made an advance northward. Once in possession of the territory, the Sioux could not be driven out.

The Sioux employed large war-parties with great effect in these attacks on the Crows. The general practice seems to have been for the people to assemble in a great camp in summer for the annual Sun Dance, and after the ceremonies were concluded a great war-party would set out to make the annual crusade against the unfortunate Crows. In 1858, the Indian agent for the Upper Missouri reported that the Sioux had killed in a battle the head-chief of the Crows and thirty of his best warriors. In 1859, the Crows told Captain Raynolds that a small camp of their people recently had been wiped out by a huge Sioux party of eighty campfires. This was evidently the war-party of Black Shield which is spoken of in the Sioux winter-counts and is still remembered by the Oglalas.[4] The winter-count of Cloud Shield relates that in 1861-1862 a large war-party led by Red Cloud engaged in a battle with the Crows, killing the Crow chief, Little Rabbit. Another Oglala count calls this chief Spotted Horse.

The report of the Upper Missouri agent for 1862 relates the conclusion of this Sioux drive against the Crows. It states that the latter tribe had been driven from its old home and was wandering about among the mountains farther to the westward. From this date the Crows did not often venture into their old hunting grounds east of the Bighorn and south of the Yellowstone.

Agent Twiss, who had charge of the Oglalas and Brulés of the Upper Platte, for some reason concealed the fact that his Sioux were warring on the Crows; indeed, he represented his Indians as peaceful people who were being raided by the unregenerate Crows. His reports when carefully examined show that he was falsifying the facts. In the report of 1856, he describes the northern boundary of the Sioux as running from Bear Butte in the Black Hills along

4. The Crows killed Big Crow, son of Black Shield, and that chief sent around a pipe and got together a great assembly of Sioux. The Oglalas still talk of this affair. In a recent book it is stated on Sioux authority that Big Crow was the son of Chief Breast of the Miniconjous. This does not agree with the Oglala statements or with the winter-counts.

the divide between the forks of Cheyenne River in a southwesterly course, thence along the divide between Powder River and the North Platte to Red Buttes above Platte Bridge. All lands north of this line were Crow territory; yet the Oglalas of Twiss' agency were hunting and camping north of the line every year and going up to the Yellowstone to attack the Crows in their own camps.

Twiss was constantly suggesting new plans to the Indian Office, plans which would require the expenditure of vast amounts of public money without apparent benefit to anyone, unless it was the agent and his trader friends. Thus in 1856 he was urging the establishment of a new agency for the Oglalas on the upper waters of Horse Creek, southeast of Fort Laramie, and one for the Brulés on White River near Butte Caché, about eighty miles northeast of the fort. The Sioux, as he put it, would thus be removed from the bad influence of the whites who traveled along the Platte road, and with government farmers to teach them they would soon settle down and become self-supporting growers of crops. Such proposals might have taken in the officials at Washington, but men on the Upper Platte must have known that the agent was trying to obtain more government money under false pretenses. Most of the Sioux had already left the Platte road on their own initiative, and were seeking new hunting grounds far away. These Indians were as wild as wolves and would undoubtedly have beaten or shot any member of their tribe who attempted to settle down and farm. Agent Twiss certainly knew this, and his proposal was probably made in his own interest rather than with any idea of aiding the Indians. The most astonishing of this man's schemes was the plan for an agency at Upper Platte Bridge for the "Crows, Snakes, and Upper Band of Miniconjous." This agency was evidently intended for the convenience of the Miniconjou Sioux, who would thereby be enabled to obtain all of the Crow and Snake scalps and ponies they required without the trouble of going from 200 to 300 miles to the camps of the Crows and Snakes.

One year later, in 1857, this strange man had forgotten all about his plan for an Oglala farm on Horse Creek, a Brulé farm at Butte Caché, and a Crow-Snake-Sioux Scalping Station at Upper Platte Bridge. Without a word of explanation he had taken the agency from near Fort Laramie and moved it up to Deer Creek, on the Overland Road about 100 miles west of the fort. He does not indicate why he chose this spot after all his objections to having the

Indians near the road and its bad influences. It may be noted, however, that by moving to Deer Creek the agent practically deserted the more friendly bands of Oglalas and Brulés, those who hunted south of the Platte and the Loafer band near Fort Laramie, and cast his lot with the wild Smoke People who were now hunting on the head of Powder River, only a short distance north of Deer Creek. John Richards, the "desperado" who had started the liquor smuggling on the Upper Platte in 1840, was now established near Deer Creek, as was also Joseph Bissonette. Both of these traders were now well-to-do. Old Joe had an Indian trading house, an emigrant store, an Overland stage station, and a postoffice, which establishments he conducted with the aid of his squaws and numerous half-breed progeny. Richards' place was similar to Bissonette's, but his Indian trade was much larger, several strong trails leading straight from his stockade to the Sioux camps on Powder River. He had built a toll-bridge across the river for the emigrant trade and was a rich man with no need to remain on the Platte; but the Sioux had become his people, and his passionate interest in their affairs kept him where he was. He had several half-Oglala sons growing up, the "Reshaw boys," that clan of joyous warriors, scouts, interpreters, and traders, of whom we shall hear more farther on. Richards had boasted in 1841 that the government would never send out an Indian agent good enough to stop his sale of liquor to the Sioux, and in 1857 he was still of the same opinion. Agent Twiss was certainly not the man, for Richards was dealing out liquor before his very eyes.

Agent Twiss evidently was thinking primarily of his own comfort and interests when he removed the agency to Deer Creek. The Mormons had built a pleasant way-station there for the use of their parties of emigrants, the locality being noted for its fine water, abundant grass, and good supply of timber. The Mormon War of 1857 had caused the abandonment of the location, and Major Twiss (all Indian agents were majors) had at once nested in the Mormon buildings like a cuckoo—he and his Oglala girl and their pet bear. Sir Richard Burton, who passed along this road in 1860, picked up several bits of scandalous gossip concerning Twiss, consisting among other things, of the assertion that "the Maj's ba'r got more sugar than the pore dam Injuns did."

The picture of this Indian agent, an honor graduate of West Point and a former army officer, hobnobbing with these illiterate

French traders and their half-breeds, drinking with them, and sharing in their shady deals, is really an astonishing one. Removed from office by President Lincoln in 1861, Twiss took his Indian wife and children to Powder River and joined the Oglalas there. In 1864 he came to Fort Laramie with the Indians, where Lieutenant Eugene F. Ware saw him and described him as a fine-looking old man with a snowy beard. Twiss joined eagerly in the officers' discussion of Grant's campaigns, exhibiting a grasp of military strategy that surprised them, for they did not know that he had been in the army. A few days later he left with his wild Oglalas, heading north for Powder river. It is not known when or where he died. Today there are many people among the Oglalas named Twiss, the descendants of this strange man.

The southern group of Oglalas felt that their father, the agent, had deserted them when he took the agency to Deer Creek. These people now spent most of their time far south of the Platte, coming up to trade each season with Beauvais, an old American Fur Company man, who had a trading place on the South Fork at California Crossing. They also traded with the Gilman brothers and Jack Marrow, who had trading houses farther down the river. Twiss and his successors accused these traders of handing out liquor and of carrying on an illicit trade in arms and ammunition, which they exchanged for horses and other property which the Indians had stolen. The truth seems to be that the traders near the forks of the Platte were on the whole less unscrupulous than Richards and Bissonette, their principal offense resting in the fact that they were too far away for the agent to have a working understanding with them and to be able to collect his customary "divvy."

The influence that the traders had over the Oglalas in the fifties and sixties was very great. Most of these men were Frenchmen from St. Louis; they had married into the tribe and spoke the language, and it was through them and their retainers that the agent and other officials had to communicate with the Indians. Very ignorant of the white man's ways and almost as credulous as small children, most of the chiefs were easily led by the nose, and the traders were adept in the art of leading, or misleading, the Indians. Before 1865 no agent could remain on the Upper Platte unless he had come to an agreement with the stronger traders. He could not even meet his Indians until he induced the traders to send out runners to coax the chiefs in. His interpreters were chosen by the traders and generally acted solely in their interest, but occasionally one of these men, somewhat more intelligent than his comrades, used his position near the agent to feather his own nest. Thus the Janis family owed its fortune to the fact that when Agent Twiss reached Fort Laramie in 1855 he selected Antoine Janis for his interpreter. Janis was supposed to be John Richards' man, but he used his position near the agent for his own advantage and soon was able to set himself up in business. The feud between these French traders was handed on to their half-Oglala children, culminating in the killing of two of old Janis' sons by the Reshaw boys. Antoine had a brother named Nicolas, and he had a half-Oglala son also named Nicholas. After 1870 Nicolas Janis was married to Red Cloud's daughter, but whether this was the older man or his son is not clear. In spite of this fact, Red Cloud was always on better terms with John Richards and his son John than with any other traders and usually followed their advice. On the other hand, Red Dog of the Oyukhpe band, the strongest group of the Northern Oglalas after 1870, would have nothing to do with the Richards clan.

These traders might have caused very serious trouble if they had desired to do so, for they had an extraordinary hold on most of the chiefs; but they also had a very wholesome fear of the United States government and a shrewd understanding of the fact that trouble is bad for trade. Their rogueries, which were many, therefore stopped short of instigating the Indians to make attacks on the whites, but it is fairly evident that Richards and Bissonette encouraged the Sioux of Powder River in their war on the Crows, a war which was good for trade; these Sioux getting most of their arms and ammunition from the traders near Deer Creek, under the eyes of the agent who was stating in his annual reports that the Sioux were honestly keeping their pledge of peace with the Crows.

A curious fact concerning these traders has not been noted by any of the authors who have written accounts of the Sioux: Bordeaux, Beauvais, the Janis brothers, and Leon Palladay were all American Fur Company men from old Fort John, on the site of Fort Laramie, and they were all closely connnected in trade and by marriage with the Southern Oglalas or Bear People and with Spotted Tail's Brulés who associated with the Bear People. On the other hand, John Richards, Joe Bissonette, and some others were former employes of the opposition company, Pratte, Cabanne & Company, the owners of Fort Platte near Fort John, and they always traded with the Northern Oglalas or Smoke People and were married to women of that group. By keeping this in mind and observing which traders and interpreters were favored by an Indian agent we can often understand what influence he was under. Agent Twiss started in 1855 under the influence of the American Fur Company men but in 1857 shifted to the other faction, going over to the Smoke People interest.

It may be noted that Red Cloud and his band of Bad Faces left Fort Laramie about the time Agent Twiss moved to Deer Creek, and we must suppose that these two events were in some way connected. Perhaps with the agent gone, the Sioux camp at the fort had to depend more than ever on the military for their support and the commandant grew tired of their constant demands and ordered them away. At this time the Mormon War caused a general shifting of troops, and the officers at Fort Laramie who had known the Sioux there for years were ordered elsewhere.

That the Bad Faces had not degenerated because of their long association with the soldiers at Fort Laramie was quickly demonstrated when they joined the rest of their people on Powder River. Led by Red Cloud, they took a conspicuous part in the closing episodes of the Crow war. Red Cloud at this period often went to Deer Creek to trade with his friend John Richards, from whom he obtained arms and ammunition for the prosecution of his warlike ventures. It was during one of these visits in the winter of 1859-1860 that he met Lieutenant (afterwards Colonel) Henry E. Maynadier, who was called Many Deer by the Sioux. In speaking of this meeting in later years, Colonel Maynadier stated that Red Cloud at the time was not a chief. The fact is evident enough. One of Old Smoke's sons was the chief of the Bad Faces of 1860 and Red Cloud was the leading warrior, a "shirt-wearer" or head-soldier. Indeed there is no evidence at all that Red Cloud was made chief until 1865 or even 1870. This question of chieftaincy is not an easy one to decide, as even the Indians themselves disagree when speaking of the matter. Red Cloud was a "shirt-wearer" in 1865, but I do not believe that this fact would rate him as a real chief.[5]

5. Stanley Vestal in his *Sitting Bull*, Chapter XIII, makes the "shirt wearers" among the Hunkpapas the "head chiefs." It is not as simple as that. The men who led in the Crazy Horse camp when it surrendered in 1877 were all shirt wearers. Crazy Horse had a shirt and was not a chief; He Dog and Little Big Man, both in this group that led the column, were shirt wearers but not chiefs. It is not quite

This movement of the Bad Faces to Powder River completed the retirement of the Oglalas and Brulés from the Platte Valley. A small group of Loafers—people who had intermarried with the whites or had acquired a taste for the white man's ways and whiskey and who shivered at the thought of going to live in the wild camps on Powder River and Republican Fork—remained near Fort Laramie. Big Mouth and Blue Horse, originally Bad Faces, had deserted their own camp when it elected to move northward and had joined the Loafer band. Old Smoke remained on the Platte. When the agency was moved from Deer Creek back to Fort Laramie in 1861, he returned to the fort to live, where in the following year he is mentioned as "the chief of the Sioux at this post."[6] The old man died in 1864, and for some years his scaffold-grave was to be seen standing on the high ground just west of the fort.

The Oglalas of the Bear People group, now established on the Republican Fork, were mainly True Oglala and Kiyuksa. They were the old leading bands of the tribe, but as they were strongly inclined to be on friendly terms with the whites they were now losing in reputation and also in numbers. In 1865, Colonel W. O. Collins estimated them at 150 lodges, whereas Francis Parkman in 1846 had given them 190 lodges. The Oglalas of the Smoke People division on Powder River had three principal bands: the Hunkpatila, "those who camp at the horn," (referring to the horn of the tribal camp circle—the position of honor) led by Man-Afraid-of-His-Horse; the Oyukhpe, "thrown down," among whom Red Dog was the rising man; and the Iteshicha, "bad faces," the band of Red Cloud, Crazy Horse, Big Road, and Little Hawk. This northern group of Oglalas had about 300 lodges in 1865 and was growing in strength. The Crow war attracted many people to the Oglala camps on Powder River, and the trouble with the whites that soon developed again increased the population of these warlike bands. The chiefs who stood out for peace could not hold their bands together. The Loafer band at Fort Laramie probably numbered less than fifty lodges. These people being pacifists were of no importance either in the eyes of their own tribe or of the whites whom they were so anxious to please.

---

clear whether Red Cloud spoke for the tribe at the Fort Laramie council in 1866. If he did, he was a chief, for chiefs alone spoke for the tribe in council. We must rank him as a chief in 1870, for he went to Washington in that year and spoke for the tribe.

6. Spring, *Life of Caspar Collins*, p. 135.

PART II

THE ERA OF WHITE ENCROACHMENT

*"You, after talking and talking and making
treaties and treaties, you go and make this evil
worse! You have set the prairie on fire!"*

—BIG MOUTH, 1867.

CHAPTER VII

"MAKING A WAR"

1861-1864

THE beginning of the Civil War made little impression on the minds of the Oglalas. They saw the troops of the regular army march away, leaving only skeleton garrisons at the posts, and they heard of great battles among the whites, but all this was very far away and concerned them little. The uprising of the Sioux in Minnesota in 1862 was something that touched them more nearly and that they could understand. They blamed the whites for taking the lands of the Santees and goading them into hostility. In the autumn of 1862, part of the Santees appeared suddenly on the Upper Missouri, their camp full of plunder and captive white women and children. These people talked a great deal of the victories they had won over the whites, but the Teton chiefs were shrewd enough to suspect that the Santees had not come to the Missouri merely to tell them the news, and it soon became apparent that the Minnesota Sioux were afraid of the troops and had come to find refuge beyond the Missouri. The correctness of this view was quickly demonstrated, for presently large forces of troops appeared, coming across the coteau from Minnesota and also up the Missouri, and the Santees who had talked so boldly now quickly moved out of the way, part of them going northward, the rest crossing west of the Missouri to join the Tetons. As the troops were little inclined to make any distinction between Tetons and Santees, and as part of the Tetons were ready enough to fight, most of the Tetons of the Upper Missouri were soon drawn into a war which they had not sought or planned but which Fate had thrust upon them.

These events of 1862 and the following year touched the Oglalas and Brulés somewhat more closely than the news of the great battles the whites were fighting among themselves, but not closely enough to cause them to take any action. They remained quiet, but the white population of the border country was far from quiet. The news of the Minnesota massacres had spread panic along the frontier from Dakota to Kansas, and from Iowa westward to the mountains. Part of the settlers left their homesteads and fled to the nearest towns, while others banded together in armed companies and began harrying the quite friendly border tribes. The governors, one after the other, wired appeals to Washington, asserting that all the Indians were hostile and demanding troops. The newspapers added their voices to the general clamor. The government, with the news of the bloody work the Sioux raiders had wrought in Minnesota still ringing in its ears, could not ignore this widespread feeling of alarm in the West, and was compelled to send large forces of volunteer troops to reinforce the posts on the Missouri, Platte, and Arkansas.

It was undoubtedly the coming of these troops that brought on the war with the plains tribes in 1864. Red Cloud used to say, "the white soldiers always want to make a war," and there was a good deal of truth in that statement. Life at a frontier post was a very humdrum affair, and we have abundant evidence to show that most of the soldiers and the younger officers longed for the day when the Indians would give them some little excuse for starting a fight. This was true of the regular troops on the Upper Platte in 1852-1854, and it was equally true of the volunteer cavalry who came to this region ten years later. Sent to maintain peace and keep the tribes quiet, many of the officers and more of the men were soon trying to break the dreadful monotony of garrison life by starting a little Indian excitement. The Colorado cavalry and other troops recruited on the frontier regarded the Indians as wild animals and thought nothing of killing them, and many of the soldiers from the East soon developed this attitude. Lieutenant Eugene F. Ware tells us that the Kansas troops at Camp Cottonwood on the lower Platte, wishing to have a bit of practice with their artillery, dropped a number of shells on a party of Sioux Indians who were seen on an island in the river. This happened before there was any trouble, the Indians being perfectly friendly. In the *Life of Caspar Collins,* by A. W. Spring, we find this youthful officer dwelling on the eagerness with which the men and officers of his regiment, the Eleventh Ohio Cavalry, looked forward to an opportunity to show what they could do in an Indian fight. These Ohio men, stationed along the North Platte with headquarters at Fort Laramie, were listening enviously to the tales of the frontiersmen. Most of the soldiers soon discarded their uniforms, decking themselves out in buckskins, moccasins, and Spanish spurs, and having provided themselves with hardy Indian ponies out of their own pay they awaited eagerly a chance to exhibit their prowess as Indian fighters. That they did not bring on a war with the Sioux in 1863 was largely due to the fact that their commanding officer, Lieutenant Colonel Wm. O. Collins, was under a strong impression that he had been sent to the Upper Platte to keep the Indians quiet and that the way to do that was to treat them fairly.

The plains tribes were friendly in 1862 and judicious handling would have kept them so, but the Indian Office officials were asleep and there was nothing judicious in the conduct of the military men who were in control in the West. Major General S. R. Curtis, who commanded the troops on the Platte and Arkansas rivers, was a pompous man who knew nothing about Indians but imagined himself an authority on the subject. Brigadier General James Craig, who commanded along the Overland Road on the Platte in 1862, knew nothing about Indians when he came West and made no attempt to learn. Brigadier General Robert B. Mitchell, who succeeded Craig on the Overland, was a good-hearted, easy-going man, but he did not understand Indians and frankly said so. Lieutenant Colonel H. M. Chivington of the First Colorado Cavalry was a frontier product of the best Indian-hating type. He looked on the Indians as wild beasts, to be hustled out of the way of progress, and to be killed if they resisted. Lieutenant Colonel Wm. O. Collins, who commanded the Eleventh Ohio Cavalry along the North Platte, was by far the best commander in the plains in 1863. He knew nothing of Indians when he came out, but he learned quickly; he honestly desired peace, made friends with the principal chiefs, and never missed an opportunity to learn more of the tribes, their location, numbers, and disposition. Just when he was equipped to do splendid service he was relieved of command and ordered East.

The ignorance of some of these superior officers was really amazing. General Craig in July, 1862, reported that some small raids on the Sweetwater were the work of Indians whose camp was on Beaver Creek in Kansas, about 400 miles from the scene of the attacks. General Curtis reported in May, 1864, that the Minnesota Sioux were massing to attack Camp Cottonwood on the Platte, and he wished to rush a regiment of cavalry and an entire battery of artillery to that post. There was not a Minnesota Sioux within 400 miles of Camp Cottonwood and no one with the slightest knowledge of Indians would have supposed it possible for the Santees to attack that post. General Mitchell took all the prizes when he innocently reported in August, 1864, that "the Snakes, Winnibigoshish, and Minnesota Sioux" were raiding west of Fort Laramie, and the Yanktons and Kiowas were doing likewise on the lower Platte. How poor Mitchell got the idea that Lake Winnibigoshish was an Indian tribe will always remain a mystery.

While these army officers were sending alarmist telegrams and moving troops back and forth, the Oglalas and their friends were in their hunting grounds pursuing their usual business of hunting buffalo and fighting their Indian enemies when they felt the urge. On Powder River the Crow war was still the main interest. There were no whites in that country, and with only a few on the Platte and far away eastward on the Missouri the Indians on Powder River were no longer worried about white encroachments. The council they had held in 1857, when they had pledged themselves to turn back any parties of whites who attempted to enter their lands, had been forgotten by most of the Sioux, and when a wagon-train came from the Platte and moved northward across the heads of the Powder, Tongue, and Rosebud and then on westward across the Bighorn, the event attracted little attention. To these simple-minded people it was only one wagon-train going through and did not matter. If they had realized that it was the opening of a new road, the Bozeman Road to Montana, they probably would have taken a different view of the matter.

The situation of the Oglalas, Brulés, Cheyennes, and Arapahoes in the country south of the Platte was not so good as that of the bands on Powder River. The buffalo herds in their country were beginning to shrink very perceptibly in size, and the Indians attributed this to the heavy travel along the Overland Road to the north and the Santa Fe road to the south. By 1862 parties of white hunters were at work slaughtering the buffalo for their hides alone. Beginning in 1859 there had been another great rush of whites across the plains, this time to the new gold fields in Colorado, eighty thousand persons having gone to that region in three years.

These Indians south of the Platte were now surrounded by the Overland Stage Road up the Platte, with the branch line up the South Fork to Denver, and by another stage line up the Arkansas River to Denver and Santa Fe. On the Platte there were stage stations every twenty or twenty-five miles; coaches were constantly passing, and emigrant parties and trains of huge freight wagons were always in sight. As if this were not bad enough, a new stage line was presently opened from Atchison and Leavenworth straight through the Indian hunting grounds to Denver. By 1862 the bands between the Platte and the Arkansas were very much concerned over white encroachments, and they were not reassured when they discovered that a "paper" which some of their chiefs had been coaxed into signing in 1860 gave most of their lands to the whites. That these Indians were in the main very friendly was obvious to all fair observers, and it was known that practically all of the chiefs were opposed to war, for they had a deep conviction that a resort to arms would only hasten their own ruin. By the close of 1863 the situation had become a delicate one requiring careful handling, but some of the Indian agents and superintendents were too ignorant and the rest too venal to accomplish any good, while the military seemed obsessed with the idea that a vigorous use of force on all possible occasions was the best way of keeping the Indians quiet.[1]

In April, 1864, Irwin & Jackman's herd was reported as having been run off by Cheyennes from the Big Sandy east of Denver, and soon after that a party of Cheyennes had a brush with the Colorado cavalry near Fremont's Orchard on the South Platte. General S. R. Curtis, in command of the military department, then did the unwise thing and ordered Colonel H. M. Chivington to go after the Indians and punish them. Chivington, who believed all the evil that had been spoken against the Cheyennes, went after them with a will. His cavalry detachments chased the Cheyennes all along the South Platte, found two or three little camps and destroyed the lodges. The troops found it impossible to catch up with any large camps or to strike a real blow, but they certainly stirred up the Indians. Then in May came the rumor of a rebel force advancing from Texas, and Chivington ordered his troops withdrawn from the South Platte and concentrated on the Arkansas River. He

1. An excellent account of the growth of these troubles with the tribes south of the Platte will be found in George Bird Grinnell's, *The Fighting Cheyennes*, p. 124 *et seq.*

stated, rather carelessly, that the militia could deal with the Indian troubles, which were not serious. At that moment the first real war-parties were starting from the Cheyenne and Sioux camps to make the first real attacks along the Platte. These war-parties found the troops gone, and they reaped a rich harvest in horses, plunder, and scalps with practically no loss to themselves. The war was now on in earnest.[2]

I have been assured by old Cheyennes who were in the camps on the Republican Fork at this time that their people did not run off Irwin & Jackman's oxen, that they had plenty of buffalo, and had no use for oxen. The evidence strongly supports their claims. They believed that the oxen had stampeded. The fact that these Indians remained in their camps within easy reach of the troops was a clear indication of their friendly disposition—once they became hostile the troops could not get within sight of their camps. Two Crows and other Cheyennes stated that the war-party which had the brush with Chivington's men at Fremont's Orchard was on its way to Powder River to join an expedition against the Crows. The members of the party were amazed when the troops came up and attacked them.

At about the time when he ordered Chivington to start after the Cheyennes, General Curtis, with his usual brilliant understanding of Indians, instructed General R. B. Mitchell, commanding on the Platte, to summon the Sioux to Camp Cottonwood and to order them to keep out of the Platte Valley. The Sioux to be dealt with were Little Thunder's and Spotted Tail's Brulés and the southern group of Oglalas under Bad Wound and Little Wound. The Sioux chiefs came to Cottonwood on June 8 with the evident idea that a big council was to be held; but General Mitchell had not even troubled to come, merely telegraphing his orders to Major George M. O'Brien. This young officer spoke to these proud chiefs as a bad-mannered master might to his servants. He ordered them to keep out of the Platte Valley, instructed them that they might occasionally come to trade in small groups only, warned them that they must not linger near the road, and required them to report promptly all raids contemplated by the Cheyennes and other hostiles. The chiefs, who were notoriously friendly, agreed to do as

2. Consult the *Official Records of the Union and Confederate Armies,* serial numbers 19, 62, 64, and 83. My Indian information comes mainly from the Cheyennes and closely follows the narrative given by Grinnell. In the main the Indian story is certainly true.

they were ordered. They expressed fear of being attacked by the troops who might mistake them for Cheyennes, asked that a white man be sent to their camp to protect them, and begged for a trader.

They said that Agent John Loree at Fort Laramie allowed only one favored trader in their camp of over 200 lodges, a man with a little stock, asking high prices. They also asked that their annuities be delivered on the Platte near Camp Cottonwood as they were too poor to go all the way to Fort Laramie and were afraid that they would be attacked by troops if they tried to go. These chiefs were evidently determined to put up with harsh treatment for the sake of peace. A man skilled in dealing with Indians could have held these bands in his hand, quiet throughout the troubles of 1864; but no one bothered to put such a man in control.[3]

By the middle of the summer the raiding had spread along the North Platte and Sweetwater to South Pass, but here the raids were not frequent and ware mostly small affairs carried out by a handful of young warriors. The Indians along the North Platte in Colonel Collins' district had not had the provocation that those south of the main Platte had experienced, and the chiefs, who were generally friendly, were still holding the young men well in hand. But on the South Platte and below the forks matters were going badly for the whites. The Cheyennes, Arapahoes, and Sioux of the Platte who, according to Colonel Chivington, could be dealt with by the local militia, broke out in a series of savage raids along the road, from Little Blue in eastern Nebraska to within a few miles of Denver. The havoc they created was terrible, and in the end they broke the road and completely blocked all travel. The stage line ceased to operate, the trains of the emigrants and freighters collected in large groups for mutual protection and remained in camp. The mail for California had to be sent back down the Platte and finally reached its destination via Panama. During the whole of these six weeks of frightful raids the troops did not succeed once in striking back at the Indians.

The utter failure of the troops to get at the hostiles led to the adoption of several ingenious schemes, the most remarkable of which was the great prairie fire plan. Lieutenant Eugene F. Ware gives

3. Eugene F. Ware in his book, *The Indian War of '64,* states that there were two councils and that General Mitchell was present. Ware, who was also present, asserts that Spotted Tail defied General Mitchell. These statements, and the dates given by Ware, do not agree with the official records.

the wrong date for this event and is incorrect in attributing the scheme to General R. B. Mitchell. It was Colonel R. R. Livingston's plan. On October 22 he had detachments of cavalry fire the grass on the south side of the Platte at short intervals for a distance of 200 miles, the theory being that the fire would sweep the whole country as far as the Arkansas River and burn out all the hostiles. I have inquired of old Indians who were in the camps south of the Platte at the time as to the effect of this great fire. They never heard of it.

As winter approached, the roads were reopened and there were signs that a large part of the Indians wanted peace. With careful management at this time the friendlies could have been separated from the wilder bands who intended to continue hostilities; but there was the question of punishment for past wrong-doing. General Curtis had started punishing Cheyennes in April, and in November he was still determined to punish them. It does not seem to have occurred to him that before stirring up the Indians again he should have provided adequately for the protection of the settlers and travelers on the Platte road.

In most of the Indian tribes we find the tragic figure of a chief who had been to Washington, or to the white settlements, and had come home utterly convinced that the whites were too powerful to be opposed successfully. These men were always for peace and would go to any length to maintain it. They were usually misunderstood by most of their own people, who looked on them as fainthearted and even traitorous, and they were just as often misunderstood by the whites, who did not believe their professions of friendship. Among the Cheyennes there were three chiefs of this type. Lean Bear, the first of the three, was killed in May, 1864, when he rode forward to shake hands with Lieutenant George Eayre, and that young officer, mistaking his intentions, ordered his men to open fire. The other two peace leaders, Black Kettle and White Antelope, during that summer and fall did all that was possible to keep the young men of their bands from joining the raiding parties; and as soon as matters quieted down they seized the first opportunity to go in near Fort Lyon, Colorado, with a camp consisting of all the most friendly Cheyennes and Arapahoes, who wanted peace. Whether these people had been promised the protection of the troops or not is a difficult question to decide; but the friendly intentions of the Indians were perfectly apparent, and there can be no question that what they had heard from certain officers had put them off their guard.

Yet it was on their camp that the punishment General Curtis demanded was meted out by Colonel Chivington and his Colorado volunteers. The blow was terribly effective. The Indians were completely surprised; their herd was captured, and they were left on foot to face an overwhelming force of whites. Men, women, and children were shot down in the camp, and those who made their escape into the dry bed of Sand Creek were quickly surrounded and had to fight for their lives. Many of the people were killed; others escaped. That night the remnant of the group made their way afoot through bitter cold weather toward a Cheyenne camp on the head of the Smoky Hill Fork. White Antelope was one of the first men killed in the village. He made no attempt to fight but stood in the center of the camp until shot down. Black Kettle made his escape only to be "thrown away" by his angry tribesmen who blamed him for leading the people into a trap.

The Indians had all settled down in winter camps when the news of Sand Creek stirred them into new activity. As soon as the remnant of Black Kettle's people reached the Cheyenne camp on the Smoky Hill, chiefs assembled a council and decided to send around a war-pipe. During all the summer raiding the chiefs had wanted peace and whenever possible had tried to check their young men; but now, with the exception of Black Kettle and two or three others, they were all for war and ready to take the lead.

The pipe-bearers went to the Sioux camps on the Solomon Fork, then to the Northern Arapahoes on the Republican, and the chiefs of both these tribes smoked the pipe. Early in December the three tribes met on Beaver Creek.[4] Here between 800 and 900 lodges were assembled: Southern Cheyennes, Northern Arapahoes, Oglalas and Brulé Sioux. An officer who examined a deserted camp of these Indians in February, 1865, stated that there were 800 lodge fires. There were in the village probably 150 lodges of Oglalas, 250 of Brulés, and 80 of Northern Arapahoes; the rest were Southern Cheyennes.

Late in December the Indians moved north and camped on Cherry Creek, a tributary of the Arickaree Fork, and from here they set out on an expedition to Julesburg on the South Platte, to

4. The Northern Arapahoes had come down to visit their relatives, but learning that the Southern Arapahoes had retired south of the Arkansas and that it would be dangerous to go down there, they went into winter camp on the Republican Fork.

strike the first blow in revenge for Sand Creek. The chiefs took one thousand picked warriors for this attack on a stage station and one-company post. This expedition was a formal affair, with the war-chiefs or pipe-bearers marching in front and the warriors following in column; the men of certain soldier-societies guarded the front, rear, and flanks to prevent anyone leaving the column. This peculiar column formation appears to have been used only when war-chiefs led a great party on an important expedition, and it would seem that this method of going to war was copied from the old-time tribal hunt in which the hunters were kept in column under guard to prevent any of them slipping away to hunt alone and frighten the game. Even the sending out of decoys to draw the enemy into a trap was evidently copied from the tribal buffalo hunt.

The Sioux chiefs, who had been the first to accept the Cheyenne war-pipe, led the march. The warriors reached the vicinity of Julesburg the evening of January 6 and concealed themselves in the hills south of the stage station and post. The next morning a decoy of seven picked warriors was sent into the valley. They rode around near Julesburg until the cavalrymen at Camp Rankin saddled up and came out after them; they then retired toward the hills, drawing the soldiers into the trap. As so often happened when this ancient trick was tried by the Indians, some of the young warriors could not be restrained, and they charged out of the hills before the troops were well into the trap. The whites (some citizens were with the soldiers) turned at once and started back toward the stockade at a gallop, the Indians charging out of the hills with their whole force. They ran the troopers into the stockade, killing fourteen soldiers and four civilians. After this fight the Indians withdrew to Julesburg, one mile east of Camp Rankin, where they spent most of the day in plundering the station, the store, and the stage company's warehouse. Pack-ponies, which had been brought along for this purpose, were loaded with the plunder, and late in the day the Indians started on their return home with the ponies so heavily burdened that they could move but slowly.

Soon after the return from Julesburg, the Indians broke camp and moved north to a stream which the Cheyennes term White Butte Creek.[5] In this new camp the chiefs held a council and decided to make a great raid along the Platte and then move north

5. This stream has not been identified, but it was north of the Arikaree Fork and south of the South Platte, not far from Summit Springs where General Carr had the fight with Tall Bull's band a few years later.

to Powder River and there join the Oglalas and Northern Cheyennes. Black Kettle was still determined to take no part in the war, and the day the village started for the Platte he left with his band of Cheyennes and moved south toward the Arkansas. The start for the Platte was made about January 26, war-parties going ahead of the moving village, the Sioux striking northeast, the Cheyennes northwest, and the Arapahoes about due north. The war-parties and the village struck the South Platte on January 28, creating pandemonium in the valley. Ranches and stage stations were attacked and burned, wagon-trains were captured, and whites were killed wherever they were met. The soldiers were cooped up inside their stockades and usually did not venture out. The huge Indian village crossed the Platte near Harlow's Ranch, twenty-three miles west of Julesburg, and pitched camp on the north bank of the river, the lodges extending from Moore's Creek nearly four miles up the Platte. The glare from the campfires could be seen at night far along the valley, and the beating of the drums was heard miles away. All night long the Indians were dancing scalp-dances and holding feasts; the village was packed with captured cattle and with food supplies of every description from looted stores and the large wagon-trains that had been plundered. The Indians remained here for six days without being bothered at all by the troops; which is a queer commentary on General G. M. Dodge's report that his troops attacked the Indians and drove them from the road northward.

On February 2, the village started for the North Platte, and a party of one thousand warriors went down the South Platte to have a final visit with the soldiers at Camp Rankin. The chiefs hopefully sent out a little decoy party to lure the troops into a trap, as on the previous occasion; but the officers had learned a lesson on January 7 and kept their handful of troopers inside the stockade. The Indians soon gave it up and went down to Julesburg, where they plundered the buildings for the second time in a month and then burned them.

During this great crisis along the Platte the ignorance and incapacity of the higher military officers was shockingly apparent. The Indians were moving slowly along well known trails, crossing the Platte road exactly where any trader or interpreter who knew them would expect them to appear, yet all of the superior officers, including General G. M. Dodge who had just been appointed to succeed the blundering Curtis, stood bewildered and helpless in the face of the hostile attacks. They had plenty of troops with which they could control the situation, but after the first attack on Julesburg General Mitchell had stripped the Platte road of troops with the object of striking the Indians in their own camps on the Republican Fork. He marched from Camp Cottonwood, about one hundred miles east of Julesburg, on January 16, scouted the Republican and its branches, by some miracle of inefficiency just missed the hostile camps at White Butte Creek, and returned to Cottonwood on January 26 with his men and horses exhausted. He had just broken up his force, ordering the troops back to their little posts along the road, when the news came that the Indians had struck the line west of Julesburg in huge force and were creating havoc. General Dodge now took command, ordering Colonel R. R. Livingston to assemble the troops, which Mitchell had just dispersed to their old stations, and to lead them up the road to deal with the hostiles. Livingston reached Julesburg just after the Indians had burned the place and withdrawn northward. If General Dodge was referring to Colonel Livingston's action when he represented that his troops had attacked the Indians and driven them north he was slightly exaggerating the facts. Livingston found one hundred miles of road completely wrecked, all stage stations and ranches burned, the horses and cattle carried off, the telegraph poles destroyed, and much of the wire removed. He was so aghast at what he saw and heard that he took no action further than to send out detachments to scout the country cautiously and learn which way the hostiles had gone.[6]

At Mud Springs, near the North Platte, the Indians found a detachment of the Eleventh Ohio Cavalry, with whom they skirmished for the greater part of a day. Here they ran off a herd of cattle and obtained a large number of horses and mules; they then went on and crossed the North Platte on the ice. They camped in the high bluffs north of the Platte to prepare for the journey through the Sand Hills, but the next day scouts signaled from the hilltops that soldiers were coming. This was Colonel Collins who had come from Fort Laramie to assist his men at Mud Springs. The Indians streamed back across the frozen Platte in the hope of getting more horses; but Collins corraled his wagons, put the horses inside the corral, and made it very clear that the Indians would have to work for any horses they obtained from his command. The war-

6. The reports on these events will be found in the *Official Records of the Union and Confederate Armies*, serial numbers 101 and 102. Eugene F. Ware's account, as usual, does not agree with the original reports.

riors fought the soldiers here all day, and some of the more hopeful Indians returned the following morning and shot up the corral again, but they failed to bring off any plunder.

This was their last meeting with the soldiers. The Indians now moved northward through the Sand Hills and the desolate plains of western Nebraska to the Black Hills where, according to the Cheyennes, Spotted Tail and his Brulés left the village. The rest of the people moved around the northern edge of the Black Hills and westward to Powder River.

The march of this village of 700 to 1,000 lodges was an amazing feat. These Indians had moved 400 miles during the worst weather of a severe winter through open, desolate plains taking with them their women and children, lodges, and household property, their vast herds of ponies, and the herds of captured cattle, horses, and mules. On the way they had killed more whites than the number of Cheyennes killed at Sand Creek and had completely destroyed one hundred miles of the Overland Stage Line, plundering and then burning all the stations and ranches.

In reviewing these events one cannot avoid the conviction that the people of the border states and territories would have been much better off if General Curtis and most of his troops had been elsewhere in 1864. Curtis was as astonished as a small child with its first Jack-in-the-box when the Indians responded to the Sand Creek pressure by suddenly jerking up the lid and flying in his face. When he had recovered a little from the shock, he produced the ingenious explanation that it was the habit of all the plains Indians to retire into the mountains to winter, but being harried by his troops in 1864 the Indians were unable to lay up a supply of food for winter and in January, driven by hunger, they rushed from the mountains into the plains and wrecked the Overland Stage Line to obtain food and clothing![7] This able presentation of the case did not get General Curtis out of the very hot water into which the raids had plunged him. Merely through luck, the Indians in striking at Julesburg had hit the nerve in the funny-bone of the Overland Stage Line and that company, which had great influence at Washington, shrieked and wailed and would not be pacified until Curtis had been relieved and General G. M. Dodge put in his place with General P. E. Connor, an Indian fighter from California, as Dodge's commander in the field.

7. General Curtis to General Halleck, January 31, 1865.

CHAPTER VIII

POWDER RIVER

1865

WHILE the Indian war was raging on the Platte and South Fork in 1864, the Sioux on Powder River were engaged in hunting buffalo and raiding their old enemies, the Crows. A few minor depredations had been committed along the North Platte road by the wild Miniconjous, Sans Arcs, and Blackfoot-Sioux, and the little detachment of troops at Upper Platte Bridge had had some sort of trouble with the Oglalas in which an Indian named Grass was wounded and a number of Oglalas and their families were taken as hostages. This affair is not remembered by the Oglalas today, and all that we know about it is contained in some references to the hostages in the correspondence of the Indian agent, John Loree. Among the hostages were Reshaw (Richards) and family of seven, the family of Black Tiger, brother-in-law of Richards, Stone Belly with six persons, Milk with five, Rocky Bear, a chief in later days, with five, and the family of Red Shell who had died while being held at Platte Bridge. These people clearly were retainers of John Richards, and the fact that they had been arrested and held indicates that this old reprobate was very much out of favor with the new Indian agent and the new commandant at Fort Laramie.[1]

In 1864, Richards and Bissonette were still up near Deer Creek, trading with the Oglalas and other Indians on Powder River, but

1. Agent Loree's report, in *Report of the Commissioner of Indian Affairs,* 1864. It may be that old Richards was himself the hostage held by the troops. His half-Oglala son John was a young man who had been married to an Oglala girl at Fort Laramie in the fall of 1862, and he could hardly have had a family of seven. The Oglalas today say that the younger John Richards was married to the sisters (*plural*) of Yellow Bear.

the Upper Platte Agency was now located east of Fort Laramie, just below Bordeaux's trading place, which was still where it had been at the time of the Grattan fight in 1854. The agency was known as the Wakonpomny, from a bastard Sioux word referring to the handing out of gifts. Loree spent all of his time here or at Fort Laramie and seems to have been a good father to the Laramie Loafers; but the Sioux south of the Platte and those up on Powder River hated him, openly calling him a thief and complaining that he gave trading licenses to only a few of his favorites and permitted them to charge high prices for the poorest of goods. In the spring of 1864, this agent made the first attempt at farming, having a short irrigation ditch dug and planting fifteen acres. Old Smoke evidently approved this undertaking, for the Oglalas today state that he was the first of their chiefs who ever attempted to farm. His farming was very likely similar to that of Red Cloud in 1875—he gave permission for the women to try their hand at it.

When the Indian war broke out on the Platte and Arkansas in the summer of 1864, Colonel W. O. Collins, in command at Fort Laramie, took Smoke's band, mostly Loafers, under his wing and protected them from the emigrants, who were inclined to shoot first and inquire as to whether the Indians were friendly or not after they had shot them. This officer did not permit his troops to indulge in the indiscriminate chasing of Indians such as was then going on in Colorado, Nebraska, and Kansas, and the result was that the Indians along the North Platte gave no serious trouble. There were a few small raids, and the colonel considered it necessary to forbid the traders to supply the Indians with arms and ammunition. Old Smoke died at Fort Laramie during the fall, and his body was placed in a cloth-covered box on a scaffold which stood on the high ground just west of the fort.

In 1864, the wild Tetons in the country north of the North Platte were divided into two distinct groups. The southern group, consisting of the Smoke People Oglalas, and part of the Miniconjous and Sans Arcs, frequented the headwaters of the Powder River, hunting northward to Tongue River. With them were associated the Northern Cheyennes and Northern Arapahoes. Man-Afraid-of-His-Horse, of the Oglalas, and One Horn, of the Miniconjous, were the best known of the older leaders, both of them being regarded as men of sense who were strongly inclined to keep on good terms with the whites. As late as the spring of 1865, Colonel W. O. Collins, who knew these Indians well, hoped that they could be kept out of the war which was so quickly spreading through the whole plains region.

The northern group of Tetons, led by the fierce Hunkpapas, had been unfriendly as far back as 1856, and when the Minnesota Sioux came into their country in 1862 they allied themselves with them and became bitterly hostile. Led by such chiefs as Four Horns, Black Moon, and Sitting Bull, this group of Tetons roved from the Missouri westward to lower Powder River. On April 30, 1864, one thousand lodges of these Indians were on the Missouri above the mouth of Heart River. They declared that no more whites should come through their country; they would attack emigrants, steamboats coming up the river, or any troops that entered their lands. Brigadier General Alfred Sully was preparing a strong expedition to move against them, and in July he had a big fight with them on Upper Knife River (Battle of Killdeer Mountain), inflicting considerable losses. This same summer Captain James L. Fisk, while attempting to lead a wagon-train of armed men through the country of these Hunkpapas to the Montana gold fields, was attacked east of the Little Missouri by a Sioux war-party which almost succeeded in destroying the train. In the end, Fisk's party was rescued by a force of 850 infantry from Fort Rice who escorted them back to the Missouri.

Thus in the fall of 1864 the friendly Oglalas on the head of Powder River were caught between two Indian wars, one on the Upper Missouri and the other south of the Platte. In both of these struggles their own kinsmen were engaged and the vital question of preventing further white encroachments on their lands was the main issue, yet the bands on Powder River seem to have been quite unaffected until the great group of hostiles from south of the Platte joined them early in March, 1865. The story these southern Indians told of the outrages the white soldiers had committed against them while they were still friendly and of the retribution they had exacted from the whites, the sight of the great numbers of captured horses these hostiles had in their possession and the plunder that filled their camps greatly excited the Powder River bands, and it must have been at this moment that Man-Afraid-of-His-Horse, who had stood firmly for peace with the whites, began to lose his hold over the people. Indeed, there is every reason to suppose that the hostiles now offered a pipe to the Powder River

{116}

Indians and that in a council the friendly chiefs were over-ruled and the pipe was accepted.[2]

These Indians seem to have been quite unaware of the stir the great raids along the Platte had made among the whites. The people of the West, the great stage companies, the freighting firms, and many other influences were demanding that the government now subdue all of the plains tribes. Consequently, at the moment when these Indians on Powder River were celebrating their successes along the Platte with dances and feasts the military authorities were hard at work assembling troops for the invasion of their country. The Civil War was ending; troops could now be spared in large numbers for service against the Indians, and it was planned to send five or more heavy columns of cavalry into the Powder River country where they were to unite and operate against the hostiles. Two forts were also to be established, one on Powder River and the second on the Yellowstone. This program would have resulted in the conquest of the Sioux and the permanent occupation of their country by a force sufficiently strong to control their every movement; yet the Indians seem to have suspected nothing, and when grass came up in April, 1865, they went about their usual occupations as if no war existed. The killing of four Crows, who ventured into their camp to steal horses, put them in a fine humor. They had great scalp dances and were happy. Presently they broke up their winter camps and separated, the different bands setting out to hunt buffalo on the Powder and Little Powder. In May they moved to Tongue River to hunt, and from there some small war-parties went to raid the Crows. On Tongue River, according to my best informant, George Bent of the Southern Cheyennes, the heads of the soldier societies, the men whom the whites termed the "war-chiefs," held their first council to consider action against their white enemies. Young-Man-Afraid-of-His-Horse, the son of the old chief, and Red Cloud were present at this meeting, which was attended by the head-soldiers of the Sioux and Cheyennes. The decision reached by this council was that in midsummer an expedition should attack the whites on the North Platte, and meantime several small war-parties were to conduct raids along the road. The leaders of

2. This is evident from the formal attack made at Platte Bridge in the following July. Such formal affairs were undertaken after the presentation of a war-pipe. The Sioux who came in and surrendered at Fort Laramie in April stated that the hostiles from south of the Platte were trying to induce the Indians on Powder River to join them in the war.

these groups were to bring back information which would enable the head-soldiers to decide at what point to strike with their large expedition in July. From this it is evident that these Indian leaders were oblivious of the fact that the military were rapidly assembling great forces for the invasion of the Powder River lands. Red Cloud and his friends were planning to fight the United States with all its power exactly as they had always fought their Crow, Pawnee, and other Indian enemies, by sending one large war-party against them in July and then letting their interest in the war subside until the following summer. The authors who speak with admiration of the "generalship" of these Indian chiefs are merely exhibiting their ignorance. From their habits of thought and way of life the Sioux could not conduct offensive warfare in any other manner, for it was only in midsummer and early winter that they could raise a large force, and even then they could not hold their warriors together for a longer period than a week or ten days. Conditions in 1866 and 1876 were not normal. In 1866, the troops were holding forts in the heart of the Powder River country and the Indians had to make extraordinary efforts to force them out. In 1876 these Indians won their great victories while they were on the defensive and apparently without any plan at all for offensive action.

General P. E. Connor, the new commander on the Platte, was pushing his preparations for the invasion of the Powder River country when the first little raiding parties struck the road west of Fort Laramie in April. Colonel Thomas Moonlight with a large force of cavalry set out at once from Fort Laramie, marching as far up the road as Platte Bridge. He saw no Indians but heard that the raids were being made by a camp of Northern Cheyennes who were on Wind River. Making a hard march, Moonlight attempted to strike these Indians but could not find them, and while he was on this wild goose chase and the road was partly stripped of troops, two hundred warriors from the camps on Tongue River attacked Deer Creek, below Platte Bridge. This was on May 20. According to George Bent, who was with the Indians, there were two parties, one of Cheyennes who attacked Deer Creek, the other of Sioux, led by Young-Man-Afraid-of-His-Horse, who raided the road farther to the east. At Deer Creek the Indians ran off some horses but were then attacked by a body of Kansas cavalry who drove them off with some losses.[3]

3. George Bent, the half-Cheyenne son of William Bent, was seen by the troops among the warriors. They mistook him for Bill Comstock, an outlaw who

These raids were hardly over when the troops at Fort Laramie performed the remarkable feat of exasperating the Loafers and other Sioux, members of the friendly camp located near the post, to such an extent that they actually turned hostile. These Oglala and Brulé pacifists had been loitering near the fort all through the troubles of 1864, trying very hard to keep on good terms with the whites and often being shot at by nervous emigrants who regarded all Indians as hostile. Colonel Collins sympathized with these Sioux and tried to protect them, but as long as they wandered about in small groups he could not be of much assistance; consequently, he formed them into one large camp on the north side of the Platte ten miles below Fort Laramie and placed Charlie Elliston, a Virginian who had a Sioux wife, in command of the camp with a force of Indian soldiers or police, to aid him in controlling the people. Spotted Tail, who had gone north with the hostiles in February, 1865, had not accompanied them to Powder River, for he was still determined to keep out of the war if he could do so. He wintered on White River, east of the Black Hills, and in April came down to the Platte and joined the friendly camp. With him were probably all of the most friendly Brulés and Oglalas, the followers of Little Thunder and Bad Wound.

Two Face, a very friendly Oglala chief, had been met with his band on the Platte by General Mitchell in August, 1864, and had been sent under a guard to Camp Cottonwood. Becoming frightened, this chief and his followers ran away. But these friendlies could not bear to be absent from their white friends for long, and Two Face having bought or ransomed a white captive from the hostiles started in the spring of 1865 to take her to Fort Laramie, evidently hoping for a reward. Near the Platte his party ran into some of Elliston's Indian police, who rounded them up; and having learned that Blackfoot, another friendly chief, was on Snake Creek with a small camp, Elliston went with his Indians and brought in this band also. Colonel Collins, their friend, was no longer in command, and Colonel Moonlight who had succeeded him was still on the road in pursuit of the hostiles when these Indians were brought to Fort Laramie. The temporary commandant, a drunken brute who hated Indians, listened to the hysterical statements of the white captive, Mrs. Eubanks, who had been brought

---

a few years later became a hero while serving as a scout in Colonel Forsyth's company in Kansas.

in by Two Face, and then ordered that this chief and Blackfoot should be hanged in artillery trace-chains, a command which was promptly carried out.[4]

The Sioux in the friendly camp were greatly shocked by this horrible act of injustice, but they were as much opposed to war as ever and remained where they were. General G. M. Dodge, the new commander of the military department, now discovered the fact that there was a camp of Sioux within ten miles of Fort Laramie and telegraphed to General Connor to ask why these Indians were not attacked at once. Connor replied that they were friendlies, under the protection of the military, and could not be attacked. An able officer would have regarded these friendly Indians as valuable allies whose warriors could be utilized as scouts, but Dodge regarded them as an intolerable burden and nothing else. He now telegraphed the War Department for instructions and received the wise answer that the Indian prisoners should be sent to Fort Kearney on the lower Platte. General Connor was at Fort Laramie, and knowing something of these Indians he protested that they should not be sent down the Platte. That meant moving them into the country of their bitter enemies, the Pawnees, and most of the Sioux would regard going there as a march to death. The order, however, was not changed, and on June 11 the 185 lodges of Sioux—1,500 to 2,000 people—were started eastward under the guard of 135 men of the Seventh Iowa Cavalry, Captain Wm. D. Fouts being in command. The simple precaution of disarming the warriors and separating them from the women and children was not taken.

The hanging of the two chiefs, the mistreatment they had themselves experienced, and their fear of this march into the Pawnee country had greatly alarmed these Sioux, part of whom wished to run away, but some of the chiefs opposed this. They evidently were quarreling among themselves, and at night they held secret councils. Elliston and his Indian police were in the camp, and there were also twenty-five to fifty white citizens, mainly men who were married to Sioux women. These whites were all trying to reassure the Indians and keep them quiet.

On the evening of June 13 the column reached Horse Creek,

4. Charles A. Eastman, in *Indian Heroes and Great Chieftains,* gives the names of the men who were hanged as Two Face and Thunder Bow. With his customary effort to make Spotted Tail out to be a toad, he states that this chief handed over the two men to the soldiers. The official record proves this is not true.

the troops crossing and camping on the east bank, the Sioux halting and putting up their lodges on the west side of the stream, on the very ground on which they had encamped during the great peace council of 1851. Little Thunder and the older men must have had some queer thoughts as they looked again at this ground where the whites had made so many pledges of peace and brotherhood. That night the malcontents held another secret council and decided on action, but they evidently did not trust the chiefs and their followers and kept the plan to themselves. At three in the morning on June 14 reveille was sounded in the soldiers' camp and orders were issued to march at five. Captain John Wilcox moved down the road, halting about two miles from camp until the wagon-train came up. Captain Fouts with part of the soldiers recrossed Horse Creek to get the Indians started. They were watching for him. The plan was to permit the troops to come into the camp and then kill them all, but some of the young warriors grew impatient and started firing before the soldiers were well into the trap. Captain Wilcox hearing the firing, corralled the wagons and prepared to defend himself. He made no effort to aid Fouts, and presently a messenger came up with the news that Fouts had been killed and that the Indians were fighting each other. A man was now sent to Camp Mitchell, eighteen miles east, for aid. Fouts' men, led by Lieutenant Haywood, now reached the wagons, and Wilcox angrily demanded the reason for their retreat. The lieutenant stated that no ammunition had been issued to the men before they had started for the Indian camp and that they were practically without cartridges. Wilcox then took seventy picked men and went far enough up the road to observe the Indians. They were crossing women and children to the north bank of the Platte, but at sight of the troops the warriors made for them, and Wilcox hastily retired to the wagons, pursued by a swarm of charging and circling Indians. Coming out again, the Indians once more drove him back; but at nine in the morning a company of cavalry arrived from Camp Mitchell and Wilcox ventured across Horse Creek again, only to see the last of the Sioux swimming their ponies across the river. He made no attempt to follow, but burned the Indian camp and withdrew to his wagons again.

In this affair the troops had one officer and four men killed, seven men wounded. The only Indian reported as being killed by the soldiers was a Sioux who was with the wagon-train, under arrest and in irons. How a prisoner in irons happened to be the only casualty the reports fail to record. The Sioux in fighting among themselves in the camp had killed four of their own chiefs, who evidently attempted to stop the uprising. The names of these chiefs are not given, but it is very probable that poor old Little Thunder was one of them and that old Bad Wound of the Oglalas was another.

Colonel Moonlight contributed a rather comic ending to this little drama by gathering all the forces he could assemble at Fort Laramie and pursuing the fugitive Indians to the head of White River, only to permit them to surprise him in camp and run off nearly all of his horses, leaving his men to walk home, a distance of about eighty miles, through a desolate and almost waterless country. General Connor was very angry at the blundering of Colonel Moonlight and the officer who had ordered the two chiefs executed. He requested that they both be relieved of command, and General Dodge soon after had them mustered out of the service. Spotted Tail had been cured by this unfortunate occurence of any desire to associate further with the volunteer troops. He remained on White River until the spring of 1866. Part of the Sioux from this friendly camp went to Powder River. They had been cured of pacifism, but others had not and soon turned up again near Fort Laramie to be gathered into a new friendly camp.[5]

Early in June the hostiles were encamped on Lodge-pole Creek: the Clear Fork of Powder River. Here the Cheyenne war-party came in, and two days later Young-Man-Afraid-of-His-Horse with a large party of Sioux returned to camp. These parties were the ones which had made raids on the Platte road in May and the first days of June. After the return of the warriors the head-soldiers announced that no more parties would be permitted to go on raids, for they intended now to prepare a large expedition and lead it themselves. Indian soldiers were appointed to police the camps and to see to it that no warriors slipped away to make little raids, which would alarm the whites and put them on their guard. The Sioux now held their Sun Dance and the Cheyennes their Medicine Lodge ceremonies. At this season the Indians always kept near camp, and

5. The best account of this affair is in *Official Records of the Union and Confederate Armies,* serial numbers 101 and 102. The military at this time also ordered the camps of friendly Indians at Fort Halleck and Fort Collins, in Colorado, to be sent to Fort Kearney, and these Indians ran away, all except Friday, a well-named Arapaho who loved the whites too dearly to leave them.

experienced frontiersmen knew that they could approach quite close to a hostile camp with little risk of being discovered. The ceremonies concluded, the camps began to move slowly up Powder River, shifting their location a short distance every few days to get fresh grass for their ponies. In every camp the preparations for the expedition to the Platte were in progress.

The expedition was to be a full-dress performance, and every man was busy with his equipment. Shields, bonnets, war-shirts, and every article and weapon the warriors needed received careful attention; most of the warriors required the aid of the older men who knew the proper ceremonial and sold their services to the young braves. Even the ponies had to be provided with special paint which would protect them from wounds and other injuries. At last all was ready, and the men of the different soldier-societies held war-parades. All of these proceedings were carried out according to the ancient customs, and this is one of the last occasions on record in which the Indians sent out a large expedition with all the old formalities and ceremonies. There must have been over 1,000 lodges in the village, composed of Oglalas, Miniconjous, Northern and Southern Cheyennes, Northern Arapahoes, and some Brulés and Sans Arcs. The lodges were placed in the form of vast circles, and it was inside these circles that the warriors held their final parade, dressed in all their war-finery, and with their ponies painted and decorated with eagle feathers. They rode around inside the circles, singing their war songs, and then rode out of the camp circles and started up Powder River. The men of each soldier-band formed a column by themselves; each band had its specified position in the line of march, and the soldiers who had been selected as police were formed up in front, on the flanks, and in the rear of the column, keeping order and directing the movements of the warriors. The head-soldiers or pipe-bearers marched in front of all, carrying the war-pipes and controlling the march. They halted now and then, and all the warriors dismounted and sat around on the grass, smoking and talking. On the march the men sang war-songs. Toward the end of the day the leaders selected a place to camp for the night. Our best account of this march comes from Cheyenne informants who, unfortunately, did not give the minute details which would enable us to name all of the leaders. George Bent of the Southern Cheyennes informed me that he saw in the line of men who led the march Roman Nose of the Northern Cheyennes and Young-Man-Afraid-of-His-Horse and Red Cloud of the Northern Oglalas. Pawnee Killer of the Southern Oglalas (a Kiyuksa man) and the elder Hump (High-Back-Bone) of the Miniconjous were probably also in this line.

These leaders had selected the little garrison at Upper Platte Bridge on the site of the present city of Casper, Wyoming, as the object of their attack. They made two or three night camps on the way, and on the evening of July 24 they encamped on the little creek which ran into the North Platte some distance below Upper Platte Bridge. The plan for the coming fight was the same that had been employed at Julesburg in the past winter, that ancient trick of sending out a decoy party to draw the enemy into a trap. The stratagem was so simple that it seemed almost childlike, but these Indians were such adepts in setting the trap and varying the details to fit each occasion that even the most experienced enemy was likely to be caught, and once in the trap he could escape only with heavy losses.

At dawn on the twenty-fifth a decoy party was sent into the valley to attract the attention of the troops. In the meantime the great mass of warriors was marched to their position behind the hills on the north side of the river. Here they were kept in close formation by the Crazy Dogs, who had been selected to maintain order and prevent any men slipping away to operate independently.

The decoy party had not been out very long when a company of troops with a howitzer crossed the bridge and started after them. The Indians withdrew toward the bluffs; but the soldiers seemed unwilling to follow them, halting and firing some shells from the howitzer. At the sound of the firing the mass of warriors grew excited, and they soon broke through the lines of Crazy Dogs and rushed up to the tops of the hills. The troops evidently did not observe this movement, and continued to pursue the decoys. The cavalry, however, would not venture far from the bridge, and the Indian leaders decided to return to camp and try the plan again on the following day. The Crazy Dogs now herded the warriors away from the hilltops, striking some of them with quirts, and marched them back under guard to camp. The leaders sent an order for the decoy party to come in; but these warriors disobeyed, swam their ponies across the Platte, and made a charge on some cavalry which was marching up the road on the south side of the river. Here one Cheyenne was shot dead, the only man killed that day.

The following morning, July 26, the same procedure was repeated, but this time the warriors were divided into two or more parties, some being hidden near the mouth of the creek below the bridge, while the others massed behind the hills, near and above the bridge. The decoys went out as on the first day, and again a company of cavalry soon crossed the bridge. This troop was commanded by Lieutenant Caspar Collins, Eleventh Ohio Cavalry, but he was not coming over, as the Indians supposed, to attack the decoys, but to go up the road westward to the assistance of a wagon-train which it was feared the Indians would discover and attack.

As soon as Collins had crossed the bridge and started up the road the signal was given for the body of warriors below the bridge to get in position to cut off the retreat of the troops, while the Indians above the bridge rode around behind the hills to get in front of them. The warriors below charged first, and at sight of them swarming into the valley Collins ordered his troopers to gallop their horses, evidently thinking that he could get to the wagon-train before the Indians overtook his command. But almost at once Indians appeared on the hills on his front and flank, and a moment later he found himself being charged from every direction by a swarm of warriors. At sight of the Indians more troops had been rushed across the bridge with a howitzer, and these men were now firing rapidly.

According to the Indians, Collins attempted at first to fight his way through the warriors on his front; but his men were soon driven back and rushed down the road toward the bridge. The Indians were charging in from every side, yet most of the troopers fought their way through. The lieutenant and four of his men were killed; the rest reached the bridge safely. The Indians were still charging about and shooting when some warriors on the hills signaled that more whites had been discovered up the river. This was the train Collins had gone out to reinforce.

Unaware that Indians were in the vicinity, the train went into camp and the teamsters were leading the mules to the river to drink when the first warriors charged them. Abandoning their mules the teamsters rushed back to the corralled wagons; the warriors charged them but were driven back by soldiers who were hidden in the wagons. An Indian meantime had captured the bell-mare, and as he led her away all the mules of the wagon-train came rushing after her. Roman Nose came up soon after the fight began and organized the attack. He ordered the Indians who had guns to open a heavy fire on the wagons, and after a time he led a charge of mounted warriors which overwhelmed the whites, all of whom were killed among the wagons except two or three men who swam the Platte and got away.[6]

After this fight the Indians returned to their camp. They were greatly excited over the events of the day and stayed up most of the night dancing and talking. The next day most of the party started back to Powder River, but some of the men formed small war-parties and made raids along the Platte road.

In this full-dress performance at Platte Bridge, according to Indians who were present, about 3,000 warriors took part. It will be noted that no attempt was made to cross the river and attack the troops in the posts on the south bank. This is not surprising. The Indians had no comprehension of that kind of fighting; their whole idea was to take some horses and mules, get some scalps, and return home with as little loss as possible. There is no question as to their courage. This was their way of carrying on war. The fact that Collins' little troop of cavalry managed to break through this huge mass of Indians with such small loss is surprising. This may have been due to the fact that the Indians had few good guns at the time and that they would not face the losses inevitable in any attempt to stop the cavalry by meeting them in a hand-to-hand combat. If the troops had stopped to fight they would have lost their lives, but they charged with their horses at a dead run and managed to get through. It seems to be true that most of the warriors were massed in front of Collins and on his right flank and that when the sudden flight began only a few Indians were able to get between the troops and the bridge to head them off. The Cheyennes state that the Sioux were massed below and north of the bridge and the Cheyennes westward; the Cheyenne Dog Soldiers were the first to attack Collins, the Sioux led by the Crazy Dogs then came down on his flank and rear, and it was through the Sioux ranks that the soldiers broke a way to reach the bridge. The Sioux at this time had had much less experience in fighting troops than the Cheyennes, and they were not as well supplied with guns as that tribe.

6. This account of the fight at Platte Bridge is largely derived from information given to me by George Bent, who was with the Cheyennes during the march and engagement. The Indian accounts seem very fair, differing from the official reports only in minor details.

The Indians had just returned to their villages on Powder River when General Connor at last started his columns against them. His movement had been delayed and the original plans had been greatly altered. No column from the Missouri River was now to come to Connor's aid; his own columns had been reduced in strength and it seemed for a time that he might not be able to take the field at all. His plan for guarding the stage line and wagon-trains had failed. From the Little Blue in eastern Nebraska to South Pass the Indians had raided the roads at their pleasure, and the stage company demanded so many troops to guard its line that it seemed doubtful if Connor could get together any force for field service. The Civil War had just ended and the volunteer cavalry regiments which were ordered to the plains marched with snail-like slowness, hoping that orders for their muster-out would over-take them before they reached the Indian country. Some of the regiments received such orders far up the Platte, and at once turned about and marched for home. One Kansas regiment reached the vicinity of Fort Laramie, but the men mutinied on being ordered to march against the Indians. Connor surrounded their camp with loyal cavalry and artillery and so frightened them that they agreed to go on the expedition. They marched, but that was all that they did. They made a sullen promenade of several hundred miles through the Powder River country and back to Laramie without attempting to find or attack the Indians.

Connor's own column moved from La Bonté's Crossing straight north to the head of Powder River. Here he built a post, Camp Connor, later known as Fort Reno. He had some Pawnee Scouts with him, and these Indians soon discovered the trail along which war-parties returning from raids on the Platte to the hostile camps were making their way. By setting ambuscades the Pawnees suc-ceeded in surprising several war-parties, killing some of the enemy and retaking many horses and much plunder.

General Connor had informed his superiors in April that he intended to start for Powder River before the new grass should strengthen the Indian ponies and make it possible for the hostiles to move. When he wrote these words it was already too late; the Indians were moving and their ponies had recovered from the winter's privations. Connor regarded the Cheyennes as the greatest trouble-makers, and his main object was to punish them, although he intended to give the Sioux a lesson also. He stated that he would locate the hostile camps and then make rapid night marches and strike these Indians blows which they would never forget. When he reached Powder River the Indians whom he was so anxious to attack had been camping on that stream for nearly two months and were still there, two or three days' march north of his position; his Pawnees discovered the trail leading to the hostile villages and had several fights with raiding parties returning home from the Platte road; yet Connor now went over to Tongue River to attack a camp of Northern Arapahoes. With the best commander the government could find blundering about in this way, we can hardly criticize the Indians on Powder River for failing to move at once against Connor and attempting to drive him from their country. These Sioux and Cheyennes had had their fighting at Platte Bridge, and according to their way of thinking that was enough. They were now engaged in hunting buffalo to supply their families with meat. That they were not alarmed by the attacks the Pawnee Scouts made on their war-parties is, however, somewhat astonishing. The Pawnees were uniformed like cavalry, but they stripped for a fight, and the hostiles who saw them perhaps did not realize that they were part of a military expedition.

Connor's attack on the Arapahoes fell on the camp of Medicine Man, who as late as the spring of that year had been regarded as head-chief of the Northern Arapahoes and a friendly. There is no evidence that his people had been with the hostiles. The troops surprised his camp and ran off most of his pony herd, but the Arapahoes came back at the soldiers with surprising vigor and in a hot running fight compelled them to drop most of the captured ponies. Having completed this operation, Connor marched down Tongue River to meet the columns of Colonel Cole and Colonel Walker, who had orders to rendezvous near the northern side of the Panther Mountains, the Wolf Mountains of modern maps.

Although three large columns of cavalry were moving through their country and hunting for their camps, the hostiles on Powder River were quite unconscious of their danger. They were first alarmed by the Sawyers road building party. This was a large wagon-train going to the Montana gold fields, of which James A. Sawyer of Sioux City, who had been a colonel in the army, was in charge. By terming themselves a road building party these men obtained a government subsidy and a military escort; as for the road building, they did no work, merely coming up the Niobrara River to its head and then striking across for Powder River. Near Pumpkin Buttes they became confused in the badlands, and to add to their troubles the hostiles now learned of their presence and paid them a visit.

It was a party of hunters who first saw the wagons. These men went back to camp and reported to the chiefs, and Red Cloud of the Oglalas and Dull Knife of the Northern Cheyennes then led a party of warriors to the place where the wagon-train had been seen. George Bent of the Southern Cheyennes was present and did the interpreting for the Indians. He informed me that Red Cloud told Colonel Sawyer that he must keep away from Powder River with his wagons, which would disturb the buffalo, but that if he would give the Indians some supplies he might go on straight west, thus keeping out of the Sioux hunting grounds. Over the protest of the officer who commanded his military escort, Sawyer now gave Red Cloud and Dull Knife a wagon load of provisions, and they went away; but they had hardly gone when another party of Indians came up, and being refused provisions attacked the wagon-train and kept it corralled for several days. This story of the wagon-train indicates that as late as the middle of August, 1865, Red Cloud and his friends were not aware of the fact that the whites were attempting to open up the Powder River country by the establishment of roads and posts.

The great plan to send several columns of cavalry into the Sioux country and have them unite at a certain moment and strike an overwhelming blow at the Indians had been evolved at the War Department, General G. M. Dodge and the other western commanders contributing some thoughts to the scheme. In the first days of September the troops were at last in position to close in on the hostiles. General Connor with 1,000 men was marching down Tongue River to the northwest of the Indian camps; Colonel Nelson Cole with 1,400 men had come up from the lower Platte, passing east of the Black Hills to the Little Missouri, where he found Colonel Samuel Walker who had come with 600 men from Fort Laramie, via Rawhide Creek and the Black Hills. Cole and Walker, according to the plan, were now to communicate with General Connor at the northern base of the Panther Mountains, and all three columns were then to set upon the Indians from different directions and make a swift end of the business. On the map the War Department strategy was working perfectly, but in reality Connor's column, which was the only one that exhibited the slightest desire to fight Indians, was too far away to get at the hostile camps on Powder River. Colonel Cole and his men were all from the East, with no experience in Indian fighting; the men were sick of the campaign by the time they reached the Little Missouri, and their grain-fed horses and mules which had had nothing but grass for several weeks were worn out. Colonel Walker's regiment was the one which had revolted and refused to go on the expedition. Compelled to march, they had tracked dolefully up to the Black Hills, and running into Cole's outfit had followed along with it when Cole turned westward toward Powder River. These two commands passed directly between the hostile camps on Powder River and those of the Black Moon and Sitting Bull group of Sioux, who were encamped on the Little Missouri, yet they had not seen an Indian and were quite ignorant as to the location of the camps. Reaching Powder River, a detachment was sent to Panther Mountains to communicate with General Connor, but no trace of his column could be found, and Cole and Walker now found themselves practically lost in the wilderness, with their animals breaking down and supplies running low. While they were still wandering about sadly on the lower Powder, trying to decide on a course of action, they were discovered by the hostiles on the Little Missouri, who at once swarmed over to Powder River, eager for fight and plunder.

In July, at the time when the Powder River hostiles had gone to Platte Bridge to set a trap for the troops there, this other group of Sioux, led by Sitting Bull and others, had gone to Fort Rice on the Upper Missouri to try the same trick, which seems to have been the only military maneuver known to Sioux generalship. They sent out a decoy party on July 28 to lure the soldiers into their trap, and failing on that day they tried again on the thirtieth, but with no success. They then withdrew in an unpleasant humor and moved toward the Little Missouri. When they discovered Cole and Walker on Powder River they attacked them like hungry wolves.[7]

With 2,000 troops under their orders, Cole and Walker made no attempt to do anything further than to defend their camps. Day after day the Indians appeared and charged in on the troops, trying to run off the horses and mules and delaying the march of the

7. Colonel Pattee's account of the Sioux attempt to draw the troops at Fort Rice into a fight will be found in *South Dakota Historical Collections*, Vol. V. General Sully stated that Sitting Bull led 500 warriors to Fort Rice to make this attack (*Official Records of the Union and Confederate Armies*, serial number 102, p. 1173).

columns. Many men and horses were lost in these fights. On the night of September 2 a severe storm came up and lasted all night. Two hundred and twenty-five horses and mules died during the storm, and a large quantity of supplies had to be burned, as there was no means of transporting them. From September 1 to 4 the commands were being constantly harried by Indians. These warriors came up from the direction of the Little Missouri and from the mouth of Powder River.

On September 6, Cole and Walker began to march up Powder River, with the idea of ultimately reaching Fort Laramie. They had no news of Connor and no plan except to get out of the country. They now appear to have been out of reach of the Missouri River Sioux, who were in their rear; but on this day they ran into the Oglalas, Miniconjous, Sans Arcs, and Cheyennes near the mouth of the Little Powder. These Indians had been in camp here for some time, with no knowledge that Connor had built a fort on Powder River to the south of them or that Cole and Walker with 2,000 troops were marching toward them from the north. It was purely by accident that a few warriors going down Powder River ran into the troops and returning to the village reported their presence to the chiefs. The Indians were having dances and ceremonies in their camps, which may account for their failure to discover the troops sooner; the record of these wars, however, proves conclusively that the old theory that Indians were constantly on the alert was not correct. The Indians rarely set a guard about their camp or sent out scouts to look for the enemy, and time and again we find the troops actually riding into the hostile villages before they are discovered.

As soon as the Indians learned that troops were near, the warriors in little bands and groups rode down the river to meet them. This apparently was on September 5, but both Cole's reports and the Indian accounts are so confused that it is difficult to obtain a clear view of these events. There was a big fight in which about 2,000 warriors were engaged; but the ground was very much broken by ravines and ridges, which tended to confuse the fighting. The Indians had no plan and no general leadership, but came into the fight in small parties, each band intent on obtaining as many horses and as much plunder as they could. A party of Cheyennes had wonderful luck. They chased some cavalry into a thicket, only to find that the troops had abandoned their horses and waded across to the other bank of Powder River. The Cheyennes found eighty cavalry horses, with saddles and full equipment on their backs, tied to the bushes. This fight is the one the Cheyennes called Roman Nose's fight. While the troops were in line of battle in front of their corralled wagons faced by several hundred warriors, Roman Nose rode along the line of soldiers from the river to the bluffs with the whites firing at him all the way. He repeated this performance three or four times, until his horse was finally shot under him. The Indians then charged the troops, but could not break through to get at the horses, which was their main object.

After this affair the Cheyennes moved toward the Black Hills to hunt buffalo; but the Sioux remained near the mouth of the Little Powder, and Cole and Walker on September 8, almost blundering into their village, had another encounter with the Indians. During the fighting the lodges were taken down by the women and the camps were moved out of the line of march of the troops.[8] After this fight a storm of cold rain came up and lasted thirty-six hours, killing 414 of Cole's and Walker's horses and mules. Wagons, supplies, harness, and cavalry equipment had to be burned before the columns could resume their march. On the tenth large bodies of warriors appeared, completely encircled the troops, and escorted them on their way. Firing was kept up during most of the day, with little damage to either side. Indians who were present have informed me that they could not fight the troops very successfully at this time because they had few guns and little ammunition. This statement is borne out by one of Colonel Cole's officers, who states in his report that on this day, September 10, the Indians had four or five good muskets. That would be about one really good gun to each one hundred of the Sioux warriors.

The troops now crossed the Little Powder, and just above its mouth found the remains of an immense Indian camp of 1,500 to 2,000 lodges. This village the Cheyennes and Sioux had abandoned

8. Stanley Vestal, *Sitting Bull*, Chapter XII, states that Sitting Bull with about 400 warriors had this fight with the troops on September 8. He seems to have the wrong date—the Sitting Bull fight was probably several days earlier. Sitting Bull was supposed to be a good deal of a patriot and considerably superior mentally to most of the other Teton chiefs, yet he seems to have had no idea at all of uniting the Indian forces or of having some plan of common action, until it was too late to accomplish anything. Except for one fight in 1865, which had no results, he took no part at all in the attempts of the southern or Red Cloud group of hostiles to defend the country during the period 1865-1870. When three military posts were established on the Powder and Bighorn in 1866, Sitting Bull took no action whatever.

a few days before. The Sioux were still in the immediate vicinity, and it was their men who fought the troops on September 8 and 10.

On the eleventh Cole and Walker began to slaughter horses for meat. The commands were nearly out of supplies and almost unable to march because of the condition of the few horses and mules still left. The Indians were still hanging to the columns and harassing them constantly. The situation was a gloomy one and disaster seemed very near, but at this moment a messenger from Connor came into camp with the cheering news that the general's column was only sixty miles away, on the Tongue, and that there was a new post with abundant supplies some distance farther up Powder River. The men resumed their march, and as the Indians had now withdrawn their main force, the columns finally reached Fort Connor in safety. But the troops were in a frightful condition, mere crowds of ragged, hungry, and footsore men. Captain Palmer of Connor's staff stated that they looked like tramps.

Thus ended the great Powder River Expedition of 1865, which had cost such huge amounts of money.[9] With the exception of the capture of part of the Arapaho pony herd not a thing had been accomplished. General Dodge had the optimism to report the expedition a great success. He pictured the frightened and spiritless columns of Cole and Walker as a victorious army advancing up Powder River, driving a multitude of Indians before them. The men on Powder River knew better than this. Cole and Walker were too dispirited to make reports, and Connor too disgusted with them to ask for any. The Indians have always spoken of their meeting with the Cole and Walker columns as one of the brightest incidents of a happy summer. Their camps were full of cavalry horses and mules branded U S and they had many good carbines which they had taken from the soldiers.

9. Secretary Stanton telegraphed to General Grant, July 28, 1865, that the mere cost of transporting the supplies which General Dodge was ordering for his troops in the Indian country had risen to two million dollars per month.

CHAPTER IX

RED CLOUD'S WAR
1866-1867

At the close of the Civil War the Republican group in Congress, who were sometimes termed the radicals, were rapidly gaining control of both houses. Basing their program on what they regarded as justice to the negroes, these men were determined to discard Lincoln's plan of reconstruction and to give the former slaves a dominant position in the South. To this principal objective they soon added others, for the groups of humanitarians, idealists, and church associations from whom this bloc in Congress drew much support had many interests. Some of the churches had been concerned for years over the welfare of the Indians, and when in the winter of 1864-1865 Congress began to delve into Indian affairs they threw themselves into the discussion, demanding that the old wicked method of dealing with the Indians should be abandoned and a Christian policy substituted for it.

The noise of this debate soon attracted the notice of the politicians in the West who had long specialized in obtaining Indian appropriations and the pleasant work of expending them, but who had come upon lean years with the outbreak of hostilities and the taking of control by the military. These western worthies now began to develop Christian longings to come to the aid of the Indians and promote the dawn of peace and appropriations. By the spring of 1865 they were in touch with the group in control at Washington, and thus with practical politics wedded to high ideals the new Indian policy swept on the flood-tide toward success.

By the month of May, 1865, the astonishing spectacle was presented of the military straining every nerve to prepare strong cavalry columns to be dispatched against the Indians on Powder River, on the Upper Missouri, and in the country south of the Arkansas, while at the same time the leading group in Congress was declaring vociferously that these Indians were all good friendly folk who would be only too glad to make peace if the military would let them alone. Senator J. R. Doolittle had now taken the field with a select committee to investigate Indian affairs, and by boldly denouncing the military and appealing to his friends at Washington he actually obtained an order suspending the movement of troops against the southern plains tribes and then had a peace commission appointed to make treaties with these Indians.

At this time Major General S. R. Curtis, whose order to Colonel Chivington to begin chasing the Cheyennes in April, 1864, had started all the trouble in the plains, was in command of the Department of the Northwest. Brigadier General Alfred Sully, who was under his orders, was prepared to attack the Sitting Bull group of Sioux in the country west of the Missouri, a movement which was intended to support General Connor's advance to Powder River; but just as Sully was ready to march General Curtis discovered a mare's nest in another direction and had the column diverted into the country north of the Missouri. For two months Sully marched through an empty wilderness, from the Missouri to Devil's Lake, from Devil's Lake to Mouse River, up to the Canadian line, and then back to the Missouri again, without seeing a hostile. The expedition had cost millions of dollars and had accomplished nothing, due to Curtis' meddling. Sully got back to the Missouri early in August, learned of the location of Sitting Bull's camp and was planning to attack him when he received the astonishing news that General Curtis had accepted the chairmanship of a Sioux peace commission and with Newton Edmunds as his principal adviser was coming up the river with a steamboat load of presents, intent on making a cracker-and-molasses peace with the Sioux.

Father DeSmet, who was always ready to act as bellwether in leading the Indians to a treaty signing, had been delegated to collect the Sioux chiefs in the district below Grand River. This was supposed to be a treaty with the hostiles, but DeSmet did not go twenty miles away from the Missouri, picking his chiefs from the camps of what the wild bands of Sioux contemptuously termed the "stay-around-the-fort" people. As for the upper bands, Colonel Pattee at Fort Rice was ordered to gather a delegation, and he merely summoned the friendlies to the post, picked his chiefs, and hustled them down the river to meet the peace commission. General Curtis and his brother commissioners came up the river about the middle of October, met the Indians in council, coaxed the chiefs into signing the treaty, and then handed out the presents. They concluded the work at Fort Sully, near the mouth of Cheyenne River, on October 28 and at once started on the return journey.

Thus was the great new Peace Policy inaugurated among the Teton Sioux. No one could criticize the making of peace with these friendly bands along the Missouri River but the men who made this treaty compiled a list of all the hostile Sioux, and without the name of one chief from the hostile camps appearing on their treaty they falsely announced that they had made peace with the Sioux bands who had been engaged in war.[1] There is no excuse to be made for General Curtis and Newton Edmunds; no plea that they were ignorant of the facts can be made in their behalf, for they had been engaged for several years in dealing with the Sioux, knew which bands were friendly and which were not, and they had information at the moment they were concluding the treaty that Sitting Bull with 2,000 lodges of hostile Sioux was out near the Little Missouri and that on Powder River there were from 1,500 to 2,000 additional lodges of hostiles.

With the signing of the Sioux treaty, peace was supposed to have been established with all the plains Indians, for treaties had been concluded with the tribes on the Arkansas River. The visionaries who were now in control of Indian affairs at Washington really believed that they had ended the Indian wars. The doctrine on which they based their policy was that the Indians were always in the right and the frontier white population always in the wrong, that the Indians were good people who would never cause trouble if dealt with in a Christian spirit of kindness and forebearance. As for the frontier whites, they were regarded by the group now in control of Indian affairs as miscreants who must be forced to respect the Indians' rights. With their heads in the clouds, these humanitarians and idealists were quite unconscious of the fact that

1. They listed 10,300 Sioux, only a small fraction of whom were represented by the chiefs who signed the treaty, the rest being hostiles who knew nothing of the treaty. At this time the hostile camps had at least 3,000 lodges, at a low estimate 18,000 persons. Some queer statements concerning the making of this treaty will be found in the Dawes Report (Senate Documents, Forty-eighth Congress, first sessions, 1884), where it is said that Newton Edmunds was the head of the Dakota "Indian ring" which made the treaty for its own profit.

a great crisis had come in the plains region, where the tribes were determined to oppose any further encroachment on their lands and the whites were firmly bent on opening up the region to settlement. Here was a situation which blind faith in the goodness of the Indians could not control, and a day would undoubtedly arrive when the government would have to use force either against the Indians or its own citizens. The very treaties which hastily had been signed to start the new Peace Policy contained the germs of conflict. The Sioux treaty provided that the government should have the right to open roads and build posts in the Sioux country, and at the moment the tame chiefs on the Missouri were agreeing to this there were 3,500 to 4,000 lodges of Sioux on the Little Missouri and Powder River who were determined that no whites should enter their lands.

In October, 1865, when the peace treaty was signed on the Missouri, the hostiles on Powder River were still celebrating their successes against Colonel Cole and Colonel Walker. They now began sending parties out to raid the Platte road, and General Connor had no sooner left Powder River with his dispirited troops than he was forced to take fresh measures to protect travel from Indian attacks. By this time someone with a bit of sense had realized that a peace treaty with the Sioux which did not include any of the Sioux hostiles was rather an anachronism; a copy of the treaty was therefore sent to the commandant at Fort Laramie, and he was instructed to use every method possible in an effort to induce the chiefs in the hostile camps to come to the post and sign the agreement. No trader or mixed-blood at the fort was willing to risk his life by going to Powder River, but after a time Big Mouth and some of the friendly Oglalas of the Loafer band were persuaded to go to the hostile camps with a message. If, as the peace crusaders in the East asserted, these Sioux on Powder River were eager for a treaty, they did not show it. Not an Indian was seen for nearly three months and then, in the middle of January, 1866, Swift Bear and his band ventured to approach the fort and send in a message. But were these people hostiles? Swift Bear and Standing Elk were the chiefs of the Corn Band of the Brulés, the most friendly of friendlies, who had been unwillingly forced to leave the whites when the other Indians of the friendly camp had attacked their guards on Horse Creek in the spring of 1865. These chiefs signed the treaty and informed Colonel Henry E. Maynadier, now in command at the post, that the Oglalas were talking of coming in; but they did not come. This winter was a severe one and the Indians suffered much and lost many ponies from cold and starvation. Nothing more was heard from the camps until early in March, when Spotted Tail sent in word that his daughter had died and that at her request he wished to bury her beside Old Smoke on the high ground just west of the fort. Colonel Maynadier readily gave his consent, and when this friendly chief came to the post he was shown every possible consideration. Spotted Tail spoke to the colonel with great bitterness of the wrongs which had driven the friendly Sioux out to the hostile camps. He said that for four years his people had been mistreated by the whites, and particularly by the volunteer troops, until it had grown unbearable.

The government now was in the peculiar position of having a new peace treaty with all the Teton Sioux tribes at a time when practically all of the Tetons were on Powder River and so bitterly hostile that no white man in the country dared to enter their territory. On the instigation of the Peace Party the treaty had been hastily ratified and proclaimed, and the public had been assured that the new road to Montana, via Powder River, was safe for travel. This was an outrageous falsehood. Any party that tried to use this road would have to fight Indians from the moment they crossed the North Platte. The peace advocates in the East thought that all that was necessary was to send a copy of the treaty to Fort Laramie and the hostile chiefs would throng in to sign it. By the spring of 1866 it was apparent even to Peace Party leaders that the hostiles did not intend to come in. Something had to be done at once.

Mr. E. B. Taylor of the Indian Office now came out to Fort Laramie with a document appointing himself and Colonel Maynadier commissioners to deal with the Sioux. Taylor had been directed to put the Peace Policy into effect among these Indians, and he was determined that nothing should interfere with the program. The men at Fort Laramie tried to talk sense to Taylor; but he would not listen, stating again and again that he had been sent to make peace and that he was going to do it.

Taylor sent messengers to the hostile camps calling the Indians in for a peace talk and promising plenty of presents, including arms and ammunition. So far Swift Bear and his Brulé Corn band had signed up, as had also Big Mouth and the Oglala Loafers and the chiefs of Spotted Tail's camp. Not one real hostile had signed, but the news of the rich store of presents at Fort Laramie and the offer of arms and ammunition now began to have effect, and in June the Sioux came down from Powder River in full force. Even Man-Afraid-of-His-Horse and Red Cloud came; but these men were no traders' chiefs, who would take the pen when told to do so.

They demanded to have the treaty carefully explained to them, and the moment the clause referring to roads was read they balked. Commissioner Taylor, determined that nothing should block the signing of the treaty, seems to have attempted to deceive the Indians. He is reported to have told them that there was to be no new road through their country and that the roads mentioned in the treaty were really one road which already existed. The point at issue was clear enough. The road he had in mind was the Bozeman road to Montana, via Powder River, and the Indians were determined that this road should not be used by the whites. Since the government had pledged itself to keep this road open to travel, it is difficult to say how Mr. Taylor would have fared in his negotiations with the Sioux if he had been left to deal with them in peace. For an incident now occurred which broke up the peace council and sent the Indians flying back to Powder River.

A large body of infantry was marching up the North Platte accompanied by a train of wagons. On June 16 the column went into camp a few miles below Fort Laramie, and that evening a friendly chief of the Corn Band visited the camp and talked with the commanding officer, Colonel Henry B. Carrington. The chief asked where the soldiers were going and was informed that they were marching to Powder River, where they were going to build posts and guard the new road. This Brulé chief went straight to the Sioux camps with this news. A dramatic scene ensued at the peace council, the chiefs accusing Commissioner Taylor of deceiving them; they then abruptly left the council, and ordered their camps taken down and started for Powder River, sending back word that they would fight any whites who came into their country.

This incident was hushed up by Commissioner Taylor, who reported that all had gone well at the council. Not even the officials at Washington had any suspicion of the truth, for Taylor worded his report to give the impression that most of the chiefs had signed the treaty and that Red Cloud who had refused to do so was an unimportant leader of a little group called the Bad Faces. At this time Red Cloud was the principal leader of the all-important warrior class in the Powder River camps, and Man-Afraid-of-His-

Horse, who had also refused to sign the treaty, was the accepted peace chief of these Indians. In this affair Mr. Taylor assumed the attitude which men who are sure of the virtue of their purpose often adopt, that any act is justifiable if done in a worthy cause.[2]

Colonel Carrington's march to Powder River had been decided on months before. He had received his orders in April, and General W. T. Sherman had later come to Fort Kearney, Nebraska, to discuss with him the march and the building of the new posts in the Powder River country. That the high military commanders supposed the Sioux would sit quietly while their country was invaded and posts built in their best hunting grounds is astonishing. All the hostiles that Connor had dealt with on Powder River in 1865, except the Southern Cheyennes, were still there. Connor's force had been 3,000 cavalry, and now Carrington was sent into that same country with 700 infantry, including bandsmen, and not a single cavalryman. This seems queer, but things were queer in the Indian country in 1866. The peace crusaders had preached so vociferously that the Sioux were friendly that even the military commanders seem to have adopted that view. Colonel Carrington was not a fighting officer, but just the man to build posts and organize a system of road patrols, and his orders and the make-up of his force clearly indicate that this was all that he was expected to do. Yet every man of sense at Fort Laramie must have known when the Sioux left the council in a rage and headed north that trouble of the worst sort was brewing on Powder River. That parties of peaceful emigrants and freighters were permitted to go into that country without proper warning was shocking, and that after these first parties had been attacked the officials should have encouraged others to take the same route was still more shocking. The peace mania had by this time developed such momentum that the mere thought of war with the Sioux was taboo; the raids on Powder River were attributed to a little group of malcontents, and the officials deluded themselves and the public into believing that if no action was taken the Indians would soon quiet down. The government had accepted the Indian Peace Policy, but it was already straddling—trying to please the peace crusaders by giving them a free hand in making peace with the Sioux, and at the same time trying to please the frontier population by giving it a new

2. *Report of the Commissioner of Indian Affairs,* 1865. As Taylor did not write his report until October 1, his concealment of the facts was deliberately planned.

road to Montana. The new road meant war, but the men in control of affairs refused to see that fact.

Carrington reached Connor's old post, now called Fort Reno, at the head of Powder River June 28 and there found several wagon-trains awaiting military escort on their way to Montana. To these trains he issued a set of regulations for their movement through the Indian country. He asserted that the road would be made perfectly secure, that no escorts would be necessary, that the trains must organize and keep together, and that care must be taken not to annoy the Indians. From the tone of these regulations it is apparent that Carrington even after reaching Powder River had the same strange belief as the other military and civil officers, that there would be no serious trouble with the Indians. Two days after he issued these regulations seven Sioux warriors ran off the sutler's herd within two miles of Fort Reno. Pursued by mounted infantry, the Indians had to abandon a pack-pony which was so heavily laden with presents from the Laramie peace council that it could not keep up with the party. On July 10 Carrington marched from Fort Reno and on the thirteenth reached Piney Fork. Here, forty miles from Fort Reno, he began the construction of Fort Phil Kearny. On the fourteenth the Cheyennes sent in a messenger to ask if Carrington wanted peace or war. The colonel made a friendly response, and on the sixteenth the chiefs came in for a talk. They were very friendly, and informed Carrington that their village, 176 lodges, was hunting on Goose Creek and Tongue River. They said that the day Carrington reached Piney Fork a party of Sioux from Red Cloud's camp came to them and told them of Carrington's march, describing his movements in detail, and then demanded that the Cheyennes help them fight the troops. The Sioux had said that if Carrington would go back to the old fort, Connor's post on the head of Powder River, and not open a road through their hunting grounds they would leave him alone. The Cheyennes stated that Red Cloud had 500 warriors, indicating a camp of 250 lodges, and that Man-Afraid-of-His-Horse was camped on Tongue River one day below Red Cloud, and that the Sioux were all busy holding a Sun Dance.[3]

It may be noted here that in this year, 1866, for the first time both the whites and the Indians begin to speak of Red Cloud as

3. Here, and in all this account of events near Fort Phil Kearny, I am making use of the *Carrington Papers*, in Senate Documents, Vol. I, Fiftieth Congress, First session, Document 32.

the big man among the Sioux of Powder River, giving Man-Afraid-of-His-Horse, the old head-chief, a second place. In January Colonel Maynadier had stated that Red Cloud had 250 lodges of Oglalas under his control, now in July the Cheyennes gave the same information. The Crows reported that the Oglalas had 500 lodges on Tongue River this summer; therefore Man-Afraid-of-His-Horse also had 250 lodges, the same as Red Cloud. The reason for the sudden rise of Red Cloud is obvious. He was a popular war leader and had now taken a strong stand in favor of fighting the whites if they invaded the Sioux hunting grounds. Man-Afraid-of-His-Horse knew the power of the whites and desired peace if it could be obtained on favorable terms. At this time the Southern Oglalas who had come north to Powder River in February and March, 1865, were still there. They wanted peace, taking about the same stand that Man-Afraid-of-His-Horse did, and it is probable that most of the 250 lodges that made up his camp were Southern Oglalas.

The account of the peace council at Fort Laramie given by these Cheyenne chiefs is very interesting. They said that the Sioux told them that Red Cloud and Man-Afraid-of-his-Horse were at the council, but that before the treaty could be signed the Little White Chief (Carrington) came with his soldiers to build new forts and open a new road through their hunting grounds. They contended that the commissioners had tried to deceive them, putting in the treaty that new roads were to be permitted but in their talks speaking of only one road and saying that this would not run through the Sioux hunting grounds.

The Cheyenne chiefs had taken a great risk by going to pay this friendly visit to Carrington, and they very soon had to pay for it. They went from Carrington's camp to the camp of a trader, French Pete (Pierre Gasseau), on Reno Creek. A war-party of Sioux soon appeared at the camp and angrily demanded what the Cheyennes had been doing at the soldiers' camp. The Cheyennes replied that they had been visiting the Little White Chief, who was very friendly; he had given them presents and had told them that there were many presents at Fort Laramie for the Sioux, if they would go there and touch the pen for the treaty. On hearing this the Sioux, who were seated around the Cheyenne chiefs glowering at them, rose in a fury, took their bows from the bow-cases and began striking the chiefs on their bodies and across their faces, crying *Coo! Coo!* as when counting coup on enemies in battle.

The chiefs bore this insult in silence and the Sioux still raging, left the camp. The Cheyennes sat there as if frozen. Never had their chiefs suffered such an insult, but they were not strong enough to fight the Sioux and could do nothing. After a time they spoke to old Gasseau, telling him to get his people over to the soldiers' camp as quickly as he could. They then left him. Gasseau, who had a Sioux wife and felt secure, stayed in his camp; and at dawn the following morning the Sioux rushed in, killing him and all his men. The women and children escaped into the bushes and were later rescued by Carrington's men.

Colonel Carrington busied himself with the building of his new post. He also sent two companies to the Bighorn to build a post, Fort C. F. Smith, on that stream. The troops for the Bighorn and the first lot of wagon-trains seem to have slipped past the Sioux on Tongue River while they were in ignorance of their movements; but the Sioux soon began raiding vigorously all along the road. Every wagon-train was attacked, and the Indians boldly pushed in close to the forts, running off stock and attacking detachments of troops wherever they were met. Colonel Carrington's reports were full of optimism. He considered the situation good, and gave the assurance that wagon-trains would be safe if they were well organized and used precautions. This was his report on August 29; yet in the same report he stated that thirty-three white men had been killed along the new road in the past five weeks, during which period the Indians had made daily attacks, stealing seventy head of government animals near Fort Phil Kearny alone. The hostile camps were on the Tongue and Powder rivers, to the northwest and northeast of Fort Phil Kearny; but the raiding parties were going around the fort and making attacks along the road for a hundred miles to the south.

During all of the raiding in July and August, when his troops could not go a mile from the fort without being attacked, Carrington appears to have had no idea at all of taking the offensive. His plans were purely defensive. He was asking for reinforcements, but for only four companies of infantry and two of cavalry. This force would render his position secure. His idea of security appears to have been peculiar. On July 17 the Indians coolly dashed up within sight of his troops, ran off the bell-mare and 174 mules from Hill's train and got away, killing two men and wounding three of their pursuers. The same war-party killed six whites in

French Pete's trading camp within a few miles of Carrington's camp. Day after day all through the latter half of July and the whole of August reports of this kind were coming in; but the colonel considered the situation good and travel reasonably safe.

That Carrington was not a fighting officer is all too clear. In six weeks he issued seventy-five special orders regulating petty details concerning doors, keys, and an order for the soldiers not to walk on the grass. The elaborate care which he utilized in the details of his work of building Fort Phil Kearny and the regulating of every small activity of the garrison show the true bent of his mind. From a reading of the documents one gets the view that the military authorities knew that Carrington was not a fighter, and that he was kept in command partly for that reason. The proposal to abandon the building of Fort C. F. Smith, made to Carrington by the higher command in July, is really extraordinary. If this post had been abandoned the road would have been guarded as far as Fort Phil Kearny; but on the Tongue and Bighorn, where the hostiles were actually encamped, no protection would have been supplied to trains. The result would have been a road leading from Fort Laramie to Piney Fork and there ending in the heart of a hostile Indian country. The government evidently did not intend to take the offensive, and we have further evidence of this in the attempt Carrington made in August to get in touch with Red Cloud and the other Sioux leaders with the evident purpose of negotiating for peace.

Three old mountaineers, Jim Bridger, Bill Williams, and Jim Beckwith were the men he employed in this service. They made contacts with the Crows and attempted to open communication with the hostiles through that tribe. The Crows were in three camps, one near Fort C. F. Smith on the Bighorn, one on Clark's Fork, and a small one on Pryor's Fork. They, like the Cheyennes, were willing to help fight the Sioux, but Carrington would not accept the services of either tribe. He was demanding Indian scouts to assist his troops, but he did not want the Cheyennes and Crows who knew every inch of the country and who knew the Sioux. With almost unbelievable foolishness he refused the services of these Indians and demanded Omaha and Winnebago scouts from eastern Nebraska.

From the report Jim Bridger and Bill Williams brought back, it appeared that the Sioux during the summer had attempted to induce the Crows to join them and had offered to return to the Crows part of the hunting grounds which they had taken between 1856 and 1863. The Crow chiefs said that some of their young men were in favor of joining the Sioux against the whites. Red Cloud and Man-Afraid-of-His-Horse had both visited their camps, and the Crows had returned these visits. They reported that Man-Afraid-of-His-Horse, the head-chief of the Oglalas, had said to them that tobacco had been sent, that he would go, and that they must wait for him. This is very interesting, as it indicates that Man-Afraid-of-His-Horse was still considering signing the treaty. What he meant was that tobacco, symbolizing an invitation to a council, had been sent from Fort Laramie, that he would go there to talk to the officers, and that the plan of an alliance between the Sioux and Crows, aimed at the whites, must wait until his return. Something must have happened in early fall to alter his plans, for he did not make this journey to Fort Laramie.

From the Crows and Cheyennes it was learned that the hostiles consisted of the camps of Red Cloud and Man-Afraid-of-His-Horse on Tongue River, comprising about 500 lodges, and Buffalo Tongue's camp on Powder River, north of the mouth of Clear Fork. These were the main camps. The wilder bands of the Northern Cheyennes had joined the hostiles, and Medicine Man, the Arapaho whose camp had been attacked by General Connor in the fall of 1865, had also joined them.

The Cheyennes and Crows in giving information during the summer had stated that the Sioux were planning two big fights which they spoke of as "Pine Woods" (near Fort Phil Kearny) and "Bighorn" (near Fort C. F. Smith).

With their autumn buffalo hunt over the hostiles were ready in mid-December to strike in earnest. Colonel Carrington noted the increased Indian activity about the post, but it did not alarm him. His reports reflect his perfect confidence in his ability to deal with the situation. On December 20, still immersed in his love for routine detail, he went out and inspected the wood hauling arrangements, made some slight changes in the system, ordered a little bridge built over a creek, and returned to the fort much satisfied with everything. The next day the blow fell with stunning suddenness.

During the past twenty years many books have appeared which have given Indian accounts of the fighting near Fort Phil Kearny in December, 1866; few of these Indian statements agree with each other or with the reports circulated in 1866 and the years immediately following, and one cannot escape the conviction that the Indians either have been misquoted or that they have a poor recollection of the events they were describing. From the contemporary Indian information we learn that in July Red Cloud was planning to go to the vicinity of Fort Reno with a large war-party, as soon as the Sun Dance was over, and stop travel on the road by making raids. And it is evident that he executed this plan to the best of his ability. In August he and the other Sioux leaders were planning two large attacks, one at Fort Phil Kearny, the other at Fort C. F. Smith. The fight at Fort Phil Kearny had therefore been planned months ahead, by the Red Cloud group, yet some Miniconjous who were present when the fight occurred state that Red Cloud was not with the warriors. This is denied by the Oglalas, who say that Red Cloud and many other Oglalas were in the fight. It would appear from Colonel Carrington's reports that the Indians made two attempts to entrap the troops; this may explain why the Indians themselves do not agree as to who their leaders were.

On December 6, the Sioux certainly made an attempt to entrap the soldiers, and Red Cloud was seen on a hill directing the movements of the warriors by signals. The Indians failed that day, but they organized a second expedition two weeks later and came back to try again. That this second, and successful, attempt was primarily a Miniconjou affair is admitted by all the Sioux, but the Indians do not agree as to who the leaders were. White Bull of the Miniconjous was present, and he states that Crazy Horse led; He Dog and his brother Short Bull of the Oglala band to which Crazy Horse belonged were present, and they say that High-Back-Bone of the Miniconjous led. Many other Oglalas have the same view. They contend that Red Cloud was present but that High-Back-Bone was in general charge. Old Two Moon of the Northern Cheyennes was also present, and he stated in 1912 that Crazy Horse led the decoy party.

It seems that this misunderstanding arises from the failure of the Indians themselves to make any distinction between general and active leadership. This fight was a formal affair, similar to those at Julesburg and Platte Bridge in the previous year, and we know that in all such expeditions the column of warriors was led by a group of older men—the Pipe Bearers, Walking Chiefs, or

War Chiefs. High-Back-Bone would have been in this group, and Red Cloud also would have been there if he had participated. Crazy Horse, who was about twenty-two years old, would certainly not have been among the chiefs, but as he was a prominent young warrior and a favorite of High-Back-Bone, it would have been natural that he should be given the position of honor as leader of the decoy party.[4]

The Miniconjous, Oglalas, and Cheyennes came up Tongue River and encamped at the mouth of Prairie Dog Creek. On December 20, they went up Prairie Dog Creek to a point near the scene of the next day's battle, and here, according to the Cheyennes, the Sioux leaders consulted the fates, employing a strange method of divination. They had with them a "half-man" (hermaphrodite or bardache).[5] With a black cloth over his head, this person rode over the hills, zigzagging his pony. Presently he rode back and fell off his pony, flat on the ground, crying out that he had a small number of soldiers in his hand. The Sioux leaders gravely told him that he had not enough enemies in his hand. Three times more this creature rode over the hills and returned, each time with a larger number of enemies in his hands. The fourth time—four being the Sioux sacred and lucky number—this half-man came rushing back greatly excited, and falling off his pony he cried out that he had both hands full—over one hundred enemies. The Indians gave a great shout and returned contented to their camp.[6]

The next morning the Indians rode up Prairie Dog Creek and took a position around Lodge Trail Ridge, the Oglalas and

4. He Dog, Short Bull, and Black Elk all lived in the same camp with Crazy Horse. If he was the principal leader in this fight, why should these men take the honor from him and give it to a Miniconjou? It seems strange that White Bull of the Miniconjous should say so little concerning the part his fellow-Miniconjou, High-Back-Bone, took in the fight. The Oglalas today still talk of High-Back-Bone as one of the finest leaders the Sioux ever had. He is the man Mr. Vestal calls High Hump and High Back. The name refers to the ribs in the buffalo hump. This name was also borne by the Miniconjou chief who is generally known as Hump. He is said to have been either a son or nephew of High-Back-Bone.

5. The Sioux had great respect for these half-men and often consulted them, particularly in matters concerning war. According to what the Sioux told Lieutenant Caspar Collins, in 1863, one of these half-men, a "crazy man who thought he was a woman," once induced the Sans Arcs to place all their bows on a hill while he performed a ceremony. A force of enemies suddenly appeared and caught the Sioux without any weapons, driving them away in wild flight. This event greatly amused the other Sioux bands, who are said to have then given the name Sans Arcs to this group.

6. Grinnell, *The Fighting Cheyennes*, p. 228. I have heard of this half-man's performance from other Indians. He seems to have belonged to the Miniconjous.

Cheyennes, with a few Arapahoes, on the southwest side, the Miniconjous on the northeast. The leaders sent out decoys to attract the notice of the troops. Two Moon in his account given in 1912 stated that a large party was sent to attack the wood train, which was forced to corral and call for aid from the fort; troops soon came along the road, and the party attacking the train was then withdrawn by the Indian leaders and a second party, led by Crazy Horse, was sent out to meet the troops and lead them into the trap. This Cheyenne chief's account of these events seems much more sensible than the Sioux versions, and it explains why the Miniconjous insist that Crazy Horse was the leader, although we know that he was too young to be in general command. The real leaders were on a hill directing operations, and if the Oglalas are correct in their view, High-Back-Bone of the Miniconjous was the man who was actually issuing the orders.

Captain William Fetterman, in command of the hundred men who had come out to relieve the wood train, was eager for a fight and at once started after Crazy Horse's little party. Crazy Horse skillfully led the troops on, up to Lodge Trail Ridge, along its entire length and down to the lower ground beyond. This is the only occasion on record in which the decoy party trap worked perfectly. There were none of the usual mistakes; no little groups of warriors rushed out ahead of time to warn the troops of their danger, and the decoy party actually finished its work and gave the signal before any of the warriors charged.

As the Indians suddenly appeared from their places of concealment and rushed forward, the mounted troops hastily retired to the ridge, the infantry taking a position part way up the slope among the rocks. Here they fought until most of the men were down; the survivors then ran to join the mounted troops, who retired along the ridge, but they were presently surrounded near the point where the monument now stands. The troops released their horses and took cover among the rocks. Here they fought until the last man was killed.

Fetterman reached Lodge Trail Ridge a little before noon, and Captain Ten Eyck with a reinforcement of seventy-six men arrived one hour later. He heard firing, and on reaching the ridge found the valley below full of Indians, who challenged him to come down and fight. They made no movement in his direction, and as he did not leave the ridge they gradually withdrew. Ten Eyck found the bodies of Captain Fetterman and sixty-five others lying in a space hardly forty feet square. Fetterman's entire command, eighty-one officers and men, had been destroyed. The Indian loss was eleven Sioux, two Cheyennes, and one Arapaho.

In 1866, and for years afterwards, Red Cloud was believed by the whites to have led the Indians in this affair. We now know that he was not in command, but the Miniconjou assertion that he was not present is difficult to credit. His own band, the Bad Faces, were present, and the old men of this band contend today that Red Cloud was among the leaders. Captain James H. Cook of Agate Springs, Nebraska, the closest white friend Red Cloud ever had, states that this chief often spoke to him of being in the Fetterman fight and that many other Oglalas confirmed Red Cloud's statements.

Colonel Carrington was relieved of command immediately after the news of the Fetterman disaster reached army headquarters. His frantic appeals for more men after the blow had fallen are in strange contrast with his tone of complacent satisfaction before the event. Carrington tried to clear his skirts of blame; his superiors tried to clear theirs; the Peace Party made an absurd attempt to prove that the harmless and peaceful Sioux had been goaded into hostility by the aggressive action of the military. The Commissioner of Indian Affairs, Bogy, went so far as to state in print that the Indians came to Fort Phil Kearny to beg for arms and ammunition with which to hunt buffalo, that Carrington cruelly refused to give these starving people the means they required for obtaining a supply of meat, and that the Indians then, driven to desperation, attacked Fetterman's command. The men who flew to the defense of the Indians on such occasions as this could never be induced to understand that the Indians of the plains used bows in hunting buffalo and kept their firearms for fighting purposes.

Colonel H. W. Wessels, who succeeded Carrington in command, was ordered to make a winter campaign against the hostiles, but as his force was too small and composed mainly of infantry, and as the worst weather of the winter was now at hand, the plan was abandoned. The Indians had retired to their winter camps, and quiet settled down around the posts on the Powder and Bighorn for a brief season.

Despite the Fetterman disaster, the end of the year 1866 saw the government in a stronger position in the northern plains than it had occupied in the spring. The new posts, Phil Kearny, Reno, and C. F. Smith, were solidly set in the heart of the only good hunting grounds the northern Sioux now possessed, and if these posts continued to be held, sooner or later the wild Sioux, Cheyennes, and Arapahoes would have to come in and conform to the government's bidding. That the posts could be held was certain. The Indians had no idea of attempting to capture the forts; indeed, they had no plan beyond the usual one of harassing the whites at certain seasons by making raids. South of the Platte, where some bands of Sioux and Cheyennes seemed inclined to make trouble, the military were planning new posts which would gradually control the stuation. But to the humanitarians in control of the Indian Peace Policy any military action, even the taking of precautionary measures, was anathema and was resented as a threat that the coercion of the Indians might be resorted to. These men really believed that kindness and fair treatment were all that were necessary to keep the wild plains tribes quiet.

By the autumn of 1866, all of the friendly Sioux and Cheyennes who had formerly roved in the country south of the Platte, with the exception of the Southern Oglalas who were still up north, had signed the treaty and were back in their hunting grounds. For the moment these bands were very pleased, for the more solid benefits offered by the new Peace Policy had fallen largely into their laps. They had been loaded with presents, and what they had long desired, an agency of their own near the forks of the Platte, had been given them; but the whites were crowding in on them from every quarter, and the chiefs were very uneasy about the future. The Union Pacific and Kansas Pacific roads were rapidly advancing into their lands, and parties of white hide hunters armed with the finest modern rifles were at work slaughtering the buffalo. Could they keep their warriors quiet while the whites completed the work of destroying their means of life? To chiefs like Spotted Tail who had some realization of the crisis at hand, the friendly words and liberal presents brought to them by the new men from Washington were a small consolation, for they felt that they were being asked to remain inactive while the border whites destroyed them.

At this time, September, 1866, the first Indian agent appointed under the Peace Policy came to the Upper Platte. He was J. M. Patrick, an honest man with a real desire to assist the friendly

Indians—the first agent of this type these Indians had seen since Thomas Fitzpatrick had left them in 1853. Going first to Fort Laramie, Patrick found 373 Sioux—old men, women, and half-breed children. Big Mouth with 233 Oglala Loafers was hunting on Horse Creek, and Spotted Tail and Swift Bear with their friendly Brulés were south of the Platte. After a year of Christian forebearance and lavish expenditure of funds, these bands, which had always been friendly, were all that the peace crusaders had to show as the results of their policy among the Oglalas and Brulés, but these cheerful optimists regarded the future as bright. The Fetterman disaster in December startled but did not dismay them, and in the spring of 1867 they resumed operations with greater vigor than ever.

In February, 1867, the Sanborn-Sully commission was appointed to investigate the troubles of 1866, the Fetterman disaster, and also negotiate with the Indians. G. P. Beauvais, the old Indian trader, was made a member of the commission. He and J. B. Sanborn reached Fort Laramie in April, and after distributing $4,000 in supplies to the few Indians present, they informed the chiefs that the agency was being removed to North Platte, Nebraska, away from the influence of the hostiles on Powder River. Most of the friendlies were Brulés and Oglalas whose hunting grounds were south of the Platte and the new location of the agency suited them perfectly, for as far back as 1858 they had felt bitter about having to make the long journey to the vicinity of Fort Laramie in order to obtain their annuity goods. But the Loafers and Half-Breed band, who lived near the fort, did not relish the change. Big Mouth and his Loafers went to North Platte for their supplies but soon returned to their old haunts near Laramie. Many of the Loafers and half-breeds did not leave the fort at all. They had few horses, could not travel, and did not desire to leave the post from which they drew their livelihood.

On June 12, this peace commission held a talk at Fort Laramie with Man-Afraid-of-His-Horse, Iron Shell, and other chiefs who were said to represent two hundred lodges of Oglalas and Brulés, Iron Shell being a Brulé chief of the Orphan band. These chiefs said that the Indians had abandoned the war and were coming in to join the friendlies; but old Beauvais noted that Man-Afraid-of-His-Horse and the others were inquiring very anxiously about ammunition, and he advised Sanborn not to put too much faith in their assertion that their bands were coming in. That the hostiles were short of ammunition in 1867 is clear enough. They were trying desperately to obtain powder and lead on the Platte, on the Missouri, and by trade with the Crows and other tribes. Red Cloud was present during these talks at Fort Laramie, but the commissioners in their report do not mention this, and it is known only because Agent Patrick referred to the fact in his annual report, and Big Mouth mentioned it at a later council. Red Cloud seems to have kept in the background during the council, and this looks as if his own tribe still regarded him as inferior in rank to Man-Afraid-of-His-Horse.

When Sanborn and Beauvais were sent to Fort Laramie, General Alfred Sully was sent up the Missouri on a similar mission: to fish for chiefs from the hostile camps, and to bribe them into signing the treaty. When a Sioux was told that if he touched the pen he would receive so many guns, so many pounds of powder and lead, so many blankets, axes, kettles, and knives, and that if he did not touch the pen he would get nothing, it was bribery. Sully heard of a big hostile camp near the northern edge of the Black Hills and sent men out to call the chiefs in. Iron Shell, who had been at Laramie with Man-Afraid-of-His-Horse a short time before, came in with some other chiefs; but they did not come to touch the pen, rather to dictate terms to the government. They said they did not want any white men except traders in their country; they demanded that the posts in the Powder River country be abandoned and the road given up; after that had been done and all the whites were out of their country they would talk peace. General Sully, who had some feeling for his country's honor, told the Sioux bluntly that the troops would remain on Powder River until the Indians stopped fighting and signed the treaty. Little did he know the men in control of the Peace Policy, to whose hands the nation's honor had been entrusted.

By this time it was somewhat difficult to determine what treaty it was that the Sioux were being so earnestly urged to sign. The peace treaty of 1865 had been ratified and proclaimed more than a year previous; still there was no peace, and not a chief from the hostile camps had signed that treaty. Was the commission of 1867 peddling that old treaty or a new one? The chiefs were puzzled. Many of the traders' chiefs who had signed in 1865 wished to sign again and receive a second helping of presents. Sully found these chiefs still hanging about the posts. They were a choice collection. He found near one of the posts those Oglala Loafers who had signed for that tribe in 1865. There were twenty-eight lodges of these people; their three chiefs had signed the treaty, after which it had been announced that peace with the Oglalas had been made, the peace commission ignoring the fact that five hundred lodges of Oglalas were on Powder River, still dancing the scalps they had taken from Cole's and Walker's troopers and preparing for further raids on the Platte.

While Sully was on the Missouri, a friendly Brulé came in with news from the hostile camps. This man had been on one of those little visits, of which the Sioux were so fond. Setting out from the Missouri sometime about 1865, he had rambled about for 500 miles, visiting various camps. The spring of 1867 found him at Red Buttes on the North Platte; from here he had gone to Powder River, then to the Black Hills, where he visited a camp of hostile Oglalas. Finally, going along the old trail northward, he came to the Low Pines at the head of Heart River, and there he found the biggest camp he had seen in all his life—Sitting Bull's camp. He was very enthusiastic in his description of this camp. These hostiles were rich people, not like the poor friendlies on the Missouri, living on handouts from the white man. They had had a very successful spring hunt and their huge camp was crammed with dried meat and skins. They had innumerable herds of fine horses and mules, many of the animals branded US. *Waugh!* No Indian on the Missouri had ever seen such a camp: *rich people, and happy!* Planty buffalo! Planty horse and mule! Planty good time fighting white man and getting more horse and mule! Peace? *Ah, nah!* The people of the big camp did not care for peace; but they cared for powder and lead, and soon after the friendly Brulé had told his tale, a large village of Miniconjous and Sans Arcs from the hostile camp he had described moved down Moreau River and sent in word to Old Fort Sully that they were inclined to do a little trading. They were permitted to come in and replenish their powder horns and bullet pouches, with the idea that this might put them in a good humor and that they might then be coaxed into signing the treaty. They came in with 200 to 300 mules loaded down with robes and other articles of trade. These Indians were wild, defiant, and dangerous. They looked on the friendlies they found at Old Fort Sully with a mixture of contempt and pity; and having traded for arms,

{153}

ammunition, and blankets, they brushed aside all talk of peace and abruptly departed for the hostile camp.[7]

During the years 1866 and 1867 the army had such dreadful luck in dealing with the Indians that it almost seemed as if the peace people were right when they claimed that the military were the cause of most of the trouble in the Indian country. The Peace Policy had been attached to the leg of the army like a ball-and-chain; it was constantly tripping the soldiers up; and, as if this were not enough, officers who had made their reputations on the battlefields of Virginia were now being sent to commands in the West, where they had to deal with Indians although they had not the least experience in that department of military art.

General W. S. Hancock was one of these commanders from the Army of the Potomac. The Indians in Kansas were giving some trouble at this time, and the government decided in the spring of 1867 to send Hancock out to deal with them, not rudely, as some brutal persons in Kansas were advocating, but in a kindly manner befitting the true spirit of the Peace Policy. Hancock, in fact, was expected to overawe the Indians by a display of troops and fine uniforms, but he overdid it. The Indians were very nervous about seeing large bodies of troops approaching their camps; and when Hancock marched up—horse, foot, and guns—the Cheyennes and Sioux left their lodges standing and ran away. Hancock regarded this as a proof of their hostility, and forgetting that he was serving under the Peace Policy, he burned the Indian camps. The Indians, regarding this as a proof that Hancock had a bad heart, began to raid. Hancock, regarding this as further evidence that the Indians were hostile, turned Custer and his Seventh Cavalry loose. The Indians considered this as a final indication that Hancock did not like them, and skipping nimbly out of Custer's way began to raid harder than ever. And here was a lively new Indian war, and whose fault was it? The peace people naturally stated that Hancock was solely to blame, while Hancock just as naturally retorted that they lied and that the Peace Policy agents were handing out government arms and ammunition to Indians who were using these weapons to kill the government's citizens.

When Man-Afraid-of-His-Horse and Red Cloud came to Fort Laramie during the spring and failed to obtain ammunition, their followers quarreled and split up, part of the people leaving the

7. Sully's report is in the *Report of the Commissioner of Indian Affairs*, 1867.

hostile camps and going southward. These were mainly Southern Oglalas, people who had gone up to Powder River in March, 1865, after being driven into hostility by General Curtis. Little Wound was their principal chief, but Pawnee Killer, who was their war leader, was better known to the whites, who usually termed these Oglalas Pawnee Killer's band. They were camped on the Platte near Fort McPherson trying to trade with Jack Marrow and some of their old friends when Custer arrived after his futile pursuit of the Cheyennes and Sioux who had run away from General Hancock. These Oglalas had already heard of the burning of the camps by Hancock and of Custer's activities, and they were nervous. Custer, always optimistic, cast loving eyes at their camp and set to work to demonstrate that they were not really friendly.

The Oglalas took down their lodges and started for the Republican Fork, saying that they were going to hunt buffalo; but Custer had by this time convinced General Sherman, who was at the fort, that Pawnee Killer was a suspicious character who required watching, and Sherman ordered Custer to follow the Indians with his regiment. Wherever they went the Oglalas found Custer mousing near their camp. They avoided him without any difficulty, but were by this time very much annoyed. How could they hunt with this devilish, long-haired Soldier Chief following them about with his blundering regiment, frightening the buffalo? Pawnee Killer at length took his warriors out and forced Custer to show his hand. There was quite a fight, and the Oglalas having learned what to expect skipped out of the way again. They had few guns and the troops were too strong for them, but Pawnee Killer made rather a fool of Custer. He actually tried the old, old decoy party trick on this smart cavalry general and caught him, Custer sending Captain Hamilton with twenty men straight into the trap; but again the troops had such a great superiority in arms that the Indians could not act effectively and had to open the trap and let Hamilton go.[8] The Indians then discovered a party of soldiers who were coming from Fort McPherson with orders for Custer, surrounded them and killed them all. With these men was Red Drops, a sub-chief of Man-Afraid-of-His-Horse's band, who had unwisely consented to serve as guide. During the fight Red Drops kept shouting to be released, crying to the Sioux that he was an Oglala, but they paid no attention, and he was killed.

8.   General George A. Custer, *My Life on the Plains* (New York, 1874), pp. 83-84.

This new war annoyed the whites very much, for it was not on distant Powder River but in the center of the lands which the Empire Builders were so busily tilling. How could the country be settled and the railroads built with an Indian war going on? The Indians were very active, attacking stage coaches, wagon-trains, and ranches and frightening the construction gangs away from their work on the railroads. One chief, seeing the new iron trail, piled some ties on the track to see what would happen. He saw. A train went into the ditch, and the Indians broke into the cars and acquired the finest stock of hardware, groceries, and dry goods they had ever seen. They loaded their ponies down and got out of the way before the troops arrived. All this while the Peace Policy agents were declaring angrily that the Indians were friendly and that the troops must be withdrawn.

The government now found itself caught between the aroused public opinion in the West, which wanted the Indians dealt with severely, and the stubborn insistence of the humanitarians and church groups that the policy of kindness and bribes should be continued. An attempt at a compromise was made and a new peace commission, composed of N. G. Taylor, the generalissimo of the Peace Policy, J. B. Sanborn, and General W. S. Harney, the last supposed to represent Western interests, was sent out to make a final attempt to settle the Indian troubles. They were to offer agencies on the Upper Missouri to the Sioux. If the Indians went up there they would be fed and well treated, if they refused to go a cavalry force of several thousand men would be sent against them.

The Indians were informed by runners that a great council was to be held at Fort Laramie on September 13; the richest presents ever seen in the Indian country were to be handed out; everyone should come without fail. Traveling over the new Union Pacific line the commission reached North Platte, then the end of the track. Here a talk was held with the Sioux under Spotted Tail, Man-Afraid-of-His-Horse, and other chiefs. The commission's discreet report informs us that at the North Platte talk a "difference" with the chiefs arose which almost disrupted the meeting, but that in the end a "perfect agreement" was reached. The truth hidden behind these careful phrases was this: In July these same Indians had come to North Platte to demand arms and ammunition, and on being refused had created an uproar and had gone away in a very bad humor. Later they had been asked to come back and meet

{156}

the commission. At the start of the meeting the chiefs again demanded powder and lead, and on being refused created another wild scene. The perfect agreement which the report mentions was arrived at when the commission gave in and, over the protest of the military officers, supplied the Indians with ammunition.[9]

From this first victory at North Platte the peace party hastened to Fort Laramie, fully expecting to find Red Cloud and all the northern clans awaiting their coming. They found no Indians there, but received a message from the northern Sioux to the effect that they were too busy to come in now; that they hoped to meet the commission sometime, maybe next year. This neat affront should have discouraged the hardiest of peacemakers, but Taylor and his comrades decided to take Red Cloud at his word and to come back the next year. They put out some set-lines around Laramie, in the hope of catching a few chiefs, and then departed for the Arkansas River where they were scheduled to make peace with the southern Indians in October.

It was on this occasion at Fort Laramie that Sanborn and Harney lost their tempers and shocked Mr. Taylor by asking General W. T. Sherman what military force would be required to give the Powder River Indians a sound whipping. Sherman, after consulting with General C. C. Augur and General Alfred Terry, replied that the force required for a Sioux campaign could not be spared from the South, where the crusaders had the soldiers on duty trying to keep the whites down and the negroes up. He also believed that the cost of an Indian campaign would be too great. The policy of pampering the Sioux and giving in to them was therefore continued. Taylor suppressed this incident in writing the commissioner's report, but the facts came out in 1870 when Sanborn wrote a letter on the subject to the Board of Indian Commissioners. It would be interesting to know what force Generals Augur and Terry considered necessary to deal with the Powder River bands. These Sioux had very few guns in 1867 and were almost out of ammunition. A force of three thousand good cavalry would have been sufficient, and with the three forts on the Powder and Bighorn to be used as bases of operations the troops should have made

9. Henry M. Stanley, *My Early Life and Experiences*. Stanley was at this council and reported it for a newspaper. The report of this commission is in Volume XI, Executive Documents, Fortieth Congress, second session. The evidence indicates that these Sioux had been friendly in the spring, but that since then their warriors had made some raids. They should not have been given ammunition.

short work of the hostiles. The peace crusaders were claiming that 50,000 or even 100,000 troops would be required, but it is to be hoped that Sherman did not accept these handsome figures and the slur at the United States army which was hidden behind them.

It is not difficult to learn what it was that kept Red Cloud so busy that he could not meet the peace commission at Fort Laramie. All through the spring and summer of 1867 he pressed his campaign to force the whites out of the Sioux country. Frequent attacks were made on wagon-trains on the Montana Road, and much of the time the three forts were so closely blockaded that the troops had to fight even to obtain wood and water. In May, Mitch Boyer and John Reshaw, Sioux half-breeds, brought news to Bozeman, Montana, that Fort C. F. Smith on the Bighorn was in a desperate condition. There were only two hundred men at the post; the horses had all died, or had been run off by the Indians, and the post was short of provisions and must have help at once. They also stated that the Sioux were holding their Sun Dance on Powder River and would start out in force on the warpath about June 1. A party of forty-two volunteers guided by Boyer and Reshaw set out to relieve the post and slipped safely through the hostile country, probably because the Indians were holding their Sun Dance. They met several small parties of Sioux, with whom the guides talked. These Sioux were hovering around the lower Bighorn, trying to open a trade with the Crows for ammunition.[10]

The government was still deluding itself with the idea that only a few malcontents in the Sioux camps were making trouble and that there was no war on Powder River. Instead of strengthening the garrisons and sending a cavalry force against the Indians, it kept the military strictly on the defensive. There was no war, yet the road via Powder River and the Bighorn had been abandoned by both the emigrants and freighters as too dangerous for use, and only military supply trains completely armed and heavily guarded were using the road. These wagon-trains fought their way to the posts which they were supplying. The posts protected themselves— nothing more. The road they were supposed to protect had been deserted by the public.

10. Granville Stuart, *Forty Years on the Frontier,* Volume II, pp. 64-66. Mr. Stuart's date for the Sun Dance is incorrect. The Sun Dance had been ended only a short time before the Indians set out for Fort Phil Kearny, the last week of July. Reshaw was the half-Oglala son of old John Richards. This young man in 1870 killed Yellow Bear at an Oglala camp on Tongue River and was at once cut to pieces by the Sioux.

After their Sun Dance, the Sioux of the Red Cloud group and their Cheyenne friends began to discuss plans for an attack on the troops, but they could not agree, some of them wishing to go to Fort Phil Kearny, others preferring to make an attack at Fort C. F. Smith. Finally part of the warriors, mainly Cheyennes, started for the latter post, where they made an attack on August 1, while Red Cloud with about 1,000 men set out for Fort Phil Kearny.

At this time, Captain J. N. Powell was on duty guarding the wood cutters at Phil Kearny. He had his men take the boxes from a number of wagons and place them on a hill in such a way as to form a small fortress, and here he stationed his infantrymen. The Indians made their appearance on the morning of August 2. They were mainly Oglalas, Miniconjous, and Sans Arcs, under Red Cloud, High-Back-Bone, and some other leaders. Their intention was to try the old decoy party trick again, and Crazy Horse had been picked as the active leader. The warriors, however, as so often was the case, could not be restrained; they rushed out of their places of concealment before the plan could be carried out, about two hundred of them stampeding the herd of horses and mules belonging to the fort; while a second party, which Crazy Horse was with, attacked the wood cutters' camp, killing some men and setting the camp on fire. Some of the workmen fled to the fort; a few joined Powell, who now had two officers, twenty-six soldiers, and four citizens. His men were all armed with the new breech-loading rifles, and from their shelter in the wagon boxes they fired rapidly on the mass of mounted warriors who now charged up the slope to attack them. The Indians made no attempt to come in close but began circling, and this they kept up until the chiefs ordered them to draw off. They then left their ponies, got into a ravine, and attempted to advance on foot; but the fire of Powell's infantry drove them back each time. At about noon a force of one hundred troops was seen coming from the fort, and the chiefs now ordered the engagement broken off.

The Sioux have never regarded this fight as a defeat. They had captured a great many horses and mules, and although they had six killed and six wounded they had inflicted a heavier loss on the whites, killing several workmen, one officer, and five men in Powell's force. Captain Powell reported that he thought about sixty Indians had been killed. Colonel Richard I. Dodge in his stupid book, *Our Wild Indians,* started the story of the huge losses suffered by the Sioux in this affair, and the tale has grown with the years until today it is sometimes stated that 1,500 warriors, twice the entire force of Indians engaged, were killed by Powell's thirty men.

This war on Powder River was the kind the Sioux liked. The soldiers did not bother them, permitting them to take matters into their own hands and run the war to suit their own convenience. They went to Fort Laramie in the spring to talk, and to attempt to obtain ammunition; then they had their buffalo hunt and Sun Dance; after that they went to Fort Phil Kearny and had a good fight, then to Fort Reno and made some raids, obtaining more horses and plunder. The autumn hunt ended the year's activities, and they then retired to their winter camps, happy and in perfect trust that the white soldiers would not come out and force them to fight at this season, when they wished to be quiet.

The importance of the wagon-box fight really lay in the fact that it at last opened the eyes of the officials to the realization that Red Cloud was not merely the leader of a little sub-band of malcontents as Mr. Taylor had officially reported, but was at the head of several thousand hostiles. Superintendent H. B. Denman of the Indian Office reported after the Powell fight that the display of strength made by Red Cloud on this occasion indicated that the government must either make peace with these Indians on their own terms or else flood their country with troops and fight a long and costly war.

Mr. Denman was quite right. The government now had either to whip the Sioux or to give in to them, and it was growing more apparent every day that the officials at Washington meant to give in. They were seeking excuses to justify such a policy, and naturally found many plausible ones. One official stated that by humoring the Indians and keeping them quiet the Union Pacific could be rapidly completed, and then the Powder River road would be of no importance, for a shorter and better road to Montana could be run from the railroad line west of the Bighorn Mountains. Powder River would then be of no interest to the whites. Why not please the Indians and avoid a costly war? This view did not take into account that the Northern Pacific had to be built along the northern edge of the Powder River country; that the Indians if left undisturbed would certainly block the building of that road, and that the whites already had their eyes on this desirable portion of the Sioux lands, for there was a growing belief that gold was in the

Black Hills and the Bighorn Mountains. Give in to these Indians now, and sooner or later the government would find itself in the unenviable position of arbiter in a struggle between the Indians and the whites, a struggle which would not be arbitrable and which must end in the government's taking either the Indians or its own citizens by the throat and compelling obedience. As was shown later, in the Black Hills matter, the government did not dare to attempt to discipline its own citizens. It therefore was necessary to discipline the Sioux, and if this was to be done it should have been in 1867 when the hostiles were almost out of ammunition, had few guns, mainly old muzzle-loaders, and were clearly beginning to tire of the war. One sharp blow in the winter of 1867 would have cleared the Powder River country of the greater portion of the hostiles.

In making a decision, the government was evidently much influenced by the report of the commission which had been appointed in February, 1867, to investigate the causes of the Indian war in the Powder River country. In its report, this commission made the astonishing assertion that the government had no right to open a road through the Sioux lands and, as J. P. Dunn put it, they attempted to bolster up this opinion by quoting decisions of the Supreme Court which did not apply and by referring to treaties which had never been in effect. The humanitarians and church groups accepted this peculiar view at once and urged the government to abandon the Montana road through the Sioux country. No one suggested abandoning the Union Pacific which was being built through the Sioux country.

The talk of justice to the Sioux and of respecting the treaties was rather absurd. The hostiles on Powder River had no treaty with the government, the old treaty of 1851 having expired and their chiefs having refused to sign the treaty of 1865. The truth of it was that in 1867 the immediate interest was to keep the Indians quiet until the Union Pacific could be completed, and with the idea that they were being clever, the officials accepted the views of the Indian Peace Party and decided to give in to the Powder River hostiles. In fact these Indians in no way threatened the Union Pacific line, which ran too far south of their country to be within the reach of their raiding parties.

CHAPTER X

RED CLOUD COMES IN
1868-1870

IN the autumn of 1867 the officials at Washington decided to
abandon the Sioux treaty of 1865, which the hostiles had so
stubbornly refused to sign, and to offer to the Sioux and the
other plains tribes a new treaty so generous in its provisions
and accompanied by the distribution of such lavish presents that
none of the Indians would be able to resist the temptation to sign
the agreement. Conceived in a spirit of kindliness and liberality
toward the tribes, this treaty was as balm to the souls of the good
men of the Indian Peace Party, and it also satisfied practical men,
for the treaty was so drawn that the tribes in complying with its
terms would be compelled to remove from the plains of Nebraska
and Kansas, thus rendering easier the great task of building the new
railroads and settling the country. As for the future, the humanitarians and idealists of the Peace Party had the brightest hopes, while
the practical men, as is too often the case, considered only the immediate advantages which they hoped to gain.

As far as the Teton Sioux were concerned, this treaty of 1868
provided that all of the present state of South Dakota, lying west
of the Missouri River, should be formed into a Sioux reservation
to which these Indians should be removed; agencies would be
established on the Missouri River at which the people would be fed
and clothed for four years, during which time they would be
educated and trained to enable them to become self-supporting. As
it had been learned definitely in the autumn of 1867 that the wild
bands in the Powder River country would refuse to sign any agreement until the troops had left their land, a new clause was added
to the treaty, at the special urging of the Indian Peace Party men,

which provided that the forts should be abandoned and the troops march away, that the Powder River and Bighorn countries should be recognized as unceded Indian territory into which no whites might go and where the wild Sioux and their Cheyenne allies might hunt and rove undisturbed. Thus after two years of struggle Red Cloud and his friends on Powder River had won their battle.

In recent years a tendency has developed among some authors of books on Indians to deprive Red Cloud of all credit for having led in the war of 1866-1867. If he did not lead, who did? Neither Sitting Bull nor any of the chiefs of his northern group of Sioux hostiles appear to have taken much interest in the struggle; indeed, Sitting Bull who is supposed to have been so wise and far-seeing had no thought of uniting with Red Cloud but waited placidly until his own hunting grounds were invaded before he took any real action. Red Cloud put himself at the head of the opposition to white encroachments on the Sioux lands at the Fort Laramie council in the spring of 1866, and he held firmly to his position until the last soldier had left Powder River. The years 1866 and 1867 were Red Cloud's day, and the struggle that took place in the Powder River country in those years will always be known as Red Cloud's war.

The treaty of 1868 was the child of the Taylor, Sanborn, and Harney peace commission of 1867, and it was to this body that the task of inducing the Indians to accept the agreement was delegated. The Sioux were being given, as it seemed, almost everything except their ancient liberty to wander as they pleased in their own lands, and the bands on Powder River were to receive even that favor; yet the men in charge of the treaty expected to have considerable trouble in persuading the chiefs to accept the agreement. In 1865, the leaders of the Indian Peace Party had much to say concerning the old wicked method of bribing and cajoling chiefs into signing treaties, but during the past three years these gentlemen had learned by sad experience that no treaty could be consummated except by the use of such methods, and feeling strongly the justice of their cause they soon discarded most of their scruples concerned with fair and open dealing. In the spring of 1868 the leaders of the party hired many emissaries to talk to the Sioux—a strange crew of chief-catchers, made up of traders who had been promised new licenses, squawmen, interpreters, and half-breeds. To these were added Father DeSmet and the Reverend S. D. Hinman, missionaries and specialists in the art of talking Sioux chiefs into signing papers.

These men soon had the Sioux country echoing with the news of the coming treaty councils.

But most of the Sioux were at first strangely apathetic. The treaty commissioners came west in April, expecting to find the Sioux gathered in force at Fort Laramie awaiting their coming, but on the way through Nebraska they learned that almost no Indians were at the fort. Near the forks of the Platte they met Spotted Tail and his friendly Brulés, but they had to bribe these Indians with a large assortment of goods, including arms and ammunition, before they would consent to go to Fort Laramie. At the fort the commission held a council with Spotted Tail's band and obtained the signatures of the chiefs; runners were then sent to the other Sioux bands, urging them to come to the council, but day after day the commission dawdled around the post with nothing to do. At last they decided to leave one of their number, J. B. Sanborn, at Fort Laramie to obtain the signatures of the Oglala chiefs, while the rest of the party hastened to Fort Rice where they had arranged to meet the Upper Missouri Sioux in council.[1] Early in May Sanborn got the Oglalas of the friendly Bear People group, led by Little Wound, to come to the fort and sign the treaty. They received the usual presents, including arms and ammunition, and went away again. Man-Afraid-of-His-Horse was with Little Wound and signed when he did. This northern chief had been south of the Platte since April, 1867, but he now returned to his own country on Powder River. So far not a chief from the hostile camps in the north had come in; and Sanborn, after waiting for some time longer, gave up hope of immediate results and left Fort Laramie.

Thus far the campaign of the treaty-makers had been a failure. The public had heard a great deal about the Sioux during the past three years and could no longer be deluded into thinking that peace had been made when a number of quite friendly chiefs had signed a treaty. Rightly or wrongly, the people regarded Red Cloud as the great chief of the Sioux, and any agreement with these Indians that did not bear his name was looked on as worthless. Red Cloud had not only failed to come to Fort Laramie, he had sent no reply to the messages of the treaty commission.

When Sanborn tired of the poor fishing at Fort Laramie and departed for the East on May 28, he left at the post a copy of the

1. The final copy of the treaty implies that all of the commissioners were present when the Oglalas signed, but the report and letters of the commission show that this was not the case.

treaty and a professional fisherman, Charles Geren, an interpreter, who was instructed to do everything in his power to get the chiefs in and sign them up, especially the chiefs of the Smoke People group of Oglalas: Red Cloud's Bad Faces and Red Dog's Oyuhkpes. By the end of May the news had reached the hostiles on Powder River that the peace commission was handing out arms and ammunition, and Mr. Geren at Fort Laramie soon had visitors. Forty lodges of Bad Faces came in, under chiefs Yellow Eagle and Little Hawk, the latter being Crazy Horse's uncle. They signed the treaty, and Geren gave them the regulation payment—arms, ammunition, army rations, blankets, kettles, axes, and knives. These Bad Faces at once returned to Powder River, and until the day, nine years later, when Crazy Horse led them in to surrender to General Crook, they were the most hostile of all the Sioux. These people were soon followed by twenty-six more lodges of Bad Faces under chiefs Tall Wolf, Sitting Bear, and Mad Wolf, who signed, received their pay and immediately left for Powder River. Geren's report that these Indians were destitute and in great need of arms and ammunition is a strange comment on the view of Sherman and the other military leaders that the Sioux hostiles were too powerful for the United States to risk a war with them. The officers at Fort Laramie must have wondered as they watched this agent of the Peace Policy handing out guns and ammunition to these hostile Indians.

Geren remained at the fort for some weeks, in hope of getting Red Cloud in, but in this he failed. Man-Afraid-of-His-Horse, after signing the treaty, went up the North Platte to Fort Fetterman to visit his friend Major Dye; he then went to the head of Powder River. Red Cloud with the Bad Faces, Oyuhkpes, Miniconjous, and some others, was on Tongue River; messengers having been sent to his camp urging him again to come to Fort Laramie, the reply was sent back that he was going to the Rosebud where buffalo were plenty and that he would sign the treaty only after the last of the troops had left his country. Geren now gave it up. That Sanborn in leaving this man at Fort Laramie had only one object—the catching of Red Cloud—is apparent, for the names of the minor chiefs who were paid by Geren to sign the treaty were left out when the final copy of the agreement was made.[2]

While Geren was operating at Laramie, the peace commission was proceeding up the Missouri with a steamboat load of presents.

2.   Geren's report is in the *Reports of the Commissioner of Indian Affairs* for 1868.

It had long ago engaged a number of skilled men to go to the Indian camps and urge the chiefs to attend the coming councils. De-Smet at the head of a party of Indians and whites had gone all the way to the mouth of Powder River to take the news of the treaty-making to the hostile camp of Four Horns, Black Moon, and Sitting Bull. He came back to the Missouri with a number of Indians, reporting great success; yet we search the treaty in vain for the names of Four Horns, Black Moon, and Sitting Bull, and in the following year we find this hostile camp in the same locality in which DeSmet visited it and just as hostile as ever. The great council with the Upper Missouri Sioux was held at Fort Rice, July 2 to 4. It took an entire day to distribute the presents after the chiefs had signed. One author in speaking of this Fort Rice council states that the display of rich presents "almost put the chiefs and head-men under duress to sign the treaty."[3] Indeed, it is much to their credit that Red Cloud, Sitting Bull, and the other real leaders of the Sioux so firmly resisted the shameless attempts that were made to bribe them and kept away from these treaty councils.

We now come to a very mysterious matter which was carefully suppressed when this peace commission made its report. From Fort Rice the party went down the Missouri to Fort Sully, where they met some friendly bands of Sioux in council. They then started for home, but on the way down the river they appear to have received Geren's report with its disturbing news that Red Cloud had not signed the treaty. What the commission did next we can only conjecture; but it is to be noted that DeSmet, who was ill and wished to go straight home to St. Louis, gave up his plan and went to Fort Laramie, and with him went two other crack chief-signers from the Upper Missouri: Reverend S. D. Hinman, and the Sioux interpreter Frank LaFramboise. These men remained at Fort Laramie for several weeks, and as they evidently had been given a *carte blanche* by the commission, they must have put Red Cloud and his brethren under a dreadful temptation; but these chiefs held stubbornly to their purpose, waiting for the government to fulfill its promise to abandon the forts in their country. When at last they saw the troops marching away, they set fire to Fort Phil Kearny and came swarming down to Fort Laramie—Red Cloud and his

3. L. F. Crawford, *Rekindling Camp Fires* (Bismarck, N. D., 1926) contains a long account of this Fort Rice council, p. 161 *et seq.* Mr. Crawford is in error in stating that the Oglalas, Brulés, and Cheyennes were present at Fort Rice. He has failed to notice that the treaty was signed at various places and on different dates.

folk, and also many Hunkpapas, Blackfoot-Sioux, and others from the Sitting Bull camps. These Sioux signed the treaty November 6, DeSmet and his comrades signing at the same time as witnesses. Thus the great Sioux peace crusade of 1868 ended.

The good feeling that followed the distribution of the treaty presents among the Sioux hardly lasted until the beginning of winter. The Indians on Powder River had not traded since 1864; their camps were full of fine buffalo robes and other pelts, and they had been assured that as soon as the treaty was signed they would be permitted to trade freely again. But this was not true, the military having received strict orders not to permit any Sioux to approach the Platte road; and now when a band of Oglalas came down to trade near Platte Bridge, west of Fort Laramie, they were first warned away and then fired on, one chief being badly wounded. The Indians and the traders were enraged. The traders had been ruined by the Indian war. Now, in 1868, their aid had been solicited in getting the chiefs to sign the treaty, and they had been promised that as a reward for their services they would be given the right to trade again with the Sioux. These men had bought large stocks, some of them on credit, and they were now ruined by the military order forbidding the Indians to come in to trade. Naturally, both the Sioux and the traders cried out that they had been lied to and tricked, but it really seems that this was not the case. General Sanborn, one of the treaty commissioners, explained in a letter written in 1870 that the government's object was to keep the Sioux away from the Platte until the railroad had been completed, and that for this reason the treaty commission had made a plan for traders to go up to the Black Hills, where the Sioux might come and trade with them freely. This matter of trade was of first importance, if the Indians were to be kept quiet, yet nothing was done except to order the military to prevent trade on the Platte.[4]

Even the Sioux friendlies were soon accusing the government of bad faith, for they now learned that they were to be taken from their old haunts along the Platte and removed to the Missouri. Like the hostile bands of Powder River, the friendlies did not know the contents of the treaty, and they were clearly under the impression that removal to the Missouri was optional. Therefore, after signing the treaty, Man-Afraid-of-His-Horse took his band to Powder River and the friendly Brulés and Southern Oglalas re-

4. Sanborn's letter is in the *Report of the Board of Indian Commissioners*, 1870.

turned to their hunting grounds south of the Platte. Not even the Laramie Loafers had any intention of going to the hateful Missouri River agency.

Determined to remove these Indians from the vicinity of the Union Pacific line, the officials now began to exert pressure on them. The Squaw Camp at Fort Laramie and the Loafer band were the first to be affected. Their old friends at the fort grew cold to them, and presently told them bluntly to leave. The Indians seemed bewildered and did not know what to do. Traders and squawmen were now induced to coax these bands away from the fort and lead them to the new agency on the Missouri.[5]

The Indians and whites from Fort Laramie started their sorrowful march toward the Missouri in June, 1868. On the thirtieth they reached the Indian agency at North Platte, Nebraska, and were given some supplies by Agent Patrick. He calls them by the handsome name of "the Laramie Snipes." Here they were joined by 150 persons "of the same sort," and the caravan proceeded on its march to Whetstone, the new agency on the Missouri. The Oglalas and Brulés were hunting south of the Platte and showed no inclination to leave their home and go to the Missouri. To put pressure on them, the North Platte agency was closed, no further supplies were issued to the Indians and other sharper means were taken to force them north of the Platte. The Brulés finally started, in a very sullen humor, and Spotted Tail and the other chiefs had a hard time to prevent some of the young warriors giving expression to their feeling by making raids. The Indians all claimed that they had been tricked into going to the Missouri, a country which was not theirs and to which they had no desire to go.

These happenings, coming so soon after the signing of the great pact, are really amazing, especially when we consider the amount of breath the humanitarians of the Indian Peace Party had recently expended in denouncing men who in the past had deceived and swindled the Indians in making treaties with them. It is so apparent that none of the Sioux chiefs knew the contents of this treaty that there is no escaping the conviction that they had been tricked into

5. Charlie Elliston was one of the men who led these Indians to Whetstone. He said in 1875 that he and other men left good homes at Fort Laramie and Denver to go with the Indians, being promised trading licenses, teams and wagons, farm equipment, and free farms. They received nothing, and when they asked redress were told that they had no right to be on the reservation, where their influence was bad. Some of these men, like Elliston, had performed invaluable services for the government.

signing it. Red Cloud said in 1870 that he was told that the treaty was an agreement to restore peace and trade, nothing more, and many of the chiefs bore him out. They said that the treaty had not been read to them. We cannot accuse the local traders and interpreters at Fort Laramie and on the Platte of this deception, for nothing is clearer than the fact that they were also tricked, and cheated out of the trade and other perquisites which had been promised them.

The Sioux who went to Whetstone were all friendlies. The expectation of the peace people that the hostiles on Powder River, now no longer hostile because some of their chiefs had touched the pen, would also go to the Missouri, rapidly faded. General C. C. Augur, commanding the Department of the Platte, reported that he could see no change in the hostiles on Powder River; and as for the friendlies, he stated that when the Brulés under Spotted Tail started for Whetstone Agency, the friendly Oglalas under Little Wound, Whistler, and Pawnee Killer stubbornly refused to leave their hunting grounds south of the Platte and troops would probably have to be employed against them. We have no means of judging whether the chiefs were right in claiming that nothing had been said at the peace councils to indicate that they were to be driven from their old home south of the Platte. The officials in 1869 insisted that the Indians had agreed to give up these hunting grounds, and they were even ready to use troops to drive them from that region; yet after 1870 the Indians' right, under the treaty, to hunt south of the Platte was admitted. They hunted and wintered there, and in the end they relinquished this right by formal agreement in 1874 and were paid for doing so.

During the great peace crusade of 1868, the battle cry of the Indians' Friends had been, "Feed them or fight them." A lurid picture of the horrors and cost of a Sioux war was drawn (Commissioner N. G. Taylor said officially that 100,000 troops would be required and the cost would run into billions of dollars) and the government, convinced or overwhelmed with the clamor, accepted the feeding policy; but Congress when it voted the funds for feeding and clothing the Sioux passed over the peace people who had control of the Indian Office and insisted that the War Department should disburse the money. The new Sioux agencies on the Missouri were therefore formed into a military district with General W. S. Harney in command. The western newspapers were very acid in their comments on these proceedings. Since Harney had whipped the Brulés on the Bluewater in 1855 he had been the hero of the West, and the people had long desired to see him in command, cracking it to the Sioux. They now beheld him in charge—a new Harney, speaking the smug language of the peace crusaders and handing out rations, clothing, guns, and ammunition to the Sioux. "The acme of childishness, mawkish sentimentality, and general silliness," wrote one angry editor, and he was expressing the view of the Peace Policy generally held in the West.

The Whetstone Agency, on the Missouri above the mouth of White River, and the Grand River and Cheyenne River agencies higher up the Missouri, were the stations to which the government expected the hostile Teton Sioux to flock as soon as the treaty was signed; but not a hostile came in. At the two upper agencies the Missouri River friendlies assembled to draw rations and clothing, and at Whetstone the tame Loafers who had formerly hung about Fort Laramie made up the population. The Brulés under Spotted Tail were not at this agency. Forced to leave the Platte, they had gone up to White River and camped on the South Fork. Here they wintered, their camps never less than thirty miles from the agency. Spotted Tail and some of the other chiefs did all in their power to induce the people to move nearer the Missouri, but the Brulés would not budge, and all the supplies they had that winter were hauled to their camp at much expense. The people at the agency were the Laramie Loafers, the mixed-bloods, and the squawmen with their families. Not a family from the wild, roving camps was there. The winter was one of hardships and many deaths; and for years after the Sioux had the bitterest memories of Whetstone, the place to which they had been dragged by the whites, away from their own land, where they had buried over one hundred of the children and old people who suffered most from the hardships to which all were exposed.

The coming of spring only increased Spotted Tail's trouble. His people wanted to go on a hunt south of the Platte, and when told that the government had forbidden them to go, they were defiant and declared that they would go anyway, contending that it was their land and that the whites had no right to order them out. Some were also talking of going to Powder River to join Red Cloud. On the new Sioux Reservation where they now were, there were no buffalo and even small game was very scarce. It was all very well for the Loafers and Interpreters' Children (mixed-bloods) at the agency to live on what the white people were pleased to hand them, but the Brulés were not beggars and would not live that way. Spotted Tail, who knew the power of the whites and knew that the buffalo would not last much longer, understood that the Sioux must change their way of living; but he could not make his wild followers understand. The camp was filled with quarreling; bitter factions were springing up, and only by constant effort could the chiefs prevent serious trouble.

News now reached Spotted Tail's camp that the troops were combing the country south of the Platte, driving out the remaining bands of Oglalas and Cheyennes. From General Augur's report for 1869 we learn that General E. A. Carr with the Fifth Cavalry started to drive the Indians out of the hunting grounds south of the Platte in June, and routed Tall Bull's band of Cheyennes in a fight at Summit Springs. In August, Colonel W. B. Royall combed the country again and found a camp, but the Indians fled across the Platte and did not stop until they reached the Niobrara.[6] In September, the troops made a third expedition and destroyed a camp of fifty-six lodges, the Indians fleeing. By these operations the Sioux and Cheyennes were cleared out of the region south of the Niobrara. General Augur reported that the Sioux on Powder River were still hostile and showed no inclination to go on the reservation.

It has been stated by some authors that Red Cloud began to lose his influence over the fighting men among the hostile Sioux the moment he signed the treaty in 1868, but this does not appear to be the fact. The treaty had been signed by several other hostile leaders who clearly did so merely to obtain ammunition, blankets, and other necessaries; and there is no reason to suppose that Red Cloud was ostracized by the warriors while these other men were not. In 1869, we find him leading a large war-party against the Shoshonis.[7] It is true that in 1870 he came in and went to the agency, but that is not evidence that he had lost his power among the hostiles. When the treaty was signed, these hostiles on Powder River expected to be permitted to visit and trade on the North Platte, as

6. Little Wound's Oglala camp seems to have been destroyed during these operations. He said in 1870 that the white soldiers "cleaned me out."

7. Grace R. Hebart in her book, *Chief Washakie,* states that in 1868 Red Cloud's son led a war-party against the Shoshonis and was killed. If this is correct, Red Cloud's expedition in 1869 must have been intended as an act of vengeance for this killing.

in the old days. The officials, however, closed the trading places with the object of forcing the Indians to go to the new agencies on the Missouri. The Powder River bands stubbornly refused to do this, and when in 1869-1870 a new crisis seemed to be at hand, the officials summoned Red Cloud down to the Platte. They still regarded him as the leader of the Powder River bands, and the Indians themselves acquiesced in this view.

Red Cloud's attitude toward the government at this period, as in later days, is rather difficult to understand. In the autumn of 1869, Big Partisan, a Brulé, came to Whetstone with the news that Red Cloud was near the Black Hills and was trying to coax his people to go to the agency on the Missouri. There is no reason to doubt Big Partisan's statement, and what he said would indicate that Red Cloud was not an out-and-out hostile like Sitting Bull, who hated the whites and refused to have anything whatever to do with them. Judging from his attitude at this time, and after he went to Red Cloud Agency, it would seem that Red Cloud's policy, if we may call it that, was to remain on good terms with the whites as far as possible, to obtain help from them, but above all to hold stubbornly to the old roving and hunting life and never to give it up. For an Indian, Red Cloud was an able man, but it is to be doubted if he ever had the breadth of vision that Spotted Tail sometimes exhibited. This Brule chief realized after 1865 that the old wild life was doomed and tried to lead his people to accept the inevitable changes in their way of living. Red Cloud could not see this, and he remained "non-progressive," as the exasperated Indian Office officials put it, until the day of his death. As an old half-blind man he clutched desperately at the Ghost Dance faith in 1890 as the last hope of winning back the old free life of his youth.

The Sioux crisis of 1870 was largely due to the formation and rapid settlement of Wyoming Territory. The Peace people had been wrong in their supposition that the Sioux of Powder River would go to the new agencies as soon as the treaty was signed, and they erred also in describing the Powder River and Bighorn regions as a country which the whites did not desire. The adventurous and enterprising men who comprised most of the population of Wyoming in 1869 certainly did desire the lands in question, and from the moment the treaty was made public they deeply resented the fact that the greater part of their territory lying north of the Platte River should be recognized by the government as Indian country into which they could not go. Plans were soon made for parties of armed citizens to go north of the Platte to prospect for gold and other minerals and to seek good timber and grazing lands. The government's opposition to such invasions of the Indian lands enraged these men, who regarded the Sioux as hostile and denounced the Indian policy as the height of absurdity. The Indians were also growing very impatient, for they were still barred from trading on the Platte and considered this a violation of the promises made to them in 1868.

General Grant was president at this time, and he seems to have listened to certain wicked men who were more interested in developing the resources of the territories than in a policy of Christian forebearance toward the obstreperous Sioux of Powder River. The Indian Peace Party had gone off guard for the moment, following its successful campaign of 1868; but in the early spring of 1870 these good people in the East were rudely disturbed by reports in the Western papers that a Sioux war was about to begin and that the military leaders were moving troops into positions from which they could quickly take the field. Furiously denouncing this attempt to revive "the wicked old Tomahawk Policy" of dealing with Indians, the peace people pleaded for the Sioux and stormed against the frontier white barbarians, but their friends who still controlled the Indian Office at Washington seemed strangely helpless in face of this growing danger of a new war with the Sioux.

We now come to one of the strangest episodes in Indian history —the Red Cloud peace crusade of 1870. The government, caught between the Indians' Friends in the East who demanded peace and the clamor in the West for stiff action against the Indians, was seeking for a way out of its difficulties when a Mr. Benjamin Tatham of New York City suggested bringing Red Cloud to Washington in an effort to forestall any trouble by a personal conference with President Grant and the Secretary of the Interior. The Secretary of the Interior seemed in doubt as to what to do—perhaps he thought that this plan had too much the appearance of the government asking peace of Red Cloud—but while he was considering the matter someone must have telegraphed to Fort Laramie, for presently a message came from Fort Fetterman, west of that post, stating that Red Cloud had requested permission to come to Washington. The idea that Mr. Tatham and Red Cloud had conceived the same plan at about the same moment is absurd. The matter was evidently arranged in this manner in order to save the government's face. Red Cloud blurted out the truth when he said during the councils at Washington that he had been sent for and had come.

The officials at Washington snatched at this opportunity to avoid war with the Sioux. Messages were sent to Fort Laramie and Fort Fetterman arranging for the coming of Red Cloud and a large delegation. General John E. Smith, who had known Red Cloud at Fort Phil Kearny in 1868, was ordered to proceed at once to Fort Laramie and there take charge of the Sioux delegation. Spotted Tail and his chiefs were also summoned to Washington. The standing order to the military that no Indians were to be permitted to approach the Platte Valley was also set aside, and the Sioux and Cheyennes who were supposed to be on the point of starting a great Indian war came eagerly down to Fort Laramie and Fort Fetterman. Their camps were crammed with buffalo robes, but trade was still forbidden.

When Red Cloud reached Fort Laramie, he went into conference with the old traders who were his friends: Nick Janis, John Richards, and W. G. Bullock. Red Cloud also wished to see Jules Ecoffey, who was up the road at Fetterman, but General Smith objected, saying that the party was too large already; but Red Cloud had a telegram sent, and when his party reached the railroad there was Jules, bland and polite. He talked himself into the good graces of General Smith and accompanied the party to Washington.

This expedition to Washington to meet the Great Father was Red Cloud's show. He and not Man-Afraid-of-His-Horse or Sitting Bull or any of the other Powder River chiefs had been asked to come, and he had picked his own delegation from among his own friends—Bad Faces and Oyuhkpes all of them. There were twenty-one Indians in the party, all Oglalas, Red Cloud and sixteen other men and four women. The principal men were Red Cloud, Brave Bear and his son Sword, of the Bad Faces, and Red Dog, Yellow Bear, and High Wolf of the Oyuhkpes. Not one of these Indians had ever seen a town or a railroad. They were wild people, and had very little comprehension of what lay before them on this adventure into the land of the whites.

General Smith's orders were to avoid the town of Cheyenne, the nearest point on the railroad, probably from a fear which the officials had that Red Cloud's party might be lynched. This robust frontier metropolis, now about a year old, was full of the type of Western men who had no earthly use for Indians and who were regrettably prone to hasty action. The Sioux were therefore taken rather secretly from Fort Laramie to the little station of Pine Bluff, forty miles east of Cheyenne, where on May 27 they boarded the east-bound train.

That was an epic journey down the Platte Valley. By the time they reached the Missouri the Oglalas had grown accustomed to train life; but now they came to Omaha, a hive of white people with hundreds of buildings, some of them very high—four, five stories! The Oglalas liked Omaha; but Chicago stunned them, and as they traveled on their ideas of the world, one by one, toppled and fell in ruins. They reached Washington dazed and rather frightened; that they had any courage left was a splendid compliment to their breed and training.

Comedy and tragedy were mingled together in the incidents of this great journey. At Washington Red Cloud's folk met Spotted Tail and his chiefs. As has been stated in the earlier chapters of this book, there is considerable evidence to indicate that the Brulés were regarded among the Teton Sioux as an elder or parent group to which the Oglalas were inferior in rank. These Indians had no sooner met at the hotel than they began to bicker over the question of precedence, and as the Oglalas all backed Red Cloud while the Brulés to a man supported Spotted Tail, the quarrel grew and threatened to develop into a fight. At last the white traders and interpreters took the two angry chiefs to a bedroom, locked the door, and let them have it out. When they came forth again, Red Cloud and Spotted Tail were distantly polite to each other. Spotted Tail, with his usual good sense, had given way. He said that if his people, the Sioux, would benefit through Red Cloud's elevation by the whites to the position of head of the nation—a rank to which he had no real claim—he, Spotted Tail, would stand aside. The foolish officials, failing to realize the delicacy of the situation, praised Spotted Tail in public for his noble conduct and presented him and his chiefs with horses, thereby enabling them to dash about Washington mounted and in glory, while Red Cloud and his men were compelled to ride in carriages, which they despised as shiny black wagons. Red Cloud, inflamed with an agony of jealousy, demanded to be taken home at once. He said that he could not face the Great Father and his chiefs after being publicly shamed in this manner. The leaders of the Peace Party were so alarmed that they promised Red Cloud that they would buy his party horses and equipment with money from their own pockets if he would only remain and talk with the Great Father. Red Cloud sulkily assented, but there was some delay in obtaining the promised mounts and during his stay in Washington he and his chiefs had to ride in carriages.

The Indian Office had planned a program for Red Cloud and his chiefs, who were to be conducted about the city and shown the sights and wonders. They were to be impressed with the vast power and riches of the whites; and after this had been accomplished it was expected that the chiefs, feeling properly humble, would conform to the government's wishes and all would be well. At the first meeting with the Secretary of the Interior on June 3, Red Cloud asked that a telegram be sent to Fort Laramie to inform the Sioux that the chiefs had arrived safely, and he also asked that food be provided for his people whom he had left in camp at the fort. This day the chiefs wanted to talk business, but the secretary put them off. From this meeting the chiefs were taken in carriages on a tour of the city. They refused to enter any of the big buildings. On the next day, June 4, they were taken to the arsenal where they saw more guns of different types than they had supposed the whole world contained. The old armor impressed them; but most of all they admired the 15-inch Rodman gun which was fired for them. The great shell went screaming down the Potomac and could be seen skipping over the water four or five miles away. Red Cloud measured the muzzle of the gun with his eagle-tail fan and examined the huge grains of powder with much interest. At the navyyard a regiment of marines was paraded for the chiefs and they were shown the iron-clads anchored in the river. Admiral Dahlgren's wife invited Red Cloud to lunch, but he politely declined, saying that he was in Washington on business and not for pleasure.

On June 8, a council was held at the Indian Office, and the Oglalas were told that the government expected them to go on the reservation. If Red Cloud had been impressed with the power of the United States by being taken about Washington he did not show it at this council. He had come east to prevent a new war and to procure for his people the right to trade on the Platte. What was this talk about going on a reservation—to the Missouri? "I have said three times that I would not go to the Missouri, and now I say it here for the fourth time." No roads should be made through his country, Fort Fetterman which stood on his land must be moved, and the Oglalas must be given the right to trade at Fort Laramie. This was not the talk of a man who feared the power of the United States, and the glum officials began to realize that dictating to Red Cloud was not going to be the easy task they had anticipated.

The next day the chiefs were taken to see President Grant, and Red Cloud spoke to his Great Father in a quite unfilial tone. He demanded again that Fort Fetterman be removed from his land and asserted that the treaty of 1868 gave the Oglalas the right to trade at Fort Laramie. He then demanded two trading posts on the Platte. President Grant's response was mild and rather dull. He suggested that the Oglalas go to the Missouri and start farming. The chiefs were glum but polite. That evening they dined at the White House with the diplomatic corps, and the cabinet members and their wives.

On June 10 the conference reached a crisis, the Secretary of the Interior attempting to beat down Red Cloud's opposition to going on the reservation. The treaty of 1868 was brought out and flourished to prove that the Oglalas had no right to trade at Fort Laramie or to have an agency there. The effect of the reading of the treaty was not at all what the officials had expected. Red Cloud in a sudden fury shouted for them to put that paper away. It was all lies and a swindle. That paper had not been read to the chiefs when they signed it. They now for the first time heard all the false things that were in it. He, Red Cloud, had been coaxed into signing by a certain curly haired interpreter who had told him that it was only a peace agreement which would take the white soldiers from Powder River and give the Oglalas a chance to raise their children in peace. He had also been assured that the paper provided that his people could trade at Fort Laramie, where their fathers had always traded. "The bones of Oglalas are there all around that fort." He and his chiefs had traveled a long trail to this town to prevent a new war and the spilling of more blood, and now they were shown this lying paper and were told that they must give up their own land and go to the Missouri. The other chiefs backed up Red Cloud: not one of them had known the contents of the treaty until this day. They left the council in a black mood. That night one of them tried to kill himself, saying that he could not go back to Powder River and tell the people how they had been swindled.

The Oglala chiefs now demanded to be taken home at once. Many of the newspapers predicted that if Red Cloud went home in his present state of temper his arrival on Powder River would be the signal for war. The Indians' Friends were aghast. They had believed that in bringing Red Cloud east they were making the Peace Policy safe; and now they heard these Sioux denouncing the treaty of 1868, that masterpiece of the humanitarians, as a lie and a swindle. The council of June 10 made it clear that neither the chiefs nor the officials would give in; and here was Red Cloud in a rage demanding to be taken home at once. But peace crusaders are resourceful folk, and within twelve hours the men in charge of the Peace Policy at Washington evolved a new scheme. They planned to take Red Cloud to New York and bring him before a mass-meeting of the friends of peace in the hope of creating so much sympathy for the Sioux that the government's hand would be forced. Telegraphing to New York, arrangements were made to hold the meeting in the great hall of the Cooper Institute, and the Secretary of the Interior was induced to give his assent to this plan. Another meeting was then proposed between the secretary and the chiefs. The chiefs were still very angry and did not desire another meeting, but Jules Ecoffey, Bullock, and the interpreters won them over after hours of coaxing. On meeting the secretary, Red Cloud expressed some regret for the scene he had made when the treaty was read. "It made me mad and I suppose it made you the same." The secretary told the chiefs that they were to go home by way of New York, but Red Cloud objected. "I do not want to go that way. I want a straight line. I have seen enough of towns and want to go to my people. Waking or sleeping I have them on my heart." Red Cloud stated during this talk that there were thirty-two nations; that the chiefs of these nations had held a council before he left Powder River, and that the demands he was now making were those the council had instructed him to make. He evidently meant that thirty-two bands of Sioux had assembled in council to decide what he should say at Washington.

The Oglala chiefs were now practically kidnapped and placed on board a train bound for New York. At Philadelphia the Indians' Friends wished to hold a reception for the chiefs, but Red Cloud and the others were in such a temper that General Smith dared not take them off the train. They went straight through to New York, where they were dragged around much against their will to see new sights. Among other things they were shown over a French warship.

Then came the great meeting at Cooper Institute. The Indians' Friends had had but one day in which to spread word of the meeting and were afraid that they would not have a large gathering; yet when the time for the reception came, at noon on June 16, the great hall was so crowded that many could not get in. The *Herald* stated that a larger meeting had never been held at Cooper Institute. Red Cloud and his chiefs were on the platform facing this great multitude of white people. When the proper time came, Red Cloud arose and stretched both arms toward the sky, then swept them down toward the earth and began to pray. The effect on the audience of this prayer and of the speech that followed it cannot be better described than it was in the newspapers of the day. The *Times* on June 17 contained the following account:

"No one who listened to Red Cloud's remarkable speech yesterday can doubt that he is a man of very great talents .... He has spent his life in fighting the battles of his people, and one day he is transplanted to Cooper Institute, and asked to put on a clean shirt, a new waistcoat, a high crowned hat, and then make a speech. Among all vicissitudes of his life, this must be the most startling, and, perhaps, not the most agreeable .... Although the audience labored under the disadvantage of not knowing what Red Cloud said, until his words were filtered through an interpreter .... still his earnest manner, his impassioned gestures, the eloquence of his hands, and the magnetism which he evidently exercises over an audience, produced a vast effect on the dense throng which listened to him yesterday. 'You have children, and so have we. We want to rear our children well, and ask you to help us in doing so.' It seems to us that this is not an unreasonable request even though it does come from a 'savage.'"

The *Tribune* on the seventeenth printed this report:

"The remarkable triumph of Red Cloud yesterday in the great speech he delivered before the assembled multitude at Cooper Institute, was one of the most striking incidents in the history of the aboriginal race .... His opening invocation to the Almighty Spirit was solemn, earnest, and highly dramatic; and as he went on to recount the wrongs of his people and to demand justice for them, in words that were at once simple, strong, and heartfelt, the audience was greatly impressed.... During the intervals of translation he stood statuesque and impressive, which was quite as striking as his animation in the more earnest passages of his appeal."

After Red Cloud had finished, Red Dog made a shorter speech. He is described in the papers as the orator of the Oglalas, a man with a fine intelligent face, and rather plump in figure. His style of speaking was not that of Red Cloud. He said: "When the Great Father first sent out men to our people I was poor and thin; now I am large and fat. This is because so many liars have been sent out there and I have been stuffed full with their lies." When the speeches were over, the audience thronged to the platform to shake hands with the chiefs, and many "rich and appropriate gifts" were heaped upon them.

The hopes of the Peace Party that the meeting at Cooper Institute would turn the scales in their favor were more than justified. The chiefs who had reached New York in very bad humor now departed for home in high spirits, loaded with gifts, and heartened by the assurance that a multitude of white people in the East were on their side. A number of the leading Eastern papers and thousands of individuals now demanded that the government should alter its policy toward Red Cloud's people and make the necessary sacrifices to avoid war. The Western editors raged. They could see little sense and less fairness in the speeches of Red Cloud and his chiefs, and they expressed a vast astonishment that the childish complaints of the Sioux should have made such an impression in the East. They derided the throng that had crowded into the Cooper Institute to hear Red Cloud as "Quakers" and "humanitarian greenhorns" but the Eastern editors replied by asking blandly what had become of the Sioux war which the Wyoming and other Western papers had been so confidently predicting and which the military leaders had regarded as unavoidable. The war had vanished into the thin air from which it had been conjured. Urged on by a public demand which the peace people had so adroitly created, the government was preparing to be very good to Red Cloud and his folk. The humanitarians pushed their advantage, inducing the Secretary of the Interior to appoint a commission of their own men to go to Fort Laramie with a train-load of presents and the power to make a final settlement with the Powder River Sioux.

Meanwhile Red Cloud's party was speeding homeward by way of Buffalo, Chicago, and Omaha. At Omaha the chiefs remained several days, selecting the horses, saddles, and other gifts which the government had decided to present to them. They reached Pine Bluff on June 24, and at once started on their horses for Fort Laramie. A great assemblage of Sioux and Cheyennes had been at the fort for some time, anxiously awaiting their arrival; but the pony herds had eaten the grass for miles around, and the Indians had now withdrawn to Rawhide Butte Creek, forty miles away. There were about 1,000 lodges of these Indians; their camps were full of buffalo robes, and they were perfectly confident that Red Cloud would obtain for them the right to trade. General Smith, who was still with Red Cloud, now sent in a special report urging that the Indians be given permission to trade and stating that in his opinion if trade was forbidden the whole agreement with Red Cloud would fall through. The agreement referred to was that the Oglalas should accept an agency on the Big Cheyenne River, eighty miles north of Fort Laramie, where the tribe had wintered so often during the later fifties. Red Cloud was to be permitted to choose his own agent and trader. He picked Ben Mills for agent and Bullock for trader, but they were not appointed.

The government again gave in, and the Indians did their trading. They then went north, in great fettle, held their Sun Dance, and then organized a great war-party and joyously drove the Crows into the mountains. The Crows now had an agency and a company of United States troops to guard it. The Sioux expended a considerable portion of the ammunition they had obtained at Fort Laramie in shooting up the soldiers at the Crow agency. The agent, a brutal military man, wished to arm the Crows so that they might defend themselves and the Montana border from the Sioux, but the Indian Office took no action and the friendly Crows were left to their fate.

The peace people had been quite right in putting faith in Red Cloud. He spent the late summer in going from camp to camp in the Powder River country, holding councils, and explaining what he had heard in the East. The Indians now learned for the first time the true contents of the treaty of 1868, and Red Cloud must have had a hard time to convince the chiefs that any dependence could be placed in the good intentions of the government. While he was still engaged in this labor, John Richards came out from Fort Laramie with word that two good men were coming from Washington to hold a great council and cement the agreement which Red Cloud had made. There would be many fine presents. The Indians received this information in varying moods. Some cried that they would not have the chiefs touch any more papers—they had been deceived often enough. Others wished to know if there would be guns and ammunition; many were satisfied with the mere promise of plenty of white man's food and presents.

The Cheyennes and Arapahoes were the first to come in. By mid-August they were arriving at Fort Fetterman, bringing news that 1,000 to 1,800 lodges of Sioux were gathering at the Bear's Lodge, in the Black Hills. Grass, an Oglala chief, came to Fort Laramie to report that Red Cloud would reach there about the middle of the next moon—September 15.

The two good men, F. R. Brunot and Robert Campbell, reached Fort Laramie September 21, only to learn that Red Cloud had not arrived. This chieftain was in camp on Minipuss, the Dry Fork of Cheyenne River, waiting to learn what these white men wanted before he would move in. The commissioners sent him a reassuring message that they only wished to give him about a train load of presents and an agency where his people could obtain free food and clothing. Man-Afraid-of-His-Horse was less suspicious. He was already ahead of Red Cloud, in camp on Lance's Creek, and on the thirtieth he came in with his band, accompanied by a camp of Miniconjous and Medicine Man's band of Cheyennes.[8] He had heard of the white men's coming while on Tongue River, 300 to 400 miles away; he had hurried in as fast as he could travel, and where were the guns and ammunition? When told that these were about the only things the Sioux could not have, he was considerably crestfallen. Having been assured that there was no paper to sign, Red Cloud at last came in on October 4, in the midst of a whirling dust storm, and went into camp on the Platte three miles above the fort.

The council was held at the fort on October 5. Red Cloud carried things with a high hand. He brushed aside the commission's plan to hold the council in a large tent, insisting that it be held on the commandant's veranda, and he stopped his speech to order that a photographer be chased away. His speech was full of com-

8. Not the Arapaho chief of this name. The man here mentioned was at times called "the medicine man of the Cheyennes." I think that he was old Maple Tree, the ventriloquist. His band, later known as Two Moon's camp, was made up of the wildest of the Northern Cheyennes, about fifty lodges. They associated with the Bad Face Oglalas, and High-Back-Bone's band of Miniconjous were with them in the Fetterman fight in 1866, with Crazy Horse in March, 1876, and were the only Cheyennes present in the Crook and Custer battles in June, 1876.

plaints, particularly about the old California road which for a few miles ran along the north bank of the Platte in Sioux territory. He said that this road was a small matter not worth making a war about, but it made him feel ashamed before his own people. Evidently he had told the Indians that the treaty made all lands north of the North Platte Sioux country into which no whites could come, and some Indians had then cried out that Red Cloud had been deceived again, for was there not a road on the north side of the river with whites passing along it every day? Red Cloud was angry; he kept referring to this piece of road, and the two good men from Washington kept referring to the rich presents they had brought to the Oglalas, and the other chiefs kept asking where were the arms and ammunition? The chiefs were constantly conferring among themselves during the council, and when the whites asked the interpreters what the chiefs were saying, the reply was that they were discussing various schemes for obtaining arms and ammunition.

The real controversy was reached when the council began to discuss the location of the proposed Oglala agency. Red Cloud had gone east with instructions from the tribe to obtain an agency, or the right to trade, near Fort Laramie, and he and the other chiefs were still holding out for this location, while the commissioners had received explicit instructions not to consent to an agency near the fort. They suggested a site near Rawhide Butte, but the chiefs would not hear of it. Red Cloud finally explained that they had once had an agency at this point, which had been struck by lightning and destroyed. They all regarded this as an evil omen and would not accept the location. After endless arguments, Red Cloud admitted that the warriors, who were the real masters of the tribe, would not permit the chiefs to agree to an agency away from Fort Laramie. The warriors had also selected Ben Mills for an agent, and Bullock, Richards, Ecoffey, and Brown for traders. They said that these were their old traders who had been left alone here on the Platte during the years when the Sioux were not permitted to come down to trade with them; they would now have their old traders again, and if the Great Father sent them some poor rats from the East to take their places, the Oglalas would drive the rats away. They had selected the site of the old Ward & Guerrier store, on the south side of the river a few miles west of the fort, as the location of their agency, and they would not listen to any other suggestion. Finally, after hours of wrangling, Man-Afraid-of-His-Horse said: "There is too much talk. Give us our presents and let this other matter lie where it is." The commissioners suggested gently that the Oglalas talk over the location of the agency during the winter and return in the spring with their minds made up. This seemed to the chiefs a foolish saying. Their minds were already made up.

On October 7, the commissioners went to the Oglala camp with their wagon-trains of presents. Five thousand Oglalas were standing and sitting in a great circle. Red Cloud ordered the goods unloaded in the center of this circle and placed in four piles for the four bands. He, Man-Afraid-of-His-Horse, Red Dog, and American Horse received the goods for their respective bands.[9] Watching the proceedings rather unhappily was a great crowd of Brulés, Miniconjous, Sans Arcs, and Cheyennes, who had been told that the presents were for the Oglalas only. As the Oglalas watched the great bales being tumbled out of the wagons and cut open they grew happy. Calicoes, domestics, and woolen cloth in bolts; tinned kettles by the hundred. (*Hey-a-hey!* But why do we not get iron kettles such as the white soldiers have?) Blankets by the thousand. (But see the white ones! We do not want white blankets, only dark colored ones!) Coats, shirts, hats. (*Hey-hey!* We are not white men! We do not want these things!) Steel needles and awls; butcher knives. (But where are the guns and ammunition?) Having divided the goods into four great mounds, the commissioners and other whites discreetly withdrew to permit the Oglalas to divide the rich spoil. What a wonderful quarrel it was! No one was killed, but Red Dog's pony was shot dead by an enraged sub-chief who thought that he had not been given a fair share of the presents.

Thus was terminated Red Cloud's great campaign of 1870. War had been averted and at a trifling cost, but the government had been let in for a policy of humoring this chief and his followers, and where the policy might lead no man could judge.[10]

9. The four bands present evidently were the Bad Faces (Red Cloud), the Oyuhkpes (Red Dog), the Hunkpatilas (Man-Afraid-of-His-Horse), and the True Oglalas (American Horse). Little Wound was present, but his Kiyuksa band seems to have been at or near Whetstone Agency. Red Leaf and his Wazhazhas were present, but were rated as Brulés.

10. The authorities for this chapter are the official reports and contemporary newspapers. I also have some information from the Oglalas and from Major Jordan who was a trader at Pine Ridge after 1880 and knew many of the Indians and whites who accompanied Red Cloud on his journey East.

PART III

RED CLOUD AGENCY

"The land in which we stand is full of white men; our game is all gone and we have come on great trouble."

—Spotted Tail.

CHAPTER XI

BEING GOOD TO THE OGLALAS
1871-1873

I<small>N</small> the spring of 1871 the Indian Office sent out an agent for Red Cloud's people. It set aside the chief's oft repeated desire to have Ben Mills of Fort Laramie for his agent and sent a Mr. J. W. Wham who had been recommended by the Episcopal Church as a good man and a Christian. That he was all this we cannot doubt, but it does not seem a cogent reason for throwing him to the Oglalas, who at this period were as wild as wolves and no fit associates for a good man with church affiliations.

At this period all of the plains tribes had agents who had been nominated by the churches. The church and humanitarian groups had so persistently denounced the political appointments of agents that Congress had at length passed an act providing that Indian agents should be selected by the churches themselves. By this arrangement most of the Teton Sioux were put under the wing of the Episcopal Church, which chose the agents from its own membership and was to a certain degree responsible for their conduct. Within eight years the church had burnt its fingers so often that it was only too glad to drop out and permit someone else to select Indian agents and be responsible for them. One of the Sioux agents, who went to church twice on Sundays and twice during the rest of the week and spent most of his time in communion with ministers, had been indicted on thirty-two counts, charging larceny, embezzlement, conspiracy, fraud, falsification of public records, and forgery in all their degrees, while several other church agents had been publicly accused of frauds and thefts and had been removed from office. During these trying years all of the churches had to face the fact that a good church-goer might be a very inefficient and even dishonest Indian agent, and it hurt them dreadfully.

Mr. Wham was a good, serious minded Christian, an Indians' Friend man of the type which trustfully held that if treated kindly and fairly the Indians would, within reason, do whatever was required of them. He found the Sioux gathered at Fort Laramie in large force. Red Cloud, Red Dog, High Wolf, Little Wound, Red Leaf, and White Tail were there with their bands, and as they were all drawing rations at the fort after having been assured by the commission in the previous October that they could never be permitted to do this, they were in high good humor. Unaware of what a hornet's nest he was stirring up, Mr. Wham now attempted to carry out his orders and induce the Sioux to accept an agency north of the Platte—so far north that they could never get down to the river again. Calling the chiefs into council at the post, Wham brightly suggested a removal to White River. The chiefs indignantly refused, and would not talk of it. Mr. Wham now, as he reports, discovered that renegade white men (the Sioux traders) at the fort had persuaded the Indians not to move north, advising them that if they moved to White River the country north of the Platte would soon be occupied by settlers, and that it would not be long until the whites would be demanding the Black Hills. The agent denounced these unscrupulous men, charging in his report that they wished to keep the Sioux on the Platte so that they might trade with them; yet every word the traders said at this time came true as soon as the Red Cloud people consented to go to White River.

At these talks at Fort Laramie Red Cloud repeatedly asked for time to consult with Black Twin—he insisted that it was impossible for him to name the site of an agency until he had talked with this chief. This is really astonishing. Here was Red Cloud, accepted by the government as the head-chief whose word was law to these Indians, anxiously protesting that he could make no decision until he had seen a chief whose very name was unknown to the whites and who has now been forgotten even by the Oglalas themselves. Black Twin never signed a treaty, did not come to the agency, and is not even mentioned in the Sioux winter-counts. He seems to have been at the moment a leading chief among the wild Oglalas of Powder River, and Red Cloud was evidently afraid that if he offended Black Twin he would lose the support of these bands.

Mr. Wham now proposed as a compromise that the agency should be established at Rawhide Butte, forty miles northeast of Fort Laramie. The chiefs refused, pointing out that Rawhide Butte was halfway to the Black Hills. They stated their determination to accept no agency whose location would permit whites to approach the Hills. The Indian Office officials evidently did not share the church peoples' faith that the Indians would listen to reason if they were treated kindly, for they had given Wham secret instructions to cut off rations if the Sioux refused to move north of the Platte. Still, Wham did not like to resort to such hard measures, and he made another attempt to talk sense to the chiefs, asking if they would accept an agency on the immediate north bank of the Platte. No, they would not. The agent then followed his instructions and cut off their rations. This appeal to the supreme court—their stomachs—brought the Indians around in short order. On the twenty-ninth of June the chiefs came to Mr. Wham and said that they had chosen an agency site on the north bank of the river, thirty miles below Fort Laramie: and when would they begin to eat again?

Wham was jubilant. He wired to Washington, asking that supplies be sent at once, but the Indian Office did not even reply until July 8. During these ten hungry days the Indians grew more and more irritable and the agent had all he could do to prevent most of them from going to Powder River to hunt, which would have spelled ruin for the Indian Office's favorite scheme of settling Red Cloud and his following at an agency. Many of the Indians had already gone to the new agency site, where they were anxiously waiting for the wagons with supplies. By the middle of August, Wham was camping in tents at the agency where rations in abundance were being delivered by wagon-trains coming from Cheyenne, Wyoming.

This first agency to bear Red Cloud's name was located on the north bank of the North Platte just west of the Nebraska-Wyoming line and very near the site, on the south bank, of the old Upper Platte Agency of 1860-1864.[1] The proximity of the new agency to the old one can be the only reason why the Indians selected the site,

1. This first Red Cloud Agency was in section three, township twenty-three, range sixty west, at a point about one mile west of the present village of Henry, Nebraska. It was in Wyoming, just across the state line, and Agent Wham stated that it was thirty-two miles east of Fort Laramie. Irrigation has changed this district almost beyond recognition, the placid sugar beet having replaced the wild Oglala as the principal feature of the landscape.

for the country was very unsuitable for Indian occupancy. North of the river lie heavy ridges of barren sand hills; nearby is Spoon Hill Creek; some miles to the westward is Rawhide Butte Creek, and over toward the east Spotted Tail Creek and some other little runs. Water was in sufficient quantity, but wood was scarce and grazing for the huge herds of ponies was difficult to find.

Wham was compelled to accept the site, for the Indians would not go an inch farther from Fort Laramie, and the government would not permit them to settle down an inch nearer to that post. A contract for putting up warehouses and other buildings was let, and before winter the agency was in a livable condition, the buildings being surrounded by a high, strong stockade of log pickets, which was very necessary as the agent, his employes, and traders were constantly being threatened by the wilder of the Sioux, and were really living inside their stockade in a state of siege. It was an exciting life, but not especially enjoyable. The least trifle aroused the Indians' ready suspicions and fanned them into a flame of wild passion. Whenever Wham was seen on a horse, coming out of the gate of the stockade, a wild uproar was immediately started in the Indian camps nearby. "Why is the white man on a horse? Where is he going? To the hills, perhaps? Indeed, this is very suspicious!" The warriors run to catch their ponies, mount and come racing toward the agent in a cloud of dust. *"Hey! Hey!"* they yell. "Back! Go Back! you cannot go to the hills!" Seizing his horse's bridle they lead him with furious threats and considerable reckless firing of guns back to the stockade. Wham admitted in his annual report that he knew almost nothing of the country near the agency, as the Indians would not permit any of the whites to go far from the stockade.

Wham had just reached the site of the new agency late in July when all the Indians were thrown into a wild state of excitement by the news that a wagon-train with many white men was at Fort Laramie preparing to cross the Platte and go north to Spotted Tail's new agency (the old Whetstone Agency). While in Washington in the summer of 1870, Spotted Tail had demanded the right to move the agency from the Missouri, and on being permitted to do this he had taken the agency, in the autumn of 1870, to a point on White River two hundred and twenty-five miles west of the Missouri. Finding it very difficult and expensive to supply this agency from the Missouri River, the government was now attempting to establish a road from Fort Laramie to White River. The Sioux, of course, violently objected. The warriors armed, mounted, and proceeded to whip themselves into the usual fury, hey-heying, firing their guns, and threatening the lives of the agent and his men. The fact that the wagon-train was loaded with supplies for Spotted Tail's people did not make any difference. The government was expected to perform the miracle of feeding and clothing Spotted Tail's Indians, two hundred miles from a base of supplies, without any wagons or white men crossing the Sioux lands.

Spotted Tail and his agents were at Fort Laramie when this train arrived, and they refused to assume any responsibility. The agent would do nothing. Spotted Tail was perfectly friendly, but refused an escort of Indians to accompany the train to his agency. He stated that the moment the train crossed the Platte there would be a war; yet he must have the supplies at his agency. He and the agent then left Fort Laramie; but Swift Bear, the chief of the Brulé Corn Band, remained at the post, and he offered to obtain permission from the Brulés for the train to go through. D. J. McCann, the freight contractor, accepted Swift Bear's offer and agreed to wait eight days. The time passed by and Swift Bear did not even send a message. McCann then applied to the commandant at Fort Laramie for a military escort and was granted one.

On the north bank of the Platte, at Red Cloud's agency, and up near Fort Laramie, the Sioux were armed and mounted, riding and circling and kicking up the dust like heat-devils on a hot day. "Hey! Hey! Everybody get ready! The white men with the wagons are coming to our side of the water! Hey-ahey! Now they have made a camp, but soon they will be coming across! What liars all white men are! They fix that paper with our chiefs, saying no white man can ever come on Sioux ground, and now they are coming! And these white soldiers—all the time trying to make a war! Let the white soldiers come to our side of the water! We are ready!"

But the white soldiers did not cross the Platte. Richard Smith, who was acting for Agent Wham at Fort Laramie, wrote the commanding officer a solemn protest against sending troops into Sioux territory. He stated that a war would be the immediate result. The commandant had abundant evidence that this was true, and he wired to headquarters for new instructions. Meanwhile Smith wired the Indian Office, asking if Spotted Tail could not have his supplies delivered on the Platte for the sake of peace. The Indian

Office at this period would do almost anything for the sake of peace; therefore, it consented again and the wagons were started out to deliver Spotted Tail's supplies at Red Cloud's agency.

This wagon-train, which the Sioux intended to prevent crossing their lands even if they had to fight a war, was bringing Spotted Tail's annuity goods. Among the articles it carried were 2,450 pairs of fine Indian blankets, two cases of blue Indian cloth, three of scarlet, nine of prints, two of Melton cloth, and eight of blue drill; a score of cases of shirts, socks, coats, pants, and hats (all very good to trade to whites for ammunition and whiskey); forty-eight cases of camp kettles, forty-eight dozen axes, and many more articles. It must be understood that at the old Upper Platte Agency these Indians had received only a very few annuities and nothing more. They had to obtain most of their blankets, kettles, axes, and other needs from the traders, and they had to feed and clothe themselves, trading buffalo robes and other articles for what they required. The new policy now in effect provided them with a liberal daily ration of beef, pork, bacon, flour, coffee, sugar, and even tobacco, with all the blankets and other clothing they required, camp equipment, and even canvas for lodge covers. Western men who saw these Indians being supplied with everything that they required and witnessed the vicious spirit in which they snatched at whatever was given them and threatened war if more was not forthcoming, were filled with disgust and contempt for the policy that permitted such a situation to continue. As for the Sioux, there can be no doubt that most of them believed the government was giving in to them through fear.

The few Oglalas who had remained on Powder River when Red Cloud went to his new agency were mostly Bad Faces under Big Road, Little Hawk, and some minor chiefs.[2] In the spring of 1871 they joined forces with the Miniconjous and Sans Arcs and hunted on the Tongue and Rosebud. Presently they met the Black Moon and Sitting Bull group of hostiles on the Yellowstone, near

2. These Bad Faces who remained in the north had a winter population of about fifty lodges, but in summer they were joined by large groups from the agency which sometimes increased their camp to two hundred lodges or more. They "ran with" the Miniconjous and the wildest band of Northern Cheyennes—"Medicine Man's" band, later known as Two Moon's camp. Crazy Horse, their principal warrior, was generally spoken of as the leader of these Bad Faces. Until Red Cloud went to the agency, the Oglalas, Miniconjous, and Northern Cheyennes of this group had had little to do with the Black Moon and Sitting Bull hostiles, but after 1871 they began to associate with that group.

the mouth of the Rosebud, and camped with them for a time. In 1870, High-Back-Bone, who had been in charge of operations during the Fetterman fight, December 21, 1866, had led a war-party against the Shoshonis and had been killed. Now, in the summer of 1871, the Oglalas, Miniconjous, and Sans Arcs, after holding their Sun Dance, organized a large party and went to seek vengeance for the killing of High-Back-Bone. Finding the Shoshonis difficult to attack, these Indians made raids along the North Platte, killing some whites and running off many horses and mules. At the time, it was reported by the Sioux themselves that Red Cloud's son-in-law, evidently Crazy Horse, was the leader of the Oglalas who took part in these attacks. The whites, presuming that the raiders came from the Red Cloud Agency, were very angry.

In this year, 1871, the Indian Peace Party was in more complete control of Indian affairs than ever and was being very good to the Sioux. After signing the treaty of 1868, the friendly bands of Oglalas and Brulés in the country south of the Platte had been told that they could not remain there, and when they ignored the warning, Carr's cavalry had set upon them, destroying their camps and driving them north of the Niobrara. They had then been told that they could never go to the Platte again; yet in 1870 the government had let Red Cloud come to the Platte, not with the friendly Indians who belonged there but with all the wild bands from Powder River. To complete this strange performance a further surrender was made to these Sioux in 1871. Spotted Tail, after waiting all summer at his agency on White River for the annuities, was informed that he could get his goods at Red Cloud's agency on the Platte. Down he came with his Brulé bands, and having received complete outfits of clothing and camp equipment, he and his folk decided to go back to their old home south of the Platte! With them went Red Cloud and Little Wound with their Oglalas, and Red Leaf with his Wazhazhas. There were 1,200 Brulés and 4,800 Oglalas and Wazhazhas in the camps. Brushing aside the agent's protests, the Indians journeyed down through western Nebraska to the Republican Fork, where they happily hunted buffalo all fall and then went into winter camps. It was a hard winter with deep snow, and when they ran short of meat the Sioux helped themselves from herds of cattle which were ranging near their camps. In 1868, the humanitarians had stated boldly that if their policy of feeding the Sioux at agencies should be adopted they would turn these Indians into self-supporting farmers in four years. This performance of Spotted Tail and Red Cloud in the autumn of 1871 completed the third year of the four-year period. With only one year left, the humanitarians had not yet learned the basic fact that these Indians regarded farming as such a degrading occupation that they would not even permit their women to engage in it.[3]

Red Cloud's hunting excursion to Republican Fork, where he had never been before, discloses the fact that a new shifting of the Oglala bands had been brought about by the establishment of the agency on the Platte. Most of Red Cloud's own Bad Faces had remained on Powder River; he had only a small personal following at the agency, but he was now leading the True Oglala band, sometimes called the Head band. Their old chief, Bad Wound, had died soon after they had come north with the hostiles in February, 1865, and in the following year these people had come under Red Cloud's influence, remaining with him until he came to the agency in 1871. In the autumn of this year the band induced him to lead them to the Republican Fork and spend the winter there. Red Cloud was not the chief of the True Oglalas—they accepted his leadership for a time and then deserted him. Among their own chiefs seem to have been Sitting Bear and his son, young American Horse, and the latter soon became the real leader of the band.

This winter of 1871-1872 was a relatively quiet season at Red Cloud Agency, most of the wilder bands being away, either on the Republican Fork or north on Powder River. Some of the Loafer band, the mixed-bloods, and a few of the tamest of the Oglalas were camped near the agency, and Mr. Wham and his employes zealously cared for those ewe lambs, even hiring the squawmen to cut and haul wood to the Indian camps. Since history began, no Oglala had ever before had a white man to cut and haul wood for him. But by this time some of the squawmen realized to what surprising lengths the government was ready to go in spending money, and they were eagerly scheming to obtain their share.

Every fifth day the Indians all flocked to the agency to draw their rations and to tell the agent what they thought of him. Officially he was in charge of the Indians, but in the eyes of the Sioux he was a kind of butler who had been given them by the Great

3. See Spotted Tail's affidavit *in re United States* vs. *Coe & Carter, printed in Nebraska Magazine of History,* Vol. XV, No. 1, pp. 50-51. Spotted Tail and Leon Palladay both swore that Red Cloud was with them on the Republican all winter.

Father to hand them their food. "Our white man" was their name for him, and they treated him much of the time like a slave, ordering him about and uttering fierce threats. They were full of suspicion, and every warrior was a self-constituted detective, constantly spying on the agent and his men. No circumstance was too trivial to require their careful scrutiny. Here was one of the clerks carrying a box from one warehouse to the other. "What is our white man doing with our goods? Perhaps he is stealing them!" Instant uproar would result. The chiefs would go to Wham and complain bitterly of this dishonest employe. Why had the white man brought these rats to steal their goods? They did not like these clerks and employes. They were all strangers, and undoubtedly very dishonest There were plenty of white men married into the tribe, men they knew well, men who were their own relatives. These strangers must go, and their own white men must run the agency and look after their goods. Agent Wham, being quite well acquainted with many of the squawmen by this time, was aghast at the idea of putting such men in control of the huge stock of government supplies piled up in the big warehouses. Some of these squawmen had already established ranches on the south bank of the Platte, beyond the agent's control, and had opened a lively illicit trade with the Indians. The fur trade was dead, even buffalo robes were growing scarce; but the trade in U. S. Indian goods was a very profitable one, and all through the winter bad whiskey was going across the frozen Platte to be exchanged for clothing, blankets, flour, and bacon. When the Indians sobered up, they went to the agent and complained of the lack of blankets and shortness of food. They were cold and hungry and their white man must do something for them.

Oglala politics were very active at the agency, and very puzzling to the much-bedeviled Mr. Wham. The squawmen were pulling for certain chiefs. These white men came to the agent and talked to him with open, childlike frankness. They were full of honest good will, their only desire was to help him out; and when he followed their advice he fell into a pit from which he could extricate himself only with the greatest difficulty. These men spent most of their time devising schemes to try on the agent, for their own benefit and the benefit of the chiefs to whom they had attached themselves. Ecoffey, the trader, knew all of the ins and outs of these matters, but he kept himself aloof from the intrigues, and probably was of little assistance to the puzzled Mr. Wham. Ecoffey was the man to whom Red Cloud had sent the secret message, asking him to be on the train which was to take the chiefs to Washington in the spring of 1870. He was now the agency trader, with his own buildings, goods, and men established inside his own stockade at Red Cloud Agency. He was a Swiss who had been educated at the University of Freiburg and who had been trading with the Sioux near Fort Laramie since 1854. If Red Cloud had a true friend among the whites it was Jules Ecoffey, and after the Red Cloud Agency was established these two strangely assorted gentlemen collaborated in various schemes, some of which resulted in a great deal of trouble for the Indian agents.

Although Mr. Wham maintained a friendly relationship with the Oglalas by giving in to them, he was fast losing his illusions and could no longer agree very heartily with the Eastern humanitarians who held that the Sioux were friendly and sensible people who would be well behaved if treated kindly. In January, 1872, Mr. Wham was quietly removed and another Episcopal church man, Dr. J. W. Daniels, was appointed to his place.

Dr. Daniels, like Mr. Wham, was a good sensible Christian man, a close friend of Bishop Whipple of the Episcopal church. His orders were to induce the Oglalas to remove to White River, and he came to the agency with the firm conviction that he could accomplish this task by explaining matters to the chiefs in a reasonable way. He quickly learned his error. When he arrived only the tamest of the Indians were at the agency, yet the moment he broached the subject of removal to White River he was met by a solid wall of opposition. Daniels talked to every chief that he could find, but not one of them would consent to a removal.

In early spring the wild bands began to drift back from the buffalo range, Red Dog and his Oyuhkpes coming among the first. This chief's son, a fine young warrior who was very popular, now died. Red Dog was broken-hearted over his loss, and Dr. Daniels was very kind to him, sending him messages of sympathy and presents, having the agency carpenter make a coffin, and giving the chief scarlet cloth to cover the box. Presently Red Dog came to the agent and told him with much feeling that he was his friend for life and would always support him. He agreed to remove to White River and to use his influence with the other chiefs and gain their consent. This incident was reported at length by the

Indian Office. It was the kind of Sunday School story the Indians' Friends loved, demonstrating as it did the truth of their view that the Sioux if dealt with in a Christian spirit could be easily led into the ways of peace and progress. It was a pretty story, but Red Dog soon went back to his old ways, and until the day of his death was rated by the church people as a wicked old heathen.

Aided by Red Dog, Daniels now set to work to win over the other chiefs. The warriors from the wilder bands gathered at the agency, yelling threats, circling wildly about kicking up the dust; but Red Dog was not the man to be intimidated by such antics. He stuck to the agent, provided him with a guard from his own band, and aided him in winning over the other chiefs. Liberal presents and promises were employed by Daniels in this campaign, and by April he seemed to have won. The chiefs now admitted that an agency in the fine country on White River would be much better than this location on the Platte, but they were afraid of the wild bands on Powder River and on the Republican Fork and would make no final decision until they heard from those camps. Red Dog now sent tobacco and a message to Powder River and received a reply favorable to the removal of the agency.

Then Red Cloud came in from the Republican Fork with his wild followers. Go to White River? Had he not said more than four times that he would have no whites on his land? This agency was on his ground, and he was now going to take it up and throw it to the other side of the Platte! Aided by the warriors from the Powder River bands, who were now at the agency in considerable force, he at once set about the execution of this threat, and to such good purpose that Agent Daniels was compelled to send a message in all haste to Fort Laramie, asking for troops.

From the moment they gained control of Indian affairs in 1865, one of the characteristics of the humanitarians and church people was the tendency to censor the news whenever it was not favorable to their cause. They now in 1872 hushed up the trouble at Red Cloud Agency as far as possible. From the official reports no one would suppose that there was any difficulty with the Oglalas during this spring and summer; yet Agent Daniels had to summon troops from Fort Laramie on two or three occasions to protect the lives of the whites at the agency. The uproar ended in an impasse. Neither Red Cloud nor the government really wanted war, and the question of moving the agency, either to the south side of the

Platte as Red Cloud demanded, or to White River as the officials insisted, was dropped. Red Cloud was then induced to repeat the performance of 1870 by going to Washington with a large delegation to talk things over with the Great Father. At Washington Red Cloud was talked into promising not to oppose the removal of the agency.

Having persuaded Red Cloud to go to an agency, the Indian Office was determined to do the same for Black Moon, No Neck, Sitting Bull, and the other leaders of the northern or Missouri River group of hostiles, and in this summer of 1872 a commission was sent to Fort Peck, Montana, to hold councils with the chiefs from the hostile camps and induce them to go to an agency. Agent Daniels was appointed to this commission, and while Red Cloud was on his way East, Daniels, accompanied by Red Dog, High Wolf, and a renowned young Oglala warrior named Wolf Ears, went up to Fort Peck. While the agent was away his clerks started a new removal campaign and soon had most of the chiefs at the agency won over. These men were mainly tame Sioux and could be talked into anything, if proper presents were offered to them. The clerks were on the point of removing to White River when Red Cloud came home from Washington and, forgetting the promises he had made, threw the agency into a fresh uproar. Little Big Man, "a wild little devil from up north," was at the agency during the summer with a large party of his comrades, and they joyously flocked to Red Cloud's support, turning the agency upside down. Crazy Horse with the rest of the Bad Faces was said to be hovering near the agency, and his warriors made some little raids along the Platte road. In excusing himself for breaking his promise not to oppose the removal to White River, Red Cloud gave the curious reason that Spotted Tail was being paid by the government for consenting to the removal of his agency to a better location and that he, Red Cloud, also wished to be paid before he would consent.[4] Red Cloud was now beginning to lose the perfect confidence of the Eastern humanitarians and church people. In 1870 he had been their darling, but by 1872 some leaders in high-thinking circles

4. Spotted Tail was imitating Red Cloud's policy of obtaining all he could from the government. He was permitted to choose the site for his own agency in 1870, and he put it at a point on White River where there was little wood and the water was bad. For the Indians' own comfort, the government now wished to move them a few miles to a better location, and Spotted Tail demanded and received a large bribe in presents before he would consent to move.

were beginning to express a doubt as to whether kindness and Christian forebearance were the only things required to bring this chieftain around to a reasonable state of mind.

Like Mr. Wham, Agent Daniels soon lost his illusions concerning the Oglalas. In the autumn of 1872 he reported that these Indians were divided into three groups. The first group was composed of a small peace party headed by Red Dog who stood by the agent through thick and thin and told the trouble-makers to their faces that they were fools. The lives of these men were constantly in danger. The second division comprised a large neutral party who wanted peace but were very conservative; they were suspicious, uneasy, opposed to any innovations, and would undoubtedly all flee to the hostile camps in case of trouble. These first two parties were made up of men over thirty-five years of age. The third group was composed of all the men under thirty-five; it was larger in numbers than the other two groups together, and included all the warriors. They had no respect for any of the agency chiefs, and regarded the chiefs in the hostile camps on Powder River as their true leaders. They spent their time at feasts and dances, and in recounting their exploits in war; they were ever ready to join in any trouble-making, and when any wild Sioux came in from the northern camps this group joined them in turning the agency upside down. Daniels reported 6,320 Sioux drawing rations at Red Cloud, though not all were there at any given time. Part of these were Wazhazhas, Miniconjous, and Sans Arcs; therefore it is not known how many Oglalas there were. From the moment the agency was established, groups of miscellaneous Sioux had flocked in; this mixing process went on year after year, and today there are whole districts at Pine Ridge inhabited by people calling themselves Oglalas but who are not Oglalas by blood. There were also at Red Cloud Agency in 1872, 1,342 Northern Cheyennes and 1,515 Northern Arapahoes. These numbers were the Indians' own estimates. They flatly refused to be counted and compelled the government to issue supplies on their own assertion as to the number of people. Daniels shrewdly remarked that if the Indians could be enrolled by families and all supplies issued direct to heads of families instead of to the chiefs of bands, it would result in breaking down the power of the chiefs. This method was used in later years, and it did break the power of the chiefs. But without leaders of their own blood the Oglalas have drifted like a hulk.

At the end of his report for 1872, Daniels stated that at every Sioux agency west of the Missouri conditions were the same as at Red Cloud, and that, in his judgment, if the government continued its attempt to control these wild people by gentle methods and to remove their savage prejudices by generous gifts "we shall be startled by a massacre and shall awake to find that their war spirit is not to be controlled by kindness alone." One wonders what the church people who nominated Daniels to be agent at Red Cloud thought when they read these words. Most of them looked upon the use of force in dealing with Indians as a horrid crime.

During the summer of 1872, the hostiles on Powder River attacked Colonel Baker's troops who were escorting the Northern Pacific survey party and compelled them to abandon their work. Before the troops blundered on them, the hostiles had collected in one big village to hold a Sun Dance, after which they planned to attack the Crows. This ancient pastime of attacking the Crows every summer was being religiously kept up by the hostile Sioux and their Cheyenne and Arapaho allies. This summer, in large force, they drove the Crows from the buffalo range toward their agency and then sent little war-parties to hover about that place. The whites at the agency were cooped up, helpless to oppose the hostiles, and the Crows began to ask disdainfully if the white people were afraid of the Sioux. Judging from the Commissioner of Indian Affairs' report for this year, the white officials certainly were afraid of the Sioux.[5]

During the summer of 1872, news of the handsome treatment the Sioux were getting at Red Cloud Agency spread to the camps on Powder River, and as winter came on bands of wild Sioux from that country came down to visit their relatives at the agency, to "taste white man's food," and to assist their agency friends in making trouble. They created such a hubbub that troops from Fort Laramie again had to be called in. At this time General John E. Smith, who had gone to Washington with Red Cloud in 1870, was in command at Fort Laramie. He evidently had been sent there with the idea that he would be less inclined to resort to brute

5. Information gathered by the Sioux commission at Fort Peck at this time indicated that No Neck, with four hundred lodges of hostiles, was on Powder River preparing to attack the Crows. Sitting Bull and Black Moon, each with about thirty lodges of personal followers, were away from the main camp. It would appear that Sitting Bull returned at the end of July and was with these Indians when they fought Colonel Baker.

force in dealing with the vagaries of the Sioux than some less experienced officer might be. The government was still determined to control the Indians by gentle methods. Where Red Coud was this winter is not quite clear. He may have been at the agency, but he was more than likely with the hunting camps on Republican Fork. Agent Daniels spent the winter trying to win the chiefs' consent to remove to White River. By the liberal issue of extra rations and promises of guns and ammunition for all who would promise to remove, he won over the agency bands, but they were afraid to give their consent openly as long as the wild Sioux from Powder River were present. The Cheyennes and Arapahoes were at the agency in large force this winter, but they took little part in the talk of removal. They were afraid of the Sioux, who treated them as interlopers who were permitted to come here and eat the Sioux rations on sufferance. Watching for his chance, Daniels waited until the wilder bands had gone to hunt buffalo, and then in August he packed up the agency and moved it to White River before the fickle chiefs could change their minds again.

The distance from the old agency to the new one was about seventy-five miles, the trail running through the Sand Hills, north across Snake Creek, the Niobrara, and to White River. D. J. McCann had the contract for moving the supplies, and his big freight wagons with their long teams of oxen did the work. On the last trip the wagons were loaded with Indians; perhaps poor people who did not have many horses. The site on White River had been selected by the Indians themselves, but Agent Daniels approved it, stating that no better location was to be found anywhere on the Sioux reservation. He reported that water and wood were abundant, that good farm land was to be found in the creek valleys, and that there were immense tracts of the finest bunch-grass pasturage on both sides of White River and between the buttes and pine ridges. This picture of the new home of the Oglalas was a trifle too rosy. True, the land was a fine one for Indians to camp in; but the men in charge of Indian affairs had promised to turn the Oglalas into self-supporting farmers in four years and were now in the fourth year of that term, and for agricultural purposes they could hardly have found a worse location than this one at the head of White River. The district was notoriously subject to severe drouths and plagues of grasshoppers, and the farm lands of which Dr. Daniels spoke were small in extent, poor in quality, and difficult to work.

However, the officials had at last succeeded in removing these Indians from the Platte, and at the moment that was considered a great feat. Dr. Daniels had been promoted and Dr. J. J. Saville, a physician from Denver, had been selected by the Episcopal church as his successor at Red Cloud. Saville arrived while the moving of the agency was in progress, and Daniels hastily turned everything over to him and left.

Red Cloud was away when the agency was moved. Perhaps he was again with the True Oglalas who had gone with the Kiyuksas and Spotted Tail's Brulés to hunt on Republican Fork. These Indians did not have a successful hunt. There were still considerable numbers of buffalo south of the Platte, but white hide hunters were killing them wholesale, ripping off the hides and leaving the great carcasses to rot on the ground. During this hunt the Oglalas fell afoul of some of the white hunters and Whistler (*Zoh-lah*), a very friendly Kiyuksa chief, and two other Oglalas were killed by the whites.

The Pawnees were also hunting south of the Platte this summer. In 1872 the Sioux had forced them to abandon their hunt and go home without any meat or skins. The Sioux had played their old trick, waiting until the Pawnees were scattered into little groups while hunting and then dashing from their hiding place in force. Now in 1873 the Sioux repeated this performance with terrible effect. The Pawnees had had a good hunt and were starting homeward with the meat and skins of about one thousand buffalo, when the Sioux discovered them. It was early in the morning; the Pawnee camp was on the march and part of the men had gone out hunting when a force of about a thousand mounted Sioux suddenly appeared and charged the camp, other parties of Sioux attacking the Pawnee hunters. The Pawnees, after a vain attempt to make a stand, fled, their enemies pursuing them for several miles. Over fifty Pawnees, mostly women and children, were killed, and about the same number were badly wounded. They lost about a hundred ponies, all their personal belongings, and the meat and skins from their hunt. Eleven women and children were carried off by the Sioux. It was a stunning blow to the Pawnees, and it at last opened the government's eyes to the fact that it owed some protection to this friendly tribe, many of whose men had been enrolled for years in the Pawnee Scouts, who did good service against the hostile Sioux and Cheyennes. The Indian Office stated that the Sioux would never again be permitted to hunt south of the Platte; yet the next year, 1874, the Sioux not only hunted there but the Indian Office established a special base of supplies for them on the South Platte and had a wagon-train hauling rations to their camp while they hunted. The friendly Pawnees might have waited until the end of Time before the Indian Office would have taken any such solicitous thought of their comfort.

The hostiles on Powder River were also making much trouble in the summer of 1873. The Bad Face Oglalas, led by Red Cloud's son-in-law, raided on the Sweetwater and Platte, while the main body of hostiles, up near the Yellowstone, made their usual attacks on the Crows and on the Northern Pacific survey parties and their escort of troops. Near Tongue River, on August 4, the Sioux set a trap for Custer and his small advance force, but did not succeed in drawing him into it. Custer then attacked them and drove them off. On the eighth, a great Indian village was seen near the mouth of the Rosebud, and Custer with the Seventh Cavalry pursued the Indians until the tenth, when they crossed the Yellowstone in skin boats near the mouth of the Bighorn. That night a large force of Sioux recrossed the Yellowstone, and at dawn attacked Custer again, but he drove them off after a stiff fight. The bluffs on the south side of the river were thronged with Sioux, watching the engagement. This expedition went as far as Fort Peck before turning homeward.

This same summer a party of one hundred and fifty citizens, led by a Colonel Brown, left the Montana settlements to explore the Powder River country for minerals. They ran into the hostiles on the Yellowstone below the mouth of the Bighorn, but continued their examination of the country, fighting the Indians off whenever they appeared. It seems shameful that our government should have acted so timidly in dealing with these Indians when small bodies of determined men could defy the Sioux with impunity.[6] Agent Daniels at this time was called on for a special report as to what opposition the Powder River hostiles were likely to make to the building of the Northern Pacific. He replied that these Indians would certainly attempt to prevent the construction of the line

6. H. H. Bancroft, *History of Montana,* gives an account of Colonel Brown's expedition. The government over-rated the Sioux in 1873 and under-rated them in the spring of 1876.

through their country, but that there was little likelihood that they could cause serious trouble, for they had not enough arms and ammunition for a real war. Daniels had talked to some of the hostile leaders at Red Cloud Agency in the winter. Among these leaders were Red Thunder, a chief, and four head-soldiers: Thin Soup (Sitting Bull's son-in-law) of the Hunkpapas, Hump Ribs (better known as Hump, son or nephew of old High-Back-Bone), a Miniconjou, Ashes, and Little Chief. These men told Daniels that they would oppose the building of the railroad, and that they wanted no whites in their country except a trader who must bring them arms and ammunition regularly. They regarded the agent at Red Cloud as a friend and expected him to help them, for like nearly all of the wild Sioux they seem to have believed that the whites near the Platte were one tribe and the whites near the Yellowstone another and different people, and they saw nothing unreasonable in asking the whites near the Platte to supply them with arms to be used in fighting the whites on the Yellowstone.

CHAPTER XII

THE NORTHERN INDIANS
1873-1874

URING the removal of Red Cloud Agency in August, 1873, Jules Ecoffey the trader had a "run-in" with the Indians. Ecoffey claimed in 1875 that the trouble was started by a half-gallon of whiskey which he kept in one of his wagons for his own use. Some Indians discovered the whiskey and the chiefs, some of whom did not like Ecoffey, ordered him to leave. They also informed the new agent, Dr. J. J. Saville, and he at once revoked the trader's license. As Ecoffey was leaving, three hundred warriors charged up and stopped him. They made a great uproar, threatening the trader, and then ordering him out of the country, but at the same time demanding that he return with new goods and give them three dollars in trade for beef hides. On his refusal, they drove him away.

This affair had important results in several directions. Red Cloud, who was Ecoffey's close friend, was not at the agency this summer, and the rival chiefs seem to have joined the new agent in a scheme to drive away the trader before Red Cloud could return and protect him. Saville naturally wished to have a trader of his own appointment who would be loyal to him, and he was probably only too pleased to remove Ecoffey, who was Red Cloud's ally; but the little doctor lived to regret his hasty action on this occasion. This incident turned Red Cloud against him, and Ecoffey soon afterwards went to Washington on business and while there offered the officials some affidavits concerning frauds in the beef issues at Red Cloud Agency, evidence which they could not very well refuse to take. Thus were sown the seeds of much trouble for Agent Saville.[1]

1. Ecoffey's testimony concerning this affair will be found in the report of the Red Cloud Investigation Committee, 1875.

Having revoked Ecoffey's license and put in a friend of his own named Deer as trader, Dr. Saville set about building an agency. The wagon-trains had piled the huge stock of supplies on the ground, covered them with tarpaulins, and then departed, leaving the agent and his large force of men to cut trees on the pine ridges, haul them in, and erect the buildings. The agency site was on the south bank of White River, near the mouth of White Clay Creek, about seventy-five miles north of the old agency and the same distance northeast of Fort Laramie.[2] This place was supposed to be in Dakota, inside the Sioux reservation, but the Indian Office's bad luck continued, and when a survey was presently made it was found that the agency was just south of the Dakota line, in Nebraska. The people of Nebraska at once sent up a loud wail, demanding that the Indians be moved again. To the south of the agency rose the high cliff-like bluffs bordering the valley of White River; beyond these lay a series of low, rough ridges, much broken, and with all the slopes dotted with pines. This was the Pine Ridge country, extending from the edge of the Black Hills eastward along the northern border of Nebraska. To the north and northeast of the agency lay the Big Badlands; and over toward the northwest, a short day's ride away, rose *Pa Sapa,* the hills which were the heart of the Sioux land, from which the Indians with such jealous care had excluded all white intruders. The "old white men" (the traders and squawmen), who were their friends and relatives and whom they trusted, had warned the Oglalas in 1871 that if they consented to an agency on White River the white men would be in *Pa Sapa* before they knew it. Some of the wiser Indians remembered this saying of their old white men; the rest, like the children they were, had forgotten it. They had been promised more food and guns and ammunition if they would go to White River; so here they were, camped by bands on pleasant small streams, with good grass and wood, watching their new white man, Dr. Saville, and his men as they worked at building the new agency.

The summer and fall passed quietly. There was little excitement. Once in five days the people all moved to the agency and

---

2. The site of this agency was marked by a monument on May 9, 1932. Some slight traces of the buildings still remain. The location is one and one-half miles east of Fort Robinson and the same distance west of the town of Crawford. Agent Saville in his report for December, 1873, states that the buildings stand on an elevation 125 feet above the river, and that water is obtained from a spring about a mile away.

pitched camp nearby to receive their rations. This was a pleasant time. The beef cattle were turned out of the corral, and the young men hunted and killed them like buffalo. The butchering was quickly accomplished, and then there was feasting. The small boys went through the camps carrying messages to come and eat, for now everyone could give feasts to their friends. Some of the rations were not good. The mess-pork was good for white men, who had queer tastes, but the Oglalas could not stomach it. They left it on the ground. Even the dogs, with plenty of beef pickings, would not eat it. The flour they did not know how to cook, so they left the big sacks on the ground or traded them to the squawmen for what they could get. The bacon was not of much use either, but some of the women knew how to render the grease out of it and mix it with flour into a mess which they cooked in a skillet and termed bread. Then too the tobacco was not good. It was in big plugs, black, sticky, and strong. Why did not their white man give them the kind of yellow leaf tobacco the old traders used to have? These matters the chiefs took up with Dr. Saville in long, long conferences which were sometimes friendly and sometimes acrimonious. Saville had orders to take a census, but every time he broached the subject there was an uproar. Like the Children of Israel, the Oglalas had a violent prejudice against being numbered. They had never been counted from the beginning of time, and why should they be counted now? Perhaps it was some kind of evil magic the whites were trying to work against them. The agent was severely reprimanded and ordered to drop the subject, but this little white medicine-man was a fool. He kept bringing up the hateful matter.

All during this summer and fall huge trains of wagons were bringing supplies to Red Cloud and to the Spotted Tail Agency farther down White River. The country north of the Platte was full of white men. The beef contractor had a vast herd on the Platte, and every few days his cowboys drove cattle up to the agency for the beef issue. Three roads to Red Cloud had already been opened and there was talk of a fourth.[3]

Winter came, and with it a swarm of wild Sioux from the camps on Powder River. By the Indian Office officials, these people

3. The road most used by freighters ran from Cheyenne, Wyoming, to Old Red Cloud Agency on the Platte, eighty miles, crossing at a good ford a few miles below the agency, then ran down the river some distance to avoid heavy sand ridges, turned northward and ran straight to the new agency; a total distance of about 155 miles. The Mail Road crossed at Nick Janis' place opposite the old agency

were termed nontreaty-Sioux, the name hostiles being taboo, as it seemed to hint that the Peace Policy was not altogether a success. At Red Cloud Agency these wild bands were called the Northern Indians. They had been a trouble to the agents and the more friendly agency chiefs from the first, but never until this year, 1873, when the agency was moved up within easy reach of the Powder River camps, had it been realized what pests these wild people would become.

Led by Lone Horn of the North, a Miniconjou, and many famous chiefs, in little groups and large bands, these people began to sift down from the north with the coming of cold weather. They slipped in quietly and put up their lodges near those of their agency relatives. Little Dr. Saville knew nothing of their coming until the Indians all moved to the agency stockade for the next issue of rations. Then he knew. The uproar was prodigious, for the northern bands had not come to the agency to beg but to make demands, and they were in a bad temper over the invasion of their country during the past summer by the troops escorting the Northern Pacific surveyors. As the Indians had refused to be counted, the government had been compelled to estimate the quantity of rations that would be required, and this estimate now proved far short of the real need at Red Cloud and Spotted Tail. There had not been very many Northern Indians at these agencies during the previous winter; but those who had come had evidently taken the good news of free food in plenty to the northern camps, and by January, 1874, several thousand wild Sioux had come in at Red Cloud and Spotted Tail. The Indians themselves estimated the arrivals at three hundred or more lodges, and when we consider the fact that other wild bands were flocking to the two big agencies on the Missouri, it becomes apparent that by 1873 most of the hostiles had adopted the practice of going to the agencies to winter, leaving only a few camps in the Powder River country.[4]

and ran straight north to White River. During the June rise in the Platte, the trains usually crossed at the Fort Laramie ferry and took the old traders' trail or Fort Pierre trail to the agency. This road was said to be a little longer than the others. A new road from Sidney Barracks on the railroad straight north to White River was coming into use in 1874.

4. It was charged that the agents at Red Cloud and Spotted Tail had listened to the devil this winter and had padded their rolls to make it appear that they were issuing supplies to many more Indians than they really had on hand. One inspector was told by Lone Horn that only 300 lodges of Northern Indians had come to the agencies—about 2,100 people. This inspector pointed out that the agents had increased the enrollment between summer and early winter by 12,000 Indians,

These hostiles had hardly settled down at Red Cloud when, with the aid of the wilder young men of the agency bands, they took control and ran things practically to suit themselves. It was the same at Spotted Tail; indeed, there is reason to believe that these wild Sioux shifted their camps back and forth, getting supplies at both agencies. The Eastern humanitarians, by their desire to keep the Sioux quiet by liberal feeding, had created a kind of Indian heaven on White River, but it was not quiet. These Indians smothered the unfortunate agents with demands, especially for beef and blankets in unlimited quantities, and when they did not get all they desired the warriors rushed to the stockades, armed and painted for war, and forced the whites to give them what they demanded. The Indian Office was continually requesting the agents to take a count of the Indians, and Dr. Saville at Red Cloud was unwise enough to attempt to make an enumeration in spite of the Indians' threats. He had hardly reached the first camp when warriors came streaming over the hills from every direction. He was surrounded in a moment by a throng of fierce Sioux, who turned his horse about and drove him like a dog back to the stockade. There with Little Big Man and Pretty Bear, two fierce young devils from Crazy Horse's wild camp, acting as judge advocates, they court-martialed Saville. In the midst of these riotous proceedings, Red Cloud and Little Wound, the two leading agency chiefs, came in with rifles in their hands and gave the warriors to understand that they were not to push matters to extremes. They probably saved the little doctor's life, for he was presently released after being warned by his captors that they would kill him if he displeased them again. They then set a dead-line about the agency, forbidding the whites to go beyond it on pain of death. No white man dared go far from the stockade even in the daytime unless accompanied by an escort of agency Indians, a few of whom were bold enough to take the agent's side. Pumpkin Seed, head-soldier of the Wazhazhas, offered to form an agency guard if his men were provided with breech-loaders. He said that these wild fellows

and he termed this proof of fraud. The agency chiefs, however, flatly denied Lone Horn's assertion; they said that a great many more Northern Indians had come in, and that other Sioux from the poverty-stricken bands on the Missouri were flocking to their "fat" agencies. They estimated the total visitors this winter at 8,000; and when we consider that a large part of these Sioux were joyously passing back and forth, drawing rations and blankets at both agencies, we can hardly blame the agents if they supposed that they had more Indians than were really present. That the situation was one which invited fraud is obvious.

from up north had a great deal of respect for a good gun in the hands of a man who evidently meant to use it.[5]

The trouble at Red Cloud this winter was started in October. Man-Afraid-of-His-Horse and some of the older men tried to support the agent; but Red Cloud, at the head of the agency warriors and backed up by all the Northern Indians, busied himself in stirring up strife. The agent reported that this chief openly said that when new grass appeared in the spring it would be the right time to start war. Red Cloud was furious because the agency had been moved to White River without his consent, and he was just as determined to drive all whites out of the country north of the Platte as he had been during the previous year. He interfered to save the agent when the Northern Indians were about to kill him because he did not wish the fighting to begin until spring.

The ugly spirit displayed by these Indians clearly demonstrated which way the Peace Policy was leading. Kindness and generosity had only bred a conviction among them that the whites feared them, and while the humanitarians and church people were dreaming of turning these people into gentle Christians, earning their living by cultivating the soil, the Sioux were preparing to go back to their old wild life and to rid themselves of the hated whites who had entered their country and were trying to alter their way of living.

Agent Saville had to take a delegation of Cheyennes and Arapahoes to Washington in November, 1873, and he must have told the Indian officials of the dangerous condition of affairs at Red Cloud, but these gentlemen still had their heads in the clouds and they took no action. When Saville returned to White River on December 15, he found conditions even worse than before. On Christmas Day he gave a great feast to the chiefs and told them again that the Great Father insisted that the Indians submit to being counted. Red Cloud, speaking for the Oglalas (he had been instructed by the council as to what he should say), replied that he would not have a count taken until the guns promised to them if they moved to White River had been given. He was applauded by the Indians. Red Dog, who had become a good Indian a year before according to Agent Daniels, backed Red Cloud, as did also

5. This account of events at Red Cloud is based on the agent's monthly reports, reprinted in the report of the Red Cloud Investigation Committee, and on the Hare Commission's report. I also have Indian accounts, some material from Major Jordan, and the Rowland manuscript.

High Wolf, another of Daniels' pets. The friendly chiefs, who had promised Saville their support at this council, sat in silence, not daring to say a word. At this time the Indian soldiers were bent on making more mischief and the chiefs were competing with one another in an effort to win popularity among the soldiers. Every beef issue was a wild riot, the Indians wrangling fiercely over the cattle that were given them. Between issues they quarreled continually over the day to be set for the next issue.

Saville thought that the Northern Indians were trying to goad the agency Oglalas into war, that Red Cloud was for war, but that a majority of the agency Indians silently opposed it. Lone Horn finally announced that he and his northern hostiles were disgusted with the agency Sioux and were planning to leave. Saville, in a last talk with this chief, explained the treaty of 1868 and offered him some presents if he would comply with the treaty terms. A Miniconjou soldier yelled a fierce warning, and Lone Horn refused the proffered presents. The Miniconjou soldiers then held a council and decided to send out war-parties to raid. Therefore, early in February one party of over one hundred men set out for the settlements along the Platte where they killed Lieutenant Robinson and Corporal Coleman of the Fourteenth Infantry who had strayed from the wagon-train while hauling fuel from Laramie Peak to Fort Laramie. On the Laramie Fork they killed a man named King and on the Niobrara a teamster named Gray. They also ran off a large quantity of stock.

Bill Rowland, who was married to a Cheyenne woman and was employed as Cheyenne interpreter at Red Cloud Agency, told a story years ago that apparently refers to the starting out of these war-parties in February. He said that at this time the stockade was not finished—there was no gate that could be closed. One day the men at the agency heard singing, and upon going out discovered a body of two hundred or three hundred mounted Sioux slowly advancing four abreast in a regular column, singing war-songs. The men were all armed and painted and had their ponies' tails tied up with eagle feathers, as in war. The whites ran back into the buildings and barred the dors; and they hardly had done this when the Sioux rode into the stockade, singing, yelling, and firing their guns. They rode around and around the buildings, whipping themselves into a wild fury until they seemed to lose all control of themselves. They shot out all the windows, narrowly missing some of the whites who did not dare fire a shot in return. The Indians finally rushed out of the stockade and away over the hills. This performance was typical of the kind of war-parade the Indians usually indulged in before setting out on a large war-party, and these warriors were probably the ones who made the raids on the Platte after leaving the agency.

After this incident, according to Rowland, Agent Saville ordered a heavy gate built and kept it closed most of the time. One dark night a warrior from Lone Horn's camp dragged some loose lumber to the stockade and leaning the boards up against the pickets managed to climb over and into the yard. There he began to halloo, with the intention of drawing Agent Saville to the door and killing him. But Saville was not sleeping in the little room back of the office that night, and it was his clerk, Frank Appleton, who opened the door at the Indian's halloo. Appleton was standing in the door with a lamp in his hand when the wild Sioux rushed forward and shot him dead with a pistol. The Indian then climbed back over the stockade and made his escape. The next day a wild crowd of Sioux was riding around the stockade and firing their guns; but the whites had appealed to some of the chiefs, and they had rushed a strong force of warriors into the stockade where they were now standing guard. The killing of Appleton had aroused the agency Indians to action; they now guarded the stockade day and night and served notice on the trouble-makers that they were ready to fight for their white man.

Rowland's story asserts that it was the killing of Appleton that convinced Agent Saville that the time had come to call for troops. Rowland volunteered to take the message to Fort Laramie, a task that few men would have cared to assume. The Indian camps dotted the country for miles around, small parties of warriors might be met anywhere, and they undoubtedly would kill any white man that they happened to encounter. Rowland picked a roan mare, a strong, fast animal, and slipped out of the stockade at midnight to start his dangerous ride. The first ten or fifteen miles he had to be very cautious, for the Indian camps were all about him and he might be discovered if he made the least noise. Three or four times he had to pass very near the camps, but he slipped by safely and having passed the most dangerous area he put the mare to a faster gait. Three times during the night he unsaddled the mare and permitted her to roll, to freshen her, then mounted and rode on. He was within twenty miles of the Platte when day dawned. He rode into the ravine of a dry creek, and here he saw in the frost gathered on the sand the fresh tracks of three ponies which had passed not fifteen minutes ahead of him. The sight of the pony tracks made Rowland very cautious. His mare was in no condition to run and if the Indians saw him they would certainly kill him. He went on very slowly, keeping a lookout in every direction; but he did not meet the Indians, and at last, crossing the Platte on the ice, he rode into Fort Laramie and tied his mare in front of the sutler's store. He went straight to the commandant's office and handed the dispatch to General Smith, who had conducted Red Cloud's delegation to Washington in 1870. The agent's dispatch had the date and hour written on it, the hour eleven P. M., and it was then a little after eight on the following morning. "You must be riding a good horse," said the general. "Are you tired?" "No, sir," said Rowland, "I ain't tired right now, but I allow I will be after while." Rowland asserted that the troops started for Red Cloud the following morning, but he told this story thirty years after the event and his recollection was at fault concerning the exact day the troops marched.

At this moment, February, 1874, the High Priests of the Indian Peace Policy—the Board of Indian Commissioners—were meeting in Washington. They had just voted the Peace Policy a great success when they were horrified by the news that the agents at Red Cloud and Spotted Tail had called for troops. They could not prevent the sending of troops, but they demanded that the agents' conduct should be investigated, and since the Episcopal church had nominated the agents a bishop of that church was sent, evidently in the full expectation that he would request the removal of the agents for daring to summon troops.

When General Smith marched from Fort Laramie, he did not take a small force of troops which the Sioux would be tempted to attack and overwhelm, but a strong column including six companies of cavalry, eight of infantry, and a large wagon-train of supplies. He was ready to fight, and men who did not know the Sioux very well expected a pitched battle with these Indians. Warned by their roving parties of warriors that troops were coming, the Sioux at the two agencies had two or three days in which to prepare, but all that they did was to break up into hostile factions, quarrel fiercely, and almost start fighting among themselves. Some were in favor of going to attack the troops, some for killing the whites at the agencies, burning the buildings and retiring to Powder River; but most of the agency Oglalas and Brulés seem to have advocated peace, and being pushed too far by the hostile factions they rallied to the agents' support. There were wild scenes at both agencies, but when the troops drew near the Northern Indians, who had caused so much trouble and had threatened war so fiercely, took down their lodges and suddenly fled northward into the sheltering badlands. With them went Red Cloud and a portion of the agency Indians.

Rowland states that he requested permission to go ahead of the troops to visit his family, when the column was within a few miles of Red Cloud Agency. Perhaps he hoped that the Indians did not know that he had gone for troops, and that if he were not seen with the soldiers his life in the future might prove a happier one. He had ridden but a short distance toward the agency when a Cheyenne relative of his named Fisher rode into sight and hailed him. Fisher told him that the Indians knew he was the man who had gone for the soldiers and that they were threatening to kill him. Fisher had been waiting in the hills to warn him. Rowland, being a wise man, rejoined the troops. Some time later he was nearly murdered by a Cheyenne named Crawls-in-the-Water who entered his house at night and fired a pistol point-blank in his face. Rowland knocked up the muzzle of the weapon and killed the Indian. He then fled to Camp Robinson for protection. Agent Saville, taking all his white employes, went out and rescued Rowland's wife and children, but the Indians burned Rowland's house and haystack.[6]

General Smith camped at the Red Cloud stockade, placed sentinels, and warned the chiefs that the guards had orders to shoot if any Indian tried to cross their beats. Criers rode through the Indian camps announcing the news: "Do not go near the white soldiers! The chief of the white soldiers has told his warriors to shoot if any Sioux comes too near! Do not go near the white soldiers!" Some of the young men rode up to the sentries and attempted to block their paths with their ponies so that the men could not walk their posts. The officers led the ponies away and warned the young men not to do that again. No one was anxious

6. Rowland told this story to Dr. George Bird Grinnell, who wrote it down and later very kindly gave me the manuscript. Rowland was U. S. marshal at Red Cloud Agency in 1875.

to fire the first shot and gradually things quieted down. The troops soon moved a mile and a half up White River and went into camp. They called their encampment Camp Robinson in honor of the officer of the Fourteenth Infantry who had been killed recently by the Sioux near Laramie Peak. It soon became apparent that they were to remain, and the building of a post was begun.

When the Sioux made their raids near the Platte early in February, there was great excitement in Wyoming and Nebraska. Fears of an Indian outbreak were freely expressed, and some of the newspapers started a story that the agents at Red Cloud and Spotted Tail were defrauding the Indians of their rations, that the Sioux were starving and were compelled to raid the ranches to obtain food. This was at the moment when the Indians had taken control of the agencies, were holding the agents as prisoners inside their stockades, and were forcing them by threats to hand out rations and blankets in unlimited quantities. The Indian Office thought it strange that the agents had called for troops, and at about the same time the troops started, Bishop Hare and three other men were asked to go to the agencies and report on conditions. The agents had been nominated by the Episcopal church, which was to this extent responsible for their actions, and for this reason Bishop Hare was asked to head the commission. Councils were held with the chiefs at both Red Cloud and Spotted Tail, and the Indians took advantage of the occasion to make a fresh display of war spirit. Bishop Hare stated in later years that at this time his life was more in danger than at any time during his long experience with the Sioux. Guarded by a small troop of cavalry, the commission was surrounded by thousands of armed warriors who were yelling and shooting their guns in the air, evidently waiting eagerly for the signal to kill the whites. Although the chiefs were angry and threatening, they had enough sense not to give the signal.

The Hare commission exonerated the two agents from all blame and gave a fair account of the uproar created by the northern Sioux at the agencies in December, January, and February. They approved the sending of troops, for which approval Bishop Hare was bitterly attacked by the sentimental Indians' Friends in whose view troops were mere butchers whose use against the Indians was never justifiable. Bishop Hare was a man of peace, but what he saw and heard at the agencies utterly convinced him that the presence of soldiers was the only means by which any kind of order could be maintained. Without the backing of the military the agents would soon become the slaves of their Indians, and the agencies would prove to be the breeding places of a fresh Indian war.

The government had established the Red Cloud Agency with the idea that it would attract Sioux from the hostile camps, who would come in for rations and would soon settle down at the agency, thus removing little by little the danger of a new war in the Powder River country. The Hare commission found that the hostiles certainly were being drawn to Red Cloud and Spotted Tail in thousands; but far from settling down, these Northern Indians were stirring up the agency Sioux and rapidly creating a condition which threatened serious trouble, not on distant Powder River but in the very edge of the Nebraska and Wyoming settlements. Bishop Hare and his companions therefore suggested that a new agency for the wild Sioux be established north of the Black Hills or elsewhere in their own country, and that an attempt be made to induce some of their chiefs to go to Washington, where a better understanding with them might be reached. This proposal was approved, and the Hare commission was requested to undertake the work of establishing the new agency and to bring a delegation of the northern chiefs to the East.

The government had paid heavily for the Peace Policy which had been thrust upon it by the groups of humanitarians and church people. In pursuing this policy it had spent a vast amount of money.[7] It had permitted the peace people to dictate the terms of the shameful treaty of 1868, and when all except the most abjectly peaceful of the Sioux had refused to sign this treaty in which they were offered everything, the government had sent men to coax them and to offer bribes of presents, guns and ammunition, in order to induce them to sign. The government had endured the vagaries of Red Cloud and the other chiefs, and had given in to the outrageous demands of the Sioux at all the new agencies. Now, in the spring of 1874, it seemed that something good might come of all this, for if the hostiles could be induced to come to an agency near the Black Hills they might gradually settle down, and thus another war on Powder River might be averted. But at the very time when the Hare com-

7. The cost of feeding and clothing the Sioux was: 1868, $142,490; 1869 (first year under the treaty of 1868), $485,784; 1870, $1,608,600; deficiency bill, 1870, $120,000; 1871, $2,024,800; 1872, $1,911,800; 1873, $1,900,000; deficiency bill, 1873, $350,000. The estimate of rations alone for Red Cloud, fiscal year 1875-1876, was $726,522.25.

mission was writing its report, up on the Missouri River in Dakota fresh reports of gold in the Black Hills were being eagerly discussed; and when Bishop Hare returned to his home in Yankton, he learned that Custer was to lead an expedition to explore the Hills and that parties of prospectors were being organized at various towns on the Missouri with the openly avowed intention of following in the wake of Custer's column and invading the Hills in search of gold.

On June 9, Bishop Hare wrote to President Grant reminding him that the report of the Hare commission had been approved and that the government had decided to make a special effort during the summer of 1874 to conciliate the northern Sioux and draw them to a new agency. He informed the president that the Western newspapers were filled with articles "inciting the public" to form parties to enter the Hills with Custer, and stated that in his opinion if the Custer expedition were not stopped the Sioux country would be invaded by a swarm of adventurers in defiance of the government's solemnly pledged word to the Indians. It would then be useless to attempt to conciliate the northern Sioux, and war would certainly result. A few days before he wrote this letter, Hare had been in conference with President Grant at Washington, and at this interview the plans for drawing the northern Sioux to an agency had been approved by Grant. On hearing of the plan for the Custer expedition, Hare wrote first to the Secretary of the Interior, but that official either could not or would not stop the Black Hill expedition. He "invited" the bishop to write to Grant and give him his views. This incident at any rate shows that the government was warned in time of the certain results to be expected if Custer went to the Hills. The fact that this expedition was not stopped proves that very strong influences were back of the project, influences which were willing to risk a Sioux war in carrying out their program. There can be no question whatever that the sending of this expedition was a violation of the treaty of 1868, and after Hare's protest to the Secretary of the Interior and then to President Grant himself, how can we doubt that this violation of the treaty was deliberately planned and executed. The truth seems to be that both Congress and the public were tired of the policy of giving in to the Sioux, of constantly buying peace and never getting it, and that they were no longer ready to hasten to the aid of the humanitarians whenever they raised a cry that the Peace Policy was in danger.

Men in the West and certain eastern groups, such as the promoters of the Northern Pacific Railroad, had patiently waited for this change, and they were not slow in bringing pressure on Congress and the officials at Washington to induce them to let down the bars.

The Custer expedition was advertised as a purely military undertaking with the object of exploring routes and locating sites for future posts. That work had been done by Captain W. F. Raynolds in 1859 and 1860, and a reading of the Raynolds and Custer reports will convince anyone that from a military standpoint the Raynolds report was far more useful than Custer's. Minerals, timber, and agricultural possibilities are the matters most emphasized in Custer's report, and this may indicate what influences were at work to induce the government to forget its solemn treaty obligations.

Custer marched from Fort Lincoln, near Bismark, North Dakota, with the Seventh Cavalry, two companies of infantry, some Gatling guns and artillery, sixty Indian scouts, and a staff of scientists and newspaper men. He had 1,200 men in all and a train of 110 wagons. A party of gold hunters was permitted to accompany this column. He was back at Fort Lincoln in sixty days, but before his return he sent long dispatches from the Hills, in which he spoke enthusiastically of the riches of this region. The newspaper men also sent messages. The public was informed that in the Hills gold was to be found "from the grass roots down."

The western papers featured these reports, and parties of gold hunters began to organize quite openly for an invasion of the Sioux country. The military stopped one party which was setting out from Montana, but another group from Sioux City reached the Hills and started prospecting. Before winter hardened the ground they had found enough gold to encourage them to remain and winter on French Creek near Harney Peak. The military later made an attempt to remove these trespassers from the Sioux lands, but they were still in the Hills when new parties began to arrive in the spring of 1875. The Sioux, especially those at Red Cloud who were nearest the Hills, were furious at this invasion. They called Custer "the Chief of all the Thieves" and his trail to the Hills "the Thieves' Trail." They threatened to attack the whites if they were not kept out of their country. In November, 1874, the Commissioner of Indian Affairs placidly reported that the exaggerated accounts brought back by the Custer expedition had now been corrected by more reliable information which showed that there was no gold in paying quantities in the Hills and that the region was valueless for agricultural purposes. He expressed the opinion that if the military and the Indians themselves could not turn back the gold hunters, these people would find little gold and would soon leave the country. This complacent ostrich was soon to have his head jerked out of the sand with considerable violence.

After the arrival of the troops and the stampede of the wild Sioux into the badlands north of White River in March, 1874, Red Cloud Agency was quiet for a time. The troops moved to a location a mile and one-half up White River and began building a post. The agency buildings were also finished. They completed a log stockade ten feet high, enclosing a space two hundred by four hundred feet. Inside this stockade was a warehouse thirty by one hundred feet with an "L" thirty by sixty feet; a barn, thirty by one hundred feet; three offices, sixteen by sixteen feet; four rooms for employes, sixteen by sixteen feet, and the agent's home, twenty-five by thirty feet, two stories high. Deer, the trader, had his own stockade and buildings near the agency, and a steam sawmill was set up on White River nearby. This mill had first been placed in the timber ten miles away, but had to be moved to the agency to prevent the wild Indians from destroying it.

The whites were closing in on the Oglalas in 1874. The troops were still at Red Cloud Agency. They were building a post and preparing to remain. Custer was in the Black Hills to the north with over a thousand men. A commission was coming to purchase the hunting rights, so that the Sioux could no longer claim the right to go south of the Platte or even into the country between the Platte and the agency. The northern line of Nebraska was being run this summer, and when the surveyors found that both the Red Cloud and the Spotted Tail agencies were south of the line, an agitation was started in Nebraska and the legislature demanded that the agencies be removed beyond the borders of the state. The Big Badlands north of the agencies were considered good enough for the Sioux. No one proposed giving them the Black Hills for a permanent home. One of the innumerable commissions which the government was sending out had the brilliant idea of solving the problem by removing the whole Sioux nation to Indian Territory, but when they proposed this to the Red Cloud Indians they were met with a flat refusal. It was finally decided to permit the Indians to remain at their present agencies for the time being. The chiefs at Red Cloud had their own solution of this boundary line question. They solemnly proposed to the commission to dig up the surveyors' posts, load them on wagons and set them down in the middle of the Platte River. That was where they wanted the Nebraska boundary. They did ·not want any white men to come north of the Platte.

The four years during which the humanitarians had promised to train the Sioux and turn them into self-supporting farmers had expired in 1873. In May, 1874, the Oglalas held a grand council and after endless wrangling decided to protect anyone who wanted to farm. Up to this time the young warriors had threatened to maim or murder any Oglala who dared even to pick up an agricultural tool. Agent Saville coaxed about twenty-five men into enlisting as farmers. They bravely volunteered to let their wives try it. The agency farmer, who had so long drawn his pay in idleness, now had his white laborers build a small dam in White River, dig an irrigation ditch, and plow a few acres. The Indian women planted their little gardens and went through the process which was to become so familiar to them in later years. They cared for their little patches, watched them eagerly as the young plants grew, and then in midsummer saw all their hopes swept away by drought and grasshoppers.

The wild Sioux from the northern camps arrived at the agency earlier than usual in 1874. They began arriving in September, and by October were there in full force. They were in the usual bad humor and started making trouble at once. Custer's invasion of *Pa Sapa* still rankled, and there was talk of going with a war-party after the white miners who were still in the Hills. The presence of troops near the agency acted as a restraint on the wilder Indians and no serious trouble seemed likely, but Saville, by an act which seemed quite harmless at the time, threw all the Indians into a wild outburst of fury.

In October, he decided to put up a flagpole inside the agency stockade. Whether he merely wished to fly the United States flag over the agency or had arranged with the officers at Camp Robinson to use the flag to signal for troops in case of need, we do not know. The testimony taken in 1875 does not agree as to his object. The fort was within sight of the agency, and it would have been easy enough to use the flag for signaling. On October 22, the agent had his men cut a tall pine in the hills, trim it, and haul it in. The Indians saw the pole lying in the stockade and asked about it. They were told that the agent was going to put up a flag. The chiefs were promptly informed and came to the agency to council with Saville. They said they did not want a flag at their agency; it was their place and they did not want a flag or anything else that soldiers had. Saville did not take their objections very seriously, and after the council set his men to work finishing the flagpole.

The next day, October 23, a large number of wild Sioux came to the agency. They went inside the stockade and sat on the ground, sullenly watching the agent's men at work. Someone noticed that these warriors were armed and painted. Saville was called from the office but had hardly stepped through the doorway when the warriors leaped up and rushed with furious yells at the flagpole, which still lay on the ground. With tomahawks and axes they began cutting the pole to pieces. Saville shouted at them to halt, but they paid no heed. He ran back to the office where Red Cloud and Red Dog were sitting and appealed to them. They either were afraid to interfere or did not choose to do so. Saville now lost his head and excitedly ordered one of the employes to ride to the fort for assistance. The man walked out of the stockade, got a horse, and rode for the fort. Somehow the warriors found out that the agent had sent for the soldiers, and they left the stockade with a rush, jumped on their ponies, and started for their camps which were dotted over the country for miles around.

At the fort, Lieutenant Emmet Crawford was ordered to proceed to the agency at once. He was given only twenty-six men. As he marched down White River valley he could see a mass of Indians gathered around the Red Cloud stockade, while from every direction bands and little parties of warriors were coming over the hills right lively. The moment the Indians sighted the troops they rode towards them. Firing their guns and yelling their war-cries, they rushed up to the soldiers, swerved aside, and began circling. Crawford and his men continued to advance, with several hundred Sioux wildly circling around them in an immense cloud of dust and powder smoke. Some young warriors began riding in close, forcing their maddened ponies to collide with the troopers' horses, hoping thus to precipitate a fight. One shot from the troops was all that was needed, and it seemed that the shot would not be long in coming, when a fresh mass of Sioux came pouring over the hills. They rushed straight toward the troops, broke through the circle of warriors, turned, and began beating back the Indians with their war-clubs and quirts. It was Young-Man-Afraid-of-His-Horse, the head-soldier of the Oglalas, and young Sitting Bull, the nephew of Little Wound, with a picked body of agency warriors. They formed a protective wall around the soldiers and forced a way through the swarm of warriors to the stockade; but the troops had hardly gone inside when the warriors, with bundles of hay and matches, rushed forward to set the agency on fire. The Oglala warriors forced them back again, and presently Old-Man-Afraid-of-His-Horse and Red Dog came out and harangued the crowd, finally inducing most of the warriors to withdraw. Red Cloud took no part in quieting the Indians. The military bitterly blamed Agent Saville for leading Crawford and his men into such a situation. In his note to the commandant, Seville had asked for one troop of cavalry and had not said a word to suggest that serious trouble might be brewing.[8]

It was the wild Northern Indians who had cut the flagpole and who had later made the attempt to stop Lieutenant Crawford's march. The agency Indians, amidst scenes of the wildest excitement and anger, now told the northerners that they would not tolerate any further trouble making at their agency. The wild Sioux were very perturbed at this sudden desertion of the agency bands to the side of the whites. All that night they were packing up their possessions, taking down their lodges, and tracking off northward into the badlands. Some of them joined their relatives in the agency camps. By morning the northern camps had disappeared.

This affair of the flagstaff upset the Sioux dreadfully and the agent upset them still more by telling them that, on orders from Washington, their annuities were to be withheld until they submitted to being counted. The Oglalas counciled for an entire week, and then at ten o'clock at night on November 4, Red Cloud sent for the agent and in the presence of all the chiefs, scolded him

8. The account of this affair printed in J. G. Neihardt's *Black Elk Speaks* is a typical illustration of the kind of memories many Sioux have. Black Elk was present during the trouble. He says some little boys cut the flagpole and a large force of troops came and were about to attack the Sioux, who were hopelessly outnumbered, when Red Cloud made a speech in which he said that grown men did not fight over pranks played by little boys, and this shamed the officers into withdrawing the troops. The "little boys" were the fiercest of the northern warriors; the numerous troops were twenty-six cavalrymen. Red Cloud made no speech and did not try to stop the trouble.

severely for insisting on counting the people. He said this would not be permitted, and he threatened trouble if the agent continued to attempt a count. Saville wrote to the commandant at Camp Robinson asking how many troops were available and stating that he expected trouble with the Sioux. The commandant, who had about 145 men, withheld his answer. But now Sword, Red Cloud's nephew, and Young-Man-Afraid-of-His-Horse called a council of the Oglala soldiers; they sent for an interpreter and instructed him to tell the agent that part of the Oglalas had decided to move in close to the agency and be counted. Saville was jubilant. The movement once started, one band after another gave in and came to the agency to be counted. The wild northern people who were mixed in among the agency Indians fled suddenly across White River to hide in the badlands, as if being counted was a dreadful matter, like getting cholera or smallpox. The counting was done by the interpreters, agency clerks, and squawmen who went from lodge to lodge and counted every member of each family. The Indian Office, after struggling for two years in an effort to compel these Indians to accept a count, found that it had been taken in again. It had suspected all along that the Indians' own estimate of their number (around 6,500), was grossly exaggerated; but by actual count it was found that there were 9,339 Sioux at Red Cloud, to which number eight hundred to nine hundred Kiyuksa Oglalas, who were hunting south of the Platte, had to be added, and 1,202 Cheyennes, and 1,092 Arapahoes. On November 10, the Indians received their blankets, cloth, kettles, knives, and other annuities and went happily back to their old camp grounds, while the agent sat down to write the bad news of the counting to the Indian Office.

Red Cloud was having his troubles. The Oglalas were becoming accustomed to agency life and were steadily losing the old wild spirit which he was anxious to preserve. They still dearly loved a quarrel, with plenty of riding around and yelling and kicking up of dust; but when big trouble loomed ahead they shied and refused to face it. For a moment after the flagstaff affair the people had followed his leadership, but finding that he was leading them toward trouble they quickly deserted him. It had been the same in the affair of the counting; even his own band had refused to follow his lead in that matter.

But Red Cloud was determined to keep up his opposition; and now, with almost devilish ingenuity, he hit upon a scheme.

If the Oglalas would not help him in his struggle against the agent, he would get the white people to help him. So he took his way to Camp Robinson to open a new campaign. His friends, the chiefs of the white soldiers (he said), knew what a bad man this agent was. They had seen how badly he had acted in that foolishness about the flagpole. There had nearly been a war that day. He insisted earnestly that the agent was stealing from the Oglalas—he and his friends were stealing every day. The rations were small and very poor. The blankets, the cattle, and everything else were small and of a bad quality. He, Red Cloud, wished to go to Washington to tell his Great Father what a bad man he had for an agent, but that little rat of an agent would not let him go. Would his friends the chiefs of the white soldiers please telegraph and tell his Great Father that Red Cloud was anxious to see him and talk of these things?

The officers at the post refused to telegraph. All this matter was outside their duty and they would not meddle with it. But their sympathies were with Red Cloud. They had suspected for a long time that all was not as it should be at the agency. They knew that Saville had relatives on the payroll and had given contracts to others. They knew that the rations were of poor quality. One of the officers had inspected some shelled corn, which was a part of the rations to be cooked and eaten by the Indians, and he told the other officers that the corn was so bad that the army would refuse to accept it for the horses. There were many other things at the agency that had a peculiar appearance, and there was the flagstaff affair also, which had turned all the officers at the post against Saville. Their view was that his hasty and rather foolish conduct had almost caused the massacre of Lieutenant Crawford's little command and they felt bitterly about it.

Inducing Red Dog and some other chiefs to join him, Red Cloud continued the practice of visiting at the post. The agent, hearing of these frequent conferences with the military, came to his own conclusions, and in one of his reports to the Indian Office complained that the military were interfering with the affairs of the agency. The officers loved him none the better after that.

By chance there came within Red Cloud's reach a champion who was to prove of more value to him than all the officers at Camp Robinson could have been if they had been willing to help him. This was Professor O. C. Marsh of Yale. Learning that the fossil bones of extinct monsters had been seen in the badlands north of Red Cloud Agency, Marsh came out during the fall and organized a party to go into the badlands. At Fort Laramie he was given a company of infantry as an escort, and several officers obtained leave to accompany his expedition. The flagstaff affair had occurred just prior to Marsh's arrival from the East, and at both Cheyenne and Fort Laramie he had been warned that it was a very bad time to go among the Sioux. There was much talk of an uprising, and fears were expressed for the little garrision near Red Cloud. The professor, however, was determined to go to the fossil beds. To the frontiersmen he was a puzzle. They called him "the bone sharp." To the Indians he was a mystery. They were rather in awe of him and also very suspicious of his intentions.

At Red Cloud he found over 12,000 Indians, most of them in a very bad humor over the recent flagstaff affair and the agent's attempt to force them to be counted. (Marsh arrived November 4 —the very day the chiefs decided to refuse to be counted.) There were about 3,000 wild Miniconjous, Sans Arcs, and Hunkpapas camped north of White River. These people were quarreling with the agency chiefs, who had prevented their killing Lieutenant Crawford's party on October 23. The Cheyennes were also in a very savage humor, for their rations had been ordered stopped until they consented to remove to Indian Territory. The Arapahoes had recently been whipped by Captain A. E. Bates on the head of Powder River and were sulking in their camp near the agency.

Professor Marsh's party went into camp near the agency, and a council was held with the chiefs to obtain permission to cross White River and go into the badlands. The council had just started when White Tail, a chief, jumped up and began a furious harangue in which he recounted all of the evil deeds of the whites during the past hundred years, concluding by accusing Professor Marsh of being a gold thief whose real intention was to slip quietly into the Black Hills. The chiefs in the end agreed to let the party go into the badlands, if they would take Sitting Bull and a party of his Indian soldiers as an escort. To this Marsh assented, also agreeing to pay the escort; but the next day the Indians did nothing, and the following day Marsh moved his party to the agency to find out when his Indian escort would be ready. At sight of the moving wagons and the company of infantry, the Indian camps began to hum; mounted warriors came streaming over the hills, and by the time the whites had reached the agency they were surrounded by a great force of angry Sioux, all armed with breech-loaders and Colt revolvers. Sitting Bull came up and said that his warriors had refused to go with the party, as they feared the Northern Indians across White River. This was plainly a fib. Red Cloud said that all the Indians believed that Marsh was going after gold, and the mass of warriors yelled their approval of this statement. Pretty Crow, a noted leader, began to shout that these gold thieves must be stopped, and the women and children present started to run. A bad sign. Some Indians cocked their rifles and pointed them at the infantry; they edged their ponies closer, forming a mass in front and rear of the whites and crowding them. Runners were sent to the camps for more warriors. The agent was badly rattled and sent an angry message to Marsh that he had better get his damned infantry up to the fort before hell broke loose. There seemed nothing else to do, and the little column started up White River. They were followed all the way to Camp Robinson by a swarm of jeering Sioux, who crowded in on them from every side with the usual display of threats and insulting gestures.

After this session at the agency everyone urged the professor to give up his expedition, but he would not. Deer, the agency trader, then suggested a feast for all the chiefs and headmen. A total of fifty hungry guests at an affair which would cost a great amount of money. The professor wanted the fossils at any price and consented to the plan; so the feast was held, and the chiefs, full of meat, rice, and dried apples, again agreed to provide Marsh with an Indian escort. Red Cloud's nephew, Sword, was appointed to lead the party, but Marsh was warned that great care must be taken to avoid the Miniconjous across White River, who were bad people indeed and would kill all the white men. The next day Marsh sent word to his Indian guard that he was ready and was informed that they had changed their minds about going. Even the white interpreter backed out, alleging fear of the Miniconjous and Hunkpapas.

The professor then lost his temper, made a night march, passed through the Indian camps without being discovered (a classic example of the supposedly always alert Indians' sleeping abilities), and proceeded to enter the badlands. He found a rich deposit of fossils and set his men to work. Indians were constantly seen and many of them visited the camp to watch what the white men were doing. Sword and Spider, Red Cloud's brother, came to inform the camp that the Miniconjous had sent their women and children to the Black Hills and were preparing to attack the white men. The following day Marsh packed up his fossils and started for the agency. There he was told that the day after he left the badlands the Miniconjous sent out a large war-party to attack his camp, but finding the whites gone they did not attempt to follow them.

And what has all this to do with Oglala history? A great deal. Professor Marsh came back to the agency in a very good humor. He had two tons of fossil bones packed away in his wagons, and many of them were bones of extinct mammals hitherto unknown to science. He had forgiven the Sioux for all the little tricks they had played on him, and when Red Cloud came to his tent and complained of the treatment his people were receiving the professor listened sympathetically. The Sioux were being starved; the small rations which they did receive were very bad; the agent was a bad man, who robbed the Indians with one hand and the Great Father with the other. The professor asked questions, and Red Cloud's answers were frank and full. This chief seemed to be telling the truth and the professor was shocked and angry at what he heard. He decided that something must be done, but that he must have real evidence before he could act. He asked for samples of the rations, and when the interpreter had explained to Red Cloud what samples were the chief arose and left the tent.

And here is an unsolved mystery. Who was it that took a sample of the none-too-good Indian flour and added to it a few handfuls of the gritty White River clay dust? Who picked over several pounds of Indian coffee and carefully selected all the bad berries as a fair sample? Who unearthed that ancient and moldy specimen of long-plug tobacco, and who picked up the piece of mess pork which had once been sweet but after being thrown away by the Indians, who did not like mess pork, had lain on the ground until it was no longer sweet? No one will ever know. It looks like a white man's work, and perhaps one would not be far from the truth in pointing to Red Cloud's pet interpreter as the artist who designed this pleasing little joke. Red Cloud, when cornered by the investigation committee in 1875, rather meanly tried to blame it on Red Dog.

Whoever chose the samples, it was Red Cloud who brought them into Professor Marsh's tent. The professor was much impressed, especially by the mess pork. He longed to take that mess pork to Washington and hold it under the august nose of President Grant; but the mess pork was really not in a condition to bear transportation. Marsh asked about the beef and Red Cloud took him out and pointed to a small bunch of lame and scrawny Texas cattle. He forgot to tell the professor that these scrubs were the rejects from a recent beef issue, animals refused by the agent and turned back to the beef contractor as unfit for issue.

Professor Marsh carefully preserved his samples during the winter and in the spring of 1875 girded himself for battle and set out for Washington, determined to force an investigation of Agent Saville's régime at Red Cloud. He might have saved himself a great deal of careful planning, for no sooner had he arrived at the capital and displayed the samples than the Indians' Friends flew to his aid. They were ready to believe anything against any Indian agent. The New York *Tribune* promptly brought its big guns into action, and the crusaders of the Board of Indian Commissioners, who had regarded Red Cloud as their own ewe lamb since 1870, demanded an investigation. Red Cloud arrived in town shortly afterward, having been summoned for a conference on the Black Hills, and the professor appealed to him for corroboration of his charges against the agent. This chief, with an air of childlike innocence, denied that he had given Professor Marsh any samples or that he had complained to him about Agent Saville. The officials now gently suggested to Marsh that he had been tricked by this Child of Nature, but the professor preferred to believe that Saville had forced the chief to change his story. In the end he had his way and an investigation was ordered. The work of this commission at Red Cloud Agency in July and August, 1875, will be considered later.

The winter of 1874-1875 was a very severe one in the northern plains, and the Indians suffered much from both cold and hunger. The great storms in January and February prevented travel, supply trains were blocked by snow, and the beef contractor was much delayed in making deliveries at Red Cloud. His cowboys had to drive the herds up to the agency on the agent's demand. They were caught in storms, the herds were scattered, and some of the men were badly frozen. Part of the Indians were camped many miles from the agency and could not come in for supplies during the worst weather, and living from hand to mouth as they did, they came very near to starvation. Many of those nearer the agency were hungry part of the time; and they flocked to Camp Robinson, begging for food and complaining of the agent.[9]

Late in the fall, part of the Oglalas and Brulés had gone hunting on the Republican. The hunting rights had been sold, but all of the Indians had stipulated that they be permitted to make one more hunt, and despite warnings that the herds south of the Platte were nearing extinction, the Brulés from Spotted Tail and the Ki yuksas and some Cheyennes from Red Cloud started on the hunt. There were several thousand people in this camp and by the time they had traveled as far as the Platte they were very hungry and took some cattle from along the river. There was no serious trouble, however, and they spent the winter quietly on the Republican. One hundred buffalo were all that this great camp of Indians killed during the entire winter, and they came back to the agencies in the spring with the sad realization that they had been on their last buffalo hunt.

9. Before they came to the agency the Oglalas often suffered from hunger in winter. Much of the suffering at Red Cloud was due to the custom of feasting, rations issued to last five days often being consumed in two days. These years from 1871 to 1878 were the "fat" years at this agency, and the Indians were much better off than they were in later years when rations were systematically cut and the people suffered from a chronic condition of semi-starvation.

CHAPTER XIII

PA SAPA IS STOLEN
1875

I N 1865, when their country was being invaded by four columns of troops, the Sioux chiefs did not seem to realize that there was a war. They made no attempt to unite their forces or to form a plan of common action, and each group remained where it was, engaging in its ordinary activities, until the troops actually came in contact with it. The Indians then fought the troops off, and as soon as they were gone returned to their usual mode of life. In 1874, when the whites invaded the Black Hills, these chiefs exhibited the same strange apathy and inability to meet a crisis by forming a plan and acting in unity. Red Cloud was engaged in a squabble with his agent when Custer invaded the Black Hills, which were within sight of Red Cloud Agency. The Sioux were greatly excited by Custer's march and talked of attacking him, but took no action. As autumn advanced, news was received that other parties of whites had gone to the Hills; the wild Northern Indians came to Red Cloud, and they and the agency bands held councils, raged against the whites, and took no action. Red Cloud went on squabbling with his agent. Less than fifty miles away down the White River, Spotted Tail and his Brulés were just as excited and angry as Red Cloud's people over the threatened loss of *Pa Sapa,* and they held the usual councils and made the usual threats, but took no action. The Sioux at the Missouri River agencies behaved in exactly the same manner. These Indians were grieved, anxious, and angry, but they did not know what to do to save their beloved Hills.

All through 1874, Red Cloud tried to obtain permission to go to Washington, his sole object being to tell the Great Father what a bad man he had for an agent. In the spring of 1875, he was asked to come with a number of his chiefs, the agent to be in charge of the party. By this time the whites were coming into the Black Hills in ever increasing numbers and the Sioux were growing more agitated every day, yet Red Cloud and the other chiefs had only one thought—the agent, whether to throw him away or keep him. They quarreled before they left the agency, they quarreled all the way to Washington, and they reached the city "apart" as they expressed it, divided into two opposing factions.

But in the Great Father's village they found a situation that blew this petty subject completely out of their minds. Red Cloud evidently thought that he was being brought East simply to give his views on Agent Saville, but on reaching the capital he found Spotted Tail and his chiefs there, and also delegations from each of the Missouri River agencies. The chiefs, on discovering the presence of all the other Sioux leaders, dropped their squabbling and were still. What was this? Why had they all been brought here? Something big must be about to happen. Presently they were all taken to see the Great Father who told them bluntly that they had been brought to Washington to decide the question of the Black Hills. The whites wanted the Hills, and the Sioux would do best to submit quietly. The whites were hard to control; they would take the Hills, no one could stop them, and the Sioux would do well to sell while they could. They were taken in hand by the Indian Office men who coaxed, bullied, and reasoned with them. In the end most of the Sioux said, rather glumly, that they had perhaps better sell; but that they could do nothing without consulting their people; yes, the people must be consulted. Finally it was arranged that a special commission should come out in the autumn to meet all the Sioux in council and bargain for the purchase of the Hills.

Red Cloud, who is described by some authors as a great soldier and statesman, made a poor display of himself on this visit to Washington. In the face of the growing crisis over the Black Hills, he persisted in pressing his petty quarrel with Agent Saville. Professor Marsh was in the city, to lay the complaints Red Cloud had made before the officials, but when he appealed to the chief to support the charges Red Cloud attempted to deny that he had accused the agent of fraud and refused to admit that he had given Professor Marsh the samples of flour, tobacco, coffee, and so on. Although refusing to back his own charges against Dr. Saville,

Red Cloud insisted on having a new agent. He said he did not want another poor rat who would steal from the Oglalas; he did not want one of these praying men (that was one for the church people), or a military man. What he desired was a nice rich agent, who would not need to steal and who would give the Oglalas whatever they asked for. The Indian Office officials seemed sympathetic, but they would make no promises and ordered Agent Saville to go back with the chiefs.

At the close of the council at the Indian Office, Face, an Oglala head-soldier, turned fiercely on Red Cloud and cried: "I told you just how this matter would be when we commenced it! We came here far apart; we have done nothing, and we have no one to blame but ourselves! Our father (the agent) is a good man. He is a brave true man. We tried to break him down and we could not. He is the man we ought to take back with us and keep." To be called a brave true man by a warrior like Face was a compliment indeed. The frank statement that Red Cloud and his wild followers had done everything in their power to break him and had failed was another compliment Dr. Saville might well be proud to hear spoken. When the investigators at Red Cloud Agency in August of this year attempted to force Bill Rowland to state that Dr. Saville lacked courage, Rowland told them flatly, "The little doctor has more sand than you'd think to look at him." Any man who would stick to his post at this agency during the wild times of the winter of 1873-1874 certainly had "sand" in abundance.

Having angered the officials, Professor Marsh, and many others, Red Cloud before leaving Washington managed to shock the church people, some of whom were still his devoted admirers. At this period there was in Washington a hotel man of shady reputation who specialized in Indian delegations. Having an arrangement with some of the clerks at the Indian Office, he was always informed when delegations were coming, met them at the station, and by bribing the interpreters usually managed to carry the chiefs off to his hotel in hacks. The Indian Office, having learned of this practice, adopted the custom of sending a trusted man to the station to meet all delegations and conduct them to respectable hostelries.

When the Oglala delegation reached town in May, 1875, they were met by this hotel keeper and by the Indian Office representative. Led into it by that child of trouble, Leon Palladay, Red Cloud now brushed aside the protests of the Indian Office man and took his chiefs and interpreters to the forbidden stopping place. During the whole stay Palladay was hopelessly drunk, and every night the hotel keeper took the chiefs out on prowls, visiting places which the officials smugly termed "bad houses." To cap it all, the hotel proprietor with almost sublime effrontery sent the great Red Cloud to the Indian Office to collect his itemized bill, which included hacks, liquor, and bad houses. The innocent Red Cloud, seeing nothing wrong in all this, presented the bill in open council, and was amazed when the Commissioner of Indian Affairs in a sudden burst of passion berated him like a naughty school boy, refused to pay the bill, and declined to give Leon Palladay one cent for services which he had been too drunk to render.

Red Cloud, the "Noble Chieftain," who had taken the East by storm in 1870, would probably have been hissed if he had now made a second appearance before an audience of church people and humanitarians in Cooper Institute. The groups of high-thinkers in the East were sadly disappointed in him. They seem to have thought, when they flocked to his support in 1870, that he would go home, turn Christian, and start raising crops. He had raised everything else, and these people were now accusing him of a queer crime, of being guilty of "obtuse and unsubduable Indianism." Great in his stubborn determination to resist all changes, if in nothing else, this chief turned his face westward again, more convinced than ever that the only hope for his people lay in keeping the whites out of their country and in holding fast to their own way of life.[1]

When the chiefs reached home they found the Oglalas greatly excited over the flocking of whites into the Black Hills. The troops had arrested some of the people and removed them, but other parties were coming in almost daily. The Sioux had tried their hand at stopping the flood by destroying the goods of a merchant who was going to the Hills to start a store. This made all the whites cry out. The treaty said that if the whites came into the Sioux

1. In writing this account of Red Cloud's visit at Washington in May, 1875, I have used the official records, the contemporary newspapers and some material from the Indians and whites at Pine Ridge. This chief has been accused of many things, but hard drinking and running after strange women were never included in the list of his misdeeds. In going about Washington with this hotel man the chief was no more in danger of getting into mischief than when he was being led about New York by the church people in 1870, and he was probably happier, the hotel proprietors having more sense than to put the chiefs into stiff white shirts and collars, black suits and shiny silk hats, which was what the church people had done to them in 1870.

country the Sioux could drive them out, but when they tried to do this the whites cried out for soldiers to protect them. And now the government had sent many white men to the Hills with a big force of soldiers. This was the Jenney expedition, which left Fort Laramie in May to examine the Hills again. The Custer expedition had reported rich gold deposits, but other authorities had denied that gold in paying quantities existed in the Hills, and the government was not going to buy a gold field from the Indians until it was assured that it was a gold field. Professor W. P. Jenney of the New York School of Mines was selected to make this new examination of the country, and he took with him a staff of scientists and experienced miners, with all the necessary equipment for a complete survey.

The chiefs told the people that the Great Father had asked them to sell the Hills, and runners were now sent to Powder River to consult the leaders in the hostile camps. At all the agencies the great question was being discussed, and not quietly. It was a quarrel three hundred miles long and two hundred miles broad. The older men wanted peace and were ready to give up *Pa Sapa,* their sacred hills, to obtain it, but they quarreled fiercely over the price they should demand. As for the younger men, they would not hear of selling *Pa Sapa*—they would fight for the Hills; they would no longer give in to these white men who were crowding them from every side and little by little taking their country.

For a few weeks in July and August the Black Hills question was overshadowed at Red Cloud by the investigation into the agency's affairs which had its true origin in Red Cloud's complaints to Professor Marsh. This commission was made up of two senators, one ex-governor, and two other men of experience in the conduct of public business. These gentlemen started their investigation in the East, then came to Omaha, to Cheyenne, and to Fort Laramie, then to the Red Cloud and Spotted Tail agencies. The commission collected sufficient testimony to fill a closely printed volume of five hundred pages, but they failed to find any legal proof of fraud on the part of the agents or the contractors who supplied the agencies. This is not surprising, as the type of men who at this period were engaged in defrauding the government on Indian contracts were too shrewd to leave legal proof of their wrongdoing lying about.

One of these men had obtained the contract to supply Red Cloud Agency with flour. He went to the Bemis Bag Company at

Omaha and asked them to make several thousand 88-pound flour sacks. The bag people expressed surprise. No one had ever heard of 88-pound flour sacks. The contractor explained that the Indian Office had specified that the flour must be in 88-pound bags. This was untrue, but it satisfied the bag company. The bags were made, filled with a specially milled low grade flour, and shipped from Omaha to Cheyenne. This had a very bad look. But when it came to proving that these short-weight sacks of flour had been passed on to Red Cloud Agency as full-weight sacks, the commission found itself lost in a maze of conflicting testimony. There was no possible explanation of the special 88-pound sacks unless one concluded that a fraud was being planned; the system for receiving and recording the flour shipments was so slovenly that any fraud might be perpetrated, but as for legal evidence that fraud had been attempted there simply was none. Another lot of flour had been shipped in double sacks, a peculiar business for which no one could give a reasonable explanation. An army officer testified that he had heard that the idea was to have the flour wheeled into the warehouse in Cheyenne, weighed, and the sacks stamped by the inspector as passed; the flour was then wheeled into another room, the outer sacks whipped off, and the same load wheeled back and weighed, counted, and stamped by the inspector again. Of course, such a scheme would mean that the warehouse would have on hand only half the weight of flour the inspector had certified, and to defraud the government there would have to be an understanding with the freighters who hauled the flour to the agencies and with the agents who received and receipted for it. There were many hints of such understandings between the contractors and the agents, but hints are not legal evidence. A short time after the investigation had cleared one of these contractors, he turned up at Spotted Tail with a wagon-train of supplies fifty per cent under the weights shown in his bills of lading. He expected to find his easy-going friend the agent on hand to receipt for the goods, but to his horror he found that the agent had been suddenly removed and that a stiff, hard-hearted army officer had been put in his place. The officer refused to accept the goods, promptly reported the circumstance, and produced legal evidence on which a conviction of the culprit was procured.

There was a sufficient amount of beef being issued at the two agencies to feed an infantry division at war strength; the cost was very great and the talk of fraud in the beef contracts had been persistent and very annoying to the officials. The investigators therefore took great pains to get to the bottom of this question of the beef contracts; but after examining and cross-examining scores of witnesses it could reach no definite conclusion on any point. Strange as it may appear, these veteran Texas trail-drivers and the biggest cattlemen of Wyoming knew almost nothing of their own business. One after the other they solemnly testified that they had sold herds of Texas cattle to the Red Cloud and Spotted Tail beef contractors or that they had seen the herds or had gone through them, but not one of them knew whether the herds were mostly steers, cows, light cattle, or heavy cattle. This is really an extraordinary situation when it is recalled that it was an axiom of the cattle trade that a man who could not ride through a herd and size it up was not worth his salt, and that a man who could not look over a herd of cattle and give a fair estimate of the animals' weight on the hoof had better go into another business, in which he would have some chance of keeping his money. One of the largest cattlemen in Wyoming assured the commission that no man living could estimate the weights of cattle on the hoof, yet all these cattlemen were making their living largely through their ability not only to estimate the weights of the cattle they bought but to estimate what the animals would weigh after being on good range for six months.

The wagon-bosses who ran the trains that hauled supplies to the agencies were among the most interesting of the witnesses. Of all the liars who appeared before the commission these men easily outdistanced the rest. Many of the freighters, being very ignorant and very much worried, lied in the wrong places, and were very unfortunate in their occasional candid moments; cats were most unexpectedly let out of bags, and abler performers had to be hastily summoned to refute the testimony of these well-intentioned but clumsy romancers. One poor freighter had a little matter of a smuggled load of arms and ammunition on his mind, and he dodged questions, lied, forgot his employer's name, denied that he knew how many wagons he had, how much he was being paid, who paid him, or what he hauled in the wagons; and after prevaricating desperately for two hours he suddenly discovered to his vast relief that the commission was not at all interested in his arms smuggling but was only asking about the road to Red Cloud and the distances.

All freight was hauled to the agencies at so much per hundred pounds per hundred miles, yet for years the distance had been estimated largely on the freight contractors' assertions. An odometer was finally sent out and attached to one of the freight wagons. Naturally it was broken en route to the agency. Another odometer was sent, and on reaching the agency it registered a distance so handsome that the government refused to accept it. Report had it that the wagon boss, who held his own interests and those of his freighting brethren very dear, had at each camp along the way jacked up the wheel to which the infernal machine was attached and had set a brawny teamster to twirling the wheel. But in his enthusiasm he had overdone it, producing a figure which even the credulity of the Indian Office could not accept as the true distance to Red Cloud Agency. The army then got an order and in one week measured the road. Here again in the matter of distances and freight charges there were many suspicious circumstances but not a jot of legal evidence of fraud.

One unwilling witness was asked about the "general reputation" of a certain western gentleman whose conduct was under consideration. After pondering deeply the witness stated: "Wall, his general reputation is that he is almighty quick on the draw." He then closed up like a clam and would give no further evidence.

Agent Saville's books and papers were found in such a condition that one might say that he had evidently made a mess of things to cover up his shady operations, or that he was an honest man but a terribly bad bookkeeper. It was quite apparent that the system of accounting was so slack that if the agent cared to connive with the contractors he could easily defraud the government of large sums without leaving a trace of legal evidence to be used against him; but such conditions could be found at any Indian agency of the day, the books always being in a dreadful state of confusion. Saville was drawing a salary of $1,500 per annum; the salary of a clerk in one of the Washington bureaux. There were some 12,000 Indians to be cared for at his agency, and the estimates for their rations alone for the fiscal year 1875-1876 was $726,522.25. An army officer stated that the work the agent at Red Cloud had to accomplish and the weight of responsibility he had to bear would be considered in the army a heavy task for a brigadier general, or even a major general, while Saville was getting the pay of a lieutenant. Would an honest man take such a burden on his shoulders for $1,500 a year, and risk his life daily among wild Indians into the bargain? Why was the position of agent so much sought after, considering the slender salary attached to it? Shrewd questions, doubtless, but not exactly legal evidence of wrongdoing. Saville had three relatives on the payroll, but what of that? It was the custom of the service to put relatives and close friends on the payroll.

As for Red Cloud and the other chiefs, a very little investigation indicated that most of their complaints merited no more attention than the fault-finding talk of rather spoiled children. A dignified Oglala chief pointed to the scales as a proof of fraud in the beef issues. The scales had a platform of heavy planks. He was not a fool, he stated. Every time a steer was weighed the weight of these planks was added to the animal's own weight and the Indians were cheated out of that much beef. As to the bitter complaints about flour frauds, as far as the Indians were concerned it came to just this: they did not know how to use flour and wished to have instead shelled corn from which they could make hominy. Old-Man-Afraid-of-His-Horse complained that the agent did not give him the extra rations a man of his position should have. Many Indians in the wild camps up north still regarded him as the head of the Oglalas; when they came to visit him he was shamed because the agent did not give him the means that would enable him to be hospitable to his guests. Red Cloud, when cornered, stated that his real reason for disliking the agent had its roots in the flagstaff affair when the white man had acted foolishly and nearly brought on a war. This was clearly another lie.

As for the quality of rations issued at Red Cloud, the government had never pretended that it was supplying the Indians with first-quality, and some of the articles in the rations were a special quality, very poor grade, supposed to be good enough for Indians. Most of the rations were good enough; the Indian complaints had more to do with the insufficient quantity than the quality of the food. The Great Spirit, they explained, had constructed the Sioux along special lines so that he must eat a lot, and it was not fair to expect the Sioux in just a few years to get down to the white man's skimpy system of three meals a day.

In its final report, the Red Cloud investigation committee stated that it had failed to discover any legal evidence that Agent Saville had defrauded the government, but it strongly recommended that he be removed. Their findings were probably fair.

They had uncovered many very suspicious circumstances and there could be little doubt that frauds had been perpetrated, but who could be accused? The facts were smothered in a fog of false testimony. Probably more lying was done at Red Cloud Agency during this investigation than at any other place during a similar period in the nation's history.

Even after sixty years the historian finds it difficult to pass judgment on Dr. Saville. If his hands were not quite clean, how many of the Indian agents of his day could exhibit clean hands? Compared with most of these men Saville seems superior in many ways, for in his makeup we find little of their niggardly and mean characteristics, and in his treatment of his Indians he was far and away more liberal than those dull money-grubbers. Saville, a true westerner, was indeed generous among friends and easy-going and liberal to his underlings, and his business ethics at the worst were up to the standards of the day in the Indian country, where making money out of the government was looked upon as a noble game, about the only rule being not to get caught.

Regarding Agent Saville's régime at Red Cloud as a whole, we must admire the little doctor and his work. Time and again he lost control of the wild people, but he kept at it until he was able to manage them again. During his service he was slowly but steadily winning the confidence of the chiefs and attempting to make useful citizens of them, an accomplishment which his perhaps more virtuous, but certainly narrower and less sympathetic successors failed to accomplish. Not only did they fail in this particular, but they resorted to the very doubtful expedient of destroying the power of the chiefs, thus leaving the Oglalas adrift with no leaders to look up to and to follow.

Dr. Saville spent his last years in Omaha, living so quietly that no one knew he was there until a report of his death appeared in the papers in 1922.

This great inquiry into the agency's affairs was in progress at the same time the preparations for the Black Hills council with the Sioux were being completed. A sub-committee of the Black Hills commission came to Red Cloud Agency during the investigation, to prepare for the great council with the Sioux. J. S. Collins, who was secretary to the commission, was with this sub-committee and he states in his reminiscences that both Red Cloud and Spotted Tail at the time opposed the sale of the Hills, but willingly aided in the preparations for the council. Red Cloud was interviewed first, as the whites still considered him the Sioux chief with the greatest influence; but when the committee arrived at the Spotted Tail Agency they found a man who did not accept Red Cloud as leader of all the Sioux. Spotted Tail brushed aside the government's decision that the council should be held on the Missouri and selected Chadron Creek, a spot between his agency and Red Cloud's, as the place. He told the committee to inform Red Cloud of his decision; and as for the Sioux at the Missouri River agencies he said: "We Brulés and Oglalas have kept the Black Hills and guarded them, and we are the most numerous. The Missouri River Sioux must come here to council." Guarded by six young warriors from Spotted Tail and six from Red Cloud, this committee visited various agencies, obtaining the promise of the Sioux to attend the council in September. They also inspected the Black Hills, where they found Professor Jenney's party hard at work seeking to determine if gold could be found in paying quantities. The Hills were full of miners, taking out gold in surprising quantities, and the troops who had orders to remove all whites from the Indian lands were peacefully encamped near the miners. This had the appearance of more bad faith to the Sioux. They had been assured by the chairman of the Red Cloud investigation commission that the troops would remove all whites from Indian lands by August 15.

The Secretary of the Interior in his instructions to the Black Hills commission, June 18, showed a very fair spirit. He informed the commissioners that they were to consider themselves as representing the Indians' interests as well as those of the government. They were to try to purchase the Black Hills and also to induce the Sioux to sell their interests in the Powder River and Bighorn lands. Since the provision for feeding the Sioux made by the treaty of 1868 was for four years only, the government was now, in 1875, under no obligation to feed these people, but would have to continue the ration system in its own interest and in the name of humanity. In making any agreement with the Sioux for the purchase of the Hills, the commission was to bear in mind that the Sioux were being fed and clothed at the public expense, and that it must arrange for a portion of the purchase price to be expended for food and clothing, the remainder to be spent mainly for stock cattle, agricultural equipment, and education, with the object of making the Sioux ultimately self-supporting.

The full commission reached Red Cloud on September 4 and found the country covered for miles around with Sioux camps and great herds of ponies. Collins states that 20,000 Indians were present. This huge mass of Sioux were engaged in a desperate quarrel over the petty question of the location of the council. The Red Cloud people had gathered some of the Missouri River Sioux to their support and were demanding that the council be held at their agency; Spotted Tail and his followers were equally determined to have the council on Chadron Creek, a middle-ground twenty-five miles from each agency. From the fourth to the sixteenth the Indians quarreled over this question, working themselves into such a fury that a battle seemed unavoidable on several occasions. They were finally induced to select a large plain on White River, eight miles east of Red Cloud and immediately north of Crow Butte.

During these two weeks of quarreling, the commissioners were holding talks with the chiefs, and they soon realized that the outlook for a successful council was slim. There seemed little hope that the Indians could be induced to sell the Black Hills for a price the government could pay, and as for the Powder River and Bighorn countries, the Indians flatly refused to consider selling. They said that the wild Sioux who roamed and hunted in that country must be left undisturbed. The agency chiefs had sent runners to the hostile camps and had received a reply which had convinced them that it would be extremely dangerous for any chief to entertain the idea of selling the hunting grounds of these wild bands. The treaty of 1868 contained among its numerous provisions which were planned to place the government at the mercy of the Sioux, one which provided that in any future cessions of land three-fourths of the adult males of the Sioux tribe must give their consent to make the agreement binding. The absurdity of attempting to induce three-fourths of the raging mass of wild Sioux gathered near Red Cloud Agency to sign an agreement was obvious to all, and the commission decided to ask only for a lease on the mining rights in the Hills.

The council was set for September 17; but further quarreling, which the commission discreetly failed to explain in its report, made a meeting on that day impossible. September 20 was then set for the council. A large tent with a flat fly in front for shade was pitched under a lone cottonwood on the council grounds. The commission sat in chairs under the tent fly, with Egan's troop of cavalry drawn up in line behind the tent as a guard. Senator W. B. Allison was chairman of the commission, and General Alfred Terry, Mr. S. D. Hinman (a Sioux missionary), and old Colonel G. P. Beauvais, the Sioux trader, were among the commissioners. The others were Eastern men new to Indian councils. Tribe by tribe the warriors rode over the hills and charged wildly down upon the commission as if about to attack, but swerved aside when very near the tent and trotted off to form in line some distance away. This continued until all the warriors had assembled, forming a vast circle of armed men around the tent. The chiefs then came forward and sat down in a semicircle in front of the tent. The ceremonies of the peace pipe followed, and Chairman Allison at length rose to open the council. His speech was interpreted to the chiefs, sentence by sentence, by Louis Richards. The commission had apparently altered their plans, for Senator Allison in this speech asked for the Black Hills and also for the Powder River and Bighorn lands. When he sat down the chiefs consulted among themselves and then asked for time to council. The first session was then ended.

The Indians resumed their quarreling, and for three days the camps were in a continuous uproar, with the danger of a general rush for weapons always present. A majority of the Indians were now in favor of selling the Black Hills for a very great price; a minority opposed any agreement with the whites, and this minority was made up of all the fighting men. White men had clearly been putting ideas into the heads of the chiefs as to the great value of the Hills, and the commission expressed painful surprise in its report that government officials, such as Indian Inspector Daniels and the agent at Spotted Tail, should have "considered it their duty" to inform the Indians that the Hills were worth from thirty to fifty million dollars. After quarreling among themselves for three days, the Sioux came to the council again, still divided into two bitterly hostile factions and all armed and ready for trouble.

This last session of the council, on September 23, was classic. The commission, as on the first day, sat under the tent fly with their interpreters and with Egan's little troop drawn up behind the tent as a guard. Thousands of Indians could be seen off in the distance, riding and walking about or sitting on the hills in little groups. Noon came, then a great cloud of dust swirled up from behind the hills, and over the ridge came two hundred warriors, dressed in all their war-finery and mounted on splendid ponies. They charged down furiously toward the commission, swerved aside, and began circling the tent, singing war-songs and firing their rifles. They then formed a line in front of the commission. A signal was given and a second band charged down from the hills. This continued until it was estimated that 7,000 warriors were formed up in a vast circle surrounding the commission.

Spotted Tail now came forward from his band of Brulé warriors and sat down. Red Cloud followed him, then the other chiefs: Miniconjous, Sans Arcs, Hunkpapas, Blackfeet, Two Kettles, and Yanktonais. The chiefs sat in a circle about one hundred yards in front of the tent, smoking and talking. The interpreter said that they were trying to decide who should speak for the tribe and that no one seemed anxious for the honor as some of the warriors had been threatening to kill the chief who first spoke in council in favor of selling the Black Hills. The chiefs talked for an hour, while the commission patiently waited and the 7,000 warriors waited impatiently, milling around and indulging in quarrels, more or less violent.

Presently the excitement became greater; an opening was made in the circle of warriors and through the opening shot Little Big Man, a belligerent young gentleman from Crazy Horse's wild camp.[2] He was naked and mounted on the bare back of a fine iron gray pony, with a lariat knotted around the pony's lower jaw in place of a bridle. In one hand he clutched a Winchester, and his other fist was full of cartridges. Riding toward the tent, he announced in a voice like the roar of a cannon that he had come to kill the white men who were trying to take his land. A number of Oglala soldiers surrounded him, snatched his gun, and amid immense confusion and excitement removed him from the circle. The warriors were riding up and down making little dashes (they always did this before a fight), and some of the leaders were yelling *Hoka hey!* (the call for a charge). Egan pushed his way through

---

2. Little Big Man was also called Chasing Bear. The Sioux form of the first name was *Chasa Tonga*—an abbreviation of *Wichasha* (Man) *Tonka* (Big). This was his father's name. *Chikala* (Little) was added to the name if the speaker wished to make it clear that he was referring to the son while the father was still alive. Many of the Sioux names were much abbreviated in daily use. This man was a shirt-wearer in Crazy Horse's camp. He kept his word to General Crook after he surrendered in 1877, did not join in either the Crazy Horse or Big Road attempts to break away, and in 1879 was a policeman at Pine Ridge. His son and daughter were living at Standing Rock some years back.

the Indians and informed General Terry that his troop was surrounded and that the situation looked unpleasant. Most of the commissioners' faces were blanched, and Louis Richards, the half-breed interpreter, who knew what the Indians were yelling, was plainly scared. "It looks like hell will break out here in a few minutes," he said. "The Indians are all mad, and when they start shooting we'll be the first to catch it."

All this time the Indians had not said a word to the white men. There were, however, a great many insulting gestures and yells aimed at the high commissioners, and the warriors were calling for a charge. Suddenly there was a wild rush of mounted Sioux toward the commission; but the warriors charged past the tent and up to Egan's troopers, who were sitting their horses with their carbines gripped in their hands. It was now seen that this was no hostile movement; it was Young-Man-Afraid-of-His-Horse and his Oglala soldiers. Hearing the Indians yelling for a charge, he had rushed his men in and formed a screen between Egan's troopers and the mass of infuriated Sioux. Leaving his men, he now rode into the center of the circle and shouted to the Indians to go to their lodges and not to come to the council again until their heads had cooled. The Sioux knew that this man was not to be trifled with; he would kill the first man who opposed him. Band by band the warriors left the circle and rode over the hills toward their camps. The commissioners, escorted by Egan, went back to Red Cloud Agency in a very thoughtful frame of mind. They did not care for any more meetings with the mass of Sioux they had had to face that day, and there were no further councils.[3]

On September 26, the commission called about twenty of the leading chiefs to the agency and told them emphatically that they must cease quarreling and come to some kind of an agreement among themselves at once. On the following day the chiefs came to the agency and made many speeches which proved that they were as far as ever from an agreement. Some white men had been coaching them and they were all for the "seven generation" plan. Six generations of their people had gone before, they were the

3. J. S. Collins, *Across the Plains in '64* (Omaha, Nebraska, 1904), contains an excellent eye-witness account of this council of September 23. As a wonderful example of censored truth, the commission's own account of this council is worth quoting: "Although all were present on the twenty-third, the council was not convened. No proposition was made by the Indians, nor did any chief address the commission. All separated after some consultation held by the leading chiefs among themselves, without fixing any time for future meetings."

seventh, and in payment for the Black Hills they wanted the Great Father to feed and clothe the Sioux for seven generations to come. Red Cloud led in expressing this idea: "There have been six nations, and I am the seventh." He is said to have added to the feeding of seven generations the demand that the government pay $600,000,000 for the Hills. The Sioux would sell, but each chief named his own price and would agree to nothing else; and they wished to restrict all travel into the Black Hills to a single road, but could not agree as to where the road should be placed. One of the chiefs mentioned the Thieves' Road and when the chairman asked what road that was, he received the shocking answer that it was the trail made by the chief of all the thieves, General Custer. Red Dog said, "The trail they have made through the village [Red Cloud Agency], where the thieves come through, they may travel that." Little Bear said, "*Pa Sapa* is the House of Gold for our Indians. We watch it to get rich." Many of them spoke of the Hills as their bank and they were very bitter about the Great Father permitting his men to sneak in and rob their bank. Red Cloud had a really wonderful list of wants: "For seven generations to come, I want the government to give us Texas steers for our meat. I want the government to issue for me hereafter flour, coffee, and tea, and bacon, of the best kind, and shelled corn, and beans, and rice, and dried apples, and salaratus, and tobacco, and salt and pepper for the old people. I want a wagon—a light wagon—with a span of horses and six yoke of work cattle for each family. I want a sow and a boar, and a cow and a bull, and a sheep and a ram, and a hen and a cock for each family. I am an Indian, but you try to make a white man out of me. I want some white men's houses built at this agency for the Indians .... nice, black, shiny furniture, dishes, and a scythe, and a mowing machine, and a sawmill ...." Why not? The Oglalas did not wish to be like white men; if the government insisted on making them so, why should it not pay the bill? But the mere thought of the cost staggered the commission. After three more days of squabbling Spotted Tail abruptly asked the commissioners to put their proposals into writing, and this they did. They proposed that the government pay the Sioux $400,000 a year for the mining rights in the Black Hills, with the government reserving the right to cancel the agreement on two years' notice. They also proposed to purchase the Hills outright for $6,000,000. The chiefs refused to consider such propositions and there the matter ended.

The commission reported that no agreement was possible and that in their view the spirit and temper of the Sioux would never change until these people had felt the power of the government. It recommended that Congress decide on a course which it considered fair and, if the Sioux refused to consent, that all rations and supplies be withheld. The commission pretended to see some wisdom in the treaty of 1868, by reading into that precious document a pledge on the part of the Indians to begin farming at once and to attempt to win self-support by 1872. The commission hinted that by failing to keep this alleged promise the Sioux had violated the treaty, but we know that none of the chiefs who signed knew of the farming clause. One grows rather weary of this pretense that the treaty of 1868 was negotiated, with the chiefs dictating part of the terms. They had an unread paper laid before them, touched the pen and watched their names being signed. That was all they did. The Sioux could hardly be held responsible for the fact that the government had turned over its treaty-making powers to a group of visionaries who believed that they could take wild Indians and turn them into self-supporting farmers in four years. The attempt made by the officials at this time to shift the responsibility for the failure of the Peace Policy to the shoulders of the Sioux was unjust. These Indians were supporting themselves by hunting when the treaty was forced on them, and if they were now pauperized, living in idleness at public expense, it was because the government policy had brought them to it. In seven years the government had spent $13,000,000 on the Sioux. The idealists and church people had obtained this money from Congress by preaching on the theme, "Feed the Sioux and you will not have to fight them." The commission had just met 7,000 Sioux warriors who had been cared for under this feeding policy, and it was of the opinion that feeding the Sioux was not taking any of the fight out of them. It wished to see force employed against this tribe; but there was that treaty of 1868, which had been carefully constructed by the Indians' Friends to shield the Sioux from all the winds that blow, and especially from any possible acts of coercion on the part of the United States government. Growing almost sly in their quest for a solution of their problem, the commissioners suggested that the treaty of 1868 did not abrogate earlier treaties, but only annulled the provisions in these treaties that had to do with the government's obligations to furnish annuities of money, clothing, and other articles. They called attention to a treaty made with part of the Sioux in 1865, signed by a few cracker-and-molasses chiefs who did not represent the tribe at all, which provided that the Sioux "were subject to the exclusive jurisdiction and authority of the United States." Why not revive this old treaty, furbish it up, and use it as a justification for disregarding the 1868 treaty and for applying force in future dealings with the Sioux? Under the treaty of 1868 the government had pledged its faith to exclude all whites from the Sioux reservation, and therefore from the Black Hills; but the commission gave its opinion that the Sioux themselves had not carried out their part of the treaty stipulations with a scrupulousness that made it obligatory on the government to keep the strict letter of the agreement. Thus the refusal of the Red Cloud people to leave their own home and go to the Missouri River to live was in a way a violation of the treaty, which might justify the government in closing its eyes to the seizure of the Black Hills by an invading army of white men. The commission also pointed out that troops had to be stationed at all of the Sioux agencies to preserve order, and they seemed to have some vague idea that in this fact lay a handy excuse for slipping out of the government's pledges to remove intruding whites from the Sioux lands. These closing paragraphs in the Black Hills commission's report cannot but impress the reader with the feeling that, having failed in their attempt to purchase the Hills, these gentlemen were seeking blindly for some subterfuge by means of which the government might get out of its present dilemma either through the use of chicane or by employing force.

The government was now in a very embarrassing position. It had pledged its faith in the treaty of 1868 to exclude all whites from the Sioux lands, and had made the further pledge that if the white men disregarded the Indians' rights and invaded their territory, it would employ the military and would also permit the Indians to use force in driving out the invaders. But the whites were now in the Black Hills, disregarding all warnings and even flouting the president's own proclamation. The military in the spring of 1875 had arrested and removed some of the miners from the Hills, and had turned them over to the civil authorities who had promptly set them free. Most of these men had gone back to the Hills. The government did not dare take severe measures against its own citizens. After the failure of the Black Hills council with the Indians, the Commissioner of Indian Affairs wrote in his annual report: "However unwilling we may be to confess it, the experiences of the past summer prove either the inefficiency of the large military force under the command of such officers as Generals Sheridan, Terry, and Crook, or the utter impracticability of keeping Americans out of a country where gold is known to exist, by any force of orders, or of U. S. cavalry, or by any consideration of the rights of others."

CHAPTER XIV

SITTING BULL'S WAR
1876-1877

THE failure to purchase the Hills from the Indians only made matters worse. Up to that time the movement into the Sioux lands had been restrained; it was an enterprise for men who were willing to take any chances and to disregard the president's proclamation, but the failure to induce the Sioux to sell was looked upon as an event that let down all the bars, and the whites now began to stream into the Hills openly, in large, well-organized groups. They laid out towns, organized local governments, and began to demand that the troops protect them from the Indians on whose lands they were trespassing. The government seemed to be faced with the alternatives of employing vigorous force in driving the whites out or of attempting to justify the seizure of the Hills by reading into the Sioux treaty certain things that were not in that treaty. The government would not decide upon either of these alternatives. Instead it adopted a peculiar course of action, ordering the hostile Sioux to come in to the various agencies by a certain date and informing them that if they did not do this the military would be sent to drive them in.

This decision was reached in November at a council held by President Grant with the Secretary of War, the Secretary of the Interior, the Assistant Secretary of the Interior, and the Commissioner of Indian Affairs. Before the Black Hills trouble arose to plague it, the government's policy had been to establish a new agency for the Sioux near those Hills, and to this agency the roving bands were to be drawn by the bait of free clothing and rations. Now these Indians were to be pursued by the military and driven in to the old agencies. At the time, and afterwards, the officials denied that this order to the hostiles had anything to do with the Black Hills crisis, but an examination of the facts will convince anyone that this was not true. Grant and his officials could not very well coerce the agency Indians, but by employing troops against the Sioux in the Powder River country they evidently hoped to give the agency bands an object lesson which would break down their stubborn resistance and induce them to cede the Hills. The scheme was clever. If successful, and no one doubted the ability of the military to whip the hostile bands, it would subdue the Sioux, and gain the Black Hills, the Powder River and Bighorn countries at a nominal cost, and it would please the public which wanted these lands and also desired to have the Sioux taught their place. Some of the humanitarians would certainly make trouble, but even in that quarter many influential leaders had come to the conclusion that no progress could be made as long as the policy of dealing with the Sioux by kindness alone was continued. By making liberal arrangements for the education and training of the Sioux, the officials hoped to conciliate most of the humanitarians and church groups.

It would be absurd to pretend that Grant and his advisers began a Sioux war to cover up the seizure of the Black Hills; it is all too apparent that no one at Washington thought the Indians would put up a real fight. It was prophesied that most of the Sioux would come in like lambs when threatened with the troops; the rest would be quickly driven in by a few companies of cavalry, and all would be over before the new grass was up in the spring.

The excuse for ordering the roving bands of Sioux to come to the agencies was found in a report of Indian Inspector E. C. Watkins, dated November 9, 1875, in which attacks made by the Sioux on the whites and on the Crow Indians were set forth. There was nothing new in this—similar reports had come in every year since 1866—but the officials now wished to take strong action and the Watkins document was just what they needed. The proceedings in the capital at this moment had a marked air of secrecy, almost of conspiracy, and the Commissioner of Indian Affairs, G. W. Manypenny, in his reminiscences hints that action was decided on first and that it was after this decision was taken that generals Sherman and Sheridan consulted Watkins and obtained his report. The Indian Office then sent the message to the hostiles, informing them that their misdeeds would no longer be tolerated, that they were all to come to the Sioux agencies by January 31, 1876, and that if they did not the military would drive them in. Sufficient time was not given for these Indians to move in, and one can hardly escape the conviction that the matter was handled in this way with the deliberate purpose of giving the military an excuse to take action. The message reached the Sioux agencies just before Christmas and was at once given to reliable Indians and half-breeds who set out in the worst weather of a severe winter to find the hostile camps, deliver the message, and bring back answers. The runner from Standing Rock Agency did not get back until February 11, after the time set for the Sioux to come in had expired. He stated that the Indians (Sitting Bull's people), were near the mouth of Powder River and had received him well, but could not come in at that time. The agent at Cheyenne River also reported a favorable answer. On January 3, Agent E. A. Howard at Spotted Tail reported that he had sent out runners but had not heard from them. Agent J. S. Hastings at Red Cloud reported that Sitting Bull had gone to the Yellowstone in the autumn and was beyond his reach but that his runners had found Crazy Horse and Black Twin, Oglala hostiles, in camp near Bear Butte, and that the chiefs had said that there was too much snow and that it was too cold for them to move at present. His runners had also gone to the Cheyennes on Powder River, one hundred miles beyond Bear Butte, but they had not yet reported. From the agents' reports it will be seen that the statement of the military, that the hostiles had sent back defiant answers and practically dared the troops to come and get them, was slightly exaggerated. That the hostiles had any real intentions of coming in is very much to be doubted. These wild Sioux had not been seriously troubled by the military for many years; they did not realize at all the change in the government's policy, and if they had realized it they were too confident of their ability to fight off the soldiers to pay much attention to the orders from Washington. Some authors who have written about these events have laid much emphasis on the fact that these Indians were expected to move with their women and children to the agencies through snow and cold which were so severe that the military could not take the field at all. These writers seem to forget that the Sioux were not the military, and they overlook the fact that Crazy Horse and his Oglala camp left Bear Butte in January and instead of moving the short distance south to Red Cloud Agency made a much longer trip northward to Powder River. Sitting Bull also moved his camp at least twice between December and March. The verdict must be that these Indians did not choose to come to the agencies and were not at all impressed by the government's threat to send soldiers after them.

The bands which the military were to deal with were those Sioux and Cheyennes who desired to hold to their old hunting life, far from the whites and from everything that the whites had brought into their country, with the exception of arms, ammunition, and good blankets. A few of the chiefs in these camps had signed the treaty of 1868, as Little Hawk, Crazy Horse's uncle, had done, merely to obtain the arms and ammunition which were being handed out to bands whose chiefs had touched the pen. They then went straight back to Powder River and—unlike Red Cloud and many others—remained there. They considered Red Cloud a fool for going to an agency and becoming mixed up with the white men. But the bait of free blankets and free food was a strong temptation, and as the years went by a large number of the less stubborn hostiles acquired the habit of going in to the agencies to winter, to eat white man's food, to get ammunition, blankets and other good things. When spring came these people flocked back to Powder River, well fed and with new outfits of clothing and other necessaries. All these bands that went in to winter at the agencies were enrolled by the agents, and the optimists in the Indian Office pointed to the increase in enrollment as an indication of the success of the Peace Policy. From the figures alone it was easy to prove that the hostile camps were dwindling away as the enrollment at the agencies increased; but the men on the ground knew that this was true only in winter and that each spring thousands of Sioux left the agencies to rejoin the hostiles. The agents reported this movement back and forth between the agencies and the hostile camps but did not lay too much emphasis on the facts, hoping that these wild people, after spending a few winters at the agencies, would settle down permanently. The military had posts at all the larger Sioux agencies and were familiar with the movements of the wild bands back to Powder River each spring. Since they took no action in the winter of 1875-1876 to prevent the Sioux making their regular start for Powder River in the spring, we can only assume that either the officers were asleep or that they held the Sioux as fighting men in such contempt that they did not care how many of them tracked off to Powder River in the spring of 1876.[1]

When, early in February, 1876, the Indian Office turned over the hostiles to the military it estimated their number at about three thousand people. Inspector Watkins in his report had stated that these Indians had only a few hundred warriors, were not united, and easily could be driven in by a thousand troops. These figures, which seem liberal for the winter strength of the hostiles, were accepted by the military without comment. It was only after they had come to grief in their attempt to deal with these Sioux that the military leaders accused the Indian Office of grossly underestimating the number of hostiles. From the angry statements made by General Sheridan and the other superior officers after Crook and Custer had been defeated by the Sioux, we are evidently expected to believe that the troops stationed for years at all the Sioux agencies had collected no information of military value and that the army was depending for such information on the civilians of the Indian Office.

The military were quite ready to take over the Sioux hostiles. The army had had to endure many insults and injuries from the Indians and the Indians' Friends during the ten years of the Peace Policy, and with the Sioux in particular they had many scores to settle. A winter campaign against the hostiles on Powder River had been under discussion in army circles for several years and had been declared to be the most feasible and effective course of action. The soldiers were now given their chance, and the troops in the Department of the Platte were at once set in motion, General Crook taking the field in person and sharing in all the hardships his men had to endure. The troops on the Upper Missouri who were expected to co-operate did not move however, giving bad weather as their reason.

Bad weather did not stop Crook. He left Fort Fetterman, on the North Platte west of Fort Laramie, on March 1 with a strong

1. When the treaty of 1868 was signed, there were from 10,000 to 15,000 wild Sioux in the Powder River region. Red Cloud took about 5,000 of these to his agency in 1871, and they soon settled down and became real agency Indians. By 1874, perhaps another 5,000 of the wild Sioux had been attracted to the Red Cloud and Spotted Tail agencies, but they only came to winter and left again every spring. During this time, other bands of Sioux were going to the agencies on the Missouri, where most of them remained. The problem of the bands that came in only to winter was far more acute at Red Cloud and Spotted Tail than at the Missouri agencies. The Indian Office in estimating the winter population of the hostile camps in February, 1876, at about 3,000 persons was near the actual count, but this figure was probably too liberal.

and very mobile little column, considered strong enough to handle all the hostiles. He had ten companies of cavalry and two of infantry, a fine pack-train, a wagon-train, and all of the Sioux halfbreeds he could enlist—the Reshaw and Janis boys being among these scouts. The weather was very cold and snowy; Indians, probably not Sioux, attempted to run off General Crook's horses soon after he left the Platte but were unsuccessful. He left his wagons and infantry at a base camp near the site of old Fort Reno on the head of Powder River and advanced rapidly to Tongue River with his cavalry, scouts, and pack-train. The scouts examined the valley of the Rosebud where the Indians were supposed to be in winter camp but found nothing. This puzzled them. Pushing on down Tongue River they drew near the Yellowstone, and there found the remains of several large camps with a great deal of felled cottonwood. A few of the camps were surrounded by palisades.[2] Crook halted near the site of a very large Indian village and sent his scouts to the Yellowstone. On March 15, they returned, reporting large trails leading toward Powder River, and on the sixteenth Crook started across toward the Powder. The troops had gone but a few miles when a number of Indian hunters were seen on the hills watching the column. Crook sent the scouts to drive the Indians off and went into camp in order to deceive the hostiles as to his purpose. That night he sent Colonel J. J. Reynolds with six companies of cavalry and the half-breed scouts to find and attack the hostile camp.

The camp that Reynolds attacked was on Powder River about ten miles above the Little Powder. It was a Sioux camp, generally said to have been the Oglala camp of Crazy Horse, comprising sixty-five lodges. A band of forty lodges of Cheyennes had come from Red Cloud Agency and joined these Sioux just before the attack was made. The Cheyennes had new canvas lodges given to them at the agency, and they had brought a supply of goods, including some powder in canisters, which they intended to trade to the Sioux.[3] A party of sixty hunters from this camp had discovered

2. These camps must have been a year or more old. The palisades were probably intended to keep Crow horse thieves from getting at the herds at night.

3. My statements as to the identity of the Indians in this camp are based on the assertions made by a Sioux woman who was captured in the camp. When she said it was Crazy Horse's village she knew what she was saying. Crook's Sioux halfbreeds also knew very well whose camp it was. The Indians of today who say Crazy Horse was not present are talking nonsense. I have a Cheyenne account of this fight, obtained in 1912, which states that when the Indians fled from the camp Crazy Horse was seen running up the steep hillside with a little child on his back.

Crook's column on the sixteenth and had returned to report to the chiefs; yet these Indians with their usual apathy set no guards and when Reynolds' two leading troops entered the camp at dawn on the seventeenth the hostiles were nearly all asleep and were taken completely by surprise. The pony herd was captured and the Indians fled up the steep hillside in the rear of the camp. The warriors, having left their women and children in places of safety, rushed back into camp, attacking the troops with such fury that their advance was halted and in some places driven back. Reynolds had divided his command, evidently fearing that the Indians would get away if he did not surround them, and he failed to support his troops in the captured village. The situation seemed to him a bad one, and presently he ordered the camp set on fire and, withdrawing his troops, began a hasty retreat up Powder River, not halting until he reached Lodgepole Creek (Clear Creek). He had a number of wounded men to care for and also many others who had been badly frozen; no guard was set, and during the night the hostiles ran off all of the seven hundred ponies that had been taken by the troops. On their way home the Indians ran into Crook, who attacked them and got back about two hundred of the ponies.

Crook was very angry at what he considered the bungling of Colonel Reynolds. He had intended to utilize the captured Indian camp as a base for further operations, sheltering his men in the lodges and feeding them on the stores of dried meat that the Indians had laid up for their own use; but the destruction of the village by Reynolds had ruined this plan and the general now had to abandon his operations and return to Fort Fetterman. Some of the hostiles followed him and kept making attempts to run off two hundred Indian ponies which were still in the hands of the troops. At last, in exasperation, Crook had the ponies killed, and the warriors then left him to proceed on his way in some peace.

The failure of Crook's winter campaign left the hostiles free to take the initiative. What these Indians then did presents an interesting study. Some years previous to this campaign, as it is said by the Sioux, Sitting Bull had been created head-chief or "generalissimo" of all the Tetons in a big ceremony on the Yellowstone River. Only a fraction of the Tetons were present, and the whole affair was engineered by Sitting Bull's relatives and close friends. Crazy Horse is said to have been present and to have been made Sitting Bull's "second in command." The object of this gathering of the hostiles was to create new leaders who would take action to prevent any further encroachment of the whites on the Sioux lands. When the Black Hills were invaded by the whites, a message was sent from Red Cloud Agency to inform the hostiles that the government wished to buy the Hills, and the advice of the chiefs in the Powder River camps was asked for. Sitting Bull replied to this message, "The Black Hills belong to me. If the whites attempt to take them, I will fight." But he did not fight. With the whites swarming into the Hills, he went on a little horse lifting raid up to the Canadian border; and in the autumn when his camp was on the Yellowstone near the mouth of Tongue River, he went on another little horse lifting raid against the Crows. He then went into winter camp near the mouth of Powder River, and there he learned of the order issued to all the roving camps to come to the agencies by January 31. He and the other camp leaders took no action. These Indians were scattered, as they always were in winter. The largest camp was that which Reynolds attacked on March 17 —consisting of 105 lodges. Sitting Bull's camp was smaller than that, and there were said to be four small camps of Sioux on the Little Powder and four more on the Little Missouri. This information about the camps and their movements comes from the Sioux over fifty years after the events actually happened but seems to be correct. Sitting Bull, either at the end of February or early in March, moved eastward to the Little Missouri, but almost at once returned to Powder River, where Crazy Horse's people and the Cheyennes who were with them came in to seek aid. These people had lost most of their lodges, food, clothing, and equipment. Sitting Bull took them in.

Shortly afterwards, Sitting Bull sent a message to all the roving camps to meet him on Tongue River for a council. At this council, in April, he told the leaders that the whites wanted war and that he would give it to them. Then he is said to have sent runners "to every Sioux, Cheyenne, and Arapaho agency," summoning all the agency warriors to his aid. The Indians who tell this story seem slightly mixed as to the agencies. There were no Cheyenne or Arapaho agencies as these tribes were cared for at the Oglala agency. The statement that the agency warriors were summoned proves that today the Sioux have forgotten that in 1876 there were thousands of wild Sioux from Powder River at the agencies who had only gone in to winter and who would rejoin Sitting Bull as soon as the grass

{256}

was up in the spring. It was these people, and not the agency Indians, that Sitting Bull was counting on for support, and he knew full well that he did not need to call them from the agencies, for they always came out as soon as winter was ended.

This modern Sioux version states that when the agency Indians received Sitting Bull's message they began to buy arms and ammunition, and that when some of their chiefs, Red Cloud in particular, opposed their going to join the hostiles, they defied their own chiefs and set out for Powder River. These assertions show an ignorance of conditions at the agencies that is really surprising. No arms had been sold at the agencies for two years, and the moment the military took over the hostiles in early February all trade in ammunition was stopped. It is true that arms and ammunition could be obtained through secret channels, but the agency Indians had no money and when it came to a trade they had little to tempt the arms smugglers, who wanted very high prices for their guns and ammunition. The present day Sioux could not have made a worse choice than Red Cloud in naming the chief who opposed the war. This chief, whom they represent as trying to prevent his people from joining the hostiles, was the one chief at the Oglala agency who desired war. He was not holding his people back— they were holding him. He permitted his young son Jack to go to Powder River with the Black Elk band of Bad Faces in April, and this is now misrepresented and turned into an assertion that nearly all of the agency young men joined the hostiles, that Red Cloud could not even prevent his own son from going. This is absurd. Jack is the only Red Cloud Agency Indian who is mentioned by name as being with the hostiles. He went before the Indians realized that a real war was starting, and his father did not object to his going. Today when the Sioux speak of 1876 they should try to remember that in that year the agency Sioux were frightened, and that fear was the principal motive back of their conduct. They were no longer wild people; they could smell "big trouble" ahead and they were afraid that the wild fellows in Crazy Horse's and Sitting Bull's camps would draw them into it, which would give the white soldiers an excuse to come to the agencies and "clean them out." To picture these Sioux as flocking eagerly to the hostile camps to help in a war is a plain falsification of the truth.[4]

4. The Sioux of today who talk loosely of great bodies of agency Indians joining the hostiles in April, 1876, do not appear to realize that they are justifying

At Red Cloud Agency in the early winter of 1875-1876 the all absorbing topic of conversation was the seizure of the Black Hills by the whites. The quarrels that had featured the councils with the Black Hills commission were kept alive among the agency bands until the wild Northern Indians made their usual appearance in October and November. These wild folk from the north then had to express their opinions. As usual, their attitude toward the agency Indians was scornful, and they were full of bluster. They repeated the wise sayings of Sitting Bull, Black Moon, Black Twin, and their other leaders—big chiefs, not like these miserable white men's chiefs at the agencies. The whites should not take the Black Hills. True, the whites had already taken them; but their big chiefs were going to do something about that—next year, maybe. Meanwhile the squawmen were reading the newspapers and telling the agency leaders that the whites were discussing ways and means of punishing the Sioux. The agency chiefs were very unhappy—they desired peace, and the whites were getting ready to punish them if they did not surrender the Hills, and Sitting Bull and Crazy Horse and their men were promising to punish them if they did.

Dr. Saville was relieved as agent at Red Cloud on December 3, 1875. The Oglalas, on the whole, were sorry to see him go. They said good-bye to the little doctor and set to work hatching schemes to try on their new father, James S. Hastings, Then, just before Christmas, came the order for the hostiles to come to the agencies. Immense excitement ensued at Red Cloud and Spotted Tail; the usual denunciations of the whites were indulged in, and the young men made the usual threats, but it was observed that none of the violent acts that had featured the winters of 1873 and 1874 at these agencies were repeated. In those days the agency Sioux had threatened to kill their agents, now they went to them and asked for advice.

By the end of February the Red Cloud Indians had quieted again. At that time their main interest was in a possible shortage

---

the severe action the military took against the agency people in the late summer of that year. The military claim that the agency warriors had almost to a man joined the hostiles was without foundation, the army officers confusing the Northern Indians who only wintered at the agencies with the true agency Indians. The Sioux today make that same mistake; but they are Sioux and should know better. In 1876, almost all of the agency chiefs protested very earnestly that their people were all at home, had done no wrong, and should not be treated as hostiles. The Sioux of today might be better employed than in making it appear that these chiefs were lying.

in the beef issue. In the modern Sioux version this shortage of beef has been built up into an assertion that the Red Cloud people were starving and that the Two Moon camp of Cheyennes had to leave the agency early in March to seek food on Powder River. In the contemporary records we fail to find any evidence of real suffering at this agency, and the reasons for the Cheyenne trip to Powder River seem to be that they wished to trade to Crazy Horse's band the supplies that they had obtained at the agency, and that they were afraid the government intended to remove them to Indian Territory.

In April, the wild Northern Indians began to track off to Powder River in full force. They left the agency openly, and it is amazing that neither the agent nor the military officers at Camp Robinson a mile away realized that the removal of these bands meant a great reinforcement for the hostile camps. The Red Cloud people had already heard from their own half-breeds the story of Reynolds' attack on Crazy Horse's camp, on March 17. The Northern Indians departed, ignoring the threat of war, and if we are to believe the modern Sioux version of these events, the agency people received Sitting Bull's summons, defied their chiefs, and set out in great force to join the hostiles. But we know that nothing of the kind occurred. General Crook, not Sitting Bull, was the man who asked the real agency Indians for aid. He came to Red Cloud Agency in April and coolly asked the warriors to enlist to fight their own kindred, and they consented. Led by Sitting Bull, the head-soldier of the Oglala Kiyuksa band, by Rocky Bear, Three Bears, and other agency warriors, the young men agreed to enlist; but then Red Cloud, Red Dog, Red Leaf, and other older chiefs intervened to prevent the warriors joining Crook's forces, and Agent Hastings seems to have supported these chiefs.[5] Crook went away very angry, talking of the "disloyalty" of the agency Sioux, whom he regarded as paupers being supported by the government

5. General Crook probably lost his chance to obtain scouts at Red Cloud Agency by publicly stating in March that the hostile camp his troops captured on March 17 was crammed with ammunition and other supplies which the hostiles had received from this agency. Agent Hastings made an angry reply in the newspapers, stating that Crook's half-breed scouts had informed him that all the ammunition found in the camp was five pounds of powder, twenty of lead, and a small box of gun caps. To this he added the unkind remark that the same scouts had told him that all the Indians killed by Crook's large force were a woman and two children, and that out of 700 ponies taken by the troops the Indians recaptured all but 70. The agent was still angry when Crook came to enlist scouts, and he did not lift a finger to aid the general.

and in duty bound to aid it. The Red Cloud Indians had a different view of loyalty. They regarded the support they were receiving as just payment for lands which had been given up; they believed that their loyalty belonged to their own bands at the agency. Red Cloud and some others wanted war, but they were hopelessly in the minority and their hostility went no farther than talk. That any of these agency Indians felt the least loyalty toward Crazy Horse, Sitting Bull, and the other hostile leaders is unbelievable. Since the Sioux today tell us that most of the young warriors at Red Cloud Agency had obeyed Sitting Bull's call and had gone to the hostile camps, we must assume that the scouts General Crook was so eagerly trying to enlist at this agency were mostly old men and boys.

Captain John G. Bourke, who was with Crook during this visit to Red Cloud, stated that he had never seen any Indians as well-off as the Oglalas were then. They were well-fed and clothed. The men were clad in dark blue trousers and dark blue flannel shirts; they had very fine blankets, mostly dark blue, black, or green, and many had a band of scarlet cloth sewed transversely on the blankets, the scarlet band heavily ornamented with beadwork. They were well armed and had an abundance of ponies. Crook was of the opinion at this time that the Sioux would not put up much of a fight. Unlike the Apaches, who had nothing but their lives to lose and therefore fought desperately, the Sioux, he told his officers, were rich in ponies and other property and when they lost this wealth they would lose heart and give up. This was shrewd reasoning. The trouble was that the troops in the Crook and Custer battles, far from relieving the hostiles of their property, enriched them still further with captured cavalry horses, arms, clothing, and equipment. In 1877 an army officer stationed at the Cheyenne River Agency reported that of 1,046 horses and mules taken from surrendered hostiles 874 were branded US.

At the beginning of May, General Crook was still waiting on the Platte for reinforcements. He had decided not to take the field again until he had been given more troops and a large force of Indian scouts. General Terry, on the Upper Missouri, had not yet started his winter campaign—in May! The Indian general, Sitting Bull, had sent some small war-parties out to steal horses in the Black Hills. Moving to the Rosebud, the hostiles were now joined by the great force of Northern Indians—not agency Indians—coming out mainly from Red Cloud and Spotted Tail; they were well-fed, well outfitted, and brought good blankets, arms, and other supplies, to their relatives in the Crazy Horse and Sitting Bull camps. With them were a few agency Indians. These Indians must have known that a war was in progress, yet they did not depart in any way from their usual summer program, but continued to hunt on the Rosebud until game and grass grew scarce. About June 1, they went over to the Little Bighorn where they camped on the ground which they were occupying again when Custer came on June 25. They found little game, and returned to the Rosebud about June 5.

According to their own statements, they had seven tribal circles of lodges, and this is confirmed by the reports of officers who examined the camp sites and observed seven great circles at each camp. The Sioux today cannot agree as to which tribes were represented by these seven circles, and they say that when they moved back to the Little Bighorn after June 14 they had only five circles comprising Cheyennes, Oglalas, Miniconjous, Sans Arcs, and Hunkpapas, with whom were encamped some Santees, Yanktonais, and other people. There were also a few Brulés, but not enough to make a circle. Two circles of lodges which were present on June 14 seem to be unaccounted for on June 25. The number of lodges in these circles have been variously estimated. Today the Sioux state that the Cheyennes had two hundred lodges, the Oglalas four hundred, and that there were five more Sioux circles with two hundred or more lodges each. These figures seem much too large, perhaps fifty per cent higher than the true numbers.[6]

General John Gibbon had been ordered to move down the Yellowstone from Montana with a column of infantry to co-operate

6. To give the Oglalas four hundred lodges and the Cheyennes two hundred in June, 1876, is ridiculous. This same group of Indians, Oglalas and Cheyennes, were on the Little Missouri September 8, 1876, and had only three hundred lodges in all. That was probably their strength in June. Charles A. Eastman, himself a Sioux, made a careful study of this question about the year 1900 and gave the hostiles, in 1876, nine hundred lodges with two warriors to a lodge, some lodges having extra warriors, agency Indians who were only visitors in camp. This was the hostiles' strength when they fought Crook and Custer. Before that, in May, the hostiles were on Tongue River and had only 360 lodges, with enough additional people to make four hundred lodges. Mitch Boyer, the scout, reported these numbers after carefully examining the camp site in June. The camp on Tongue River represented all the hostiles who wintered away from the agencies; by the end of May or the early part of June they were joined by enough Northern Indians from the agencies to just about double their numbers. I believe that Eastman was right in giving the Cheyennes, who were with the hostiles this summer, only fifty-five lodges. Dr. Grinnell in giving the Cheyennes two hundred lodges overlooked the fact that nearly all of the Cheyennes were at Red Cloud Agency until after June 1—they then ran away, but too late to join the hostiles.

with General Terry, who was to move westward from the Upper Missouri. In the middle of May, Gibbon was in actual contact with the hostiles near the mouth of the Rosebud. The whole country south of the Yellowstone seemed to swarm with Indians. Terry, with Custer and his Seventh Cavalry, had at last taken the field. Terry left Fort Abraham Lincoln, near the present city of Bismarck, North Dakota, May 17, but his movements were so retarded by his large wagon-train that he did not reach the Little Missouri until twelve days later. Here he spent some time in hunting for Sitting Bull, who, as he had been informed, was wintering in this vicinity. What kind of a commander was this who would try to find Sioux in their winter camps at the end of May? To add to the ludicrousness of the situation, Terry now ordered Gibbon to hurry down the Yellowstone, and to assist him in hunting Sitting Bull on the Little Missouri, and Gibbon, with Sitting Bull almost in plain sight just across the river, had to obey.[7]

As undisturbed as if there were no soldiers in their country, the Sioux held their Sun Dance on the Rosebud in the second week of June. Sitting Bull was the principal dancer, and he had a vision of dead soldiers falling into his camp upside down. This satisfied him and he waited in perfect faith for the coming of the soldiers. Major M. A. Reno almost encountered the hostile camp while the Sun Dance was in progress. Terry had given up hunting for Sitting Bull on the Little Missouri and had sent Reno with most of the Seventh Cavalry to scout up the Powder and across to the Rosebud. On the latter stream, Reno found the trail and camp sites of the hostiles. He also saw a great trail leading toward the Little Bighorn. The Sioux at this moment were on the divide not far west of Reno's position, and the fact that they did not see him seems almost a miracle. After making this discovery he turned down the Rosebud to report his find to Terry.

7. The Indians today cannot, of course, give exact dates for the movement of the hostile camp in 1876. The military reports show that in mid-May Lieutenant J. H. Bradley of Gibbon's column saw the hostile camp on Tongue River, and that on May 19 Gibbon's Crow scouts saw the hostiles moving from the Tongue to the Rosebud. On May 27, Bradley saw the smoke of the great hostile camp on the Rosebud, the village at the time being about eighteen miles above the mouth of the stream. These hostiles were the bands that wintered in the Powder River country, their camp site on Tongue River showed 360 lodges formed into several circles—Mitch Boyer reported nine circles, but he may have been mistaken. On the Rosebud the hostiles were joined by the Indians from the agencies with approximately five hundred lodges, making the entire hostile force with extra people, who had no lodges, about nine hundred lodges, perhaps 2,000 warriors in all.

On June 16, a small party of Cheyennes discovered Crook's column near the head of the Rosebud. These young men hurried back to the hostile camp, which was then on Ash (Reno) Creek, a tributary of the Little Bighorn. They arrived in camp after dark and reported to the soldier lodge of their own camp. The leaders of the Sioux were at once informed, and a council of all the chiefs was held. The criers announced the news through the length of the great camp and the warriors prepared for the coming fight. About a thousand of them set out, moving through the darkness toward the Rosebud. They marched in the column formation which was customary on such occasions; the front, rear, and flanks of the column were guarded by men of the soldier-societies who prevented anyone from slipping away in advance and thereby putting the enemy on guard. Toward daybreak they halted for a rest, and then moved on again. At dawn they were drawn up in ranks behind a hill on the west side of the Rosebud near the southern end of the canyon. The chiefs sent some scouts up the slope to look over the top of the hill, but as the warriors moved forward several of Crook's Crow scouts suddenly appeared on the hilltop. Some shots were exchanged, and the great mass of warriors broke through the line of Indian soldiers who were holding them back and rushed up the slope. With their ponies at a dead run, the Crows made for Crook's camp, which was just beyond the hill, shouting *Lakota! Lakota! Sioux! Sioux!*

Thus the Battle of the Rosebud was begun, June 17, 1876. Crook, whose scouts had informed him that the hostiles were encamped on the Rosebud just below the canyon, was just starting his march in the hope of surprising the hostiles and capturing their village when his Crow scouts came roaring back from the hill with the hostiles swarming after them. The Indians first struck Crook's cavalry which was concentrated on the right flank near the canyon; they charged straight in and attacked the troops, sometimes in hand-to-hand encounters. They soon noticed that most of Crook's Shoshoni and Crow scouts were over on his left flank, with his infantry, and shifted their attack in that direction. Here many charges and counter-charges were made. From the Indians' account it is perfectly clear that they had no plan and no real leadership. Groups of warriors charged here and there, as they pleased. Crazy Horse was there, but he was only a warrior taking part in the general melee. Sitting Bull was there, so badly crippled from his torture in the recent Sun Dance that he could hardly ride. He took little part in the battle, but his voice could be heard encouraging the warriors.

Crook seems to have greatly underrated the Indians, even after he had witnessed their first charges. He was still determined to capture their village, and early in the fight he pushed most of his cavalry into the canyon with orders to advance rapidly and attack the Indian camp. The Sioux and Cheyennes soon made him see the error of thus dividing his forces. Their attacks on the troops and the Indian scouts which the general still had under his own hand were so fierce that disaster was narrowly averted. Crook had some cavalry on his left flank in open ground where the Indians could easily attack them. Colonel Anson Mills, who was in the battle, pictures the hostiles at this point as "charging boldly and rapidly through the soldiers, knocking them from their horses with lances and knives, dismounting and killing them, cutting off the arms of some at the elbows in the middle of the fight and carrying them away."[8] Part of the Sioux warriors broke through the line and swept around to Crook's rear. The general must have been appalled at the sight, for he abandoned all ideas of an offensive and sent a staff officer into the canyon to hasten the recall of the cavalry. This force returned just in time to break up a great charge which the hostiles were about to make. The cavalry which appeared suddenly in their rear disconcerted them; they scattered, and presently broke off the engagement.

Throughout this battle the Indians showed surprising spirit. The old method of hovering, circling at a safe distance, and taking little risk was gone; a new spirit had been born in them, and they came on with their ponies at a dead run, often breaking in among the troops and fighting hand-to-hand encounters. Many of the warriors rode up and down very near the line of troops, insulting the soldiers with gestures and daring them to come out and fight. The Indian story of the battle is made up largely of accounts of such brave acts by individual warriors, and it is only from Crook's reports and the accounts of Finnerty and Bourke that we gain an impression of the general trend of the fighting. Bourke terms this

8. Colonel Anson Mills, quoted in *South Dakota Historical Collections*, Vol. XV, p. 362. The arm cutting was Cheyenne work, and I think that this war custom, and not the practice of slashing their own arms while mourning, was the reason back of the sign language name for this tribe. Several tribes had the custom of slashing their own arms in mourning.

battle a victory for Crook and the general in his report takes the same view, stating that he drove the Indians completely off the field. This would have been very well, except for the word drove, if Crook had been on the defensive; but he was on the offensive, being determined to reach the hostile camps and strike a decisive blow. The battle stopped him in his tracks. The following day he retired to his Goose Creek base camp, where he remained for nearly six weeks awaiting reinforcements. This does not have much of the appearance of a victory. The hostiles, who had been completely driven from the field, returned at dawn in considerable force. They escorted Crook to Goose Creek, harassing his march. They hovered about his camp until June 20, then disappeared entirely and Crook saw nothing more of them until July 10. The true results of the Battle of the Rosebud were that Crook's campaign was ruined and that he was kept pegged to his base camp while the hostiles were engaged with Custer.

The Indians in this battle had from 1,000 to 1,500 warriors; Crook had about 1,300 men, including the Indian scouts. Crook reported his loss as nine killed, and twenty-one wounded, but this evidently did not include the losses among his Indian scouts, for his staff officer, Captain John G. Bourke, reported the total loss at fifty-seven killed and wounded. The Indians assert that their loss was eleven killed and five wounded. The entire lack of leadership among the hostiles in this battle, which was admitted by the Indians themselves, seems so strange that one can hardly avoid the suspicion that they had a plan which failed and that it was then every man for himself. They held a council before leaving camp, and that fact added to their procedure of marching in regular column with Indian soldiers on guard to prevent any warriors going on ahead to alarm the troops and put them on their guard, have the appearance of an attempt to employ the ancient decoy party trap. I have an account obtained by George Bent from old Two Moon twenty-five years ago which suggests that a trap was set, and it is known that Crazy Horse, after his surrender, told a reporter (see *Chicago Tribune*, June 17, 1877) that it was his plan to draw Crook into a trap. Some of Crook's officers and J. F. Finnerty, who was with Crook, were also of the opinion that a trap had been planned; indeed, they stated that this trap was in the Rosebud canyon and that the Indians had formed barriers and breastworks of fallen timber which would have made it impossible for the troops to escape once they were well into the canyon. This latter statement is probably incorrect as the Indians did not have time to prepare barriers in the canyon, these were probably old obstructions placed there in former years to prevent their ponies straying from the canyon and getting lost. But it does seem very probable that a trap was planned and that the plan was ruined when Crook's Crow scouts discovered the massed force of hostiles behind the hill and drew those warriors after them in their flight.[9]

General Terry, after wasting much time hunting for Sitting Bull on the Little Missouri during the last part of May, moved over to Powder River and lost many days in establishing a useless base camp at the mouth of this stream. It was June 21 when his entire command reached the mouth of the Rosebud, where he received Major Reno's report that the hostiles had moved farther on, to the Little Bighorn. Terry now had a conference with Custer and Gibbon and decided on a plan of operations. During this campaign every superior officer seems to have been haunted by the fear that the hostiles would run and get away from him if he did not divide his forces and surround them. Terry's plan shows this clearly. He decided to march up the Bighorn with Gibbon's infantry, to reach the mouth of the Little Bighorn June 26; Custer with the Seventh Cavalry was to go up the Rosebud, get on the trail Reno had found and follow it, thus coming in on the hostiles from the opposite direction. To further emphasize his fear that the Indians would get away, Terry ordered Custer to keep feeling to his left, to make certain that the hostiles did not slip around his flank. The orders also stated that Custer might be compelled to make a swing very far to the south, to head the Indians back into a position where both columns could strike them.

Through his own indiscretions Custer had lost much of his popularity, and he was also in disgrace with President Grant and General Sheridan. He had been compelled to humble himself and beg before he obtained permission to lead his regiment on this campaign, and he seems to have made up his mind that at the first opportunity he would cut loose from Terry and Gibbon and win a victory over the Indians with his own regiment. To carry out General Terry's plan, Custer should have made a leisurely march up the

9. Crook in his first report, June 20, states that the canyon was "covered," meaning that the Indians had a force ready to close in if the troops entered the gorge. He also says that his Indian scouts refused to enter the canyon, asserting it meant death.

Rosebud and should not have started across toward the Little Bighorn until the evening of the twenty-fifth. Instead of doing this, he made a forced march. With his men and horses tired he reached the Indian trail running from the Rosebud toward the Little Bighorn on the evening of June 24, twenty-four hours ahead of time; yet he would not permit his command to take the rest they so much needed, but started on a night march across the divide. At dawn on the twenty-fifth, in sight of the Little Bighorn valley, he told his officers that the hostiles had discovered the command, which was not true, and that no further delay was possible. He then advanced as rapidly as he could to attack the Indians. In his haste to bring on an action Custer would not wait to learn the position and strength of the hostiles; he gave up the advantage of a surprise attack at dawn, crossed the divide at 10:30 A. M. and hastened forward to assault this great Indian village in the middle of a bright June day. Every decision he made shows that he was even more confident that he could whip any force of Sioux than Crook had been before the battle of June 17. Nothing exhibits this more clearly than the order he now issued for the command to separate into three groups (four if we include the pack-train and its guard), with the object of making the attack from different directions. He was afraid that this huge mass of Sioux would run away if they were not surrounded!

The hostiles were encamped on the west bank of the Little Bighorn, their great village extended along the river for three or four miles. The lodges were set in five circles. Sitting Bull's Hunkpapa circle was farthest up stream, opposite and a little above the mouth of Reno Creek. The Miniconjou circle was below the Hunkpapas, and just to the southwest of them the Oglalas had set their circle. Below the Miniconjous were the Sans Arcs, and farthest down of all was the Cheyenne circle. Although these Indians knew that troops were near they were quite undisturbed. From their own statements we learn that two or more small parties of their people saw Custer's column advancing, yet the troops were almost in the village before any alarm was given. Sitting Bull had taken no precautions, nor had any of the other leaders.

Major Reno with three troops (112 men) and a handful of Arikara Indian scouts had been ordered to attack the upper end of the village. He crossed the river four miles above the Hunkpapa camp and advanced to attack, his horses' hoofs raising a great cloud of dust. It was the approach of this rolling cloud down the valley that first warned the Indians. As the alarm was shouted the Sioux women and children began to scream and run, and joined by all the older people they fled in great confusion down the west side of the river. The warriors were seeking arms and ponies, and as soon as they were mounted they rode to the upper end of the Hunkpapa camp to meet the soldiers. With most of the Hunkpapa warriors facing him and hundreds of Sioux and Cheyennes hurrying up from the lower camps, Reno had no chance of success and he seems to have known it. He dismounted his men before reaching the Indian camp and formed them into a line on foot. The Arikaras were expected to run off the Sioux pony herds, but the sight of this vast hostile village had taken the heart out of them, and when presently the Sioux made a charge in their direction they started for home. Most of them did not halt until they reached the Rosebud.

By this time the hostiles had several hundred warriors facing Reno's little band. Sitting Bull was there, and Crazy Horse, Black Moon, Big Road, Gall, and many other famous men; yet there was no leadership. The Indians admit this—it was the Crook fight all over again, the warriors acting as individuals or in small groups. But there was no need for leadership. Reno was quickly forced back into the timber near the river, where he found it impossible to hold out and soon mounted what men he could gather and started to retreat. The Indians chased the soldiers across the river like fleeing buffalo. By this time Captain F. W. Benteen's three troops had come up on the hills east of the river, and Reno with the survivors of his band now joined him. Benteen, who saw the end of the Reno fight, estimated that about nine hundred warriors were engaged. This fits in well with the Indian accounts. The hostiles seem to have had a total of about 1,500 warriors, but part of the men remained with the women and children, to guard them and the camps. The Indians were still engaged in escorting Reno across the river when messengers reached them with the news that more soldiers, Custer's command, were approaching the village farther down the river. Sitting Bull was certainly having luck. He had waited patiently for his Sun Dance vision to be fulfilled—for the soldiers to drop into his camp from the sky—and here it was occurring twice in less than one hour's time.

There is no mystery about Custer's march and the fate of his command. Most of our doubts concerning what happened after Custer left Reno may be traced to the fact that Captain E. S. Godfrey, in writing his narrative of the battle, set aside the evidence and based his story on a theory of his own as to the line of Custer's march. All of the official reports, made at the time, indicate clearly the line of advance, and fifty years of controversy have not shaken the evidence of these first reports. It is true that within the past few years several Indian versions of the battle have appeared which seem to bear out Captain Godfrey's views, but these narratives not only ignore the official reports, but they disregard many earlier Indian statements.

There is nothing in these present day Indian accounts to suggest that Custer came down to the ford near the Miniconjou camp and attempted to cross there, yet the evidence gathered immediately after the battle clearly showed that he did. His trail (which Captain Godfrey alone refused to accept as his trail) led to that ford. Custer left his command when it turned toward the ford and rode up on a hill, where Reno's men saw him. He waved his hat and rode out of sight, and they thought they heard cheering. It was at this moment that Custer sent back the famous message: "Benteen, come on. Big village. Bring packs." To which was added the excited postscript, "P. Bring pac's." The pack mules were carrying the extra ammunition. Seeing the Indian women and children fleeing toward the lower end of the village, Custer and his men clearly believed that the hostiles were all on the run. The two men who brought Custer's last message to Benteen were enthusiastic; they cheered the other troops as they passed them, calling out that the Sioux were "skedaddling."

Some of the older Indian accounts, obtained years ago, indicate that Custer was seen before he turned down toward the river, and that the Indians sent messengers to inform the warriors who were fighting Reno. Some warriors who were on the spot hid in the brush near the Miniconjou camp, and when Custer's troops came down to the ford, opened fire on them and finally forced them to leave the river bank before the warriors who had been fighting Reno could arrive. Major Reno examined this ground after the battle and reported that Custer had come down to the ford, the signs indicating that he had with him "C" Troop, Captain Tom Custer, "I" Troop, Captain M. W. Keogh, and "E" Troop, Lieutenant E. A. Smith's gray horse troop. Some of the Indian stories bear this out—they saw the gray horse soldiers at the ford.

Moreover, the map showing the position in which the bodies of Custer's men were found proves that the command came down to the ford. It also seems to indicate that on leaving the ford Custer divided his command, two troops, Keogh and Calhoun, going up a ravine to a high ridge, while the others, Tom Custer, Yates, and Smith, left the ravine nearer the ford and took a route between the river and the ridge. Both of these columns were marching down the river with the evident purpose of finding a ford near the lower end of the hostile village.[10]

Custer had just left the river bank, followed by a force of Indians from the village, when the warriors from the Reno fight returned down the river. From the Indian accounts it appears that about four hundred of these warriors came down the east bank and at once rushed up the ravine, attacking Calhoun's troop as it began its march along the ridge. Meanwhile the rest of the warriors from the Reno fight came down the west bank into the village. They were led by Black Moon, Crazy Horse, and other chiefs. Watching from the village while the warriors attacked the rear of the troops on the ridge and slope across the river, the Indian leaders are said to have made their first real plan. They decided that part of the warriors, led by Black Moon and others, should cross at the ford which Custer had attempted to use, while the rest, led by Crazy Horse and other chiefs, should go to the ford near the Cheyenne camp, cross the river and attack the troops from the north.[11]

Stanley Vestal's Sioux accounts of the attack on Custer present a clear-cut picture of the fighting, yet they do not seem to cover certain features. His accounts assert that the troops on the ridge (Calhoun and Keogh) were the first objects of attack, and they ignore the march of the three troops which were moving down the slope between the ridge and the river. But the trails left by the marching cavalry seem to indicate that the three troops nearest the river were the first to be attacked, for dead bodies dotted this trail from near the ford onward, and the trail itself—dim and confused—

10. A map showing where the bodies of Custer's men were found, and his trail, is in *South Dakota Historical Collections,* Vol. XV, p. 628; another is in Stanley Vestal's *Warpath,* p. 202.

11. This was the version given to Captain Pollard at Standing Rock Agency just a month after the battle by some Sioux who had arrived from the hostile camp. They said that Black Moon was killed soon after the crossing at the ford and that Gall then took control. The Sioux today make Gall the leader from the first. They contend that Black Moon and Crazy Horse consulted before crossing the river and decided not to join the Indians who were already attacking Custer but to attack from two new directions.

seemed to prove that the troops were in open order, fighting as they marched. The Keogh and Calhoun trail on the other hand was heavy and clear-cut, indicating that these troops moved to the ridge in close column formation and were not attacked until they got to the higher ground. We can explain these trails only by assuming that warriors from the village crossed over when Custer left the ford and immediately attacked the three troops which were marching along the slope, and that it was some minutes later that warriors from the Reno fight went up the ravine and attacked Calhoun and Keogh.

The clear evidence of these trails and the position of the soldiers' bodies refute many of the Indian statements. The trail of the three troops that marched along the slope near the river ended abruptly in a pile of dead bodies at a point down the slope between the river and the hill where Custer fell. In this pile of dead were found the bodies of Captain Tom Custer of "C" Troop and Captain Yates of "I" Troop, while nearby lay a pile of bodies of men belonging to Smith's gray horse troop. It is clear that these three troops were suddenly assailed and cut to pieces. The recently published Sioux narratives do not account for this, but the older ones do, as they indicate that while these troops were on the march, harassed by warriors who were attacking their rear, a large force of Cheyennes and Sioux came across the river at the ford near the Cheyenne camp, hid in a ravine, and suddenly charged out to attack the troops in front and on the flank.

By the time Custer reached the hill on which he died he must have realized that his command was doomed. Half of his officers and men were already down; the rest had been driven into groups, each of which was hemmed in by masses of Indians who were attacking them, mounted and afoot, with deadly persistence. The Indian accounts agree that it was a hard fight, the troops fighting to the last; but from the moment they were surrounded in the final position, Custer's men did not have a chance.

From their hill, Reno's and Benteen's commands had heard the firing and had heard it die away. They waited in great anxiety, discussing the question as to where Custer was and what action they should take. The pack-train with the reserve ammunition had not come up, and Reno was unwilling to move without it. At about five P. M., the packs arrived and the command advanced cautiously along the ridge in the direction Custer had taken. They presently came in sight of the battlefield, still covered with a thick haze of dust and smoke, through which parties of Indians could be seen riding about or sitting on their horses on the hilltops. Far away a few shots were heard.

The hostiles soon caught sight of the troops, and great clouds of dust arose in the valley as they came streaking toward the bluff where the command was halted. Reno at once ordered a retirement and was soon back in his original position on the hill. Here the Indians attacked him in great force, boldly charging in, attempting to throw the troops into confusion and to get at the horses; but they now were fighting troops standing solidly in a good position, and try as they might they could not break the line or win any material success. They kept up their charges for a short time, then sent their ponies to the rear and tried fighting on foot, but still they could not shake the troops. This battle continued until dark and was resumed on the morning of the twenty-sixth; but by noon the Indians learned that more soldiers were coming up the Little Bighorn (Terry and Gibbon) and they soon left Reno's command and returned to the village. Later they were seen firing the grass in the valley, and toward sunset Reno's men saw through rifts in the smoke pall a huge column of Indians moving slowly up the river toward the Bighorn Mountains.

That the hostiles showed no desire to stay and fight Terry was not surprising. They had had enough fighting for one summer. Their defeat of Crook, their great success in the battle with Custer, and the immense amount of plunder they had taken seem to have satisfied them. They had fought hard, and now they wished to be let alone, to dance and to feast, to gloat over the plunder, and to quarrel over its division. Occupied with these ideas they left the Little Bighorn and headed for the mountains, seeking seclusion and a period of freedom from military annoyance.

The news of the Custer disaster shocked the nation into a sudden realization that a war was in progress in that same Powder River country where wars with the Sioux had been fought in 1865, 1866, and 1867. Crook's fight on the Rosebud had been represented as a victory, but there was no concealing the fact that the Custer battle was a dreadful defeat. The military who had predicted that they could easily and quickly drive all the hostiles to the reservation, were now sadly in need of alibis; and we find the generals attempting to place the blame for their failure at the door of the Indian

Office, which they angrily denounced for misleading them with false reports as to the number of the hostiles and also for permitting practically every able-bodied agency warrior to slip away to join Crazy Horse and Sitting Bull. There really seems to be no justification for such complaints. The Indian Office figures were based on the winter population of the hostile camps, and the great body of Sioux who left the agencies in the spring were not agency Indians but hostiles who had come in to winter at the agencies. The military officers stationed near the agencies saw these Sioux leaving for Powder River in the spring of 1876 and did nothing to prevent it. Crook himself learned early in March that the wild bands were beginning to move from the agencies to the hostile camps, and he did nothing to stop the movement. One gains the impression that from Sheridan and Crook down, the army men in the spring of this year were so confident of easy success that they did not care how many Sioux left the agencies.

All through the month of July, Crook's force remained in camp on Goose Creek, waiting for reinforcements. Terry, after the rescue of the remnant of Custer's command on the Little Bighorn, retired to the Yellowstone and went into camp, waiting for reinforcements. In these two commands there were about 2,000 troops, but neither Crook nor Terry considered it safe to move without a much larger force. In their anxiety lest the Sioux run away from them, the generals had planned a surround-attack, and until after the Custer disaster they seemed quite unaware that this plan of campaign gave to the Indians the inestimable advantage of operating on interior lines. In early July the Sioux had the power to whip Crook and Terry separately, but being Indians they naturally did not think of doing anything of this nature. The Indians were dancing, feasting, going to the Bighorn Mountains for lodge-poles, coming back to the plains, and again dancing and feasting. It was the greatest summer of their lives, and to realize fully how astonishing this spectacle was, we must recall that for several years many army officers had been waiting impatiently but hopefully for orders to march against the Sioux, and that some of them had expressed a willingness to give these Indians odds of five to one and still beat them. Now, in July, 1876, the army was demanding a superiority of force before it would even venture to march into the hostile country. During ten days in June the fighting spirit of the Sioux had wrought this miracle. Some of the higher military leaders, who were not being quite frank, attempted to explain their new-found love for caution by stating that there were from 10,000 to 15,000 warriors in the hostile camps; but officers who had taken part in the fighting and had examined the deserted Indian camps usually gave the hostiles about 3,000 men, and even this number seems to be too high.

Taking up again the Indian narratives which have recently appeared in print, we find the Sioux of today stating that after the Custer battle Sitting Bull sent men, riding night and day to summon more warriors from the agencies; these agency Sioux are said to have started at once, perhaps riding night and day, and soon were in the hostile camp. These statements are contradicted sharply by the contemporary evidence, and such quick thinking and action as are here attributed to Sitting Bull and the agency Indians are so unlike the Sioux of 1876 that they seem a grotesque distortion of the truth. Sitting Bull is said to have addressed these fresh recruits from the agencies and to have told them that he would now strike another blow. But he took no action. He had Crook over on Goose Creek within easy reach; the Black Hills settlements and the Montana border were open to attack, but he took no action. No one who knew the situation at the time and the methods of thought and conduct of the wild Sioux would have expected him to strike another blow.

The truth is that from the moment the Custer battle ended these Indians took up their regular annual program and resumed their habitual routine. It was then, late in June, time to go to the Bighorn Mountains for lodge-poles, and there they went. Presently the time arrived to start the autumn move eastward, and off they went, passing by the Custer battlefield, hunting on the Rosebud, and then crossing to Tongue River. From the Rosebud some of the warriors went up-river and paid their respects to Crook, shooting up his camp and making attempts to run off his horses. These Indians fired the grass as they moved, and for weeks the whole region from the Bighorn River eastward to the Powder was blanketed in smoke; the timber on the mountains was on fire, and when the autumn rains came on the country had the appearance of a dismal and blackened wilderness. The military believed that the Indians set these fires to make the movements of the troops more difficult, but it seems that the Sioux always fired the grass at this season with the idea of having new grass earlier in the following spring.

On Blue Stone Creek on Powder River, in the district termed the Blue Mountains by Stanley Vestal's Sioux informants, the hostiles broke up their gathering, in August.[12] Part of the people moved up Powder River, part northward, but most of them went eastward toward the Little Missouri. Sitting Bull's war was now over, and the Indians had no intention of doing any further fighting. Crook and Terry were at that time ready to resume operations; but when they moved, Crook coming down the Rosebud and Terry marching up that stream, they found no Indians to fight. They met, followed the hostile trail eastward to Powder River and there separated, Terry going north of the Yellowstone, where he found no Indians, and Crook following the diminishing trail eastward. The Sioux, who had broken up into several camps and were seeking their usual wintering grounds, were very indignant when Crook disturbed them by marching into the district east of the Little Missouri. The fighting spirit with which they had bubbled over in June was gone. They had suffered no defeat—they simply did not wish to fight again this season. Incredible as it may seem, most of these Indians were heading for the agencies in the beautiful faith that the government would feed them all winter, outfit them anew, and in the spring permit them to set out for another season of hunting and fighting. Crazy Horse was following his usual autumn beat, traveling up the Little Missouri to the Bear Butte district. He did not intend to go to an agency, but most of the three hundred lodges of Sioux and Cheyennes who were with him had that intention. The elder American Horse (alias Iron Shield), with forty lodges of Miniconjous was also heading toward Bear Butte, with the intention of going in to winter at Spotted Tail Agency. Over eastward at the Antelope Buttes, a large camp of Hunkpapas, Sans Arcs, and Miniconjous were in their usual autumn location, fattening their ponies on the good grass and hoping to open a trade with the Arikaras for corn and other supplies. Sitting Bull with one hundred lodges or less was also following his autumn beat near the lower Yellowstone.

General Crook tried hard to get a fight out of the hostiles, but had no success until Colonel Anson Mills accidently ran into American Horse's camp at Slim Buttes. Mills captured the camp in a surprise attack, but finding it difficult to hold, called on Crook

12. Horned Horse said in 1876 that the hostiles split up here on Powder River, and the trail followed by the troops proved that this was correct. The Sioux today disagree as to where the camp broke up. The truth is that many people left the hostiles immediately after the Custer battle, and from that time on other groups were leaving; but the main break-up was on Powder River.

for aid. The Indians had called on Crazy Horse to come to their rescue, and when Crook came up with his column he was attacked by that chief. The Indians lacked the spirit they had shown in June and were easily beaten off.

Most of the Indians had to abandon their plan of going to the agencies. Crook was annoying them, and some of the bands had also heard that troops were at all the agencies, and that if they went in they would be disarmed and dismounted. Part of the Sioux now joined Crazy Horse and moved westward to Powder River, in the evident hope of finding a quiet place to winter, while other bands went to join Sitting Bull, north of the Yellowstone. Sitting Bull was no more willing to go on with the war than the other leaders; indeed, he sent messages to the military asking them to go away so that he might hunt buffalo in peace. But they would not go. Colonel Nelson A. Miles with his regiment of infantry presently caught up with Sitting Bull. That chief had about one-third of all the hostiles with him; yet he did not wish to fight, and when Miles attacked him he made a very poor showing and was quickly driven from the strong position he held on the hills and in ravines. Miles continued to pursue the Indians. During the night Sitting Bull with his own small camp slipped around the troops and got away northward. The other bands headed for the Yellowstone, and as Miles followed after them, they presently sent their chiefs to have a talk with him and then gave hostages as a pledge that they would all go to the Cheyenne River Agency, a pledge which most of them forgot as soon as they were out of Miles' reach. On February 11, 1877, the Canadian Northwest Mounted Police reported that Sitting Bull with 109 lodges of Sioux had crossed the international line. He was soon joined by about 100 more lodges of his followers.

CHAPTER XV

THE END OF FREEDOM
1876-1877

DURING the summer of 1876 the Oglalas at Red Cloud Agency were very uneasy and worried, and many of them were clearly frightened. The whites had taken the Black Hills without any payment and had then started a war, and the older Oglalas considered this all very bad and very hard. One chief said, "Tell the white people that this is not an Indian war; it is a white man's war, and we wish them to rub it out." All except the wilder young men and Red Cloud and his handful of followers were in fear of being drawn into the war, and all were hungry. Rations at Red Cloud were very short and would soon be gone and no new supplies were coming in the wagons. The squawmen read the papers and told the Indians of the doings in the great council at Washington, and it appeared that some of the white chiefs in the great council were very angry and were saying hard things about the Sioux. They were threatening to starve all the Sioux, and were talking of compelling the tribe to move, either to the Missouri or to a strange land in the south called Indian Territory. All this worried the Oglalas. Not many of them had been at the old Whetstone Agency on the Missouri in 1868-1871; but the Brulés and Loafers had told them of the privations they had suffered there. Many people had died in that land, old people and little children who could not endure the hunger and cold, and the Oglalas hated the very name of the Missouri River country.

All that summer Congress was in session, but it took no action on the Sioux appropriation bills. The failure of the Indians to agree promptly to give up the Black Hills was regarded as an evil act. These Indians were being fed at the public expense; therefore when they clung to their sacred Hills they were angrily accused of biting the hand that fed them, and many congressmen were strongly inclined to punish them by letting them go hungry. That the treaty of 1868 pledged the nation's honor that the Black Hills should be left to the Sioux forever did not impress Congress particularly. It was considered that the recipients of "public aid" had no rights as owners of valuable property, and Congress was determined to take the Black Hills and the Powder River and Bighorn countries away from the Sioux if it had to starve all the agency bands to make them loose their hold. But as all this was to be accomplished under the cloak of legality and with the appearance at least of fair dealing, the method of procedure was difficult to determine. For a time it was hoped that the sound whipping which the military were to administer to the wild Sioux would humble the stubborn agency Indians and bring them to a better realization of their true position; but the months dragged by and the military did not whip the wild Sioux. Crook failed in March, and when he met Crazy Horse on the Rosebud in June it was only to receive a Roland for his Oliver. Then came the stunning news of the Custer disaster.

After this tragedy, Sheridan demanded that the four great Sioux agencies, Red Cloud, Spotted Tail, Cheyenne River and Standing Rock, be turned over to the military, and after some hesitation the Interior Department acquiesced and the order was issued. More soldiers appeared at Red Cloud and Spotted Tail; the agents were dismissed and their places were filled by army officers who gave the Indians to understand that they were under military rule and that no nonsense would be tolerated. The Indians were very uneasy and unhappy. They complained that they were being treated as bad people when they had done nothing wrong. The bad Indians were all up north on the Rosebud—why did not the white chiefs take their soldiers there, where there were very many bad Indians and plenty of work for the soldiers? The older people at Red Cloud were frightened; the young men were sulky. They could no longer paint themselves, mount, and rush to the agency to circle about whooping and frightening their father the agent. The saucy little soldier chief they now had for a father was disagreeable like all the other white soldier chiefs and he did not understand them. Any day he might do something very bad, and they wanted him to go away.

When the agencies were turned over to the military on July 26, Colonel R. S. Mackenzie with eight troops of cavalry came to Red Cloud. Sheridan suspected that the agency Indians were aiding the hostiles both with men and supplies of arms and ammunition, but there seems to have been no movement toward the hostile camps after April. The taking over of the agencies was a wise precaution; but in justice to the agency Indians it should be said that they were not going out to join the hostiles. Most of them regarded the hostiles as bad Indians who were causing them a great deal of trouble. There had been no arms traded to the Indians at the agencies for two years back and no ammunition after the campaign against the hostiles opened.

The military's first act at Red Cloud was to take a count of the Indians who came in for rations. The number was found to be 4,760, and the soldiers pointed with horror to the agent's certified number of 12,873 Indians. Surely, here was proof that either an immense number of Indians had left the agency to join the hostiles, or that the agent was defrauding the government. It is to be hoped that the officers at Camp Robinson, who had been stationed near Red Cloud for two years, did not join in this attempt to use figures to pervert the truth. They must have known that nearly all the agency Indians were present at Red Cloud or accounted for. A few were known to be in the hostile camps, and others were hunting near the agency, or camping some distance off, afraid of the soldiers. The 2,000 Cheyennes who had left the agency in June (too late to join the hostiles), had gone because the government had cut off their rations in a cruel attempt to starve them into consenting to remove to Indian Territory. Perhaps 2,000 more of the absentees were Northern Indians who had left in April and had really joined the hostiles. The army's silence concerning these Northern Indians seems, to say the least, very insincere. The military officers knew that these Northern Indians were not agency Indians but wild Sioux who only wintered at the agency. They also knew that the summer population at the agency was about half the winter number. The army's accusation that Agent Hastings was engaged in perpetrating frauds was absurd. Hastings had been chosen with great care as a man of probity, sense, courage, and business ability—a man with all the qualities which his predecessor, Dr. Saville, was supposed to lack. Nevertheless, the soldiers tried to make it appear that within three months of his appointment this agent was deeply involved in crooked practices. Their only evidence was the figures they produced, and if there ever was a place on earth where figures could be made to play tricks, Red Cloud Agency in the years between 1872 and 1882 was that place.

On August 15, Congress at last passed the Sioux appropriation bill. In this measure the Indians were assured that they were not to be left to starve; but this bill contained a provision that no further appropriations for the Sioux would ever be granted unless the Indians gave up the Black Hills and the Powder River and Bighorn countries and agreed to remove either to the Missouri River or to the Indian Territory. Money was provided in the appropriation for a commission which was to proceed at once to the Sioux agencies and obtain the chiefs' signatures to an agreement. Agreement was hardly the word to describe what was in reality a demand for an unconditional surrender by the Sioux of practically everything they owned that was worth lifting. As if the good and humane men who advocated the Peace Policy had not suffered enough in seeing their ewe lambs, the Sioux, turned over to the brutal military, the government decided to appoint several prominent exponents of the Peace Policy to this new Sioux commission and to send the good men out to separate the Sioux from the Black Hills and their other valuable holdings. The hands of the commission were tied before they started as they were instructed to get from the Indians what Congress had demanded and not to alter the terms of the "agreement" in any way. This, however, did not prevent their making a report in which they vainly tried to revive public interest in the old refrain which they had chanted to such good results in 1866-1870: the wrongs of the Indians; the greed of the whites; how the Sioux had been driven to hostility by hunger and bad treatment; the harsh conduct of the military. They traced all the Indian wars of the past twenty years back to these causes and did not forget to state that some of the chiefs in speaking of the government's bad faith had caused their cheeks to flush with shame for their country. In 1866, this kind of talk had stirred the country to a feeling of pity for the poor Indians and had brought forth the Peace Policy with the church people and humanitarians in full control; but now in 1876 with the news of the Custer massacre still ringing in its ears, the country turned coldly away from the pleadings of the Indians' Friends.[1]

The commission went straight to the Red Cloud Agency to begin its labors; for, whether rightly or not, the whites still regarded Red Cloud as the most important of the Sioux chiefs. At the opening of the council Bishop Whipple prayed fervently for the unhappy Sioux. The commission then solemnly informed Red Cloud and the other chiefs that they were friends of the Sioux who had come to save the people from destruction. However, when they told the Oglalas of the method by which they were to be saved —the giving up of the Black Hills, the surrender of the Powder River and Bighorn lands, the removal either to the Missouri or to Indian Territory—the chiefs were very hesitant as to whether or not they desired salvation. The government had foreseen a possibility that the chiefs might not realize the great opportunity that was being offered them, and although some of the commission were churchmen and humanitarians, it had a stiffening of men of a different character. There was, for instance, Assistant Attorney General Gaylord. When the Oglalas showed little eagerness to sign away their lands and freedom, this gentleman spoke to them with a curt and almost brutal frankness which shocked them into a full comprehension of the fact that if they refused to sign the agreement they would find themselves in extremely serious trouble. Indeed, he told them quite plainly that if they resisted the government would starve them and their women and children and might also set the troops on them. By this unpleasant form of persuasion the chiefs were induced to sign in the phenomenally short period of two days. Under ordinary conditions the Oglalas would have considered the proposition for at least a month.

From Red Cloud the commission went down White River to Spotted Tail Agency, where the performance was repeated, the churchmen praying for the Sioux and Mr. Gaylord concluding the prayers by stating grimly that if the Sioux did not sign they would be starved and bullied into submission. At this point Spotted Tail lost his temper. He jumped up and left the council room, intending to consult with Red Cloud and the Oglala chiefs who were waiting outside, and arrange with them to reject the agreement, but his talk with Red Cloud made him alter his decision. The Oglalas had

1. The commission's full report is in *Senate Executive Documents*, second session, forty-fourth Congress, document No. 9.

already signed, and Spotted Tail had the good sense to realize that resistance was useless. Rejoining his own chiefs in the council room he talked seriously to them and to Red Cloud and Red Dog for a time, then turning to address all of the Brulés he said: "If our friends above [the Oglalas at Red Cloud Agency] had not signed it, I would help them in holding out, but as they have signed it, I now ask all good men who feel responsible to come up and sign." He then went to the table and signed the agreement, and one by one his Brulé chiefs followed him. Perhaps it was just as well that Red Cloud and his Oglalas had not given Spotted Tail a chance to unite the Sioux and resist. The government meant what it said and would have starved the people into submission.[2]

In spite of Bishop Whipple's prayers and the obviously sincere protestations of some of the commissioners that they were the true friends of the Sioux who had come to save them, the Indians were very suspicious. They spoke bitterly of past treaties which meant one thing to them and another to the whites. The chiefs were all worried about the reference in the agreement to Indian Territory. It was explained to them that a Sioux delegation would visit the Indian Territory and that then the Sioux would go there to live if they desired to do so; but the Indians feared that if they signed they would be forced to leave their old home. The agency chiefs protested earnestly that they had taken no part in the war and that their people should not be treated like conquered enemies and removed from their home. As they put it, the paper to be signed was not bloody—it was not a peace treaty ending a war. One chief said, "You speak to me about another land, a country far away from this. I think you should not have mentioned this to me at all. My grandfathers and relatives have lived here always. There is no blood on this paper; we are not at war with you; and, therefore, when you speak of a strange land, a land where we were not brought up, a land far away, my chiefs and soldiers are very much displeased and they wish me to say that they are displeased with the mention

2. That Mr. Gaylord did not mince matters in speaking to the Sioux is shown by what one of the chiefs, Standing Elk, said to him in reply: "Your words are like a man knocking me in the head with a stick. What you have spoken has put great fear upon us. Whatever we do, wherever we go, we are expected to say yes! yes! yes! yes!—and when we don't agree at once to what you ask of us in council, you always say, You won't get anything to eat! You won't get anything to eat!" From 1871, whenever the government made a demand and the agency Sioux resisted it, this ugly threat of starving the people into submission was made, and on several occasions it was carried out.

of that land." Spotted Tail said grimly that he would accompany the delegation to the Indian Territory solely to protect the interests of his people, but that while there he would go about with his eyes shut and his ears and his mouth shut, for he was detemined that the Sioux should not be either cajoled or coerced into going into that country to live.

At the Sioux agencies on the Missouri the commission had less difficulty in persuading the chiefs to sign. They had to listen to a great deal of childish talk and to some rather straight speaking. All the chiefs were anxious to know what price they were to receive for the Black Hills and all the other lands they were expected to surrender. The view of Congress was that the government was under no obligation to feed the Sioux, and that the expense of feeding the tribe was about equivalent to the value of the lands they were asked to give up. To this view some of the chiefs strongly objected, and one of them (Long Mandan) expressed the shrewd opinion that when the government under the treaty of 1868 compelled the Sioux to give up hunting and cooped them up at the agencies it took from the people their means of life and made itself liable for their support, and that the Black Hills and the Powder River and Bighorn lands were a different matter altogether, and in justice should be paid for separately.

None of the Sioux chiefs on this occasion had a good enough memory to recall that under the treaty of 1868 no future cession of land would be binding unless three-fourths of the adult male Indians signed the document. The present agreement was being forced through with the names of only a few chiefs attached to it. At the time, the officials justified this by asserting that the clause in the treaty referred only to future treaties, while this was only an agreement. In 1883, when the whites again grew hungry for Sioux lands and attempted to take half of what the Indians had left by cajoling a few chiefs into signing an agreement, Congress itself grew indignant at this brazen attempt to violate the treaty of 1868 and insisted that three-fourths of the adult Sioux males must sign the document. By this action Congress branded the agreement of 1876 as an illegal act, and this fact was at once seized upon by a prominent Dakota jurist, who argued that since the seizure of the Black Hills in 1876 through an agreement signed only by chiefs had violated the treaty, a precedent had been thus created and the government was now free to violate the treaty whenever it chose to do so.

When the military took over the Sioux agencies late in July, 1876, part of the Indians were so frightened that they ran away, but they did not go far and hunger soon drove most of them back. There was little game on the reservation, and most of the agency Sioux were too afraid of their hostile kinsmen to venture into the Powder River region in quest of buffalo. At Red Cloud Agency part of the people stampeded in this way but presently returned for rations and submitted to the orders of the army officer who was their agent. Red Cloud and his friend Red Leaf would not submit to orders, took their camps to Chadron Creek, twenty-three miles east of the agency, and refused to budge. Red Cloud was very busy hatching schemes and talking about making a war, but he had little influence outside his own small band. The other Oglala chiefs made friends with the military officers and tried to coax them into taking their troops elsewhere. By this time the Black Hills agreement had been signed, and the chiefs suggested politely to Colonel Mackenzie that it would be a good idea for him to take his men up to the Hills and let them dig all the gold they wanted.

But General Sheridan had other plans. He wished to humble the agency Sioux by taking their arms and ponies from them and by forcing them to encamp close to the agencies where the troops could watch them and prevent the hostiles from slipping in unobserved to join the agency bands. Sheridan had said angrily after the Crook and Custer battles that every able bodied agency Sioux had joined the hostiles. Now, in August, he was claiming that there were such large forces of armed warriors at the agencies that his troops were too few to control them. He therefore decided to take no action until Crook and Terry had concluded their campaign and were near enough to aid the troops at the agencies.

When Crook's column reached the Black Hills from the north in September, Sheridan ordered him to leave his command and come down to the Union Pacific line for a conference. Red Cloud's recent conduct was discussed at this interview, and Crook was ordered to go to the agency and deal with the situation. Red Cloud was still refusing to obey the military, sticking to his camp at Chadron Creek, and talking war. He had been engaged in such performances since he first came to the agency in 1871, but General Sheridan and General Crook were impressed. Crook wished to wait until his own column came down from the Black Hills before tackling Red Cloud, but a report that an outbreak was about to occur induced him to act at once. On October 23, Colonel Mackenzie with his Fourth Cavalry and a force of Pawnee Indian scouts began a secret march from the agency toward Chadron Creek. At dawn on the twenty-fourth the "hostiles" in the camps of Red Cloud and Red Leaf awoke to find themselves surrounded. While they had slept the detestable Pawnees had quietly entered the camp and removed all their ponies, and here they were on foot, with soldiers all around them. Much crestfallen, the two great chiefs watched their warriors come out and lay their guns and other arms on the ground; the lodges were ordered taken down and the whole camp was marched to the agency under guard.[3]

Red Cloud's dignity was dreadfully ruffled by this affair. A touch of comedy was added when a sub-committee of the humanitarians who had induced the Sioux to sign away the Black Hills earlier in the fall appeared at the Red Cloud Agency to gather an Oglala delegation and lead it to Indian Territory in the hope of inducing the Indians to remove to that country. These gentlemen, on reaching the agency, were curtly informed by the military that they could not communicate with Red Cloud until certain operations then in progress had been completed. The next day these good men were shocked to see their ewe lamb Red Cloud and his band marched in under heavy guard. The worst of it was that some of the Sioux chiefs had suspected that a raid on their pony herds and stock of arms was contemplated by the military, and during the councils over the Black Hills agreement had referred to the subject. The gentlemen of the commission had assured them that no agency Indian would be harmed in his person or property (a promise which they had no authority to give), and they were now accused by the chiefs of having lied to them.

Crook soon called the chiefs to council and spoke very rudely to them. He did not speak as Bishop Whipple and the other good men of the Sioux commission had done, but told the chiefs that he expected a marked improvement in their conduct from that time on. He informed them that fifty-three companies of troops were at or near Red Cloud Agency, and asked them to ponder the problem

---

3. Fifty guns were taken from the Red Cloud and Red Leaf bands, which proved how little truth there was in the army claim that every warrior had at least one Winchester. The troops captured 705 ponies, which they drove to Fort Laramie and sold at auction at prices under $5 per head. Many of these animals had been given to the Oglalas the year before in payment for their hunting rights in Nebraska, the animals being turned over to them at a price of $120 each.

as to how long they could face such a force if it came to fighting. He told them that Red Cloud had been insolent on many occasions, that he was now deposed, and that Spotted Tail was to be the head of both agencies, which must have tickled Spotted Tail as there was no love lost between him and Red Cloud. Finally, the general informed them that they were being fed and cared for and that he expected some loyalty from them in their dealings with the government, not only in words but in actions. First of all, he wanted them to give him some of their young men as scouts for service against the hostiles, and he told the chiefs that if they tried to discourage the young men from enlisting he was going to be in a very bad humor.[4] The chiefs listened in silence. This man, who did not dress like a big soldier chief, spoke very bad words. How far away seemed those happy days when they had chased Agent Saville into the Red Cloud stockade, demanding unlimited rations and threatening to kill all the whites in the country if they were refused. Times were very hard now.

Red Cloud refused to head the Oglala delegation which was preparing to visit Indian Territory. He said that he could not leave his band in their present sad condition, dismounted and under the guard of the white soldiers. The characters of Red Cloud and Spotted Tail are clearly brought out during this period of crisis, and one cannot avoid the impression that Spotted Tail was the bigger man. He made no attempt to resist the military, knowing the futility of such a course. He went to the Indian Territory with no thought of advising the people to move there, but only to obtain information to use in resisting the government's attempt to take the Sioux from their own land. He had been ready to oppose the government's seizure of the Black Hills and other lands, if Red Cloud had not permitted himself to be coaxed and bullied into signing the agreement. Red Cloud's opposition to the government was persistent but not very intelligent. Spotted Tail tried to co-operate with the government when it was attempting to aid his people; he kept his opposition for such acts of injustice as the seizure of the Sioux lands in 1876, but even then he did not imitate Red

4. It would appear from this speech that the general was already in a bad humor and determined to make the agency Sioux pay for all the trouble the hostiles had given him. Back of his words lay the determination to force the agency Indians to fight their own kindred. His pretense that these Indians were living on the government's bounty was a shocking travesty of the facts. They had just given up enough lands to pay for their support for sixty years at least.

Cloud in his futile talk of starting a war but rather tried to appeal to the American public's sense of fair play. Charles A. Eastman, who as a Sioux full-blood should appreciate this difference, persistently misrepresents Spotted Tail's position. In dealing with these events of 1876, Eastman makes the astonishing statements that Spotted Tail was the only Sioux chief to accept an agency before 1876, that Red Cloud first came to an agency in that year, and that when Spotted Tail was made head-chief by General Crook the Sioux were so angry that this chief had to go to Camp Sheridan to live under the protection of the military. There was no such feeling against Spotted Tail in 1876.

The Oglalas did not respond very heartily to Crook's appeal for them to enlist to fight their friends in the hostile camp. At Red Cloud and Spotted Tail agencies Crook obtained only fifty-nine Sioux scouts, many of whom were half-breeds. James Twiss, the Sioux son of the old agent Twiss, was one of these recruits. The general also obtained at Red Cloud Agency a few Northern Cheyenne scouts and a large number of Northern Arapahoes. With his Indian scouts, eleven troops of cavalry, and a large force of infantry, Crook left Fort Fetterman, November 15, 1876, on a winter campaign.

The Northern Cheyennes known as Dull Knife's band, composed of about 175 lodges, had run away from Red Cloud Agency in June, because the government was attempting to remove them to Indian Territory. Dr. Grinnell in his *Fighting Cheyennes* includes these people among the Cheyennes who were present in the hostile camp when the Indians fought Crook and Custer; but these Indians left the agency too late to take part in the battles of June 17 and June 25, and there is no evidence to indicate that they joined the hostiles at all. At this time they were in winter camp in a canyon on the head of Powder River, and when Crook learned of their location he sent Colonel Mackenzie with the cavalry and Indian scouts to attack them. Mackenzie surprised their village on November 25 and after a hard fight drove the Indians out, destroyed the village, and captured most of their ponies. Beaten from their camp, the Cheyennes went over to Tongue River and joined Crazy Horse, who was wintering there. Captain John G. Bourke of Crook's staff has related that Crazy Horse refused hospitality to the cold and hungry people of Dull Knife's band and that these Cheyennes made their way to Red Cloud Agency, coming in small parties in late December and early January. He says that most of their men enlisted as scouts, expressing an earnest desire to fight Crazy Horse because of his bad treatment of their people. In late years the Cheyennes have denied that Crazy Horse treated them badly, contending instead that he put them into good lodges and gave them food, clothing, and many horses. The official records show that only a few of these Cheyennes surrendered at Red Cloud Agency this winter, and that most of them were with Crazy Horse and aided him in his fights with Colonel Miles; part of them later surrendered to Miles, while others came in and surrendered with Crazy Horse in April, 1877.

Captain Bourke gives too much importance to the results of the Dull Knife fight, stating that the defeat of the Cheyennes and later enlistment of their warriors as scouts convinced the Sioux that it was useless to continue their resistance. Crook's own reports show that he learned from his Sioux scouts before the Dull Knife fight that the hostiles were anxious to surrender if they could obtain some assurance that they would not be badly treated. In his narrative, Bourke states that after the Dull Knife fight Crook hastened back to Red Cloud Agency and began negotiations with the agency chiefs in anticipation of the surrender of the hostiles. Even before this, from his camp near the mouth of the Tongue River, Colonel Nelson A. Miles had succeeded in opening a peace parley with the Crazy Horse group of hostiles who were wintering on the head of the Tongue. Miles seemed on the point of inducing these Indians to surrender about the middle of December, but when five Sioux leaders approached his camp for a talk his Crow scouts suddenly rushed on them and cut them to pieces. Miles disarmed the Crows at once, took their ponies from them and sent the animals to the Sioux with a message expressing his regret at the bad conduct of the Crows.[5]

The hostiles were certainly in a bad way during this winter. Most of their people usually wintered at the agencies, those who remained in the Powder River country spending the cold season in widely separated camps of some fifty lodges each. Crazy Horse now

5. Stanley Vestal, *New Sources of Indian History*, p. 182, gives a modern Sioux version of this affair which states that the Sioux killed by the Crow scouts were not leaders but young warriors who had stolen some horses from the troops and had been ordered by the chiefs to go and return these animals. Miles in his report says that five chiefs were marching in a line some distance in advance of a large body of Sioux and that the Crows rushed on these chiefs and killed them.

had 600 lodges—fully two-thirds of all the hostiles who had fought Custer on June 25—gathered in one big group on the head of the Tongue River. It was impossible to subsist such a gathering for long by hunting in winter; the troops gave the Indians no rest and cut them off from their usual sources of ammunition and other supplies.

Colonel Miles, after failing to induce the hostiles to surrender, advanced against them with about 500 infantry, having a series of fights lasting from January 1 to 8. On the eighth, 600 warriors hopefully tried the old decoy party trick on Miles but failed to catch him, and in a five hour fight he drove them off the field. The Sioux today deny that Miles defeated them; yet immediately after this engagement Crazy Horse retired eastward to the Little Powder and some of the other camps which had been with him went still farther east, to the Little Missouri.

At the agencies, Colonel J. W. Mason, who was a very close friend of Spotted Tail, was trying to induce that chieftain to go out and negotiate with the hostiles. Spotted Tail was Crazy Horse's uncle, and the Indians had told Crook that the hostile chiefs would listen to Spotted Tail with more respect than to any other man. Spotted Tail finally agreed to go on this mission if given a free-hand, and in February, 1877, he set out accompanied by 250 picked men from his agency. He met twenty-five lodges of hostiles hovering in the country just north of the agencies and induced them to surrender. He then went to the Little Missouri, where large camps were found. After many long councils, the Indians all agreed to surrender. He then went to Crazy Horse's camp on the Little Powder and obtained that chief's promise to surrender at the end of the winter. Captain Bourke is mistaken in stating that Spotted Tail returned late in January. The official records show that he did not set out until February; he was gone fifty days and returned on April 6.

Colonel Miles was much annoyed over Spotted Tail's mission, regarding it as an attempt on General Crook's part to steal his hostiles. Miles had reopened negotiations with these Indians in February and had induced many chiefs to accept his terms— unconditional surrender. He then sent his interpreter with the chiefs to bring in the hostile camps; but on March 17, a large party of hostiles came in and told Miles that Spotted Tail was on the Little Missouri and was offering much easier terms. On April 22, three hundred hostiles (mostly Cheyennes) surrendered to Miles, but in the meantime Spotted Tail had induced at least ten times that number to promise that they would surrender to General Crook.

The Sioux should always remember this journey made by Spotted Tail to the hostile camps in the worst weather of winter to save their people from further useless suffering. During the whole of this crucial period, Spotted Tail appears to have been the only Sioux chief who was big enough to consider the interests of the people outside the narrow limits of his own band.

Red Cloud's attempt to resist the military had ended on October 24 in the surrounding of his camp by Colonel Mackenzie and the seizure of his ponies and guns. His band was marched to the agency and kept under close guard by troops. The great chief sulked, and as he was still attempting to play tricks, Crook deposed him and put Spotted Tail in charge of both agencies. By January, 1877, Red Cloud had forgotten all about his previous difficulties and was making up to the officers and lunching with Crook's mess. He and Spotted Tail were not on speaking terms, but they behaved very nicely when they met at Crook's table, ignoring each other in a gentlemanly way. It is evident that Red Cloud was jealous of Spotted Tail's growing influence and that through his attentions to Crook and the other officers and his offer to enlist and help fight the hostiles he hoped to gain his own reinstatement as a big chief. His offers of help always came a little late, and by the time he had developed the idea of enlisting to fight the hostiles, Spotted Tail was preparing to set out in an effort to persuade them to surrender. The news of Spotted Tail's success appears to have put a new idea into Red Cloud's head, and he now began to urge Crook to send him out on a mission to the hostiles. What if Spotted Tail was Crazy Horse's uncle? Was not he, Red Cloud, Crazy Horse's relative also? Crook was waiting impatiently at Camp Robinson for the hostiles to come in, and Red Cloud suggested that if he were sent out he could induce the bands to move more rapidly than Spotted Tail could. He told Crook that he wished to take rations and other supplies with him, pointing out that without food the Indians would have to delay their movement in order to hunt. The general gave his assent to this plan, and early in the spring Red Cloud set out for the north with quite an imposing caravan. He had a half-breed with him who could write, and he sent back frequent messages to Lieutenant W. P. Clarke who had direct charge of these operations. Captain Bourke has preserved this specimen:

"A Pril 15, 1877
Sir My Dear I have met some indians on the road and there say the indians on bear lodge creek on the 16th april and I thought let you know it and I think I will let you know better after I get to the camp so I sent the young man with this letter he have been to the camp before his name is arme blown off

RED CLOUD"

From the date and the very clear information given in this message it will be observed that Red Cloud set out after Spotted Tail had returned, his work accomplished. Red Cloud did nothing further than put himself at the head of Crazy Horse's column, thus assuring for himself a conspicuous position when the hostiles arrived at the agency to surrender.

Spotted Tail came home on April 6, reporting that 105 lodges crowded with hostiles were approaching and that Crazy Horse with 200 lodges was moving in but was some distance farther back. On April 14, the 105 lodges reached Spotted Tail Agency and there surrendered their ponies and arms. There were 917 people, Miniconjous under Touching-the-Clouds, and Sans Arcs under Red Bear and High Bear.

Toward the end of April some of Crazy Horse's lodges began to appear at Red Cloud—people with good horses who had been able to travel faster than the main village. Cheyennes were also arriving, and early in May news came that Crazy Horse was at last approaching. Lieutenant Clarke went out to meet the hostiles. He found the camp a few miles north of White River and was received as a friend by Crazy Horse, who smoked with him. The great Oglala warrior had already given his war-bonnet and other trappings to Red Cloud, but one of his leaders, He Dog, put his war-bonnet and war-shirt on Lieutenant Clarke, presenting them to him as an act of friendship.[6] The column of hostiles marched in at noon on May 5, Lieutenant Clarke with Red Cloud and the Oglala soldier police leading the march. Behind them came the

6. He Dog was still living at Pine Ridge in 1931 and was ninety-four years of age. He was one of the shirt-wearers in the Crazy Horse camp in 1876-1877. Mr. Vestal terms these shirt-wearers, head-chiefs. If that is correct, the little camp known as Crazy Horse's had a liberal supply of head-chiefs. In winter this camp was composed of about fifty lodges, in summer it was about four times that strength.

hostile leaders: Crazy Horse, Little Big Man, Little Hawk, He Dog, Old Hawk, and Big Road, all abreast. The warriors marched in column behind their leaders, and behind the warriors came the village—the moving camp with the women, children, and old men. All marched in perfect order and in silence. The column was over two miles long. As they approached Camp Robinson the Sioux began to sing, and they marched up proudly, singing their war-songs, and halted before General Crook and his officers. In this camp there were, as Captain Bourke states, 146 lodges, with two families crowded into most of them, between 1,100 and 1,150 people, 300 warriors, and 2,500 ponies. As the women began pitching camp the ponies were given up, and Lieutenant Clarke then went through lodges, taking all weapons. He found 117 guns, mainly cavalry carbines captured from the troops, and a few Winchesters. The search was very thorough; but, as in all of these surrenders in 1877, the number of good guns found was very small, so small that it rendered absurd the military claim that every Sioux warrior was armed with a modern rifle.

Captain Bourke estimates the number of hostiles who surrendered at Red Cloud and Spotted Tail in the spring of 1877 at a little under 4,500. Of these, about 2,250 belonged to Crazy Horse's camp and to the camp of Miniconjous and Sans Arcs who surrendered at Spotted Tail. The remaining 2,250 were partly Cheyennes and partly Sioux from the various non-agency bands. This indicates clearly how very few of the real agency Indians were among the hostiles in 1876.

After Crazy Horse's surrender, the only Sioux still at large in United States territory were fifty-one lodges of Miniconjous under Lame Deer, and on the day after Crazy Horse marched in at Red Cloud, Colonel Miles attacked Lame Deer's camp, killing the chief and some of the warriors and capturing the camp with its contents and most of the pony herd. The remnant of this band remained out for some time longer, but in September surrendered at Spotted Tail Agency. Thus ended Inspector Watkins' little scheme for sending out a few soldiers to run the wild Sioux onto the reservation. The military who had so eagerly seized on Watkins' idea had expected a few weeks of easy work in the field and, with luck, a nice little fight or two thrown in. The work had taken eighteen months, and the price paid in blood, suffering, and money was staggering. But the object had been attained at last, and under the cloud of war the government had taken the Black Hills, the Powder River lands, and the Bighorn country. The pretense of formal agreement and fair payment which Congress had devised to veil this act of robbery did not even deceive the Indians. The chiefs knew that they were being robbed and that they were forced to sign away their lands. Here are beef, flour, and blankets (said the United States) for your lands in Laramie Plains and between the forks of the Platte, which we took from you before 1865; and here (said the United States) are the same beef, flour, and blankets for your lands in Nebraska which we took before 1870; and (said the United States, with an air of vast generosity) here are the same beef, flour, and blankets for the Black Hills, the Powder River, and the Bighorn lands which we are now taking from you. In all fairness, that is very near the true meaning of the "agreement" of 1876, by means of which these last lands were taken from the Sioux.

CHAPTER XVI

HOME TO PINE RIDGE
1877-1878

THE war was over, but the Indians at Red Cloud were in a constant fever of excitement. Ever since their ponies had been taken from them in October, 1876, the camps had been concentrated close to the agency, the most remote being less than three miles out. Rumors were being spread constantly through this mass of restless and rather frightened Indians, keeping them continually stirred up. The ruthless removal of the Cheyennes to the Indian Territory early in the summer of 1877 revived the talk that the Sioux were to be compelled to go there also; and even if they were to be permitted to remain in the north, it was known that the government was determined to remove them to the Missouri River. The recently surrendered hostiles were still wild people, suspicious and uneasy in their new environment. Crazy Horse was up to something. He was saying bad things, and many people had a feeling that more trouble was ahead.

At this very time, when the last of the hostiles had just been removed from the Powder River and Bighorn lands, the Nez Perces broke from their own country, fought their way across the mountains, and came down into that region from which the Sioux and Cheyennes had just been driven. All available troops were sent against Chief Joseph and his people. There was a rumor that the Nez Perces intended to strike south or southeast into the country of the Shoshonis or even to the Sioux agencies. What would be the attitude of the Sioux if the Nez Perces came down on them, demanding aid against the white soldiers?

General Crook had ordered every man that he could spare to Camp Brown, in order to head back the Nez Perces if they should attempt to come through the Gray Bull Pass into the Shoshoni country; and he was greatly perturbed about the attitude of the Sioux, especially those in Crazy Horse's camp. On August 1, Crook had reported that Crazy Horse had grown reconciled to life at the agency, but at this time there were many disturbing reports coming from Red Cloud Agency which indicated that this wild chieftain was planning something.

There has been an attempt in recent years to prove that Crazy Horse was the innocent victim of a plot devised by Frank Grouard, Crook's favorite scout, and by the agency chiefs who were jealous of Crazy Horse, or afraid of him. There seems to be very little truth in these stories; enough, however, to lend them color and to give their authors an excuse for spinning them. If Grouard did make a slip in interpreting Crazy Horse's words to General Crook, there is no reason for supposing that he did this with the deliberate intention of betraying his old friend to his death. From the day of his surrender, Crazy Horse had shown a sullen and morose disposition in most of his dealings with the whites. He made it fairly plain that he hated the whites and that he intended to attempt to return to his old wild life in the north at the first opportunity. The significant thing is that his close friends, the leaders in his own camp, were drawing away from him, realizing that he intended to break the promise he had given to General Crook to remain quietly at Red Cloud Agency. They seem to have attempted to wean him from his plan of breaking away, but he was not the man to listen to others. His iron will and great courage were his strongest characteristics; he refused to consider the obstacles in the way of his proposed out- break, and he seemed incapable of comprehending that the people of his own band were turning against him. That the agency chiefs were against him there can be no question. They regarded him as a willful trouble maker who would get them all into serious dif- ficulties if he were not stopped. He was being watched and even spied upon by everyone. The army officers had their scouts and agents in his camp; the agency chiefs had their people reporting to them and passed on what they learned to the officers at Camp Robinson.

Crazy Horse's plan was evidently for his band and that of his old friend Touching-the-Clouds, altogether about 2,000 people, to leave the agencies and go north, there to resume their old life either on the Powder and Bighorn or farther northward beyond the Yellowstone. But late in August he discovered that he could not count on Touching-the-Clouds and his Miniconjous and Sans Arcs; indeed, that he could not count on all of his own band. They would not follow him in an attempt to break away from the agencies. Crazy Horse then demanded that his people be permitted to go on a buffalo hunt to the Bighorn. There had been some talk of such a hunt during the past spring, and General Crook appears to have made some kind of promise to the Indians; but times had changed, and with the Nez Perces on the warpath it would have been madness to permit Crazy Horse to lead a large party of Sioux to hunt on the Bighorn. His real object evidently was to obtain permission for his people to leave the agencies. Once away from the white troops he could revive the Soldiers' Lodge and bully the backsliders into obedience to his orders. They would then be compelled to follow wherever he chose to lead.

Hearing that affairs at Red Cloud were nearing a crisis, Crook dropped his preparations for striking at the Nez Perces and hurried to the agency. At Camp Robinson he obtained enough information concerning Crazy Horse's recent conduct to convince him that a crisis was at hand, but the general seems to have believed that a personal interview with the Oglala chief would smooth out the situation. He started for Crazy Horse's camp with Captain Bourke and some others; but on the way his ambulance was stopped by Woman's Dress, who bore a message from the agency chiefs, warning Crook that Crazy Horse had stated his intention to kill him in the coming council if the general did not grant his demands.[1] Crook was convinced that Crazy Horse meant what he said, and he very wisely returned to Camp Robinson, sending out a message for the chiefs to come there for the council. Crazy Horse ignored this summons. Crook told the chiefs bluntly when they assembled that Crazy Horse was leading them into trouble. They said they did not approve of Crazy Horse's conduct and were ready to follow the general's lead. He told them they should prove their loyalty by arresting Crazy Horse. They then consulted together and informed Crook that they were willing to act, but that Crazy Horse was a desperate man and it would be better to kill him.

1. Woman's Dress was a grandson of Old Smoke and the son of the chief who was nicknamed Bad Face, in whose camp Red Cloud and Crazy Horse had grown up.

Crook demurred; he said that it would be murder. An agreement was finally reached whereby the chiefs were to act in concert with the troops in an attempt to arrest Crazy Horse in his own camp; and after issuing his orders to General L. P. Bradley, in command at Camp Robinson, Crook prepared to continue his journey to Camp Brown.

These events were on September 3. Crazy Horse, either warned of what was planned against him or roused to suspicion by the happenings of the day, decided to act at once. Thus, while the friendly chiefs on the night of September 3 were assembling their posse of warriors to assist in arresting him, Crazy Horse was ordering his lodges to be taken down and was starting his flight toward the north and freedom.

That the Indians were practically all against him and solidly back of General Crook is indicated by the names of the leaders who went with the posse to arrest Crazy Horse. Red Cloud, Little Wound, Young-Man-Afraid-of-His-Horse, and Yellow Bear, representing all of the Oglala bands at the agency, led the posse. Black Coal was there with his Arapahoes; and Big Road, Little Big Man, and Jumping Shield, three of Crazy Horse's own leaders, went with the agency warriors. Eight companies of the Third Cavalry and four hundred friendly Indians left Camp Robinson at 9 A. M. on September 4, to go to Crazy Horse's camp six miles away. They found the camp taken down and most of the lodges gone; but many lodges and much camp equipment were lying scattered about on the grounds, indicating that the people had fled in haste. The friendly Indians started at once in pursuit; but it was soon apparent that Crazy Horse had entirely misjudged the feeling of the people of his own band. He had started out to lead them in a flight to the north, and most of the people had run away from him, taking refuge with the agency bands at Red Cloud or Spotted Tail. Some of the people obeyed their old leader and started northward, but they were now overtaken by the posse of four hundred and were brought back prisoners. Crazy Horse had escaped almost alone; but he soon turned toward Spotted Tail Agency, perhaps with the idea that his old comrade, Touching-the-Clouds, and the Miniconjous and Sans Arcs who had formerly been a part of his hostile camp, would aid him. There he was arrested by the agency Indians. On the fifth he was taken to Camp Robinson and turned over to the military. A group of officers and guards were in the guardroom when Crazy Horse and some of the chiefs entered. Crazy Horse instantly drew two dirks from his clothing and leaped at an officer; but his own friend and one of the shirt-wearers of his band, Little Big Man, jumped on his back and grasped his arms at the elbows. What happened after that will always be in doubt. One at least of the guards drew a bayonet and made for Crazy Horse, who was struggling and striking with his dirks, Little Big Man still on his back holding him. The usual version is that a guard made a wild lunge with his bayonet and stabbed the chief in the abdomen; but Little Big Man in 1881 told Captain Bourke that while he was on Crazy Horse's back, gripping him by the elbows, the chief struck out with one of his dirks, and that he, Little Big Man, jerked the chief's arm to prevent his stabbing someone and accidentally caused Crazy Horse to stab himself. He said that the soldier's wild lunge missed the chief and struck the guardroom door, where in 1881 the mark of the bayonet could still be seen.

Crazy Horse was taken at once to the post hospital, where the surgeons tried to save him, but he died at midnight with his mother, father, and his old friend Touching-the-Clouds at his side. When he was dead, Touching-the-Clouds put his hand on Crazy Horse's breast and said: "It is good: he has looked for death, and it has come."[2]

The killing of Crazy Horse created intense excitement among the Sioux at Red Cloud and Spotted Tail. The chiefs did not blame the white soldiers for what had happened, and Little Big Man and Jumping Shield, Crazy Horse's close friends and leaders in his camp, stated that they were convinced that the soldiers did not want to harm their old leader and that his death was due entirely to his own conduct; but the people were furiously angry. Many of Crazy Horse's own band, who deserted him on September 4, on the sixth were shouting for war on the white soldiers who had killed their great leader. The agency chiefs, however, kept a firm hand on the situation and averted serious trouble. They had their hands full. The question of removing the two agencies had to be

2. Crazy Horse was supposed to be about 33 years old when he died. His father was an Oglala named Crazy Horse and his mother was Spotted Tail's sister. One of his brothers was buried at Fort Laramie sometime before 1860; another brother was killed by the troops in 1865. This man was not a real chief—but it is very difficult to avoid calling him one—was a favorite of the Cheyennes and often joined their warriors in a fight, preferring to be with them rather than with the Sioux. He was one of the four shirt-wearers in the camp which the whites always regarded as his. His uncle, Little Hawk, was the real chief of this camp.

settled at once. Congress had attached to the Sioux appropriation bill a clause providing that the supplies for Red Cloud and Spotted Tail should be delivered on the Missouri and that these Indians should receive no further support until they moved there. The Indians were very much opposed to going near the Missouri; but supplies and rations at the old agencies were running low in the fall of 1877, no wagon-trains were arriving with fresh supplies, and it was apparent to the chiefs at least that Congress meant exactly what it said—that for the Oglalas and Brulés it was a case of go to the Missouri or starve. The chiefs had almost succeeded in talking the agency Indians into consenting to a removal when the Crazy Horse incident occurred, and a majority of the people turned right about and sullenly refused to go to the Missouri.

The situation thus created was very serious. There was real danger that part of the Sioux at least would break away and start for Powder River. The new Red Cloud and Spotted Tail agencies had been established on the Missouri and the rations and supplies piled up there, 250 miles away; but the Indians would not budge. Winter was coming on and there was no time to be lost. The chiefs were very anxious for a settlement but it must be a compromise, and they would negotiate with the Great Father and with no one else. Thus, a few days after Crazy Horse's death, Red Cloud, Spotted Tail, and the other chiefs set out once more for Washington. There they had a council with President Hayes, and in the end he promised them that if their people would go to the Missouri for the winter, in the spring they might choose any points in the Sioux Reservation that suited them and he would have their agencies removed to the places of their choice. Coming home with the Great Father's promise (Red Cloud had a printed copy of the speeches in which he had carefully marked the president's promise with a blue pencil), the chiefs induced the people to consent to move and the march toward the Missouri was begun on October 27. It was a strange sight, this exodus from old Red Cloud Agency. With two troops of cavalry in the advance, the Oglala chiefs, all in line abreast, led the march of the 4,600 Sioux who moved off down White River with their lodge poles dragging and their ponies' hoofs raising a great dust. The dismounting of the Indians had not affected all of the bands, for although Red Cloud, Red Leaf, and the surrendering hostiles had lost nearly all of their ponies, the other bands had lost but few. By gifts from friends and by trading, most of the families now had a sufficient number of animals to transport all their belongings. The people who had no ponies were taken into the wagons belonging to the squawmen and half-breeds. There were 120 big freight wagons loaded with rations, and cowboys were driving along a herd of 2,000 beef cattle. Four miles away to the southward a vast cloud of dust marked the march of Spotted Tail and all his Brulés. With him were the surrendered hostiles—Crazy Horse's Oglalas, the Miniconjous, and Sans Arcs. With him also were Crazy Horse's old father and mother who were carrying with them on this last journey the body of their great son.

The Oglala caravan had advanced about seventy-five miles east of the old agency when horsemen were seen swarming over the bluffs to the south of White River, and amid scenes of the most intense excitement two thousand lately hostile Sioux came pouring over the hills and down among the Red Cloud people. It was Crazy Horse's old band, led by Big Road, and they were making a wild break for the Little Missouri, the Powder, and freedom. With them were many Miniconjous and Sans Arcs and they were carrying Crazy Horse's remains along.[3] Appealing to the Red Cloud people to join in their movement, these hostiles created such an uproar that a general outbreak seemed unavoidable. The two little troops of cavalry could do nothing, and their officers had the good sense to keep their men out of the fierce wrangle in which a thousand Sioux warriors were engaged. Red Cloud's new agent, Dr. James Irwin, also acted wisely, quietly advising the agency Indians not to go with the hostiles and at the same time propitiating the wild people of Crazy Horse's band by giving them a liberal quantity of rations and other supplies. How much the Oglalas had changed in spirit since coming to the agency was demonstrated on this day. The hostiles coaxed, threatened, and jeered at them but could not induce any of the agency people to join in their break for freedom. In the end they gave it up, and after yelling some final taunts at the agency Indians started northward into the badlands, heading for the Little Missouri and Powder River. They actually made their escape, but they did not find the

---

3. The official report made at the time stated that the hostiles carried Crazy Horse's body with them. A modern Sioux version says the bones of Crazy Horse were taken to the new Spotted Tail Agency on the Missouri where they later disappeared mysteriously. About fifteen years ago a cheerful ghoul, writing from Pine Ridge Agency, offered to sell to an Omaha curio collector "the bones of Crazy Horse, petrified and very beautiful" for the price of a Ford runabout.

freedom they were seeking. They felt lonely on Powder River, and knowing that the troops would presently be on their trail again they soon headed northward and joined Sitting Bull in Canada. There they learned to their sorrow that the redcoat soldiers of the Great Mother would no more permit them to do as they pleased than would the bluecoat soldiers of the Great Father. When they slipped back across the line to make little raids on United States territory they were met on their return by the irate officers of the Northwest Mounted Police, who took the horses and other plunder from them and berated them for violating some foolish rule the whites had concerning a line, which you could not see but which these strange white people looked upon as a sacred thing. The Oglalas sulked. They were cold and often very hungry, they missed their own land and their own folk, and were very tired of being lectured by angry redcoat policemen. They held out for a few years, then—accompanied by most of the other Sioux—slipped back south of the line and surrendered to the bluecoats. Sitting Bull and a few diehards held out a little longer, then followed the example of the rest.[4]

After the Crazy Horse people had left them, the Red Cloud Indians resumed their march toward the Missouri. They were headed for the Great Bend, at which point their grandfathers had crossed the river a century before to start their conquest of the Trans-Missouri country. The whites who had established the new agency in that district were quite unaware that it had once been the home of the Oglalas, and the peculiar thing was that these Indians were also ignorant of that fact. They had forgotten that the Missouri had once been their home; it was to them a strange and hateful place to which the whites were compelling them to go. But they were to stay only this one winter, and in the spring they would be back in their own lands within sight of *Pa Sapa*.

Bishop Whipple and the other members of the commission which had forced the Sioux to give up the Black Hills and other lands in 1876 had laid great stress in their report on the importance

4. These Oglalas when they surrendered were taken to Standing Rock Agency, but most of them later joined their own tribe at Pine Ridge. A few of them remained in Canada, where they and their children still live. Big Road (a better translation of the name is Broad Trail) came to Standing Rock as the chief of this band. He had helped arrest Crazy Horse for planning to break away, and in less than two months had executed that plan himself. He was a fine leader in a fight but had little intelligence.

of care in selecting the new sites for Red Cloud and Spotted Tail agencies. Good land must be chosen, where the Indians could learn agriculture and eventually become self-supporting. The government solved the problem of a new site for Spotted Tail Agency by ruthlessly taking the friendly little tribe of Ponkas, tearing them from their home near the mouth of the Niobrara, and removing them to Indian Territory with the brilliant thought that, since there were some Indians in Indian Territory who spoke a language kindred to that of the Ponkas, the Ponkas should go to Indian Territory. This action did not profit the government in the end; for it was found that the Ponka lands were not sufficient for Spotted Tail's large population, and that Spotted Tail and his people were absolutely determined not to remain on the Missouri. Finally, the whites of Nebraska, to their everlasting honor, took up the cause of the mistreated Ponkas, hauled the United States government into the courts, and won a victory which made it possible for all of the Ponkas who wished to do so to return to their old home in Nebraska. The commission of three who selected the site for the new agencies were so limited in their choice by Congress and by the lack of good land along the Missouri that they made a very bad selection for the new Red Cloud Agency. The site was at the mouth of Yellow Medicine Creek just above the Great Bend. The year after the agency was built the new commission which came out to settle the Indians on the lands of their own selection stated in their report that there was some grazing land on Yellow Medicine, "but the land is of the badlands kind, full of alkali, with flats of wire grass, and unfit for cultivation. The water is alkaline were determined not to go near this new agency.
and bad. No timber for building." It was just as well that the Oglalas

They camped that winter far up White River, where they could obtain good water, wood and grass, the nearest camps being seventy-five miles from the new agency. All that winter they packed their own rations and supplies from the agency; but nothing would induce them to go to the river to live. In the spring of 1878 they began to look anxiously for the white men who were to be sent out by the Great Father to move their agency back to upper White River. The Oglalas had already chosen the lands they wished to occupy, and had fixed the site of their agency on White Earth Creek (the modern Big White Clay), as far from the Missouri as they could get without going into Nebraska, which was forbidden by Congress. The Spotted Tail people had chosen the South Fork of White River for their homeland and the Rosebud Creek as the site of their agency. The commission appointed to examine the lands in 1878 reported that the Indians had selected the best sites in the entire region.

This removal in 1878 proved to be the last one for the Red Cloud and Spotted Tail people. The Oglalas settled down about Pine Ridge as their new agency was named, and the Brulés about Rosebud, and they have remained in these districts ever since.

This final settlement of the Oglalas may be considered the closing event in the story of their wanderings. They were no longer a free people leading their own life, but a captive group who were henceforth to be coaxed or driven along the stony path toward civilization. Even in 1878 the old tribal bonds were loosening; the power of the chiefs had been undermined, and the Oglalas were hardly to be considered a real tribe. Red Cloud and some of the other chiefs tried hard to keep the tribe together, and for this they were termed "non-progressive" by the government agents. who did everything in their power to destroy their influence. One cannot help admiring the stubborn resistance to "progress" by these chiefs, and especially by Red Cloud, nor can one help wondering if the government would not have been wiser if it had sought to better the condition of the Oglalas by some other method than the destruction of the only leadership these people were willing to accept or were capable of understanding. Red Cloud and the other chiefs were shifting their attitude, slowly but in the right direction; but the officials would not wait for them, and in their impatience they quarreled with the chiefs and broke them. In those troubled times the Oglalas were led by the whites into deserting Red Cloud, Old-Man-Afraid-of-His-Horse, Red Dog, and Little Wound. Today they regard these chiefs as their great heroes.

FINIS

APPENDICES

NEW NOTES (1957)

Since He Dog's death, Joseph Eagle Hawk is perhaps the best living informant on the Red Cloud family. He says that Red Cloud's grandfather was Two Arrows, sometimes called Red Cloud, and that this man's son was also called Red Cloud. This would mean that Red Cloud's father, called Isna Wica by He Dog, had the second name of Red Cloud, and thus three generations were called Red Cloud. Eagle Hawk claims that the great Red Cloud as a boy had his grandfather's name, Two Arrows, and that when he first went to war, after he was twelve, he took the name Tall Hollow Horn, which he still bore when he killed Chief Bull Bear in 1841. Eagle Hawk states that about 1843 Tall Hollow Horn killed a Shoshoni in a battle and rode back toward the Sioux party, holding up the enemy scalp and shouting that from this day he assumed his grandfather's and father's name of Red Cloud.

As a youth Red Cloud was very wild and unruly, and his maternal uncle, White Hawk, who had a good standing in the tribe, often lectured him, telling him that if he would rule his impulses, he had the making of a great chief in him. When he grew old, White Hawk handed over his rank in the tribe to Red Cloud. After that he was killed by Chief Bull Bear in a drunken brawl, and in 1841 Red Cloud killed Bull Bear in a similar brawl.

Eagle Hawk states that Smoke had a sister named Bega who had a full-blood son named Spotted Bear and nicknamed Bad Face. Bega later married the French trader Dion and had several half-blood children—the Dion clan. Spotted Bear's wife was a shrew. She often screamed at him: *"Ita kin sil yela!"* ("Oh, you old horrible face!") The neighbors laughed and called Spotted Bear "Bad Face," and the name was later applied to the whole camp.

Black Twin. He was fourth chief of the Bad Faces in 1867, but became first chief after Red Cloud went to an agency. This was why Red Cloud refused to make decisions until he had consulted Black Twin, now the head of the Bad Faces. Black Twin is called the elder brother of No Water, and the Sioux today claim he had a twin brother, White Twin. Black Twin died in the Crazy Horse camp, after its surrender in 1877. White Twin fled to Canada with Sitting Bull and died there.

Sitting Bull the Oglala. He was one of the chiefs and headmen who marched in front of the Sioux when they went to Tongue River to talk peace with Colonel Miles, and Sitting Bull was killed by the sudden attack of the Crow scouts and his gold-trimmed Winchester was captured.

Murder of Chief Yellow Bear. Mekeel misunderstood He Dog and put this event on the head of Tongue River. It was on Rawhide Butte Creek, east of Fort Laramie, while the Sioux were camped there in 1870, waiting for Red Cloud to come back from Washington.

Agent Thomas Twiss. His Oglala wife was Wanikiyewin, a girl of Chief Yellow Bear's Spleen Band. Louis Twiss, a grandson, says that the former agent took up forty acres near Rulo, Nebraska, when Red Cloud Agency was established in 1871. Twiss tried to start a fruit orchard, but died, and his sister came from the East to settle his estate. She took one of her brother's half-blood sons (William, Louis's father) East and tried to educate him, but it did not turn out well. William came back to Red Cloud Agency and found his three brothers (Charles, James, and Frank) running wild in the Spleen Band camp. They were dressed like and looked like Indians, complete with braided scalplocks. Their mother's brother, He Crow, *alias* Drags-the-Rope, had them under his care. The boys turned out well. Two were scouts for General Crook in 1876, and one was among the first lot of recruits for Carlisle Indian School in 1879.

APPENDIX A

Estimates of Oglala Population

DATE	PEOPLE	WARRIORS	LODGES	BANDS	AUTHORITY AND REMARKS
1804	360	120	60	2	Lewis and Clark. Six persons per lodge; 2 warriors per lodge.
1825	1,500		300	4	Col. Atkinson's report.
1835	2,000				Rev. Sam'l Parker, from trader information. Bull Bear had 100 lodges.
1840	2,500		250		Rev. S. R. Riggs.
1850			400	6	Schoolcraft: *Indian Tribes.*
1856	3,200		400		Schoolcraft: *Indian Tribes.*
1857	3,680	736	460		Lieut. G. K. Warren. He seems to include the Wazhazhas as Oglalas.
1865			500		Lieut. Col. W. O. Collins.
1866		1,000	500		Sioux estimate at the time. Red Cloud 250 lodges; Man-Afraid 250 lodges.
1867	2,100		350		Ind. Affairs report. Too low; leaves out some bands.
1868	3,000				Peace commission. Too low.
1870	4,200		600		Red Cloud's own estimate of the tribe; 7 to the lodge.
1874	6,320				"Sioux—mostly Oglalas" at agency. The mixing of tribes here begins.
1874	7,000		1,000		The Oglalas' own estimate. 400 lodges added in 4 years!
1877	6,035				"Sioux" at Red Cloud Agency; Wazhazhas absent, not included.
1882	7,202				"Oglalas" at Pine Ridge—14 bands. At Standing Rock 556 Oglalas.
1890	4,452				"Oglalas" at Pine Ridge. About 600 more at Standing Rock.
1902	6,602				"Oglalas" at Pine Ridge.

APPENDIX B

Oglala Social Organization

About 1850, Prescott, who had lived long among the Sioux of
Minnesota, stated (in Schoolcraft's *Indian Tribes,* Volume II), that
before the whites came the Sioux had no tribal chiefs; their chiefs
were the heads of totemic kinship groups and, unless they were
supported by strong groups of kinsmen, they had little authority in
the tribe. That this was true seems very probable, for we find among
the Oglalas and other Teton Sioux tribes many hints of a former
organization into totemic groups of kindred whose families retained
certain old personal names, one family having bear names, another
buffalo names, a third duck names. The Oglalas and other Tetons
have always protested that the system of tribal chiefs and head-
chiefs was alien to their old organization and was forced upon
them by the United States government officials.

In Minnesota in the seventeenth and eighteenth centuries the
Sioux were organized into seven groups, variously termed tribes,
villages, and council fires. The Tetons, or Prairie Village, formed
one of the seven divisions, and the original Oglalas were evidently
a minor division or kindred group within the Teton division.

When, about the year 1700, the Oglalas and other Tetons
turned their backs on their old homeland along the Mississippi
and started their long migration across the coteau toward the Missouri, they gradually lost touch with the Sioux of the East; their
chiefs no longer sat regularly at the Sioux council fire; the ties of
mutual interest that had for centuries bound them so closely to
the other Sioux divisions were loosened and in the end severed.
These wild Tetons of the coteau, constantly on the move, gaining
a hard living by following the buffalo herds, had little in common
with the Sioux bands settled along the Mississippi and the lower
Minnesota River, who spent much of their time in fixed villages
and gained at least a portion of their support from the cultivation

of the soil. As early as 1730 we find evidence that the Tetons had thrown off the authority of the Sioux chiefs. In their wandering camps each man was the equal of any of his fellows, and the chiefs were merely the heads of kinship groups and generally had no authority outside of the little camp of kinsmen who recognized them as their hereditary leaders. When Truteau met the camp of Tetons on the Missouri in the fall of 1794 these people told him that they had no chiefs or big men in their camps. They had been wandering about the coteau in a hungry quest for food, and finding little game had come to the Missouri. The men in this camp recognized no authority; they spent most of their leisure in quarreling and fighting over horses, women, guns, and other desirable property. That same winter James Mackay met these Tetons on the Missouri and recognized some of the leaders as chiefs, giving them Spanish medals and flags. Here we have evidence that the Oglalas and other Tetons are correct when they assert that they had no chiefs with authority over all the people until the whites elevated certain men to such positions.

Among the Sioux there are two sacred numbers: seven and four. These numbers are constantly appearing in any matter which they regard as important. Thus there were seven Sioux tribes in Minnesota, and the Tetons, one of those tribes, had seven divisions. When the Tetons crossed the Missouri their seven divisions became seven separate tribes, and each of these seems to have attempted to organize itself into seven new divisions or bands, to form a tribal camp circle. This seems to have been the goal set; but the wild, roving life the people led and the constant shifting about of bands made such an organization difficult and even impossible to attain.

Before the Oglalas went on the reservation each band in winter camped by itself where it pleased and led its own life, quite independently of the rest of the tribe. In spring the bands met and formed the tribal camp circle as a prelude to the year's activities. The lodges were set up in the form of a great circle, each band encamped in its appointed position, the leading band taking the place of honor at the horn or entrance of the circle. Each band had its own chiefs and "soldiers," but these men had no authority outside their own little camps, and when the tribal circle was formed in the spring four men termed *wakicunsa* (camp leaders) were selected by the tribal council to take charge of the camp circle.

Not chiefs but prominent warriors (*ogle tanka'un*—shirt-wearers) were selected as *wakicunsa*. Red Cloud was only a shirt-wearer in 1866-1871 when the government was insisting on terming him head-chief of the Oglalas. Mr. Stanley Vestal seems to have his terms mixed when he speaks of the six hereditary chiefs or scalp-shirt-wearers of the Miniconjou Sioux in 1866. The shirt-wearers among the Oglalas were not chiefs at all. Crazy Horse, a shirt-wearer, could not speak in council because he was not a chief.

These four *wakicunsa* had supreme authority over the people until the tribal circle was broken up in the autumn. They issued orders for the moving of the camp from place to place and controlled all other activities. When the four *wakicunsa* were chosen one of the soldier-societies or warrior brotherhoods was selected to police the camp and to see that the orders of the *wakicunsa* were obeyed. The big lodge belonging to this warrior society was generally employed as the meeting place of the tribal council. To this lodge information was brought concerning the movement of the buffalo herds or the near approach of parties of enemies; all other news of the day was here discussed by the council; decisions were made by the *wakicunsa,* and orders were issued which the head-soldier (*akicita-itacan*) carried into effect. The real chiefs had no authority except in settling small matters which concerned their own camps alone. They attended the tribal councils to represent the interests of their bands, but as long as the tribal circle was in use all the real authority rested in the hands of the *wakicunsa* alone.

Such a form of organization naturally thrust the prominent warriors to the fore and, in tribal affairs, prevented the hereditary chiefs (unless they were men of very strong character) from playing an important part. The system led our own government time and again into making the mistake of supposing that some prominent warrior was a "head-chief" whose word was law among the Sioux. It was under such a delusion that the officials moved heaven and earth to induce Red Cloud to sign a treaty and come to an agency to live. They made him a "head-chief" while the Oglalas knew him only as a prominent warrior, and at a time when he was afraid to make a speech or take a decision except on orders from the tribal council, they persisted in believing that he was a kind of autocrat who could force his will upon the people.

The Oglalas on the reservation who described this system of tribal organization failed to explain what happened when the people were living in widely separated divisions, as they were most of the time from 1855 to 1877. The answer, however, is obvious—the Southern Oglalas, who lived south of the Platte, had their own tribal circle and complete organization, while the Northern Oglalas, on Powder River, had theirs. Again, when most of the tribe settled down at the agency after 1871 these agency people had a complete tribal organization, and at the same time the little camp of wild Oglalas on Powder River, composed mostly of Bad Faces, formed a tribal organization of their own, complete with four shirt-wearers, four *wakicunsa* and so on. These wild fellows pretended to regard the agency leaders as nobodies and, strangely enough, many of the agency people held the same view, stating that the only real chiefs and soldiers were in the Bad Face camp on Powder River.

Of the two Oglala bands listed by Lewis and Clark in 1804, the True Oglala and the Shiyo (Sharp-tail Grouse), the former remained at the head of the tribe, while the latter soon left and joined the Brulés. By 1825 the Oglalas had at least four large bands, of which we know certainly the names of only two; the True Oglala and the Kiyuksa. By 1835 the Kiyuksa had pushed the old "Head Band" aside, taking the lead and making their warrior Bull Bear the real head of the tribe.

The list printed by Schoolcraft under the date of 1850 shows six Oglala bands; but the list does not mention the Kiyuksa, who are known to have been with the tribe at that date. Indeed, this list makes Whirlwind, the Kiyuksa chief, head of the True Oglalas. At that date, therefore, the Oglalas had at least seven bands:

1. *True Oglala,* associated with the Kiyuksa, at the head of the tribe.

2. *Kiyuksa.* This band remained with the tribe and became the leading band of the Southern Oglalas.

3. *Minisha* or Red Water. Chief Red Water's band. They were close allies of the Kiyuksa. This band disappeared from the Oglala camp circle between 1849 and 1860. Perhaps old Red Water died in the cholera of 1849 or his band left the Platte during the Brulé war in 1854. They seem to have gone back to their old home between the Black Hills and the Missouri. Perhaps they joined the Sans Arcs, whose leading band after 1860 was sometimes called Minisha.

4. *Old-skin-necklace.* This band is not mentioned elsewhere. Wolf-skin-necklace was a common personal name among the Sioux.

5. *Peshla* or Short Hair. Still a band among the Oglalas in 1880.

6. *Night Cloud.* Nothing is known of this band of 1850.

7. *Red Lodge.* Nothing is known of this band. Some camps had a fine red lodge in which to entertain traders. Yellow Eagle was the chief of this band in 1850. He was later a chief in Man-Afraid-of-His-Horse's Hunkpatila band, but during the war of 1866-1868 shifted over to the Bad Face camp. He was then a chief in Little Hawk's band of Bad Faces.

Thus by 1850 the Oglalas had a camp circle of the ideal Sioux type, consisting of seven bands; but the tribe now split up, the Kiyuksa, True Oglala, and some minor groups moving south of the Platte; the Smoke people, led by the Bad Faces, going northward. Each of these two main divisions then organized a camp circle of its own.

When Red Cloud came down to Fort Laramie from Powder River in 1870 he brought five Oglala bands with him: Bad Face (Red Cloud's folk); Oyukhpe (the old leading band of the Smoke People under Chief Red Dog); Hunkpatila (Man-Afraid-of-His-Horse's camp); True Oglala (led by Sitting Bear and the younger American Horse); and the Wazhazha (under Chief Red Leaf). The last band was refused a share in the Oglala presents on the ground that they were really Brulés. This view was held by the Oglalas themselves as late as 1875. They always said, "the Oglalas and the Wazhazhas." Yet they gave this band a regular place in the Oglala camp circle. At this date, 1870, the Kiyuksa, the Loafers, and some other Oglala groups were at Whetstone Agency on the Missouri. They completed the seven large bands of the camp circle.

In 1875 there were at Red Cloud Agency four principal bands of Oglalas: the True Oglala (called the Head Band); the Kiyuksa, under Little Wound; the Oyukhpe, under Red Dog; and the Wazhazha, under Red Leaf. Red Cloud had only a handful of his own people, the Bad Faces, at the agency. Nearly all of this band was in the wild camp on Powder River. Man-Afraid-of-His-Horse was at the agency, but his old Hunkpatila had broken up and he had but few followers. The Loafer band was at Spotted Tail Agency with the Brulés.

The famous Red Cloud census, made I believe in 1878 by the Oglalas themselves in the form of colored pictographs, shows seven bands, or eight if we count Red Cloud and his Bad Face band, most of whom were, however, with Sitting Bull in Canada. This interesting list included the True Oglala, the Kiyuksa, the Oyukhpe, the Wazhazha, the Tapishlecha or Spleen, the Payabya (the old Hunkpatila band under a new name), and the Loafers. Add the Bad Face and we have seven large Oglala bands, excluding the Wazhazha.

In 1879, when the breakdown of the old tribal organization was just starting, the following camp circle was obtained. It is included here as an interesting picture of the social organization of the tribe just before the action of the government broke it to pieces. The numbers indicate the position of the bands in the circle, No. 1 occupying the place of honor at the horn or entrance:

1. *Payabsa* (pushed aside). Man-Afraid-of-His-Horse's band. Pushed aside and almost destroyed as a band by Red Cloud and his Bad Face followers in 1864-1874, this band, with the aid of the government agents, had now resumed a leading position.

2. *Tapishlecha* (spleen—of an animal). An old band, now strong again. Also called Shkopa (bent), and Split Liver.

3. *Kiyuksa* (breaks his own). This is said to refer to the breaking of the tribal marriage customs by people of this camp. This band was also called the Cut-off and Bit-the-Snake-in-Two. The last name is said to refer to the use of a leather snake in the old test of virginity. A woman of this band was taking the test, and on being rejected as not a virgin became so infuriated that she bit the leather snake in two. Some of the Oglalas today seem to think that the name Kiyuksa originated after Bull Bear was killed in 1841, when this band and some others split off from the rest of the tribe. Kiyuksa was, however, a band name among the Eastern Sioux as far back as 1730. These people seem to have come across from Minnesota with the Saone group of Tetons. The name must be very old as it is also found among other Siouan tribes.

These first three bands in 1878 constituted the first half of the tribe, known as the Bear People or Bear Band—most of them former followers of old Bull Bear. They settled on Medicine Root Creek and other streams in the eastern edge of the Oglala reservation and kept in close touch with the Brulés just to the east of them.

Old-Man-Afraid-of-His-Horse and Little Wound were their leading men.

4. *Wazhazha.* Meaning unknown, but I suspect that it refers to snake. That authoritative work, the *Indian Handbook,* states that Wazhazha means Osage, and when you turn to Osage you are informed that it means Wazhazha. It is a very old name, found among several Siouan tribes. The Wazhazha among the Oglalas were Brulés who joined the Oglalas at the time of the Harney expedition of 1855. They were a wild band, always siding with Red Cloud. They settled on Porcupine Tail Creek, between the two Oglala divisions, the Bear People to the east and the Smoke People to the west.

5. *Iteshicha* (bad face). Red Cloud's own band. This was a small group at Pine Ridge in 1879, most of the band being up north with Big Road. At Pine Ridge the Red Cloud band settled in the southwestern part of the reservation, near the agency and near the present village of Oglala. Red Cloud is buried there.

6. *Oyukhpe* (thrown down or where they lay down their packs). One of the oldest and strongest Oglala bands. They settled east of Red Cloud's people, on and near Wounded Knee Creek. Their great chief, Red Dog, lived to be a very old man, remaining "non-progressive" to the end.

7. *Waglukhe* (followers or loafers). They seem to have been given this name because of their custom of following emigrant trains along the Platte road in order to beg from the whites, and because they spent much time loafing about Fort Laramie. This camp included most of the mixed-bloods (the "interpreters' sons"), and the families whose daughters were married to white men at the fort. The Loafers were both Oglalas and Brulés. They first went to the old Whetstone Agency with the Brulés, then followed that tribe to Spotted Tail Agency; finally, in 1879, the Oglala Loafers rejoined their own tribe.

These last three bands in 1879 constituted the second half of the Oglala tribe: the Smoke People or Smoke Band, former followers of Chief Smoke. This division of the tribe followed Red Cloud, but in 1881 the agent made Young-Man-Afraid-of-His-Horse chief, *vice* Red Cloud, deposed for being "non-progressive." At the same time Young American Horse was put at the head of the Bear People, poor old Little Wound, who had tried so hard to serve the white people, being thrown away like an old moccasin because he could not learn new ways quickly enough to please the agent.

These seven bands of 1879 were made up of little camps, each with its own name. Among these obscure bands were the formerly proud true Oglala, now not considered important enough to have a place of its own in the tribal circle. Some of these little bands had formerly been strong and prominent, like the True Oglala. Leadership either made or ruined an Oglala band. An unimportant little camp with a strong leader would surge suddenly to the front, draw strength from the other bands and for a time lead the tribe, only to sink back into obscurity when a younger warrior from some other camp pushed the old leader aside and took his place. In the old days such changes were constantly going on, old bands disappearing and new ones taking their places.

As long as the tribes held to their old wild roving life, strong leaders were able to hold the Oglalas together in a few compact bands, the whole being knit together by the tribal system of the camp circle. On the reservation the government policy was to destroy the power of the leading chiefs; the result was a breakdown in tribal control; the large, strong bands split up, and little men who would not have dared to face Red Cloud, Red Dog, or Man-Afraid-of-His-Horse in the old days pushed forward with claims to the chieftainship. In 1879, the tribe had seven strong bands; in 1883, they had fourteen that were recognized and about one hundred little groups each claiming to be a real band as good as the Kiyuksa or Oyukhpe. An Indian wit of the day said that any man who found a bottle label with writing on it could say that it was a chief's commission which empowered him to set to work organizing a band. How the old chiefs must have longed for the authority of the *wakicunsa* and a good strong soldier lodge to disabuse these small men of the notion that they were big chiefs. But the Indian soldiers had now become policemen in the pay of the government and were aiding the agent in his work of wrecking the tribal organization.

APPENDIX C

Additional Notes

Red Cloud's Name. If the Oglalas of the past two generations ever knew the true origin of this chief's name they seem to have forgotten it, for during the past thirty-five years these Indians have advanced at least a dozen conflicting stories on this subject. The *Indian Handbook,* making a poor choice, published a tale to the effect that thousands of Red Cloud's warriors who were sitting on the hills wrapped in scarlet blankets looked from a distance like a red cloud; hence the name bestowed on the great leader. This childish nonsense came from the Oglalas themselves. It fails to account for the facts that Red Cloud bore the name when a young man without followers, and that at the time when he did have thousands of followers in the war of 1866-1868 the Oglalas had not traded for years and were almost out of blankets of any color. A recent author has stated on the authority of these Indians themselves that the Red Cloud family took their name from a vision of a buffalo and a red cloud, and that Red Cloud's father had a lodge with this vision painted on it. This tale assumes that the name was that of a family, which it was not at all. It was the name of one child in a large family. Red Cloud's father must have died about the year 1825, and it is perfectly absurd to suppose that the Oglalas of today know what kind of lodge he had. The name Red Cloud was recorded in several places in the winter-counts, and many pictographic representations of the name were made under Red Cloud's own eyes. In no instance is a buffalo shown in these contemporary Indian pictographs—they show the chief and above his head a red cloud. The true reason why Red Cloud was given that name cannot be proven, but it is nevertheless quite apparent. He was born the winter the ball of fire meteorite passed over the Sioux country from west to east. This meteorite was observed at Fort Snelling at the mouth of Minnesota River on the night of September 20, 1822; it is recorded in the Sioux counts under the date "winter of 1821-1822." The passage of this roaring, blazing star, illuminating the sky with a lurid glare, greatly impressed the Indians, and many of them named their children for the event. Red Cloud was evidently one of those to be named in this way. The name, however, was not originated then as it goes back among the Sioux beyond the year 1750. The word *makhpiya* may be translated either as cloud or sky; thus when the Sioux say blue cloud, they mean blue sky. In this instance the word may refer to the meteorite itself. Inkpaduta had twin sons born at that time, and he seems to have named them for this event. One was called Roaring Cloud, the other Fire Cloud. I once knew an old Cheyenne named Red Cloud who was about the age of the famous Oglala chief. This man's father was an Oglala, his mother a Northern Cheyenne. This Cheyenne Red Cloud was born about 1822 and, like the Oglala chief, seems to have been named in memory of the passing of the blazing star.

If one thing is clear it is the fact that Red Cloud, Man-Afraid-of-His-Horse, and the other old chiefs were not much interested in the origin of their own names. It is their descendants who are attempting to ennoble the families by devising these queer explanations of the origin of the names. These tales all exhibit a lamentable ignorance of the customs and living conditions in the old days.

Red Cloud's Parents. He Dog, Red Cloud's sister's son in 1931 gave the name of the chief's father as Ishna Witca (from *ishnala,* "lone," and *wichasha,* "man"). Lone Man was a Brulé chief, and we find that this name, Lone Man, was borne by chiefs of the Lower Brulés in later days. Red Cloud's mother was Walks-as-She-Thinks. She must have been a Saone, for Old Smoke who was a Saone always called her "sister." He also took her orphaned children into his camp, where they all grew up. He Dog's name for Red Cloud's father's band was Kuhee or Kuhinyan (Stand-offish), so called because they usually camped by themselves away from the other bands. This is clearly the Brulé band Lieutenant Caspar Collins heard of in 1863 as a group living on the Missouri: the Coolaweech-asha or Band That Lives Away From the Rest. *Coola* is He Dog's Kuhee, *wichasha,* here has the meaning of "people." I have failed to find any such band among the Brulés and suspect that this is a corrupt form of the name for all the Upper Brulé tribe: Kheyata-wichasha. The Lower Brulés were Kutawichasha. Red Cloud's father and mother must have both died about 1825. He Dog indicated that the children were all young when their mother's relative, Smoke, took them to his camp. Charles A. Eastman's picture of the care with which Red Cloud was trained and brought up by his father is pure imagination.

American Horse. In this volume I have stated that young American Horse led the True Oglala band in 1870, but a fresh examination of the records discloses that this band was represented in the council at Fort Laramie, October, 1870, by Sitting Bear, who spoke as their chief. The record in other places puts American Horse in the lead. The winter-count kept by American Horse himself records the birth of his father, Sitting Bear, in the spring of 1840. Sitting Bear was therefore the chief of the True Oglala band in 1870—a man of about thirty. American Horse, his son, could not have been over ten years old at that time, yet the American Horse of the record was a grown man and a leader of this band. The same American Horse is mentioned repeatedly as a leader at Red Cloud Agency, 1871-1877. The Oglalas themselves seem incapable of clearing up this tangle. I can only suggest that Sitting Bear may also have been known as American Horse and that in the records of the Fort Laramie councils he was set down under both names. The elder American Horse was a son of Old Smoke and was the leader of a very wild band. He never came to Red Cloud Agency, but on his occasional visits always went to Spotted Tail Agency. He Dog, who knew him well, states that he was no relation whatever of the younger American Horse, who was a Southern Oglala and son of Sitting Bear. The men who assert that the elder American Horse (killed in 1876), was the father or uncle of the younger chief usually give themselves away by venturing on further statements. Thus Eastman adds that after the death of the elder chief his band was brought to the agency by his nephew, the younger American Horse, who then for the first time came to the agency. The records prove that young American Horse was at the agency all of the time, 1871-1879; they show that he belonged to a different band and to the half of the tribe which was always opposed to the Smoke People, to which division the elder American Horse belonged.

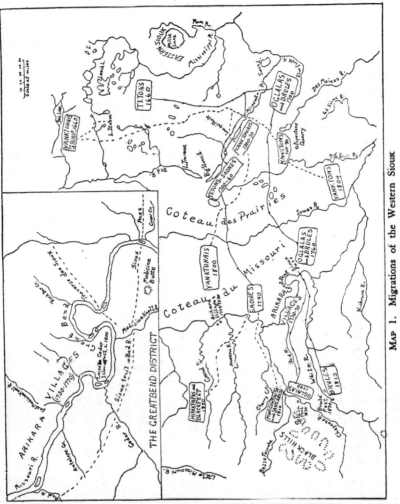

Map 1. Migrations of the Western Sioux

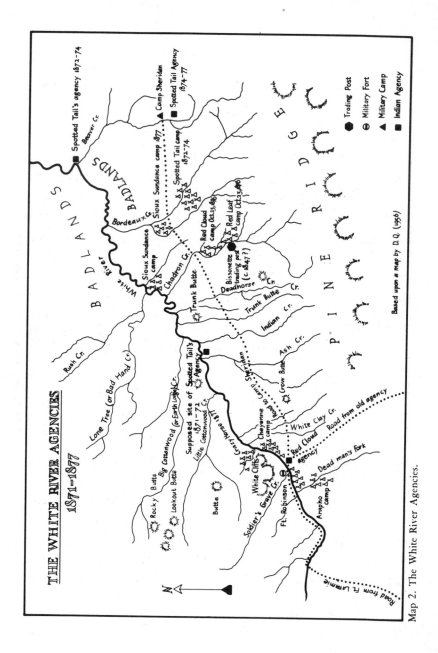

Map 2. The White River Agencies.

BRIEF BIBLIOGRAPHY

(Many sources quoted in the text are not included here.)

Allen, A. J. *Ten Years in Oregon: Travels and Adventures of Dr. E. White and Lady.* Ithaca, N. Y., 1850.

American State Papers, Indian Affairs. Washington, 1832-34. 2 vols.

Audubon, J. W. *Audubon's Western Journal: 1849-50.* Cleveland, 1906.

Beach, W. W., ed. *The Indian Miscellany.* Albany, N. Y., 1877.

Beede, Dr. A. McG. Sioux Traditions (manuscript). This material was collected among the Saone and Yanktonais Sioux groups. Dr. Beede died at his home, Fort Yates, N. D., in 1934. He gave me much interesting material on the Sioux migration to the Missouri.

Blair, E. H., ed. *Indian Tribes of the Upper Mississippi.* Cleveland, 1911. 2 vols.

Brackenridge, H. M. *Journal of a Voyage up the River Missouri.* Thwaites, ed., *Early Western Travels,* Vol. VI.

Bradbury, John. *Travels in the Interior of America.* Thwaites, ed., *Early Western Travels,* Vol. V.

Bryant, Edwin. *What I Saw in California.* New York, 1849.

Burton, Sir Richard F. *The City of the Saints.* New York, 1862.

Carver, Jonathan. *Three Years Travels.* Philadelphia, 1796. Carver seems to have invented his alleged sojourn among the Western Sioux from some information obtained from traders.

Chardon, F. A. *Journal at Fort Clark, 1834-1839.* Edited by A. H. Abel. Pierre, S. D., 1932.

Chittenden, H. M. *The American Fur Trade of the Far West.* New York, 1902. 2 vols. and atlas.

————, and Richardson, A. T., eds., *Life, Letters and Travels of Father Pierre-Jean DeSmet, 1801-1873.* New York, 1905. 4 vols.

Clark, W. P. *The Indian Sign Language.* Philadelphia, 1885.

Collins, J. S. *Across the Plains in '64.* Omaha, Neb., 1904.

Coues, Elliott, ed. *History of the Expedition under the Command of Lewis and Clark.* New York, 1893. 3 vols. and atlas.

Custer, G. A. *My Life on the Plains.* New York, 1874.

Dorsey, J. O. "Siouan Sociology," in *Fifteenth Annual Report, Bureau of American Ethnology.* Washington, 1897.

Dunn, J. P. *Massacres of the Mountains.* New York, 1886.

Featherstonhaugh, George. *A Canoe Voyage up the Minnay Sotor River.* London, 1847. 2 vols.

Finerty, J. F. *War-path and Bivouac.* Chicago, 1890.

Frémont, J. C. *The Exploring Expedition to the Rocky Mountains.* Auburn and Buffalo, 1854.

French, B. F., ed. *Historical Collections of Louisiana.* New York, 1846-53. 5 vols.

Grinnell, G. B. *The Fighting Cheyennes.* New York, 1915.

Hafen, L. R., and Ghent, W. J. *Broken Hand, the Life Story of Thomas Fitzpatrick.* Denver, 1931.

Hayden, F. V. *Contributions to the Ethnography and Philology of the Indian Tribes of the Missouri Valley.* Philadelphia, 1862.

Hebard, G. R. *Washakie.* Cleveland, 1930.

Hodge, F. W., ed. *Handbook of American Indians.* Bureau of American Ethnology, Bulletin 30. Washington, 1907-10. 2 vols.

James, Edwin. *Account of an Expedition from Pittsburgh to the Rocky Mountains ....under the Command of Major Stephen H. Long.* Philadelphia, 1822-23. 2 vols. and atlas.

Kappler, C. J., comp. *Indian Affairs. Laws and Treaties.* U. S. Document 319, Fifty-eighth Congress, second session. Washington, 1904. 2 vols.

Keating, W. H. *Narrative of an Expedition to the Source of St. Peter's River.* Philadelphia, 1824. 2 vols.

King, Charles. *Campaigning with Crook.* New York, 1890.

Mackenzie, Alexander. *Voyages from Montreal....to the Frozen and Pacific Oceans.* New York, 1802.

Mallery, Garrick. "Pictographs of the North American Indians," *Fourth Annual Report,* Bureau of American Ethnology. Washington, 1886.

Margry, Pierre, ed. *Découvertes et établissements des français dans l'ouest.* Paris, 1876-86. 6 vols.

Mooney, James. "Calendar History of the Kiowa Indians," *Seventeenth Annual Report,* Bureau of American Ethnology, Part I. Washington, 1898.

Morton, J. S. *Illustrated History of Nebraska.* Lincoln, Neb., 1905-6. 2 vols.

Neihardt, J. G. *Black Elk Speaks.* New York, 1932.

Neill, E. D. *The History of Minnesota.* Philadelphia, 1858.

Office of Indian Affairs. *Annual Reports.* The reports prior to 1827 are printed in *American State Papers, Indian Affairs;* later reports were issued in reports of the departments of War and of the Interior; sometimes also separately.

Palmer, H. E. "History of the Powder River Indian Expedition of 1865," Nebraska State Historical Society *Transactions,* Vol. II. Lincoln, Nebr., 1887.

Parker, Samuel. *Journal of an Exploring Tour Beyond the Rocky Mountains.* Ithaca, N. Y., 1838.

Parkman, Francis. *The California and Oregon Trail.* 8th ed.

Richardson, A. D. *Beyond' the Mississippi.* Hartford, 1867.

Riggs, S. R. *Grammar and Dictionary of the Dakota Language, Smithsonian Contributions to Knowledge,* Vol. IV. Washington, 1852.

——————. *Dakota-English Dictionary.* Edited by J. O. Dorsey, *Contributions to North American Ethnology,* Vol. VII. Washington: U. S. Geographical and Geological Survey of the Rocky Mountain Region, 1892.

——————. *Journal of a Tour from Lac-qui-parle to the Missouri,* South Dakota Historical *Collections,* Vol. XIII. Pierre, S. D., 1926. Reprinted from *Missionary Herald,* Vol. XXXVII, April, 1841.

Root, F. A., and Connelley, W. E. *The Overland Stage to California*. Topeka, Kan., 1901.

Sage, R. B. *Rocky Mountain Life*. Boston, 1857.

Schoolcraft, H. R. *Historical and Statistical Information Respecting....the Indian Tribes of the United States*. Philadelphia, 1851-57. 6 vols.

——————. *Narrative Journal of Travels....from Detroit.... to the Sources of the Mississippi River*. Albany, 1821.

Spring, A. W. *Caspar Collins*. New York, 1927.

Stanley, H. M. *My Early Travels and Adventures*. New York, 1895. 2 vols.

Stansbury, Howard. *Exploration and Survey of the Valley of the Great Salt Lake*. Washington, 1853. 1 vol. and atlas.

Stuart, Granville. *Forty Years on the Frontier*. Cleveland, 1925. 2 vols.

Thwaites, R. G., ed. *Early Western Travels*. Cleveland, 1904-7. 32 vols.

Truteau, J. B. "Journals." First part in *American Historical Review, Vol. XIX*, No. 2 (January, 1914); second part in Missouri Historical Society Collections. Vol. IV (St. Louis, 1913).

United States Congress, Joint Special Committee. *Condition of the Indian Tribes*. Washington, 1867. Also published as Senate Report 156, Thirty-ninth Congress, second session.

Warren, G. K. *Exploration in the Dacota Country*. Senate Executive Document 76, Thirty-fourth Congress, first session. Washington, 1856.

Wied-Neuwied, Maximilian Alexander Philipp, prinz von. *Maximilian, Prince of Wied's Travels*. Thwaites, ed., *Early Western Travels*. Vols. XXII-XXIV.

INDEX

Agency Sioux; their wildness in 1871-73, 190-92, 194-200, 208-12, 215; their vacillation and flightiness, 196-99, 205, 207, 210-14, 220-23, 225-27; their fear of "big trouble," 211, 223, 257; they decide to support the agent, 222; their conduct in 1876, 256-59, 273-86.

Agreement of 1876, 280-83.

Allison, Senator W. B., 242.

American Fur Company, 43-45, 52, 64, 96.

American Horse (the elder), 275-76, 318.

American Horse (the younger), 23, 25, 313, 318.

Antelope Buttes, 275.

Appleton, Frank, 212.

Arapahoes, 33, 46, 57.

Arapahoes, Northern, 107-11, 115, 123, 128, 182, 199, 201, 210, 225.

Arapahoes, Southern, 104, 107, 109.

Arikaras, move up the Missouri, 14-16; their villages, 15-16, 19; Sioux attacks on, 14-15, 17-19, 24, 27; their strength destroyed by smallpox, 17; relations with Tetons, 24-27, 36-37; their hostility toward whites, 34-37; they move to the Platte, 38, 49; return northward, 49.

Arkansas River, 52, 69, 83, 86, 105, 111, 136.

Ashley, General, 36, 43.

Assiniboins; early history, 4-6, 18.

Augur, Gen. C. C., 157, 169, 171.

Bad Faces, 87, 97, 165, 171, 192, 198, 203, 257, 311-14.

Bad River, 15-16, 19, 22, 28-29, 39, 41.

Bad Wound, 30, 85, 106, 119.

Badlands of South Dakota, 22, 206, 214, 219, 222-23, 225-27.

Bear Butte, 82, 251, 275.

Bear People, 40, 51, 55, 58, 85, 88, 98, 164, 313.

Bear's Rib, 82.

Beauvais, Col. G. P., 95, 151, 242.

Beaver Creek, 103, 109.

Beckwith, Jim, 144.

Belle Fourche (North Fork of Cheyenne River), 89.

Benteen, Capt. F. W., 268-69, 271.

Big Mouth, 98, 137, 151.

Big Partisan, 172.

Big Road, 98, 192, 268, 292, 297, 300.

Big Sioux River, 9-10, 14-15.

Bighorn country, 161, 163, 172, 240, 250, 278, 280-83, 293.

Bighorn Mountain, 272-74.

Bighorn River, 92, 143-44, 203, 266, 274, 296.

Bissonette, Joseph, 64, 94-96, 114.

Black Coal, 297.

Black Elk, 257.

Black Hills; early references to, 15-16, 20, 24, 41, 45-46, 82, 86, 113, 128-29, 132, 152, 161, 167, 182, 206; invaded by whites, 217-19, 230-35, 240, 247-49; council concerning, 239-49; seized by government, 277-70, 280-84, 293.

Black Kettle, 108-9, 111.

Black Moon, 116, 166, 192, 268, 270.

Black Shield, 92.

Black Twin, 251.

Blackfoot (Chief), 119.

Blackfoot-Sioux, 12, 38-39, 77, 114, 167, 261.

Blue Blanket, 35.

Blue Earth River, 7-11.

Blue Stone Creek, 274.

Blue Water Creek, 79.

Board of Indian Commissioners, 213.

Bordeaux, James, 59, 73-75, 115.

Bourke, Capt. J. G., 260, 264-65, 287-89.

Boyer, Mitch, 158.

{325}

Elliston, Charles, 119.
Emigrant-trains on Platte, 56, 58, 61-63, 69, 71.

Face, 232.
Farming among the Oglalas, 201, 220, 246.
Fetterman, Capt. Wm., 148-50.
Fetterman disaster, 145-49, 151.
Finnerty, J. F., 264-65.
Firearms, early use of by Indians, 4-5, 10; Sioux equipped with, 14, 17, 25; sources of supply in Fifties, 91; shortage in 1865-68, 132, 134-35, 149, 152, 156, 165; supply in 1876, 257, 279, 285, 292.
Fisk, J. L., 116.
Fitzpatrick, Thomas, 57, 65, 69.
Flagpole affair, 220-22, 224-25.
Fontenelle, Lucien, 45.
Ft. C. F. Smith, 141, 143, 145, 150, 158-59.
Ft. Fetterman, 165, 173-74, 177, 182, 253, 287.
Ft. John, 52, 57, 64, 96.
Ft. Laramie, 46, 54, 69-79, 85-87, 93, 96-98, 103, 107, 114-16, 118-20, 137-40, 145, 151, 157, 160, 164-68, 173-74, 177, 182-84, 187-89, 197, 200, 211-13, 225, 253.
Ft. Laramie council, 1870, 182-85.
Ft. Lookout, 39.
Ft. Lyon, 108.
Ft. McPherson, 155.
Ft. Phil Kearny, 141, 145-50, 159-60, 174.
Ft. Pierre, 8, 20, 62, 81, 83.
Ft. Reno, 111, 150, 160, 254.
Ft. Rice, 116, 130, 135, 166.
Ft. Sully (old), 153.
Ft. Tecumseh, 41.
Ft. Teton, 41.
Ft. William, 44-46.
Four Bears, 116, 166.
Fouts, Capt. Wm. D., 120-21.
Fraeb, Henry, 57.
Fremont, J. C., 57-58.

Gall, 268.
Galpin, C. E., 45.
Gaseau, Pierre, 142-43.
Gaylord, Assistant Attorney General, 281-82.
Geren, Charles, 165-66.

Gibbon, Gen. John, 261-62, 266, 272.
Gilman brothers, 95.
Godfrey, Capt. E. S., 268-69.
Good Whiteman, 25.
Goose Creek, 141, 265, 273-74.
Grand River, 27-28, 38, 135, 170.
Grant, President U. S., 173, 177, 217, 250, 266.
Grattan, Lieut. J. L., 72-76.
Grattan fight, 73-76, 85, 87.
Grouard, Frank, 295.

Hancock, Gen. W. S., 154-55.
Hare, Bishop, 215-17.
Harney, Gen. W. S., 79-80, 82-83, 85, 156, 169-70.
Harney expedition of 1855, 79 et seq., 82, 85.
Hastings, J. S., 251, 258-59, 279.
He Dog, 87, 146, 291-92, 317.
Hermaphrodites, 147.
High-Back-Bone, 146, 148, 159, 193.
High Wolf, 174, 188, 211.
Hinman, Rev. S. D., 163, 166-67, 242.
Horse Creek, 33, 65, 93, 120, 137, 151.
Hostile Sioux camps; in 1865, 130-32; in 1866, 141, 145; in 1867, 157-60; in 1868, 164-66; in 1871, 192-93; in 1872, 200; in 1873, 203-4; in 1875-76, 251-53, 256-57, 261-63, 266-68, 273-76, 287-90.
Hostiles, ordered to come in, 249-51, 258.
Howard, E. A., 251.
Hunkpapas, 116, 130, 167, 225, 261, 267-68.
Hunkpapas; early history, 12, 38-39; hostility toward whites, 77, 81, 83.
Hunkpatilas, 98, 312.

Independence Rock, 57.
Indian Territory; proposal to remove Sioux to, 219, 277, 280, 282, 285-86, 294.
Iowas, 9, 14-15.
Iron Shell, 151-52.
Irwin, James, 300.

James River, 11, 15, 20.
Janis, Antoine, 96.
Janis, Nicolas, 96, 174.
Jenney, Professor W. P., 234, 340.
Julesburg, Colo., 109-13.
Jumping Shield, 297.

Twiss, Thomas, 77-79, 83, 89, 92-96, 287.
Two Face, 119.
Two Kettles, 12-13, 18, 28, 40.
Two Moon, 146, 148, 259.

Union Pacific Railway, 150, 160, 167.
Upper Platte Agency, 69, 93-96, 114-16, 189.
Utes, 88.

Vestal, Stanley, 270.

Wagon-box fight, 159-60.
Walker, Col. S., 128-33.
Walks-as-she-Thinks, 317.
Ware, Lieut. E. F., 102, 107.
Warren, Lieut. G. K., 83.
Watkins, E. C., 250, 253, 292.
Wazhazhas, 67, 193, 209, 312, 314.
Wazikutes, 13.
Wessels, Col. H. W., 149.
Wham, J. W., 187-91, 193-96.
Whetstone Agency, 168-70, 277.
Whipple, Bishop, 281, 301.
Whirlwind, 41, 58-59, 67, 311.
Whistler, 85, 161.
White Antelope, 108-9.

White Blanket, 30.
White Bull, 146.
White Butte Creek, 110, 112.
White Clay Creek, 206.
White River, 15, 19, 22, 26, 51, 62, 67, 93, 122, 170, 188, 196, 201, 206, 219, 224-26, 230, 299, 301-3.
White Tail, 188.
Whitfield, J. W., 76.
Wilcox, Capt. J., 121-22.
Williams, Bill, 144.
Wind River, 118.
Winter-counts of the Sioux, ix, 18-20, 22-23, 25-26, 35-36, 41-42, 49, 59, 62, 88.
Woman's Dress, 296.
Wounded Knee Creek, 314.

Yanktonais, 4, 6, 13, 18, 39, 261.
Yanktons; early history, 4-6, 10, 13, 18; move to the Missouri, 26, 28; cede Teton lands, 84.
Yates, Capt. G. W., 270-71.
Yellow Bear, 174, 297.
Yellow Eagle, 165, 312.
Yellow Medicine (Minn.), 9.
Yellowstone River, 66, 90, 92, 117, 192, 203, 251, 254-55, 261, 273-74, 276.

RED CLOUD'S FOLK, *A History of the Oglala Sioux,* by GEORGE E. HYDE, has been composed on the Linotype in 11 point Granjon. This typeface, at once clear and distinctive, is named for the celebrated printer Robert Granjon, who was a typecutter as well. Granjon began work around 1523 but it was not until 1545 that his European reputation was established. Desiring to create a type representing France, he cut a typeface known as "caractères de civilité," so named from the titles of two books printed from the new characters in 1559 and 1560. This type enjoyed great popularity, especially in the Netherlands. Granjon was fond especially of typographic ornaments and did much to make their use universal in printed books. The later years of his life were spent in Rome, where he cut type for the Vatican Press, for the Medici and others. The modern Granjon type-face is not from any of his but is a modern recutting by George W. Jones of a type cut originally by Claude Garamond.

THE PRINTED PAGE IS EVERYMAN'S UNIVERSITY

UNIVERSITY OF OKLAHOMA PRESS
PUBLISHING DIVISION OF THE UNIVERSITY
NORMAN